Speaking of America

Speaking of America

Great Conversations at the Library of Congress

DAVID M. RUBENSTEIN

DUKE UNIVERSITY PRESS *Durham and London* 2026
Published by Duke University Press in association with the Library of Congress

Project Editor: Jessica Ryan
Designed by Dave Rainey
Typeset in Portrait Text and Helvetica Neue LT Std by Westchester Publishing Services

Library of Congress Cataloging-in-Publication Data
Names: Rubenstein, David M. author interviewer | Newlen, Robert R. writer of foreword
Title: Speaking of America : Great Conversations at the Library of Congress / David M. Rubenstein ; foreword by Robert R. Newlen.
Description: Durham : Published by Duke University Press in association with the Library of Congress, 2026. | Includes bibliographical references and index.
Identifiers: LCCN 2026011328 (print)
LCCN 2026011329 (ebook)
ISBN 9781478034643 hardcover
ISBN 9781478063308 ebook
Subjects: LCSH: Historians—United States | Journalists—United States | Authors, American | Interviews | United States—Civilization | United States—History | United States—Politics and government | LCGFT: Interviews
Classification: LCC E169.1 .R858 2026 (print) |
LCC E169.1 (ebook)
DDC 973--dc23/eng/20260409
LC record available at https://lccn.loc.gov/2026011328
LC ebook record available at https://lccn.loc.gov/2026011329

Cover art: Carol M. Highsmith, *Domes of the Library of Congress Thomas Jefferson Building and the U.S. Capitol, Washington, D.C.*, between 1996 and 2000. Carol M. Highsmith Archive, Library of Congress, Prints and Photographs Division.

To Jim Billington, Carla Hayden, and Robert Newlen, each of whom strongly encouraged and supported the Congressional Dialogues series and made its occurrence a reality and success

Contents

Foreword by Robert R. Newlen, Acting Librarian of Congress ix

Introduction by David M. Rubenstein 1

1. Ken Burns on Bringing History to Life 7
2. Stacy Schiff on Samuel Adams 28
3. Allen C. Guelzo on Ulysses S. Grant and Robert E. Lee 46
4. Manisha Sinha on Lincoln, Johnson, and Reconstruction 71
5. Michael Beschloss on Wartime Presidents 90
6. Chris Wallace on the Presidential Election of 1960 113
7. Mark K. Updegrove on John F. Kennedy 135
8. Max Boot on Ronald Reagan 160
9. David Maraniss on Jim Thorpe 188
10. Beverly Gage on J. Edgar Hoover 209
11. Evan Thomas on Sandra Day O'Connor 230
12. Admiral William H. McRaven on the Hunt for Osama bin Laden 255

13. Walter Isaacson on Leonardo da Vinci 281

14. David McCullough on Writing American History and *The Pioneers* 299

15. Siddhartha Mukherjee on Cancer, Cell Biology, and Mapping the Human Genome 314

16. Eric Schmidt on Artificial Intelligence 336

17. Graham Allison on the Cuban Missile Crisis and Thucydides's Trap 356

18. Arthur C. Brooks on Happiness 379

19. David Grann on *The Wager* 402

Acknowledgments 423

Credits 427

Index 431

About the Author 443

Foreword

Having spent much of my career working in the Congressional Research Service (CRS), which provides confidential, objective, and authoritative research and analysis to lawmakers, I especially value the Library of Congress's mission of service to Congress. Since its founding in 1800 as a small reference library for lawmakers, the Library has expanded its collections and efforts to support Members of Congress and their staff through lending books, informing the legislative debate through the CRS, and hosting tours and other events for Members and their guests.

Beginning in 2013, the Congressional Dialogues program has brought Members together for nonpartisan, off-the-record receptions during which David M. Rubenstein—the chair of the Library's premier philanthropy organization, the Madison Council—interviews a prominent author, usually a historian or biographer, about a timely subject of interest to Congress. Complementing the interview, our unparalleled collections are highlighted by Library of Congress staff in displays of historic books, letters, maps, photographs, and other treasures that bring to life each interview's theme. These displays showcase how the Library serves as a universal and enduring source of knowledge and creativity.

We are greatly indebted to the generosity of Mr. Rubenstein for sponsoring these events. He has supported major exhibitions at the

FIGURE F.1 The Great Hall in the Library of Congress's Thomas Jefferson Building, where Congressional Dialogues events are held.

Library over the years and was the sole benefactor of the David M. Rubenstein Treasures Gallery, which opened in 2024. His commitment to promoting literacy inspired his support of two signature programs at the Library: the National Book Festival—one of the most prominent literary events in the nation—and the Library of Congress Literacy Awards, which honor organizations that work to expand literacy and foster a love of reading. David is a standard-bearer for the American spirit of generosity, creativity, and leadership, and we deeply appreciate all he has done for the Library of Congress.

Featuring new introductions by David, this volume of nineteen interviews from the Congressional Dialogues series spans thousands of years of history, from ancient Greek warfare to the Renaissance masterpieces of Leonardo da Vinci, to key moments in US history, including the American Revolution, the Civil War and Reconstruction, and the Cold War. Topics such as military leadership, the drive for athletic greatness, happiness, and the future of artificial intelligence shape the conversations. The wide range of issues recalls Thomas Jefferson's sentiment from an 1814 letter that "there is, in fact, no subject to which a member [of Congress] may not have occasion to refer."

Although the Congressional Dialogues series is exclusively for Members of Congress, there are myriad opportunities for visitors to experience the Library and its collections. As part of its commitment to preserve and share the nation's treasures, the Library hosts a variety of scholarly initiatives, world-class performances, and engaging programs, including a weekly "Live! At the Library" series where visitors can experience the Great Hall—the same location where the Congressional Dialogues are held. I encourage you to explore the Library's offerings in person in Washington, DC, or online, at www.loc.gov, to find what inspires your curiosity.

—ROBERT R. NEWLEN, *Acting Librarian of Congress*

Introduction

In 1987, the Librarian of Congress was Dr. James Billington, a Princeton-educated Rhodes Scholar who had been appointed by President Reagan (and later confirmed by the Senate) to the then-lifetime position. Like most of his predecessors, Jim (as he was known to all) Billington was less of a librarian than a scholar—his specialty was Russia and the Soviet Union.

At the time of his appointment, the Library received essentially all of its funding from congressional appropriations, and that funding process had worked well for most of the Library's long history.

The idea of a Library of Congress had first been suggested by James Madison in 1783, when he was serving in the Congress created by the Articles of Confederation. Madison saw a library as a resource that could be very helpful to Congress. Even then, the legislative process moved slowly, and Congress (later operating under the Constitution) finally approved the idea in 1800, with President John Adams signing the legislation that authorized the new Library to spend $5,000 to purchase the appropriate materials necessary to help respond to inquiries from Members of Congress. That sum was used to purchase more than 700 books and three maps.

Over the years, the Library grew incrementally but suffered a major blow in 1814 when the British burned the Capitol Building (where the Library of Congress was then located). The entire collection burned.

To deal with this existential challenge, Thomas Jefferson offered to sell his personal library, then the largest private collection in the country, to the Library of Congress.

In time, after concluding that Jefferson's collection did not have any anti-Christian books, Congress accepted the offer and paid $23,950 for approximately 6,500 books. These became the heart of the Library's collection until 1851, when a fire destroyed nearly two-thirds of the Jefferson books. (The Library, in time, replaced most of those with other same-era copies of these books.)

Eventually, the collection grew dramatically and became the world's largest. Today, the Library holds more than 184 million items, including at least 40 million catalogued books and other printed materials.

From its inception, the Library was designed to respond to inquiries from Members of Congress and to acquire materials that could assist them in performing their legislative duties. But as the collections grew, the mission grew as well. In 1870, the Library was given the responsibility of operating the United States Copyright Office. That office ultimately required an author to submit two copies of any publication for which a copyright was sought, and that process helped to increase the collections. The Library also made large acquisitions of valuable books, maps, and letter collections and was also given large collections by Americans who wanted their items or papers to be catalogued and kept as resources for future scholars.

Funding some of these purchases often required the Library to seek funds beyond what Congress appropriated to it. In 2000, Jim Billington helped to persuade John Kluge, one of America's wealthiest individuals, to provide the Library with its largest gift—$60 million. That gift was used to create the John W. Kluge Center, which was designed to support scholarly research and to fund additional acquisitions.

As part of this process, the Library created the Madison Council, which was designed as a nongovernmental support group for the institution. Kluge became its first chair, a position that I have now been honored to hold for the last ten-plus years.

When I was first invited by Jim Billington to join the Madison Council, I began to learn more about the Library and its many different functions, including making its vast collections available to scholars as well as to anyone who would like to use some part of these extensive resources.

In time, I suggested to Dr. Billington that we might initiate a way to bring Members of Congress—from both houses and both parties—together in a social setting that would be educational for them. The Library would host a reception and dinner in the Great Hall of the Library (perhaps Washington's most ornate interior setting), and the dinner would be followed by an interview that I would conduct about an author's book, typically related to American history and leaders. But other subjects likely to be of interest to the Members in fulfilling their legislative responsibilities would also be included from time to time.

Dr. Billington liked the idea. Educating Members of Congress about American history and other important subjects relevant to Congress's responsibilities would seem to be a worthwhile goal. I agreed to bear all of the costs to avoid complaints that taxpayer funds were being used to provide elected representatives with an enjoyable evening. (I do not engage in any personal lobbying of them on any issue.)

But would anyone actually attend? We were not sure.

The first dinner was held on June 18, 2013, with Jon Meacham as the guest interviewee. Meacham is a leading expert on many presidential and history-related subjects; this dinner focused on his book about Thomas Jefferson (fittingly, the Library's great supporter), and Jon did his usual excellent job in the interview. And the Members seemed to enjoy the whole evening—but for two reasons we had not initially anticipated.

First, at the cocktail hour prior to the dinner and interview, the Library placed on display for the Members and their guests some of the Library's historic manuscripts, letters, and other documents written or edited by Jefferson. Because of the fragile nature of many of these documents, they are rarely displayed publicly.

For all the subsequent Dialogues, the Library has continued to display, prior to the dinner, historic documents and other materials relating to the featured guest's writings or subjects. And this display has proven to be an invaluable part of the evening for the Members and their guests.

Second, the Members really welcomed the opportunity to socialize with those from the opposite party, which rarely happens any longer in increasingly partisan Washington. (No press is permitted at the dinners, and they are strictly nonpartisan.) Members also welcomed a chance to meet people from the other chamber of Congress. Because there is relatively little major legislation passed these days, there are fewer conference committees where key leaders from the House and Senate get to know each other while negotiating the terms of a bill that both chambers can pass.

After the first dinner, word spread among Members of Congress, and greater numbers came to the second and following dinner interview evenings, which were called Congressional Dialogues.

There have now been more than seventy Congressional Dialogues over ten-plus years. Among those who have been interviewed are historians David McCullough, Doris Kearns Goodwin, Danielle Allen, Walter Isaacson, Doug Brinkley, and Michael Beschloss; business leaders Bill Gates and Eric Schmidt; and even Chief Justice John Roberts.

The Congressional Dialogues are naturally dependent on Congress's always-changing schedule, but there are typically about six to eight every year, with about 250 attendees on average. (Each representative or senator can bring a guest; they typically bring a spouse, a staff member, or a constituent.)

Jim Billington retired as Librarian of Congress in 2015 and was succeeded by President Obama's appointee, Dr. Carla Hayden, who had served the previous two decades and longer as the head of the public library organization, the Enoch Pratt Free Library, located in my hometown of Baltimore.

Dr. Hayden was the first woman, the first African American, and only the third trained librarian to hold the Librarian of Congress position. She earned a doctorate in library science from the University of Chicago (coincidentally the same university where I went to law school). She became an enthusiastic supporter of the Dialogues and hosted more than forty after Billington's departure.

President Trump removed Dr. Hayden as the Librarian in May 2025. Her deputy, Robert Newlen, as Acting Librarian of Congress, has continued the decade-long tradition of the Dialogues. Given the popularity of these events, they are likely to continue for quite some time.

I thought that the public would enjoy reading what has been said at a number of the Dialogues that featured some of the best-known interviewees, and Robert Newlen agreed. The result is this book, published by the Library of Congress and Duke University Press. In previous books that I have authored, I included a number of the Dialogues. However, there are a good many that have never appeared in print, and a cross section of these are included in this book. (The conversations have been lightly edited and updated in consultation with the interviewees.) I think these interviews not only enable the reader to learn what the Members heard but also provide a wide-ranging look at history (mostly American) and many leading figures who made that history.

A question frequently asked in Washington by scholars at the growing number of think tanks in the city, by organizers of policy conferences, by authors of books directly related to subjects being addressed by Congress, by writers of op-ed articles, and even by congressional staff members is simply this: "What impact does what I am doing have on what Congress ultimately does?"

The same question might be fairly asked about the Congressional Dialogues.

The answer for all of those individuals and organizations and gatherings, including the Dialogues, is difficult to know with precision. Members of Congress absorb information from many places, and they are not often precise—in floor or committee debates, or in the official legislative record that typically is drafted in support of legislation—about what has influenced them.

But, based on anecdotal evidence and conversations with Members, prior to and after Congressional Dialogues events, the Members routinely talk about the impact the dinners have on their thinking and perspectives. Indeed, more than a few have regularly commented that those evenings—the cocktail conversations, the historic documents on display, the interviews, the chance to talk with other Members in a frank, unfiltered, and private way—are among the most enjoyable and valuable parts of being a Member of Congress.

—*DAVID M. RUBENSTEIN, May 2026*

1

Ken Burns on Bringing History to Life

INTERVIEW DATE: JUNE 11, 2024

We often talk these days about GOATs, the Greatest of All Time, typically in a sports context. Michael Jordan is often said to be the basketball GOAT; Tom Brady is often said to be the football GOAT.

But there are debates about who deserves these sport GOAT titles. (For example, some might claim LeBron James has passed Michael Jordan.)

In the documentary film world, there is no need for a debate. Ken Burns is the GOAT. His body of work is staggering—more than thirty films—and those films have done more than anything else by any other filmmaker or author or journalist or performer to bring history to life.

Filmed, edited, and shown over the past forty-five years, these films have won sixteen Emmy Awards. But, perhaps more important, they have all been shown on public television to ensure the largest audience can view them at the lowest cost: zero (and, as a result, the lowest remuneration to Ken Burns).

The subjects of Burns's work are breathtaking: His best-known films cover, among other topics, the Civil War, the Vietnam War, World War II, the American Revolution, the Roosevelts, Benjamin Franklin, Muhammad Ali, Hemingway, the United States and the

FIGURE 1.1 Filmmaker Ken Burns has made documentaries on the Civil War, baseball, jazz, the Vietnam War, the national parks, and the American Revolution. In the latter, which was released in November 2025, he covers events leading up to the conflict, such as the Boston Massacre, depicted here in an engraving by Paul Revere, through the peace treaty with Great Britain and the Constitutional Convention.

Holocaust, Leonardo da Vinci, country music, Jackie Robinson, the Central Park Five, Prohibition, the national parks, Mark Twain, baseball, jazz, Thomas Jefferson, Lewis and Clark, the Statue of Liberty, and the Brooklyn Bridge.

It is hard to think of anyone who has done as much to educate Americans about their history as Ken Burns. I have known Ken for many years; have been a donor to his foundation, which helps to fund his films; and have interviewed him on multiple occasions.

This interview was done to mark the opening of the Library of Congress's new Treasures Gallery, which is designed to showcase many of the Library's more cherished and significant objects. I was pleased to be able to support the Gallery project and to lend objects from my own collection.

DAVID M. RUBENSTEIN (DR): You have a couple of things that are going to come out soon. The next documentary coming out is on Leonardo?

KEN BURNS (KB): Yes.

DR: Historically, you've done only things on America. Is that right?

KB: Only things on America. But I was with Walter Isaacson, a biographer of Leonardo. I was already making a film on Benjamin Franklin, also one of his subjects. We were having dinner, and he was trying to sell me on Leonardo. And I said, "Walter, I only do American stuff." And he said, "In the eighteenth century, the best American artist is Franklin, and he's the greatest scientist of that century. And Leonardo is an even greater scientist and artist. You've got to do it." He wouldn't let it go all through dinner.

I walk out, and I'm talking to my oldest daughter and her husband, who are collaborators with me on film projects like Muhammad Ali, Jackie Robinson, and the Central Park Five film. I said, "Walter was trying to sell me on Leonardo." They said, "We can do it." I called Walter back the next morning and I said, "Okay."

So we've made a film, two parts. It will be out in November [2024]. My daughter and son-in-law (and two of my four grandchildren) lived in Florence for a year to research, shoot, and write it. Of course, I had to visit them to make sure the film was on track.

DR: Wow, sounds like hardship.

KB: Hardship duty. I don't need to talk to you about travel. A documentary filmmaker in public broadcasting lives an incredibly exotic life. But I worry about people in private equity and how hard it is living paycheck to paycheck.

DR: It's been a struggle. But some people have to bear their cross, and I do it.

KB: Yes, and admirably. [To audience:] I went to Baltimore to see some relatives a few weeks ago, and I brought back some souvenirs. He went to Baltimore a few weeks ago and bought the Orioles.

DR: That's true.

KB: I used to go to Memorial Stadium and later to Camden Yards, and you'd see Tip O'Neill, Speaker of the House, in Memorial Stadium talking to Silvio Conte, the Republican congressman from western Massachusetts. And they would talk the inside game. I learned that the Speaker got his nickname after a catcher whose name was Tip, who could snap his fingers and convince the umpire that it was a foul tip.

DR: That's a good trick. I hadn't heard of that one. But now everything is digitized, and everything is on every video camera. It's completely different.

You did a great series on baseball. Why did you do baseball? Do you have a love of baseball as well?

KB: Yes, I love it. The first time I ever went to a major league game was at Memorial Stadium in 1958 or '59. My dad's family is from

Baltimore, as you are. Yes, I've loved the game all my life. I thought, "Finally I've got a subject that I know about." Of course, each day of the production was a daily humiliation about what I didn't know about it.

But I did it, and I called it a sequel to the Civil War series. People thought that was crazy. But if you think what the Civil War did, among a handful of watershed moments, the most important event in American history: It ended slavery in a country that had been claiming for fourscore and nine years that all men are created equal. (The guy who wrote that line owned hundreds of other human beings.) The first real progress in civil rights *after* the Civil War was on April 15, 1947, when Jack Roosevelt Robinson, the grandson of a slave, made his way to first base at Ebbets Field. Martin Luther King Jr. was a junior at Morehouse College. This is before Truman had integrated the militaries, before *Brown v. Board of Education*, before planned protests at lunch counters.

In fact, Robinson, as a teenager, had refused to get up from a lunch counter in Pasadena, California, on a number of occasions. He had also been court-martialed for refusing to give up a seat on a bus at Fort Hood, on a military base in Texas, and was acquitted. This was eleven years before Rosa Parks. And so King, when he got to be in his position in the '50s, called him the pilgrim. He said he was "a sit-inner before sit-ins and a freedom rider before freedom rides." That's the centrality of Jackie Robinson. And so to do baseball was to talk about the promise of who we were. Could it be a national pastime, if you excluded what turned out to be among the greatest players of all time?

DR: Not in your league, but I did a documentary on Fenway Park last year [*Iconic America* on PBS, episode 1, season 1].

KB: You did.

DR: And in doing that, I learned something that was amazing. Some of you may have heard of the Curse of the Bambino. For baseball fans, that meant that the Boston Red Sox had sold Babe Ruth, a native of Baltimore, to the New York Yankees for $100,000 to pay off some Broadway debts that the owner of the Red Sox had. And for eighty years they didn't get to the World Series, or didn't win a World Series.

KB: They didn't win for eighty-six years.

DR: People said it was because they were stupid enough to sell Babe Ruth. But the real reason was that Tom Yawkey, the owner of the Red Sox, was a racist. He gave a tryout to Jackie Robinson and said he wasn't good enough. He gave a tryout to another guy named Willie Mays and said he wasn't good enough. And, finally, when they had to integrate, the last team to integrate, they got a player named Pumpsie Green.

KB: Pumpsie Green, 1959.

DR: Who did not go to the Hall of Fame, right?

KB: He did not go to the Hall of Fame.

DR: Let me ask you about the thing I often ask you about. When you first became well known, you had what I'll call a Prince Valiant haircut, and it was kind of a shaggy thing. Where did you get that haircut, and where has it gone?

KB: [to audience:] So I have to tell you that this is not the first rodeo that David and I have had. It's like the tenth time we've done a public conversation—at Gettysburg, the 92nd Street Y, places like that—and every time there's a question about my haircut. Every single time. So yesterday I got my hair cut. I said, "Make it really short, because then David won't ask about my haircut."

What happened is that I was a hippie from Ann Arbor, and I cut my hair back to a John, Paul, George, and Ringo thing when I had to be respectable after college. It just sort of stuck, and it became this signature thing. Tom Brokaw, in fact, came up to me when I turned sixty, which was ten-plus years ago, and he said, "Time for a big boy haircut." Tom is like a mentor. I said, "Ouch, that really hurts." Now he's an *eminence grise*, and his hair is wild and crazy. And I said, "I thought it was seventy." So I knew that by seventy I had to do it.

DR: Okay. For those who haven't followed the Civil War series, when you made that, did you have any idea it would transform Americans' knowledge of history and interest in it? How afraid were you that your career would be over if the thing bombed?

KB: I had no idea. I was more flabbergasted than anyone in the country by it. I had made six other films. Two had been nominated for Oscars. So it wasn't like I felt like I was in the wrong profession. But I remember the Corporation for Public Broadcasting, which has been a major funder in every film, turned down my application. The argument was that your attention span for looking at old photographs is about an hour, which most of those films had been. But the idea that I had proposed was for five one-hours (and it ended up being almost twelve hours).

DR: Twelve hours. How much did it cost to make that?

KB: My part of the budget was something like $3.2 million. The National Endowment for the Humanities gave a grant of $1,439,000.50, and I eventually repaid all of it. General Motors, and a couple of other foundations, MacArthur and Arthur Vining Davis, completed the rest. I'm currently working on a history of the American Revolution, and it is—like the Vietnam and the country music series—a big, long series that is north of $30 million. [*The American Revolution* debuted in November 2025.]

A lot of the success of those films has to do with this institution, the Library of Congress. It's like standing on the rim of the Grand Canyon. It's like walking across the Brooklyn Bridge, the subject of my first film. The Library of Congress is one of the great places on Earth. For the photographs that are in that Civil War film, I went to 163 sources, including one private home in Gorham, Maine, that had just one carte de visite of Joshua Lawrence Chamberlain. But across the street in the Library of Congress's Madison Building, I spent eight or nine weeks, 8:30 a.m. to 5:00 p.m., with two scoop umbrella lamps and a metal easel, gloves and a tripod, and I rephotographed, by hand, something like 9,000 photographs of the Mathew Brady collection. Which is, of course, not just Mathew Brady, but Alexander Gardner and many other people, *right here*. Those are all in the public domain. That is to say, we—you and I and everyone else—own those photographs, which is a wonderful thing.

This is extraordinary stuff. But, David, let me ask you: What is it that has prompted, as Carla Hayden says, the patriotic philanthropy you do? Why is the Washington Monument repaired? Why does the National Archives have a gallery? Why are you involved at Monticello? What is the motivation for you?

DR: I came from very modest means, and when I got lucky in my business career, I decided I wanted to give back to the country. I kind of stumbled on the idea that one thing we could do, and you understand this as well, is to educate people about American history more. The theory behind representative government, as Jefferson said, was we need to have an informed citizenry.

KB: That's right.

DR: But we don't have an informed citizenry as much as we should. Now the human brain has evolved enormously. The human brain is an incredible device that enables Shakespeare to write those plays, or Beethoven to compose those symphonies, or Picasso to paint those paintings. But it has a lot of flaws. If you look different than me, sometimes that means I'm not going to like you as much. If you don't do something I like, I'm going to go to war with you. The human brain still doesn't work perfectly. The brain has not yet evolved to this point.

If you see a document, let's say the Gettysburg Address, we know what the text of the Gettysburg Address is. We know what the words are. So why not just destroy the originals and put it on a computer slide? Because when you see the original, three things happen. Before you see it, you're probably going to read more about it and get educated. When you go to see the original, you're going to get a curator who's going to tell you more about it. And most likely, afterward you're going to go home and read about it. The human brain still absorbs information much better if it sees an original or something preserved.

The idea is to give back to the country in some ways, and this is one way that I thought I could do it. I was surprised that many people weren't doing this. I am an original signer of the Giving Pledge. I've said many times, we should all try to make a gift to the country, to remind people of the history and heritage of it. But I've never been able to convince people there to do it. There are some people obviously doing some of the same things I'm doing, and you're obviously doing it in a different way. But I just thought that was my little contribution to remind people of our history.

Let me ask you a question, though. On the Civil War series, there are two or three things I remember. One is that you had these Southern voices. Whose idea was it to get Southern voices? I used to work in the White House with one of them, Jody Powell, and you had others. What was the idea behind that? How did you get that idea of having voices like that?

KB: I knew that as a filmmaker I had to wake the still photographs up. To "wake the dead," as my late father-in-law once said to me. So rather than just have a single third-person narrator, the voice of God as it's often called, what if you punctuated it with first-person quotes from diaries and letters and journals and newspaper accounts, military dispatches, telegrams? That would give you a sense of the style and articulation of voices in the nineteenth century. And if you didn't see them as actors playing each role but *heard* them reading with an interior voice, almost like a thought, that would add some verisimilitude to it.

And so, if you're going to do a film about the Civil War, probably half your voices are going to be Southern. I wanted to reach out beyond the actors I could enlist to do a Southern voice and use people who were really Southerners. Jody Powell was a person I knew. Charlie McDowell was a voice. Shelby Foote—now that's a talking head.

There's a little bit of difference between somebody who's on camera and someone who is reading. But we got a variety of people reading. Arthur Miller read voices, Kurt Vonnegut read voices. That was a way to help wake up those photographs.

DR: There's a second question I always ask you, and I think others would be interested in, about the music. The music was very lyrical. Do you think the music was an important part of the success of the series? Where did you get the idea for the particular song that became the most famous?

KB: What people do in filmmaking is they score a film, which is a mathematical term. It means that, after the film is edited, you hire a composer to edit to time. Musicians are playing while looking at the finished film.

We don't believe in that. I think all art forms, film included, painting, everything when it dies and goes to Heaven wants to be music. It's the only art form that's invisible. So what I did is I would take a friend who could play the piano, and I would go through hymnals of the time, and out of 300 hymns, I'd pick out ten. I'd go to the sheet music of the time, and I would listen to a melody that I liked. I collected forty or fifty tunes. Went into the studio *before* we started editing and had musicians play it numerous times different ways: Play the A music, and then repeat the A music, and then the B music (which we call the chorus), and then the C music, if it existed, and come back to the A. Let's do it just a single hand on a piano, two hands, adding instrumentation, subtracting it.

We would end up with what we called musical beds. We might have "The Battle Cry of Freedom." Everybody North and South loved it. Play it soft and funereal. Play it loud and martial with music. Play it on a tinny piano as if it was some schoolteacher playing it. We played it every which way. Sometimes forty versions of a single piece.

Then we started editing with the music first. I'd shorten a line of narration to fit a phrase of music, or I'd lengthen it to fit a phrase of music. That way, the music is baked in. It's not something that you're adding at the end to amplify emotions you hope are there. You know what it's like to turn down the soundtrack on a horror film. It's not as scary once that music is down.

In the course of making my previous films and this one, I used a session musician named Jay Ungar who had a band called Fiddle Fever. Another member of the band sent me a vinyl album. It was Rounder Records. I just would do a needle drop. I'd listen to the first track, go to the second, go to the third. The fourth song on the first side was this tune called "Ashokan Farewell." I didn't even know how to pronounce it.

Ashokan is part of the reservoir system of New York City up near the Catskills. Jay Ungar, the man who wrote this song, lived there and still has to this day a music camp there. He was a Jewish kid from the Bronx, and in 1983, at the end of the summer, everybody was going back to start the new school year, and he just sat down and wrote this beautiful Scotch/Irish lament, "Ashokan Farewell." I was stunned by it, and I don't think he even understood what he had. I called him up and I said, "Jay, I need to use this." I must have used it fifty times in the Civil War series. It has been played at a hundred funerals and memorial services and weddings and renewals of vows. It had a profound effect. That begins to illustrate the power of music. Two notes and it gets to you.

DR: One other thing about the Civil War series I wanted to ask you about. There was a letter that was found that a soldier had written to his wife. He died in combat, and the letter was found. You ultimately got hold of that letter. I think it was from Captain Ballou.

KB: Yes. Sullivan Ballou.

DR: What was so magical about that letter, and why was it so emotional for people to hear that?

KB: We had about two dozen academic and other advisors, from Robert Penn Warren and Shelby Foote to a man named Don Fehrenbacher, who was from Illinois and was a scholar of the causes of the war and of Lincoln. We had asked most of our advisors to send first-person quotes.

Nobody did, except for one, Barbara Fields, a Columbia University historian. And she was great. She'd been part of the Freedman Project and was sending the newly discovered testimony of freed Black Americans from slavery. They were good, but no other scholar had sent anything. Finally, a letter came from Professor Fehrenbacher that he had found in an archive, and I read it out loud and wept.

It's a letter from Sullivan Ballou to his wife, Sarah, in which he's describing about as many levels of love as I know. I think that every man wishes he could say the words that he said to the woman he loves. But I think, more importantly, every woman wishes her man could say those things to her. He's talking about love of country and love of cause and love of government, something we've lost. We've made the government the enemy. We've lost that civic engagement with the things that animate our purpose—love of country, love of God, love of government, love of cause, love of family, love of wife, love of children, love of the lover. All of those are expressed in this letter in which he's saying, "I know that I'll come home, but if I don't, just remember that when the soft breeze fans your cheek, it will be my spirit passing by. Do not mourn me."

I used to carry that letter around everywhere I went for twenty years—I had a Xerox copy of it—until it dissolved in my wallet. People everywhere would ask me to bring it out and read it. And I swear to God, half the times that "Ashokan Farewell" is played today, that letter is read with it, because it's an expression of our love that all of us understand.

I live in New Hampshire, which is a political state. I have a yard sign and it says, "Love multiplies." That's my political statement.

DR: *The Civil War* was an epic documentary. Then you did one, which was ten parts, on the Vietnam War, which was more controversial. People were watching it who had been alive during the war. Were you worried that it was going to inflame people? What did you learn that you most wanted people to learn about?

KB: I think the Civil War was, and is still, more controversial. It's the heart of who we are. The best way to understand how important the Civil War was is that before the war, when speaking about our country, we would say, "The United States are." Plural. It's actually grammatically correct. Now we say "The United States is." That is not grammatically correct, but we say it. And the war, for whatever it did or didn't do, made us an "is"—so far.

I thought Vietnam would be controversial. We assembled a war room of Senator McCain's former chief of staff and Senator Kerry's people. We had eight or nine people from both sides of the aisle ready to fight back with what we thought was eminently fair, completely new scholarship about the war. But there was almost no pushback. Cobwebs grew in our "war room." With the exception of what you'd expect on the far reaches of the left and the right, there was nothing, no meaningful criticism.

The film benefited from that scholarship—new stuff about the Gulf of Tonkin, newly released documents about North Vietnamese military strategy, stuff from Vietnamese civilians in the South, Vietnamese civilians in the North, soldiers in America who were talking exactly like soldiers in North Vietnam.

To answer your ultimate question, I think that if governments tell the people the truth, things are better than if they don't.

DR: What I took from your Vietnam series was that Democrats and Republicans both misled the public about the winnability of the war. Is that fair?

KB: That is totally fair.

DR: You recently gave a commencement address at Brandeis University. Generally you are fairly down the middle politically; you're not offending anybody if you can avoid it. That speech went viral. Why did you give a commencement speech at Brandeis, and what was your main message?

KB: I've given a lot of commencement addresses, and only once before had I strayed from the neutrality of just calling balls and strikes. Certainly, in my work that's all I do. You'll see it in *The American*

Revolution. For example, we're not a country without George Washington, but there's some other stuff you need to know about him, too.

We're at a critical moment in our nation's history, and I wanted to call attention to that in my address. One small part of the speech is dedicated to what I think is an existential moment for us right now in the country. But most of the speech was trying to say that maybe the reason why we are where we are is that we are so dialectically preoccupied. Everything is either rich or poor, red state or blue state, North or South, East or West, gay or straight, male or female, Palestinian or Israeli. All we know is argument. There is nothing binary in the world, actually, in nature, but we make everything binary. The novelist Richard Powers said, and I quoted this in my commencement address, "The best arguments in the world won't change a single person's point of view. The only thing that can do that is a good story."

A good story is a vehicle that allows you to tolerate contradiction and undertow, to be able to hold, as we all do in our personal lives, the features of someone that can be both attractive and unattractive. And yet in most of our civic lives—now I can't even call them civic lives, because we've stopped teaching civics—we don't even know what that means. In our political arena, we have become so dialectically preoccupied that we don't listen. What I was trying to talk about is how to undo that—to learn to tell stories, to learn to listen. I used the word *listen* as a kind of verbal trope throughout. *Listen, listen.*

And I would tell stories, and I would quote Abraham Lincoln, who spoke to the Young Men's Lyceum in 1838. He's not even twenty-nine years old, and he says, "When shall we expect the approach of danger? Shall some transatlantic giant step the earth and crush us at a blow? Never. All the armies of Europe, Asia, and Africa could not, by force, take a drink from the Ohio River or make a track in the Blue Ridge in the trial of a thousand years. If destruction be our lot, we must ourselves be its author and finisher. As a nation of free men, we will live through all time or die by suicide."

I said to the graduates that I have had the great privilege for five decades of making films about the US, but I've also made films about *us*—that is to say, the lowercase, two-letter plural pronoun. All of the intimacy of *us* and *we* and *our*, and all of the majesty, the complexity, the contradiction, and even the controversy of the United States. That's where I've operated, and that's a way to begin to understand.

I urged them to think about character. I said, "Choose virtue over vulgarity. Choose discipline over dissipation, honor over hypocrisy. If you're going to insist on a binary situation, at least choose the thing that points us in the direction of what Thomas Jefferson meant when he wrote 'the pursuit of happiness.' Which was not the acquisition of things in a marketplace of objects but lifelong learning. If we do that, we survive."

DR: With *The Vietnam War*, you educated people about the fact that the US government misled people. In *The Civil War*, you showed how destructive that war was and how much death came about. What are we going to learn from your Revolutionary War series that is going to open our eyes and make our jaws drop?

KB: We have protected the Revolution like it was a relic encased in amber. We're willing to accept the bloodshed of the Civil War, World War I, World War II, Vietnam, Korea, all of that. We are not willing to understand that the Revolution was, in fact, a civil war. There are lots of players. There aren't just fifty-five guys in Philadelphia thinking great thoughts. And some of those great thoughts forged some compromises, and some of those compromises are beyond brilliant, and some of them are beyond tragic—counting people who were enslaved as three-fifths of a person when in the previous decade you had declared that all people were created equal. There's complication in our Revolution. Fully a fifth—20 percent—of the population is loyalist, and they will start terrorist organizations to fight the terrorist organizations of the Patriots that are killing their neighbors.

Our Civil War is not a civil war. Civil wars mean large civilian deaths, and we didn't have that in our Civil War, except in Missouri and Kansas. Two people died at Gettysburg who were civilians. Very few at Vicksburg. It's a sectional war, North against South. But our Revolution *was* a civil war. Lots of stories have *not* been told, including the ticktock, if you will, of what the sequence of battles is. We know Lexington and Concord, and then we think Yorktown. But it was a long six and a half years between those battles. There are so many things about the battles that are important to understand. I would love to sit here and draw you a map of the Battle of Cowpens in South Carolina and tell you what Daniel Morgan did to the British in this fight, and to understand the larger stakes and the context of our founding.

DR: Washington lost more battles than he won.

KB: He learned something fundamental in the French and Indian War, when General Braddock was ambushed by the French and Indians at Fort Duquesne, Pittsburgh, and was mortally wounded, as was most of his staff. The command fell to Washington, and he executed a great retreat, was celebrated for it, and he learned two super-important lessons. One, the British army was not invincible. Two, you didn't have to win, you just didn't have to surrender. There was no shame in retreating to fight another day, and that's what he did. And yes, he won at Trenton, he won at Princeton, it's a draw at Monmouth, but everywhere else, it's an unmitigated series of losses. The biggest battle is Brooklyn, is Long Island, a loss. Kips Bay, a few days later, a loss. At Harlem Heights, the Americans kind of hold off the British. White Plains, a loss. All through New Jersey, losses, losses. Brandywine, Germantown, Camden, Charleston. Nothing really goes his way until the last battle, Yorktown.

DR: Historians don't like counterfactuals. But suppose we had lost the Revolutionary War and suppose the South had won the Civil War. How would history be different?

KB: The first part of the question is super complicated. I think things would have gone on in a very interesting way. The British would have to have spent a lot of money subjugating us, and probably at some point they'd have given up.

The South could not have won. As Shelby Foote himself said, the North fought the war "with one arm tied behind its back. And if there had been more Southern victories, and a lot more," he said, "the North would have just taken the other arm and swatted back." If the South had won, you would have a funny situation in North America where you would have this growing industrial power matched by something that was beginning to stagnate, and I would think that by World War I, the South would be knocking at the door to come back in.

DR: The Revolutionary War, the Civil War, Vietnam—those are important subjects, and this is an important one. How did you come to the idea of doing a film on Muhammad Ali?

KB: I hope my answer about Jackie Robinson was central. I did a film on Jack Johnson, the first African American heavyweight champion. Unexpected. Black people were not supposed to fight for the championship belt, because they might win. And he did, when he was given a chance. The reason why we have the expression "Great White Hope" was to put people up against Jack Johnson, people whom he dispatched, and when they couldn't beat him in the ring, they went after him in his personal life.

Sports is an arena in which we play out many of the larger themes in American life. In the case of Jackie Robinson, it's obviously hugely important. If you think about who he was in the 1940s and '50s, he was the ultimate symbol of Black masculinity. That changed with Muhammad Ali. If you want to continue to follow a theme about identity in America and who we are, ask yourself a question: Wouldn't you want to know more about somebody who, at the end of the '60s, was the most reviled person in America (for his refusal to be inducted into the Army), and who dies the most beloved person on our planet?

We were curious about what happened all the way through his life—private as well as public. It wasn't just the boxing matches, which we wanted to take apart. It wasn't just the personal life. It wasn't just the family life. It wasn't just the Nation of Islam. It wasn't just the opposition to the Vietnam War and the refusing of the draft and this and that. It was the totality of this person whose faith saw him through. I don't know a better story in America.

DR: How many films do you have in the works now that are coming out?

KB: I hope they all come out, God and funding willing. There's five productions. *Leonardo da Vinci*'s done. *The American Revolution*, the most complicated thing we've ever done. At one point in that film, Christopher Brown, a Black historian, for the only time in the film breaks the fourth wall. That means he's talking to us instead of answering the unheard question. He finally goes, "I don't really believe in the great man theory of history, but I don't know how we become a republic without George Washington." And it's really a sigh of relief.

We're doing a history of Reconstruction. It's called *Emancipation to Exodus*, just exactly what it sounds like, the exodus being the Great Migration, which begins at the end of World War I and goes for six decades, of African Americans out of the Jim Crow South into the North—as Richard Wright said, to "the warmth of other suns," the title of Isabel Wilkerson's wonderful book about that period. We're doing a film on LBJ and the Great Society. One of the more interesting and tragic people in the Vietnam War was LBJ. Obviously Richard Nixon as well, whom you could do endless things on.

There's a trope that if Kennedy hadn't died, we wouldn't have gotten deeper into Vietnam. That's crazy, because Johnson went to Kennedy's people after Dallas, and he said to McNamara, and he said to Rusk, and he said to Bundy, "I need you more than he needed you." Because Kennedy was an internationalist. LBJ was a disciple of Franklin Roosevelt and the New Deal, and he wanted to be the second coming of it. We wanted to back up and understand what his ambitious domestic policy was until the din of Vietnam made it harder to enact.

We've been interviewing people who knew Dr. King, not just the famous folks—John Lewis, I think we got the last interview he did, and we certainly got the last interview with Harry Belafonte—but people who would pick King up at the Albany, Georgia, airport and feed him and give him the spare bedroom and take him to church the next day. People who were doing the same thing in Birmingham and Montgomery. It's an important thing. We've lost a little bit of touch when we mythologize and make icons out of people.

I've now just started talking about it, but I've spent the last three and a half years interviewing President Obama. We've done two eight-hour interviews so far. We have one or two more to go. The idea is that, with no rush, somewhere down the line to look at the important, seminal, groundbreaking eight years of his administration.

DR: You do this from the media center of New York City?

KB: I live, as you know, in a tiny village in New Hampshire. I've been there for forty-six years, and I've made all the films there. We do have offices in New York and Brooklyn where my coproducers often are. And, of course, our beat is the country. When somebody says, "I live in this little town, Johnston or something north of Des Moines," I go, "I know where that is," because we've driven through it for one project or another.

DR: You did something on Lyndon Johnson. Is the job of being a Senate majority leader very easy?

KB: We like to think of him as the master of the Senate. If you actually go back and examine the legislative accomplishments of his Senate majority, it's not very spectacular. He's a good manipulator. He can get stuff done. He came late to civil rights. But only a Southerner could have sold the landmark Civil Rights and Voting Rights Acts to others and made it happen. And then many of the things that we take for granted today, like public television, come out of that Great Society vision, a kind of extension of the New Deal. But I think no majority leader has done more with less than Lyndon Johnson did.

DR: Your shows are on PBS. Why don't you put them on commercial television and make a buck out of it?

KB: You have to measure richness on a different scale than just what's in your bank account. I have friends who work in Hollywood and/or TV and they often complain about feeling constrained. I could go at any time to a premium cable channel or a streaming service and get the $30 million for Vietnam, but they'd never let it be eighteen hours. Maybe now they would, because everybody's bingeing. But after *The Civil War*, they all came to me and they said, "What are you doing next?" I said, "Baseball." They said, "Two hours?" I said, "I think it's going to be eighteen and a half." They passed. It had an even bigger audience than *The Civil War*. They came to me: "What are you going to do now? Jazz? Oh, no, Black stuff doesn't sell." I finally went, "I like this place here." PBS. There are no commercials, obviously. There's not a suit telling me to make it longer or shorter or sexier, less sexy, or more violent or less violent. If I went to, say, a premium channel, and I said, "I want to do a history of the Vietnam War, and it's going to be $30 million," they'd give it to me. But they wouldn't give me ten and a half years to make it. They wouldn't treat it like a university or a hospital doing research. I said, "It's going to take me ten and a half years to do it." And there is not a business model out there that would tolerate that expenditure, except in public television, where I'm raising the money. There's funding from the Corporation for Public Broadcasting and PBS itself. But most of it is going to come from Bank of America, our sole corporate underwriter, from you, and from foundations and other individuals of wealth. And we're going to work with all these scholars and we're going to take the time to do it right.

I was finishing the World War II film in 2006. It was broadcast in the fall of 2007. I'd already said we weren't going to do any more wars, and then we did the World War II film. I just said, "We're doing Vietnam." And then before the ink was dry on Vietnam, I said, "We're doing the American Revolution."

I had no idea back in 2016 that I'd be approaching the 250th anniversary of the country when it's going to be shown. It's just that these stories need to be told.

That is only one argument for public television, which is the largest network in our country. I have been in places in Nebraska, I've been in places in Tennessee where the only signal you can get is a PBS station. It's much more important to the lives of people there than it is in Nob Hill or the Upper West Side or Georgetown. It is central to their lives, with continuing education, classroom of the air, children's programming, obviously the prime-time stuff but also weather reports and homeland security. We like to think of it as some sort of liberal bastion. But let's remember William F. Buckley's *Firing Line* was one of the most popular shows on PBS for thirty-two years.

DR: It's an incredible career, and I want to thank you as an American for everything you've done to educate us about our own history and the history of so many other things that are important. I want to thank Dr. Carla Hayden for putting this all together, but also the exhibition upstairs is an idea that the Library of Congress had. Let me explain what the reason for it is.

The Library of Congress has an incredible number of artifacts. It's got the greatest number of books in the world, the greatest number of comic books, everything you could possibly think about. But when people come to Washington to visit, they often go to the Smithsonian, which is a great institution. I've been the chair of it. Nineteen terrific museums funded by Congress. People will go to the National Archives and see the great documents there. But people don't know that the Library of Congress has artifacts that are unique and that they can come see them, because there was no one place where they could all come together and see them. So Carla had the idea, with her team, to find one place where the best, most valuable artifacts could be put, so when people come to the Library of Congress, it's not seen only as a research library but as a library where you can come and learn about America by seeing these famous artifacts. Carla has also done a great deal to educate people about the importance of literacy and children learning, and so part of the money that Congress has given to redo the Library of Congress has been to make sure we have a place where children can come; they can learn how to read and appreciate the importance of reading.

2

Stacy Schiff on Samuel Adams

INTERVIEW DATE: JUNE 13, 2023

Stacy Schiff is an acclaimed essayist and biographer who won a Pulitzer Prize for her work on Véra Nabokov, wife of the famed novelist Vladimir Nabokov. Schiff was also a Pulitzer finalist for her biography of Antoine de Saint-Exupéry. She is perhaps best known for her number-one best-selling biography of Cleopatra, which has been translated into thirty languages.

In recent years, she has applied her considerable writing skills to books on American subjects: Benjamin Franklin, the Salem witch trials, and, most recently, Samuel Adams. His younger cousin John, is, of course, much better known—a leader in the Second Continental Congress, the first vice president of the United States, and the country's second president.

But, as Schiff makes clear in her book *The Revolutionary: Samuel Adams* and in our Dialogues discussion, it was Samuel Adams who was the driving force in the Massachusetts colony during the fight against various taxes imposed by the British after the French and Indian War. It was Samuel Adams whom the British army was trying to capture (along with John Hancock) as they moved toward Lexington and Concord, which led to the first skirmishes (and killings) of the war—"the shot heard 'round the world." And it was Samuel Adams

FIGURE 2.1 Though less remembered today than his cousin John, Samuel Adams was an intellectual leader of the American Revolution, invoking the ire of the British, who sought to capture him when fighting erupted in April 1775.

who authored many of the pamphlets and articles condemning British taxation and who, in many ways, served as the intellectual leader of the revolutionary movement, crystallizing its ideas and knitting the colonies together.

Samuel Adams was not interested in calling attention to himself and did not seek glory or a visible public role. But he was the acknowledged leader within and well beyond Massachusetts. Crown officers considered him the greatest incendiary in the king's dominion, the most dangerous man in America. After the war, he served as Massachusetts's governor.

His father operated a malt business, though not a brewery. Adams found little success with it and had no better luck as a Massachusetts tax collector. That had been his principal occupation prior to the war, and his failings in that role would not have suggested he would later be a hero in the Revolution.

But as Stacy Schiff made clear in our discussion, Adams was essentially unrivaled as the intellectual force behind the effort to break away from the mother country. He did this without seeking acclaim or glory. But for Schiff's book and the current Samuel Adams beer, he might well have passed into history as only a relative of his better-known cousin, who came to eclipse him.

DAVID M. RUBENSTEIN (DR): When I was growing up, John Adams was the more famous member of the Adams family. He was the first vice president and the second president. Was Samuel Adams more important in the Revolutionary War than John Adams? They were cousins?

STACY SCHIFF (SS): They're second cousins. John is thirteen years younger than Samuel, a sort of starry-eyed country cousin, whom Samuel effectively recruits to the cause. Samuel is the older, wiser Bostonian, an urbanite, from a much wealthier family. One's status in eighteenth-century Massachusetts could be read in one's place in the Harvard class. Samuel was sixth in his class, while John was fourteenth in his. John fell quickly under the spell of his cousin, whom he thought a man of great erudition, excellent judgment, and steadfast integrity. The two of them agreed from the start that American liberties stood in danger, and identified the same culprits behind those incursions. John often did Samuel's bidding over the pre-Revolutionary years, from his early writing assignments to the defense of the redcoats after the Boston Massacre.

DR: When Samuel Adams was growing up, his father was what?

SS: A maltster. He prepared the malt from which beer is brewed.

DR: His father was in the beer business.

SS: Adjacent, as we would say today.

DR: His father was a reasonably prominent person. He had how many children?

SS: There were actually twelve children, of which only three survived, a not unusual ratio for the time and place. Theirs was a wealthy family, something that Adams's enemies failed to grasp. He was not a desperado, eager—as the Crown officers tended to assume—for American independence because he had nothing to lose. He was instead the downwardly mobile son of an affluent family, which put him in a position to connect, as I think no one else could have done, the New England elite with the dockyard workers, the candlemakers, the bricklayers. He knew his way about the Boston street. At the same time, he was on intimate terms with the town's leaders.

DR: Samuel Adams went to Harvard College. Harvard in those days was designed to train ministers, I assume. Did he want to be a minister at any point?

SS: If you had an intellectually agile son, you hoped he would become a minister; it was the traditional career for the gifted, book-loving New England son. For some reason, pious though he was, Adams did not seem to be attracted to the ministry.

DR: His father gave him some money to go into business. How did that work out?

SS: The exact answer has been lost to time, but it seems the money went missing, too. Adams never in his life made a wise financial decision, something on which he prided himself. He inherited a sum of money. He squandered it. He inherited his father's business. He ran it into the ground. He briefly worked in an accounting firm, from which he was dismissed because, as his boss put it, he was a perfectly able-bodied young man, but his mind was utterly consumed by politics. He was really a man of ideas. He appeared to live on air, which on closer examination turned out to be the generosity of any number of friends.

DR: He becomes a tax collector. And if you don't collect the taxes you're supposed to collect, you have to pay it back yourself?

SS: It was an odd system. No one cared to collect taxes; most men who were appointed to the office chose to pay a fine rather than serve. The incumbents often ran as fast as they could in the opposite direction. Adams seems to have taken the job because at the time he had two small children and desperately needed the income. Essentially the way the system worked was that you received a premium on the taxes you collected but were also responsible for any funds your ward failed to deliver. After a few years of what sounds like lackadaisical collecting, Adams was approximately eight times more delinquent than any of the other delinquent collectors. I will note that the delinquent tax collector was no doubt also the popular tax collector.

DR: How did he get involved with opposing what the British were doing? To put it in context, after the so-called French and Indian War, or the Seven Years' War, the British are saying, "Hey, we put a lot of money up to defend the colonies against the French and the Indians, and maybe you could pay us back a little bit by letting us tax you." What do the people in the Massachusetts colony think about that idea? Were the British all wrong in saying that they should be getting some money back for the protection they provided?

SS: It's a little more complicated than that. The Sugar and Stamp Acts essentially are the first edicts to unite the colonies. Some historians have noted that there has been no American question on which there has been such perfect unanimity, before or since. At issue was not simply the question of taxation without representation; even Crown officers thought the Stamp Act, for example, was an example of imperial overreach. At issue was really a definition of the colonial relationship, which, oddly, had been left largely undefined and which began to beg for definition as the colonies came into their own. The Massachusetts Charter, for example, never once mentioned the word "Parliament."

So those efforts to tax the colonies are in part an attempt to delineate a relationship between the overseas possessions and the mother country, to determine how the colonies fit into the empire. Who was actually in charge? The relationship was a muddle. Throughout this period the Americans were extremely aware of the fact that they were looked upon with condescension by London, where few seemed able even to locate them on a map. No high-ranking Crown officer had so much as set eyes on America. Londoners wondered if Philadelphia were in the East Indies or the West Indies. Generally there was a cluelessness on the part of London about what to do about these far-off possessions, about who lived there, what language they spoke, and even what color they were.

DR: The British impose some taxes. How does Samuel Adams express his opposition? Does he own a newspaper, or does he write articles in other people's newspapers? Does he use his own name or does he use somebody else's name?

SS: Let me reverse the order of your questions. One of the beauties of writing about Samuel Adams, by which I mean one of the most daunting parts, is that he published under a host of pseudonyms. I've counted thirty-two, though I'm doubtless missing some. He writes under classical pseudonyms, which are easy to explain, like Vindex or Candidus. He also writes as "A Chatterer" and as "An American." But then he chooses other names, like "Alfred," more difficult for us to understand. The masquerade allowed him to audition ideas; the many pseudonyms made it seem as if the discontent was general. And they allowed him, in different voices, to address different subjects. He might use one pseudonym to advocate for freedom of the press and another pseudonym to rail against taxation without representation and another to issue an anthem to liberty. He had been known to wield an especially artful pen; the first response from Massachusetts to the Stamp Act was entrusted to Samuel Adams by the Massachusetts Assembly, of which he was not officially a member. He was tapped for his eloquence.

DR: The British impose some taxes. There's opposition. The British take those taxes off. They impose some other taxes, there's concern about that, and then, in 1773, there's the famous Boston Tea Party. Was Samuel Adams behind the Boston Tea Party?

SS: Indisputably so, though the extent is difficult to map with precision. One remarkable thing about the Boston Tea Party is that while thousands of Bostonians stood on the wharf that December evening as a group of camouflaged "Indians" jumped on the ships, hoisted up the cargo, slashed open the chests, and dumped the tea into the harbor, the next day no one had seen a thing. It was difficult to find a single witness to the Boston Tea Party, unlike the Boston Massacre, of which nearly every Bostonian was able and eager to provide an account.

That said, Adams and his closest colleagues made a conspicuous effort to avoid the wharf. The following morning the royal governor cursed that Adams "never was in greater glory." Adams had orchestrated the meetings that preceded the destruction. And when twelve men were deposed later in London by the Crown authorities, where it was safer to speak, those men named Adams among the chief conspirators behind what we know today as the Boston Tea Party.

DR: Now, the British think that Samuel Adams is behind it. Do they send troops over to capture people like Samuel Adams and John Hancock?

SS: Samuel Adams and John Hancock are the two most wanted men in Massachusetts for many years. You can read in the British archives any number of attempts, from the late 1760s on, to find a statute, any statute, by which Samuel Adams and his fellow "incendiaries" might be lawfully deported and tried for treason in London. The Crown tried over and over to do this by the book; over and over they fumbled in locating legal language that would work, save for an ancient statute of Henry VIII. At one point the solicitor general and the attorney general feuded, as one of them believed Adams could be arrested and deported and the other disagreed. But the idea for many years was that if you could simply silence Samuel Adams, "the great incendiary" as the British appointed him, you could quash a stubborn, pesky opposition. For a long time, it seemed to be the work of a few disgruntled provocateurs, Adams chief among them. That clause in the Declaration of Independence, by the way, about deporting Americans overseas to be tried for pretended offenses? I'm fairly certain that was a nod to Samuel Adams.

DR: John Hancock became famous for his signature on the Declaration of Independence, but who was the more senior person at that time? Was it Samuel Adams?

SS: Adams also serves as a sort of one-man recruiting office. If you delivered the finest Harvard commencement address on the subject of liberty anyone had ever heard, you could count on finding Samuel Adams on your doorstep the next morning. Among Adams's recruits was John Hancock, fifteen years younger. He was immensely rich. Adams seems to have calculated that the fortune would be of great use to the cause, while a political office would be of great interest to John Hancock, who thrived on adulation.

DR: The British can't find Adams; they can't find Hancock. Where did Hancock and Adams go?

SS: The night of Lexington and Concord? They spent some portion of it in a swamp.

DR: In a swamp?

SS: Ultimately, after Paul Revere had warned them that redcoats were en route, they wind up crouched together in a swamp. Thomas Gage, the general dispatched to Massachusetts to quash the opposition movement, was authorized to arrest its leaders. He soon discovered that he could not easily arrest Samuel Adams. Early in 1774 he had received specific orders to do so, by which time he realized he had missed his moment. Instead he marched his men out of Boston with orders to seize the munitions in Concord, to burn the tents and drown the musket balls in water. He may have sent an oral command to arrest Adams and Hancock as well, which was obviously what Paul Revere and their friends understood; it was the order that sent Revere flying, to warn Adams and Hancock of imminent arrest that evening.

DR: In 1773, there's the Boston Tea Party. Hancock and Adams escape from the British. In 1774, there is the First Continental Congress, and the meeting of the First Continental Congress is called in part by Samuel Adams? Who instigated the idea of the colonies meeting for the first time in Philadelphia?

SS: The idea had been under discussion for years. No one knows precisely who the genius behind it was. Early in 1774 a group of Massachusetts legislators meet, ostensibly to discuss whether the East India Company should be reimbursed for the tea tossed into the harbor. Adams and his colleagues hijacked the meeting, spiriting off those who believed in compensating the East India Company on false pretenses and holding a secret session, in which they instead agreed on a delegation to travel to Philadelphia. Adams is instrumental in shaping that delegation, in making sure that they have the funds for the trip. Philadelphia seems to have been chosen for its central location.

DR: To put it in context, at that time more of the delegates had been to London than had ever been to Philadelphia or to any other colonies. The colonies related to England more than they related to each other?

SS: At the time, if you mailed a letter from Georgia to Boston, it traveled first to London.

DR: When they get to the First Continental Congress, who are the leaders? Is Samuel Adams a leader there, or is John Adams a leader?

SS: So great was Samuel Adams's reputation at the time that, by this point, if you were the lead opposition figure in your colony, you were known as the Samuel Adams of North Carolina, or the Samuel Adams of Georgia, or the Samuel Adams of Rhode Island.

On the other hand, for the Southern colonies, and even for the mid-Atlantic colonies, there was a fear of the radical New Englanders. They appeared to many as hotheaded fanatics; some feared that they would take over their colonies as well. As the Massachusetts delegation traveled south to the congress, Adams was advised over and over that he needed to restrain himself, that he would be wise to take a backseat. Which he did; he operated behind the scenes, not that the Southern delegates failed to feel his influence there. John Adams would later say this was the reason why General Washington led the troops, why Richard Henry Lee proposed the Declaration, and why Thomas Jefferson wrote it. The New Englanders expressly assigned those tasks to the Virginians, known to be more moderate and refined men.

DR: In the First Continental Congress, the effort is to try to get the British to back down on the taxes, to appeal to King George, not to break away. At the time, there weren't many people saying we should divorce ourselves from England, were there?

SS: That's right. It's next to impossible to locate a dividing line. Several historians have claimed that Samuel Adams decided on independence in 1768, when troops first arrived in Boston. I don't see any evidence that that's true, however. The emphasis for many years was on redress rather than revolt; there really was a feeling that if everyone could just go back to 1763, to the years before Parliament's blundering overreach, all would be fine. In any event, "independence" was not a word one bandied about. Washington would say that as late as the fall of 1774 no one in North America desired a rupture with the mother country. Franklin said the same in the spring of 1775. John Adams early in 1776 balked at the idea.

DR: So, they ask King George to rescind the taxes. They appeal to him even though he's not really running the government. The Continental Congress ends. Where does Samuel Adams go between 1774 and 1776?

SS: Much of the time he's back in Boston. He believed that independence should have been declared the morning after shots were fired at Concord. Had it been declared, he was certain the Canadians would have joined the American colonies. He then returns to Philadelphia for the Second Continental Congress.

DR: The Second Continental Congress is begun in 1775. At that point, people are beginning to say, "Maybe we should break away." Is Samuel Adams a leader of that effort to break away from Britain?

SS: There's a great deal of evidence of subtle arm-twisting behind the scenes, as opposed to Adams's taking a more formal role. He takes to heart the advice that he needs to proceed patiently and delicately. At the same time, you can feel him chomping at the bit. When he returned to London, the Massachusetts royal governor would tell King George that Samuel Adams had been the first to settle on the idea of independence, though the Massachusetts royal governor also said a fair number of things about Samuel Adams that were patently untrue. But there's no mistaking Thomas Jefferson's assessment, and he called Adams "the earliest, most active, and most persevering man of the Revolution."

DR: Samuel Adams is older than John Adams by how many years?

SS: Thirteen years.

DR: Thirteen years, and he's more the revolutionary. Why does John Adams get so much of the credit for being in favor of breaking away from England when Samuel Adams was probably more of an instigator in doing that?

SS: Samuel Adams was a man without vanity who believed in selfless public service. John was a man of tremendous vanity who wrote, in my opinion, the best letters of all of the Founders. And if you write the best letters, you get best remembered; John Adams is unfailingly quotable. John did advise Samuel after the Revolution that he should not leave the heroics to others and that he should make a collection of his papers. John went so far as to wager that the papers of Samuel Adams would explain the history of America as no other documents could. And Samuel Adams never seems to have lifted a finger to comply.

Which is to say that you have, on the one hand, a diffident man who's comfortable standing behind the scenes, who doesn't play for an audience, who hails from the no-fingerprints school of revolution. And you have a man who loves the limelight, who never meets anyone about whom he fails to form a piquant, quotable opinion, who leaves behind a wealth of material—and who goes on to play a role on the federal stage, as Samuel Adams never does.

DR: In the Second Continental Congress, there's a motion to get all the delegates to go back to their colonies and get permission to break away from England. Then there's a committee formed to draft a Declaration of Independence. John Adams is on that committee with Thomas Jefferson and Benjamin Franklin, among others. Why wasn't Samuel Adams on that committee?

SS: That's a matter of conjecture. John Adams would have seemed the less radical alternative. And certainly one Adams man would suffice; very often, the British would say there were too many Adamses in Massachusetts. If you want a measure of Samuel's fame vis-à-vis John during these years, here it is: When John Adams arrived in France to assist Benjamin Franklin in raising funds for the Revolution, people assumed he was the famous Mr. Adams, by which they meant Samuel. Poor John had to disappoint them. He was a different Mr. Adams.

DR: Samuel Adams and John Adams both sign the Declaration of Independence?

SS: Under the bolder signature of John Hancock.

DR: When they sign it, they've committed treason, you could argue. Were the British going to try to hang Samuel Adams if they caught him?

SS: For years, Adams had read in the papers that he was about to hang or face deportation at any moment. This added to his allure; he did nothing to lower his profile or to curtail his activities. He did not mind walking about Boston as a wanted man, on the verge of being sent back to London in chains. He's fearless and he's incorruptible. At various earlier points there appear to have been attempts to bribe him, all of which—to the frustration of Crown officers—he resists.

DR: He's a wanted man, so he has to be careful. Does he fight in the war?

SS: He's in Congress throughout the entire war, serving on more committees than I can count. Which I suppose is a kind of war, no? He regularly wound up on committees to answer Washington's letters. At one point he was amused to find himself—among the worst-dressed and least worldly of delegates—on the committee for deciding ceremonials.

DR: So, he stayed in Congress? He hung out in Philadelphia, basically, for quite a while?

SS: Philadelphia, Baltimore, Lancaster—everywhere Congress fled, Samuel Adams lived. He especially took to Baltimore, you will be happy to know. As there was categorically nothing to do there, Congress worked more efficiently.

DR: The final battle of the war is in 1781, and they sign the Treaty of Paris in 1783. Where does Samuel Adams go after it's over?

SS: He returns to Boston and to relative obscurity. He's briefly governor of Massachusetts. He and John Hancock, who have maintained a love/hate relationship for decades, suffer yet another falling-out. Hancock does his best thoroughly to malign Adams. The relationship ultimately mellows a little bit, and they briefly serve together as governor and lieutenant governor. Hancock then dies. Adams finishes his term and serves three more terms on his own. He is by then a myth and a monument, a sort of relic, the first port of call when a foreign revolutionary lands in America. He's what Thomas Jefferson calls an apostle of liberty, the father of this revolution, who otherwise lives in perfect obscurity.

DR: Samuel Adams becomes governor of Massachusetts, but his cousin becomes president of the United States. Is there a rivalry there?

SS: None whatever. By this point, Samuel Adams has grown old; his health is compromised. There's some hesitation on his part to embrace a federal entity. He remains a true New England man; he's somewhat backward-looking at the end of his life, having fought this battle, as he sees it, for an ancient purity of principles. He's not at ease with the capitalistic, opulent direction in which America seems headed. He's on the fence about ratifying the Constitution. And he has no interest whatever in playing on a national stage. He had helped to erect America's intellectual architecture but seemed to have had little interest—unlike his cousin—in institutions.

DR: How long does Samuel Adams serve as governor?

SS: He's there for the rest of one of Hancock's terms, after which he serves three additional terms.

DR: And when does he die?

SS: He dies at eighty-one in 1803.

DR: And he has two children who survive him.

SS: One who survives him, actually.

DR: Why do you think it is that historians have given so much attention to John Adams but not so much to Samuel Adams?

SS: A great deal of the answer, I think, comes in how we like to remember our Revolution. Samuel Adams represents the messy, anarchic part. As one historian has written, the Revolution was for many years cleansed of any trace of rebellion. We have turned the destruction of the East India tea into a "party"; we have done our best to forget the acts of civil resistance, the boycotts and pickets and vandalism and extralegal institutions. The crowd actions, the street theater, we largely owe to Samuel Adams. The resistance that he organized and led for those twelve or fourteen years is something we tend to think away. We prefer to focus on the high Jeffersonian ideals rather than the raucous crowds in the streets, or the pillaging of the home of a royal governor. And after a revolution, it's essential after all to trundle off the revolutionaries.

DR: What is the message you want to convey to readers of your book on Samuel Adams?

SS: That words matter, that ordinary citizens are more powerful than they might believe, that one enlightened individual can effect a tremendous change, and that the Revolution was neither a predetermined nor a directly longitudinal event. It moves by fits and starts. There are any number of dead ends. There are some moments of pure stagnation. At one point after the Boston Massacre, Adams is alone in sustaining an opposition effort. Everyone else has either been bought off by the royal governor or is essentially exhausted by the previous years of struggle. Adams stands alone. There's a fierce integrity and a kind of noble service with him that you don't see with the other Founders. You can't wholly understand the Revolution, or at least its origins, without him in the picture. Not only does he cast it in a different light, but if you return him to the picture, you see what John Adams called the revolution in thinking that preceded the revolution in fighting.

DR: Did Samuel Adams and John Adams get along?

SS: They get along extremely well until the end of Samuel's life, at which point John thinks that Samuel has essentially grown rigid. He's not entirely wrong. But it's also John who reminds us that Samuel Adams was not a firebrand or a scold, but rather a man of tremendous erudition, of gentle integrity and a real delicacy of feeling, which is not at all the Adams of legend.

DR: When you're doing research on someone like Samuel Adams, where do you get letters or other materials? Where did you find the information about him?

SS: The Adams papers, conveniently for me, are today in the New York Public Library. That collection is especially rich, as it includes both Adamses' letters and the other side of the correspondence, which I'm not sure anyone had read closely before. You have, for example, the letters from the acquaintance who stopped at Adams's house at one point when Adams was in Philadelphia, at Congress, to cart off his papers so that, as the acquaintance writes, "those vultures will have nothing of yours, which would have provided them such hellish pleasures." You can read of the esteem in which he's held in Boston, where people go out of their way to protect him. That's something that does not emerge from his correspondence, modest as he is on every occasion, even when describing, for example, the glorious welcome he and John Hancock receive when they enter New York City in the wake of Lexington and Concord.

What one's enemies have to say about one is extremely telling, so a great wealth of the book derives from material in the British archives.

The Crown officials all reported to London regularly, often daily. They write continually about that incorrigible rogue Samuel Adams and the havoc he is working. For every possible reason, he's not writing about what he's doing. Which is to say that in the British National Archives in Kew is a mother lode of material about what Adams is actually up to or at least what the Crown officers believe he's up to. He often gets credit for things that he did not do or for essays he did not write. But you can trace his movements from what his enemies have to say about him better than you can from what he himself reports.

DR: Benjamin Franklin wrote one of the first autobiographies by an American. Why didn't Samuel Adams write an autobiography saying "how I won the war"?

SS: I should love to know the answer; it's a terrible lacuna on Adams's part. I'd also like to know a great deal more about the orchestration of the Tea Party, for the record.

DR: How long did it take you to research and write this book?

SS: A book usually takes me five years. This one took six, possibly because I spent a number of months sourcing Purell and washing down my vegetables. The papers are more scattered than they have been for my other books; the life is more difficult to excavate than, say, Ben Franklin's. And I probably spent too much time reading eighteenth-century newspapers. But I prefer to blame COVID.

DR: You've won a Pulitzer Prize, and you've written some great books, but they've all been about people who are dead. Have you ever thought of writing a book about somebody who's alive?

SS: Until recently I shied from the idea. It always seemed to me that a clinical distance was necessary to biography, that I needed to see my subject with sufficient detachment. And, too, you want the supporting cast to be able to speak freely. I may finally have arrived at the point where I'm willing to reverse myself on this. For the right subject, I do think I would take the plunge. Especially if that subject happened to have excellent handwriting. Of which Samuel Adams was decidedly not possessed.

3

Allen C. Guelzo on Ulysses S. Grant and Robert E. Lee

INTERVIEW DATE: JULY 22, 2015

Allen Guelzo has long been one of the country's leading scholars of the Civil War, based for many years at Gettysburg College, where he was the director of Civil War Era Studies, and more recently at Princeton University, where he directed the James Madison Program in American Ideals and Institutions. In the summer of 2025, he joined the University of Florida faculty as professor of humanities. He has written widely on the Civil War, including such prize-winning, best-selling books as *Lincoln's Emancipation Proclamation: The End of Slavery in America*; *Gettysburg: The Last Invasion*; and *Robert E. Lee: A Life.*

Robert E. Lee is one of American history's most interesting figures: the son of a Revolutionary War general who was a good friend of George Washington; the husband of a step-great-granddaughter of George Washington; a leading military figure in the Mexican-American War; a general in the US Army before the Civil War; and someone who commanded so much respect that Abraham Lincoln, through a close friend, asked Lee to lead the Union army in the war against the states that had seceded or were about to secede.

But Lee turned that offer down because of his deep commitment to Virginia and his belief that Virginia would, in time, secede. He could not, in good conscience, take up arms against his home state.

He ultimately became the Confederacy's lead general and led an undermanned, undersupplied, underfinanced military force to the point where, had Gettysburg gone differently, the Union might have had to reach an agreement recognizing the Confederacy.

But that did not happen. The greater financial strength, manpower, and armaments of the Union—and the military skill of Ulysses S. Grant—ultimately forced Lee to surrender at Appomattox Court House.

Lee's loss did not diminish his standing in the Confederacy. If anything, he became more of a hero as the years went forward. He was admired for his valiant effort, leadership in the face of daunting odds, character, integrity, and personification of the Southern gentleman who fought for the lost cause with all his vitality and wisdom. Perhaps that is not completely surprising.

But the spoils in wars ultimately go to the victors, and so it was with the Civil War.

Ulysses S. Grant, who was forced, probably because of alcoholism, to resign his US Army commission before the war and who was selling firewood on the streets of St. Louis when the war broke out, became widely admired in the North (and respected in the South) for being able to do what no other senior Union general could do: win.

And by winning many key battles against the Confederacy, and ultimately ending the war, Grant became such a hero that he was elected president of the United States in 1868 and then again in 1872. While his presidency was, at times, marred by the corruption of the others working for Grant, he left office after two terms as the most widely admired person in the country (and might well have won a third term had he run).

Grant's post-presidency was not as successful; he invested nearly all his capital in a firm that turned out to be a fraud. But, on the good news side of that unfortunate situation, Grant needed to make money—and he did so by writing his life's story (up to the presidency). That book is widely thought to be the best memoir ever written by a president.

FIGURE 3.1 AND 3.2 Prior to the Civil War, Robert E. Lee (*above*) had a distinguished career in the US army, while Ulysses S. Grant (*opposite*) had been kicked out, in part because of his drinking. When the war began, Lee led the Confederate army and Grant volunteered for the Union, eventually earning the rank of general—a role that Abraham Lincoln had initially offered to Lee in April 1861.

DAVID M. RUBENSTEIN (DR): In hindsight, is there anything that Abraham Lincoln could have done after he was elected president that could have prevented the Civil War from occurring?

ALLEN C. GUELZO (AG): The demands of the seceding states were very clear and very concrete. They were not going to accept anything except cooperation. Lincoln understood that they were obdurate this way. He also understood that if he made concessions like that, his presidency was over before it began. Besides, he did not believe that there was any constitutional justification for secession. The Constitution does not contain a reversion clause. There's no mechanism described in the Constitution that describes how you secede from it.

Lincoln's argument was that secession is the essence of anarchy. Because in a democracy, what are the operating principles? The operating principles are that the majority wins, and when it wins it gets its way. It agrees not to put the minority up against a barn wall and shoot it, but the minority also takes comfort in the fact that maybe a year or two later, if they are persuasive enough, they'll become the majority and then things can change. If you let people simply break away the moment there is a problem, then what you have is not democracy, what you have is "I'm taking my bat and ball and going home." That's not baseball.

DR: There was nothing Lincoln could have done to prevent the war from occurring. Is there anything he could have done to shorten it? Could he have been more effective militarily so the war didn't go on for four years?

AG: Heaven knows he tried. But one of the great difficulties he had to work with is that the United States Army, at the beginning of the Civil War, comprised only 16,000 men. It was not so much an army as it was a frontier constabulary, kind of like the Royal Canadian Mounted Police. Making that transition from the old way of doing things to managing enormous armies of over 100,000 men really taxed the abilities and the talents of the people who were commanding those armies. It took a long time and a lot of trial and error before Lincoln was able to finally identify the kinds of commanders who could take charge and perform effectively.

DR: Suppose Lincoln had issued the Emancipation Proclamation at the beginning of the war. Would that have made a difference because it would have reduced the Southern capability to fight?

AG: Probably not. If anything, it might have gone the other way, because too early in the war it would have caused an uprising in the North to say, "We're fighting to preserve the Union. We're not fighting to free the slaves." And especially in the Midwest there was a tremendous amount of resistance to the idea that you were going to make freeing the slaves a war aim. If Lincoln had moved too quickly on that, he could have sent Kentucky, Missouri, Maryland bounding into the arms of the Confederates like jackrabbits across the prairie.

DR: A former member of the United States Senate and former secretary of war, Jefferson Davis, was selected, to his surprise, as the head of the Confederacy. Is there anything he could have done to shorten the war?

AG: He could have won more battles. At the end of the day, the contest between the North and South really does come down to what happens on the battlefield. People often ask me what I think the turning point of the Civil War was. My answer is Appomattox. Because all through the war, up to that point, or at least up until November of 1864, it might have gone another way for political and economic as well as military reasons.

DR: In the first battle of the war, the Battle of Bull Run or First Manassas, it was expected by the North at least that they were going to win. In fact, people went down to watch it as a sport. What did the North not understand about the South? Why was there such misjudgment about how easy it would be to win that battle?

AG: Because nobody in the North really had any understanding of large-scale military operations, including the people who were in charge of the Union army marching to Bull Run. Watching the army on its way to its first battle would be a little bit like watching Barnum & Bailey's circus on the road. It was a strange, undisciplined mob. When they finally showed up on the battlefield, they found out that the people on the other side of that battlefield were very much in earnest and had deadly weapons, and they won the battle.

This was a terrific comedown. The assumption had been, going back to the days of Andrew Jackson, that all the federal government had to do was show up in force with soldiers in uniforms and Southern willpower would collapse. That was a mistake. Southern willpower did not collapse. Many Southerners thought it would, but the victory at Bull Run surprised them almost as much as it shocked the Union.

DR: In total there were roughly 620,000 people killed in the Civil War. Is that the right number?

AG: For a long time that was the accepted figure. Several years ago, J. David Hacker, in an essay in the quarterly *Civil War History*, called on us to revise the numbers upward, based on crunching the data from the 1870 census. His estimate pegged the deaths resulting from the Civil War as something closer to 720,000 to 750,000.

DR: The US population was roughly 20 million, so you had roughly 3 percent of the entire population of the United States dying in the war. To put it in context, we have 320 million people today. If 3 percent died, it's like more than 9 million people dying.

AG: It was a demographic catastrophe, among everything else that the Civil War was. It decimated the American population, and it crippled the American economy for many years, crippled the Southern economy for almost a hundred years afterward. The impact of the American Civil War was like the Great Depression multiplied three or four times.

DR: The North had roughly two or three times as many people as the South?

AG: That's right.

DR: That's one of the reasons they thought they would win. They had more industrial power as well as more people?

AG: Right, although we do tend to exaggerate the industrial power of the North. If you look at the 104 districts from the North that were represented in Congress, about 72 of them were farm and village districts. The North was not exactly an overwhelming industrial powerhouse. What's more, the Confederacy had the advantage of lots of open space. They could fight delaying actions. They could make it as costly as possible for the Union to keep on. And after a while, when they bled the Union army out, the Confederacy would be able to say, "You've had enough, haven't you?" and the Union would give up.

DR: Let's talk about U. S. Grant and Robert E. Lee. Would anybody have expected, at the beginning of the war in 1861, that either would rise to be the top general in their respective armies?

AG: Maybe three or four people. Grant had been a captain in the US Army.

DR: What was his real name?

AG: His birth name was Hiram Ulysses Grant. When he showed up at West Point, he was entered into the cadet book as Ulysses Simpson Grant. Someone mixed up cadet names. You know what it's like in the army—if you get a name put in there one way at the beginning, just try to change it. So, he became Ulysses Simpson Grant and simply had to acquiesce in that, and his wife simply called him Ulys.

DR: Ulysses S. Grant graduated from West Point, served in the military for a while, but left unceremoniously. Why did he leave?

AG: He was posted to a forlorn West Coast installation where he began consoling his sorrows with the bottle. It got bad enough that his commanding officer effectively said, "Either you resign your commission or we're going to institute proceedings." Grant leaves the army in disgrace as a drunk. He goes back home to his wife and to his family, and he tries his hand at a variety of civilian projects. He tries to open a store. It fails. He tries to farm. It fails. He ends up clerking in his father's leather goods store in Galena, Illinois. That's a comedown for someone who had this West Point education and who had been in the Mexican War, and here he is basically living from hand to mouth, nobody expecting very much from him.

DR: Working for your father is one thing. Before the war broke out, he was selling firewood on the street corners of St. Louis. Can you explain how that came about?

AG: Desperation. There was no other way to make money. The depression of 1858 had undercut so much of the American economy that Grant was out there selling firewood like people in the 1930s were on street corners selling apples. Anything, anything, to generate a little bit of income. That's how desperate he was.

DR: The war breaks out and he's not a member of the military. He's just selling firewood on the streets of St. Louis. How did he get into the war?

AG: Almost by accident. He wrote a letter to the secretary of war offering his services as a trained military man. Never got a reply. It wasn't until many years later that it was found that the letter had been misfiled by a clerk. But he did know a number of important Illinois congressmen, principally Elihu Washburne, and it was Washburne who persuaded the governor of Illinois, Richard Yates, to make Grant the colonel of the 21st Illinois Volunteers. This was

Grant's big opportunity. Grant took charge of the 21st Illinois, whose previous colonel had been a total loss. One officer watching Grant on the parade ground, calling men to attention, said, "This man knows what he's doing. He's a professional." From that point, Grant went nowhere but up. Eight years later, he's president of the United States.

DR: Let's shift to Lee for a moment, to put him in the same period of time. Lee also goes to West Point, but his background is better than Grant's.

AG: A little bit better. Robert E. Lee graduates from West Point, class of 1829, and goes on from there to have a reasonably successful career in the army—"successful" by the standards of the army in those days. His movement from being a second lieutenant all the way up to being a colonel took almost thirty years. It was a slow, painful process. Most of the time he spent in the Corps of Engineers. In the last few years of his service before the war broke out, he was the lieutenant colonel of the Second US Cavalry in Texas.

The curious thing is, he never actually commands troops under fire until 1859. That's when he is called by the War Department to take charge of a contingent of Marines who are going to storm the Harpers Ferry arsenal, where John Brown holed himself up during his famous raid.

DR: Lee was an engineer. He was good at building forts and changing the course of rivers and things like that?

AG: He preserved St. Louis as the great city of the upper Mississippi. In the 1830s he was sent there because the Mississippi River was playing its usual tricks. It was slowly diverting itself away from St. Louis, which would have become an inland town, and the merchants of St. Louis really didn't think that was a good idea. Lee was brought in, and he began constructing a series of dams to rechannel the Mississippi River and keep St. Louis on the map as a port city, and he was very successful at it.

DR: Lee married well, you might say. How did he marry into the family of George Washington?

AG: George Washington had no children of his own, but his wife, Martha Washington, brought to the marriage two children from her first marriage. One of those was "Jacky" Custis. Jacky married, as Washington thought, unwisely, and produced two children of his own. One of them, George Washington Parke Custis, becomes Washington's step-grandson, but even more, he becomes Washington's heir. And in the years between Washington's death in 1799 and George Washington Parke Custis's death in 1858, he becomes the guardian of the reputation of George Washington. He creates this little miniature museum at his home in Arlington.

DR: He's the one who built Arlington House.

AG: And created this little miniature museum of Washington artifacts.

DR: He has a daughter?

AG: He has a daughter, an only child, Mary Anna Randolph Custis. Robert E. Lee courts her, marries her in 1831, and so becomes connected with not only the Custis family but, through the Custis family, with the whole image of George Washington.

DR: Grant's wife was also reasonably well connected, at least financially. Can you describe how they met?

AG: The match between Julia Dent and Ulysses Grant is one of those great love stories. Julia Dent was no great beauty, unlike Mary Anna Randolph Custis. Julia was cross-eyed, a bit doughy, but she loved Ulysses Grant and he loved her, as sincerely as any two could love each other. She doted on him. She looked after him. At one point, she had him shave off the famous beard. He shaved off half of it and had a half-face photograph taken so she could remember him as he had looked before the war.

DR: She was related to a friend from West Point?

AG: She was a distant cousin of his West Point friend James Longstreet, who becomes one of Grant's opponents in the Civil War. The old army was very close-knit.

These people were all connected to each other. They all knew each other. That meant that during the Civil War a lot of army commanders had a fairly good idea of the kinds of things their opponents would be up to. Someone once told William Tecumseh Sherman that he really didn't need to worry about dealing with John Bell Hood in front of Atlanta, because this officer remembered Hood in a poker game at West Point betting a thousand dollars "with nary a pair in his hand." This is a very small community in which people have a lot of respect for each other, and yet they are clawing and fighting in this bloody standoff of a civil war.

DR: The war breaks out and Grant volunteers. You just described how he's beginning to train volunteers in Illinois. What does Lee do? Did he want to stay in the military in the US government? Does he want to go to the Confederacy? How does he decide what to do?

AG: When Lee is in Texas in January of 1861, it's making its first moves toward secession. We know from reading his letters that Lee, who was stationed at Fort Mason, was prepared to put it on a war footing and defend it against Texas secessionists. He was very clear. He said, "Secession is nothing but revolution."

He receives orders recalling him to Washington. In order to get to Washington he has to report to department headquarters in San Antonio. When he gets there, he finds San Antonio is in the hands of secessionists. He's actually worried that they're going to arrest him.

Finally, he's able to leave Texas, arrives in Virginia, and then crosses the river over to Washington. It is there that he meets Francis Preston

Blair, the great political wire-puller. Blair has been commissioned by Abraham Lincoln to make Lee an offer to command the entire federal army. Lee mulls this over. He goes to meet with the general and chief of the army, his old mentor Winfield Scott. He tells Scott, "I don't think I can do this." Scott says to him, "That's as I feared, but you will make the greatest mistake in your life."

So, on April 20th, 1861, Lee resigns from the United States Army; sends his letter to the new secretary of war, Simon Cameron; and then, a few days later, takes off for Richmond. He is offered a brigadier general's commission in the state of Virginia's forces, which he accepts. His reason for doing this was that Virginia represented his family. It represented his lineage. It represented his history. He could not draw a sword against Virginia.

DR: It wasn't the Confederacy so much. He didn't think secession was a great idea, but he didn't think he could ever invade Virginia?

AG: No. He had to protect Virginia. I think, to a certain degree, he believed that the whole crisis over secession was going to blow over. In April of 1861 that was still possible. When he sends that resignation letter in, it's only five days after Fort Sumter. There could be a lot of people who would rush in and say, "Let's smooth this out. Let's come to some kind of relationship." Compromise, of course, had been the story of the game for the previous thirty or forty years, from the Missouri Compromise of 1820 through the Compromise of 1850. Perhaps there would be a compromise now.

Carl Schurz had this interesting comparison. He said that years ago the Southerners, especially South Carolinians, had threatened to leave the Union. They threatened to walk out of the saloon and go get a drink. Then they walked back in. Well, he said, "Now what's going to happen is the Southerners are going to walk out of the saloon, take two drinks, and then come back in."

DR: Lee is working as a commander in the Virginia militia. How does he go from the Virginia militia to the Confederacy, and what type of position does he get?

AG: It's a slow process. Jefferson Davis wants him as his chief of staff, and he nails Lee to a desk in Richmond for the early months of the war. It's not until the fall of 1861 that Davis sends him to western Virginia to oversee Confederate operations there, and when he does, it is a debacle. The Confederate forces there are badly handled, and Lee is portrayed by many people as being a failure—just another one of these overhyped United States Army officers who it turns out really didn't have any gumption.

There's so much criticism of Lee that Davis has to reassign him to South Carolina and Georgia inspecting fortifications, to get him out of the way. People in South Carolina were very suspicious of Robert E. Lee. In Mary Chesnut's diary, she writes of one South Carolinian she knew who wagged his finger at her and said, "Robert E. Lee is not with us. We cannot rely on him." There's a lot of suspicion of Lee.

But in the spring of 1862 Davis calls Lee back to Richmond, and when General Joseph Johnston, commanding the Confederate forces defending the city, is wounded, Davis turns to Lee and puts him in command. From that point on, Lee takes charge of the situation, goes from victory to victory to victory to victory, becomes the great icon of the Confederacy.

DR: While this is happening, Lincoln is dealing with a succession of generals. What was the problem with them all?

AG: They weren't very bright. Lack of intelligence can be a real inhibition. When you look at the people who were in charge of the armies, especially in the East, you start at Bull Run with Irvin McDowell. Here was a man who owed his military promotion to the fact that he was politically tied to the secretary of the treasury.

Then he's succeeded by George McClellan. Now there's a man of great professionalism. The problem was that his professionalism was almost entirely administrative. Great organizer of the army, terrible combat leader. He would have made a perfect chairman of the Joint Chiefs of Staff, except that there were no Joint Chiefs of Staff in those days. And what makes it worse is that McClellan is at odds with

Lincoln politically. He has no confidence whatsoever in the Lincoln administration or in emancipation.

Finally Lincoln sacks him and replaces him, in the Virginia theater of operations, with General John Pope, who is a vigorous abolitionist but not a terribly competent commander. Pope meets a disastrous defeat at Second Bull Run. Lincoln, humiliated, is forced to put McClellan back in command. McClellan goes and wins the battle at Antietam but fails to follow up on it.

For a month after Antietam, Lincoln is pestering McClellan: "Follow up on this. Follow up on this. Follow up on this." McClellan has got one excuse after another. "My cavalry horses are fatigued." "What?" says Lincoln. "What have your horses been doing that fatigues anything?" Lincoln said that McClellan was a great engineer but his talents were mostly confined to a stationary engine.

DR: Lincoln visited McClellan once, and McClellan handed him a letter, saying, "Here's all the things you're doing wrong as president."

AG: When Lincoln comes down to visit the army where it's encamped on the James River at Harrison's Landing on July 7th, 1862, McClellan is there with a letter, which he hands to Lincoln, itemizing all the mistakes he has made and the things that have to happen for them to be put right. This is a general of the army, who concludes his letter by saying, "If we move toward the emancipation of the slaves, I just can't guarantee that this army is going to fight."

I'm thinking, when I read that, "Wait a minute. You're the commanding officer. You're supposed to be the one who makes them fight." But this is a veiled threat on McClellan's part that if Lincoln persisted in moving toward emancipation, he might have to do something about it.

DR: In trying to win the war, Lee has a strategy, which is "Let's see if we can punch them in the North. Let's see if we can invade the North." He tries once, in Antietam, and that became the bloodiest battle in the history of the war, with 30,000 casualties?

AG: Bloodiest single day of the war.

DR: And in American military history, probably. Thirty thousand casualties in one day. Lee goes to invade Maryland but pulls back, and Lincoln can consider it a victory, though a lot of people were killed. Then Lee says, "Let's go back into the North one more time. Let's try someplace in Pennsylvania." What happened?

AG: A place called Gettysburg, which I know a little bit about. Gettysburg happens because Lee believed, from the very start when he took command in the spring of 1862, that the Confederacy did not have the resources to go the distance. It couldn't absorb a fifteen-round heavyweight fight. If the Confederacy was going to win the war, it had to get in there and score a knockout in the first couple of rounds, quickly.

The way to do that is to invade the North, because if you can win a military victory on Northern soil, especially Pennsylvania, that is going to have not only military repercussions but political repercussions. The North is a divided house politically, and Lee hopes to take advantage of that.

When Lee comes north in 1863 and invades Pennsylvania, there's been a tremendous amount of dissension for the previous six months over Lincoln's Emancipation Proclamation. The state elections in New York and New Jersey have put into place anti-Lincoln governors. Now, in 1863, there are going to be gubernatorial elections in Pennsylvania and Ohio, and the people who are making the strongest bids are more anti-Lincoln politicians.

Lee believes that if he can come into Pennsylvania and score a victory—or, if not score a victory, at least show that he can't be evicted easily—that's going to give all the encouragement needed for people to vote for anti-Lincoln governors. He'll then have the governors of New York, Pennsylvania, Ohio, and New Jersey opposed to the war. With that bloc of states, people can say to Lincoln, "Let's go to the negotiating table."

DR: How did it happen to be Gettysburg? Weren't they going further and then Union troops just showed up? Why Gettysburg?

AG: Gettysburg becomes the location of the battle not entirely by accident. People sometimes say, "This happened without any planning." Lee hoped to fight a battle, as he said, somewhere between Frederick, Maryland, and Gettysburg, Pennsylvania. The reason he expected to do that was he had stolen a march on the Army of the Potomac. He had invaded across the Potomac, into Maryland, into Pennsylvania, and the Union army was trying desperately to play catch-up. It was stringing itself out on the roads, exhausting itself. What Lee hoped, being already in Pennsylvania, was that as soon as these disorganized Union units showed up, he could turn and start biting them and devouring them one by one. Even if he has fewer in the way of numbers of soldiers, he can bring more of them together in one place, and that place is going to be Gettysburg.

DR: The battle takes place over three days—July 1st, 2nd, and 3rd. What happens the first day?

AG: The first day, Lee almost gets his wish. The 1st and the 11th Corps of the Army of the Potomac are far out in front of the rest of the army. They come into Gettysburg. Lee's army concentrates and it virtually destroys both the 1st and the 11th Corps. At the end of the day, they are left hanging by their fingernails onto one prominence in the Gettysburg landscape, Cemetery Hill. Lee believes the next day he's just going to wade in and finish things off.

What Lee didn't realize was that the rest of the Army of the Potomac was a lot closer than he thought. By dawn on July 2nd, there are three more Union infantry corps that have moved up to Gettysburg, and now Lee has to retool his plan. He's committed himself. He doesn't want to back off. He invents a great flanking maneuver. Once again, he comes within an inch of success. He destroys the 3rd and the 5th corps of the Army of the Potomac. At the end of the day on July 2nd, everyone in the Confederate army is confidently predicting, "We've got them on the ropes. All we've got to do tomorrow is wade in and deliver the knockout punch."

DR: What happens on July 3rd? The famous Pickett's Charge.

AG: Lee has an entire division of Virginians fresh and uncommitted in the battle. He sends them in a gigantic attack straight at the nape of the Union neck, right behind Cemetery Hill. If he can break that, he will break through the Union army; he will isolate the Union artillery and send the rest of the army fleeing. The Union army at that point really only has four operational brigades left to call upon. Lee sees this as the great opportunity to roll forward and win.

People say, "Wasn't a frontal attack like that almost an act of suicide?" No, it really wasn't. It was well calculated, and there were plenty of good precedents for it in military affairs in the 1850s. Lee's attack at Gettysburg with Pickett's Charge looked very similar to Lord Raglan's successful attack at the Alma in the Crimean War in September of 1854.

DR: Pickett's Charge didn't work. Pickett's soldiers were slaughtered by those on the mound looking down, shooting at them. Lee decides to withdraw and go back to the South.

AG: That is correct. He realizes he has no more fresh troops to commit to the battle, so he is going to withdraw, get his army back across the Potomac, and rebuild and try another day.

DR: Does the Union general in charge, General Meade, follow him into the South?

AG: Very gingerly. George Meade had only been in command of the Army of the Potomac for three days when the battle begins. That's not a whole lot of time to get things organized. All through the battle Meade is trying to work with staffers he doesn't know, with corps commanders who a few days before had been his peers. He really has a difficult time of it, trying to put his finger in the holes in the dike all through the battle. He decides that since they've won a victory in

Gettysburg, let's not take too many more chances, because Lee's army is like a wounded animal that could turn and devour them.

DR: What did Lincoln think of that?

AG: He thought it was horrible. Lincoln believed that the victory of Gettysburg should be the prelude to Meade's immediately closing in and destroying Lee's army, especially since the Potomac was at flood stage and when Lee got to the river he couldn't cross it. He has to turn with his back to the river, facing the Union army, and try to figure out, "Are they going to attack? Am I going to survive?"

Lincoln is so anxious about this, so anxious that Meade will hesitate, that he sends his vice president, Hannibal Hamlin, to Williamsport, Maryland, with orders to Meade: "Attack, attack, attack. If you attack and it turns out badly, I will take the responsibility. If the attack succeeds, I'll stand back and you can have the credit for it." Even so, Meade will not take the chance. The river falls, Lee gets across it, and we have twenty-two more months of war.

DR: So, Lee goes back. What's happening out west? All of a sudden this man Grant, who is not even in the army at the breakout of the war, is winning some battles. How did he manage to get himself in a position to be a general commanding troops in a war?

AG: Ulysses Grant moves up to brigadier general very early, and he discovers something at the first battle he's in charge of, the Battle of Belmont, right by the Mississippi River. He realizes that he didn't actually win the battle. The Confederates withdrew in fear that they had lost. At that point, Grant said in his memoirs, he realized that the Confederates were more frightened of him than he was of them. He could use that to his advantage.

Grant said that his military philosophy was really very simple. It had three parts: Find the enemy, hit him as hard as you can, and keep moving on. The most important part of that was the third part, the initiative. Seize the initiative, always keep the enemy mystified, always keep the enemy guessing as to what you're up to. And that's what you see at every stage in the great campaign that climaxes at Vicksburg.

DR: Some people say that he had more soldiers than the South, more artillery, and he was willing to sacrifice his men. Some people called him a butcher because so many men were killed under his command. Is that fair?

AG: No, it's not. Robert E. Lee sustained higher casualty rates in his Army of Northern Virginia than Grant did in his army. Nor did Grant begin the Overland Campaign of 1864 with some huge surplus that he could put into the meat grinder.

DR: Grant is winning battles. He's winning at Vicksburg and he's winning at Shiloh and other places. Eventually, Lincoln says, "Hey, this guy can win battles. Why don't I bring him back here to fight Lee?" Is that what happens?

AG: That is what happens, although Lincoln is a little hesitant about Grant, because he has that reputation of being a drunk. There's a lot of fear that if you put him in too senior a position, he'll take to the bottle again and the consequences will be disastrous. The secretary of war, Edwin Stanton, sends a personal emissary, basically a spy, to report on Grant's behavior. This is Charles Dana, who used to be the managing editor of the *New York Tribune*. Dana writes back to Stanton and to Lincoln and he says, "Everybody asks me, doesn't Grant drink?" Dana said, "I have never seen him yet drinking."

People think that all Grant had to do was smell a cork and it would send him over the moon, and that just was not the case. Grant had his problems with drink, no doubt. He is what we might call a recovering alcoholic. But Dana assures Lincoln and Stanton, "That is not going to be a problem you're going to have to worry about with Ulysses Grant."

DR: I thought Lincoln said, "Why don't we give the other generals some of what Grant is drinking?"

AG: That may be an apocryphal story. We don't have good evidence on that.

DR: Grant comes back and he's given the task of defeating Lee. How does that come about, and how long does it take before Grant gets to Appomattox Court House?

AG: It takes approximately eleven months, most of which is consumed by a siege of Petersburg and Richmond, the Confederate capital. Sometimes people look at that and say, "That's not accomplishing much. Why didn't he just go in and win the war in a few weeks or a few months?" But understand that clamping Richmond in a siege was exactly what Robert E. Lee did not want to have happen. Lee made a comment to one of his division commanders, Jubal Early, that "if Grant gets us in a siege at Richmond, then it's all over, because we will not be able to survive that."

Both Grant and Lee understood that Grant's strategy was working. Grant lays siege, squeezes Richmond—which had been the support artery for Lee's army—squeezes it until the pips squeak. Finally, Lee is compelled to abandon Richmond. A week after he abandons Richmond, Grant runs him to the ground and the surrender takes place at Appomattox.

DR: Who decides? Does Jefferson Davis say to Lee, "You should surrender"? What did Lee actually do, and what was he surrendering?

AG: By this point Jefferson Davis is almost delusional. He gets the last train out of Richmond. He's telling people, "We're going to fight on, we have this, we have that, we're going to take to the woods," and everyone's saying, "Yeah, right. Those woods are full of Yankees." Lee himself realizes that if he gives license to his army just to disintegrate and turn itself into a guerrilla force, that will rip apart the South for the next generation.

That being the case, Lee takes it on himself—not with directions from Davis—to open a correspondence with Grant, beginning on April 7th. Grant had written to him, saying, "Wouldn't it be a good idea to prevent the further effusion of blood?" Lee responds. They go back and forth three times, and finally Lee says, "Let's meet and discuss what we need to talk about."

DR: They meet. Were the terms that Grant offered approved by Lincoln or not? What were the terms?

AG: Lincoln didn't approve the terms. He didn't see them. But he was in sympathy with them. Lincoln had advised Grant and Sherman, "Let's get this war over with. Once the Confederate armies have laid down their weapons and gone home, they're never going to get back into shape as armies. Let's give them every incentive we possibly can to disintegrate."

DR: He gives them unconditional surrender terms?

AG: No. That was exactly what Lee was afraid of, because that was Grant's reputation. Lee was convinced that if he went to meet with Grant and he started talking about unconditional surrender, Lee would say, "In that case we're going to fight this out to the last cartridge."

DR: What is it that Grant actually gives him?

AG: Very generous terms. For one thing, Grant offers to parole the entire Army of Northern Virginia, from Robert E. Lee on downward—basically give them a pass to go home and promise that they will not take up arms against the United States.

DR: When that happens, within a week or so the rest of the South also surrenders?

AG: Joseph Johnston, who commands the other major Confederate field army, begins corresponding with General William Sherman, and basically he says, "If you can give us the same terms that Lee got at Appomattox, we'll surrender this army, too," which he does.

DR: After the war, Robert E. Lee is well respected still in the South and he ultimately becomes president of Washington College. But Jefferson Davis goes to jail. Why is that?

AG: First of all, because Jefferson Davis was a civilian who was not covered by the parole. There were a lot of people in the North who would have been perfectly happy to have jailed Robert E. Lee as well, because Lee, of course, was the Confederate who was probably most responsible for prolonging the war. So there is agitation. Lee and Davis are in fact indicted for treason in June of 1865. Davis is in federal custody and he is locked up in Fort Monroe. But Lee is different. Lee writes to Grant and says, "What about these paroles? Don't these paroles protect the soldiers of the Army of Northern Virginia from this kind of arrest?"

Grant writes to President Andrew Johnson and says, "If you don't respect the paroles that I gave to these soldiers, including Robert E. Lee, I will resign as general in chief of the army." And Andrew Johnson could not afford that kind of public relations debacle.

DR: Lee becomes, after the war, president of Washington College, now Washington and Lee. He dies five years later, in 1870, at the age of sixty-three. Grant lives another fifteen years and also dies at the age of sixty-three. What did he do in those fifteen years?

AG: He served two terms as president of the United States. He was general in chief of the United States Army. And he was bankrupt.

DR: He went bankrupt because he had gone into business with somebody who was dishonest?

AG: Shady.

DR: He's bankrupt. He needs to get some money. What does he do to get money right before he dies?

AG: He writes his memoirs. He knows at that point that he's dying of cancer of the throat. All those cigars.

DR: Twenty a day.

AG: Yes. The thing is, he didn't smoke cigars before the war. His first major victory at Fort Donelson and Fort Henry was the occasion for well-wishers in the North to start sending him boxes of cigars, and that's when he starts the habit. But the habit killed him. He begins writing his memoirs in a race with the cancer that is killing him. He finishes his memoirs just days before he dies. The memoirs, when they're published, become the restored fortune of the Grant family.

DR: They are considered, even today, the finest memoirs by any person who was president of the United States.

AG: Absolutely. They are remarkable for their clarity, for the generosity of judgment. They also—probably this helps his reputation—did not enter into a discussion of his postwar presidency. But his description of life as a general in the Union army is succinct, it is clear, it is delightful to read.

DR: His publisher was Samuel Clemens—Mark Twain. Did he write those memoirs?

AG: Some people were so surprised at how well written Grant's memoirs were that they thought Mark Twain had ghostwritten them for him. Twain always made it clear, "No, this was Grant's work." And you can understand that, because if you go back and read Grant's reports during the war and his presidential messages, that same style, that same clarity is remarkable in its evidence.

DR: Why do you think that students should study the Civil War? Why is it relevant today?

AG: For one thing, it proves something about democracy. The great thing at stake in the American Civil War was the very idea of democracy itself. This is what Lincoln was getting at in the Gettysburg

Address. A democracy supposes that ordinary people can govern themselves through their representatives. It supposes that you can lodge political sovereignty in the hands of ordinary folks on the sidewalks and in the offices and on the farms. To monarchs in Europe, that was a hilarious joke. The idea that some Tom, Dick, and Harry were fully competent to run affairs of state simply seemed to them to be ludicrous.

The outbreak of the Civil War looks like the ultimate proof that democracy does not work—that the first moment democracy hits a big bump in the road, all the nuts and bolts go flying. The purpose the war serves is to show that a democracy is not weak. A democracy has strength. And all those common, ordinary Toms, Dicks, and Harrys? They were capable of rising to levels of sacrifice that all of the professional soldiers of Europe could not even match.

When Lincoln looked out at those semicircular rows of graves at Gettysburg, he was not looking at what the Duke of Wellington called his own army, "the scum of the earth." No, he was looking at ordinary people who had seen something in democracy that was special that they were willing to die for. Lincoln says from that "we take increased devotion to that cause for which they gave the last full measure of devotion." The Civil War is proof positive of the strength, the flexibility, the power of democracy, that it is not just a Greek drollery.

4

Manisha Sinha on Lincoln, Johnson, and Reconstruction

INTERVIEW DATE: SEPTEMBER 25, 2024

Manisha Sinha, a native of India and currently a historian at the University of Connecticut, has become a nationally recognized expert on American history, particularly on subjects relating to the Civil War, Reconstruction, abolition, and slavery. In this conversation, I talked to Dr. Sinha about her book *The Rise and Fall of the Second American Republic: Reconstruction, 1860–1920*. As that title suggests, Dr. Sinha does not believe Reconstruction ended in the nineteenth century but rather two decades into the twentieth.

The traditional view among many scholars of this period is that Lincoln's plans for Reconstruction never came to fruition following his assassination, because his successor, Andrew Johnson, was not someone who wanted the freed slaves in the South to be integrated into white society (there or anywhere). And, as a result, his successors either encouraged whites to create a two-class, two-race society in the South (and to some extent in the North), or they did nothing to discourage that development.

In Dr. Sinha's view, Reconstruction, as originally conceived by Lincoln, did not have a chance to succeed, and for at least sixty years after the Civil War, the United States built a two-race society—especially in the South. That this continued into the twentieth century was

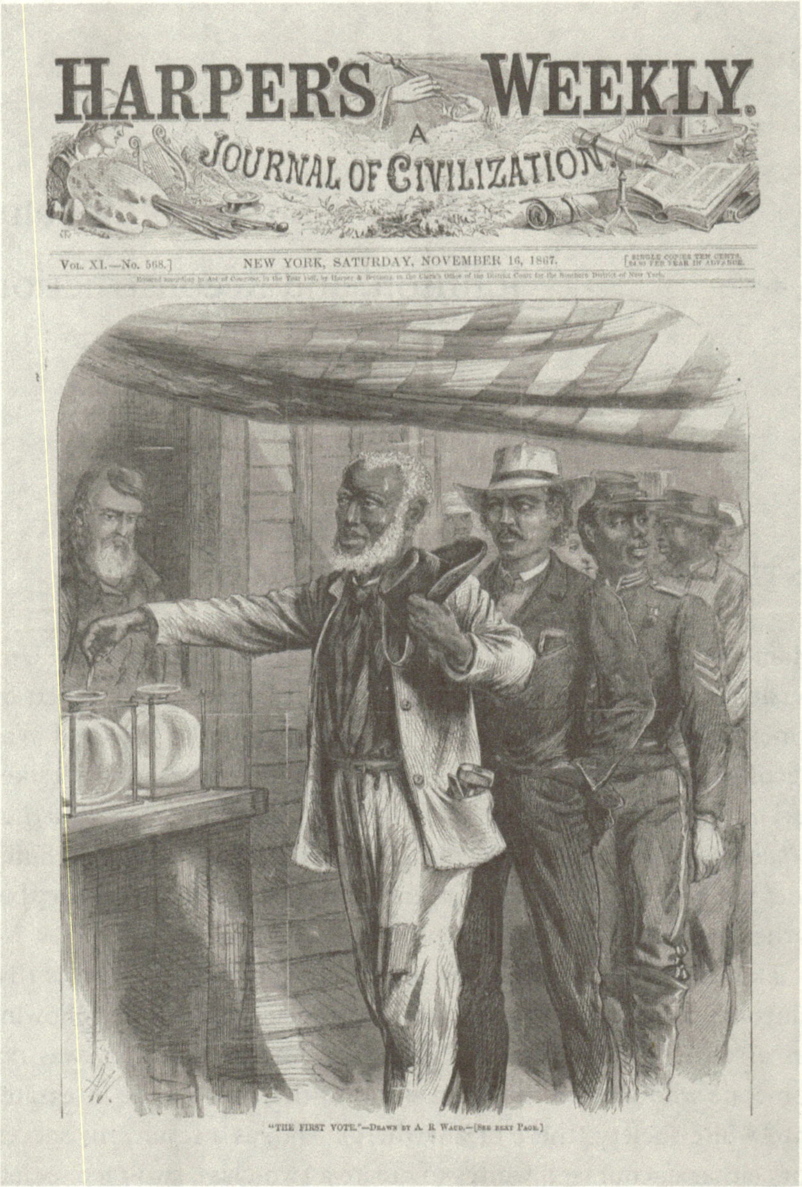

FIGURE 4.1 Three constitutional amendments were passed during Reconstruction: the Thirteenth Amendment, which abolished legal slavery; the Fourteenth Amendment, which granted equal rights to citizens, among many other provisions; and the Fifteenth Amendment, which granted the franchise to Black men. Prior to his assassination, Abraham Lincoln had publicly supported Black suffrage, a radical position for the time.

typified in Dr. Sinha's view by the fact that President Woodrow Wilson—seen as a great "reformer" at the time—fired all Black federal employees and showed a film at the White House, *Birth of a Nation*, glorifying the Ku Klux Klan.

It is hard to argue with many of Dr. Sinha's observations about how civil rights acts and constitutional amendments of the 1860s and 1870s did relatively little more than legally abolish slavery for the first fifty years after their passage. The rights and freedoms supposedly guaranteed by the Fourteenth and Fifteenth Amendments were barely enforced, leaving the country "unreconstructed" well into the latter part of the twentieth century.

Had Lincoln lived, it is not clear that he could have prevented this from occurring. But one wishes that the country had had the chance to see if that could have occurred.

DAVID M. RUBENSTEIN (DR): For those people who didn't have a course on Reconstruction, didn't learn about it in school, what was the basic concept behind Reconstruction initially, as Lincoln conceived it?

MANISHA SINHA (MS): Reconstruction is usually taught hastily or not taught at all, because it was the period following the Civil War. We know a lot about the Civil War. We don't know much about Reconstruction because it lasted for such a short time. That's why I wrote the book.

People don't think of Abraham Lincoln as our first Reconstruction president, because he was assassinated in 1865 immediately after the war ended. But, in fact, he was our first Reconstruction president, because he becomes the first American president to publicly endorse Black citizenship. That was an enormous achievement. Unfortunately, as I said, he got assassinated, and then we got Andrew Johnson, and everything went backward for a while.

DR: The night before Lincoln was assassinated, he had made a little talk at the White House in which he said it was possible that some free Black men, if they were educated, could be allowed to vote. And

John Wilkes Booth, who was there, didn't like that. He listened to it and it set him off.

But when you're talking about citizenship, the Thirteenth Amendment only freed the slaves. The Fourteenth Amendment made them citizens. The Fifteenth Amendment gave them the right to vote. Before his assassination, had Lincoln conceived, assuming the war was won, and it was about to be won, what he was going to do with Reconstruction? What did he want to have happen in the South?

MS: Lincoln was quite clear, before he died, in endorsing Black male suffrage, especially for the educated and former Union army soldiers. Remember, Lincoln was an antislavery moderate politician before the Civil War. He had opposed the Mexican War as a land grab for slavery. But he was a moderate. So, for him to endorse Black citizenship was a tremendous thing. It shows the evolution of the man from the nonextension of slavery to abolition, and then from advocating colonizing Black people out of the country to Black citizenship.

They say some men are born great, some have greatness thrust upon them, and some become great. And Lincoln did become great, for just being the first American president to endorse Black rights. Also, his administration oversaw the expansion of the federal government during the Civil War. The Internal Revenue Act, we often forget, established a progressive income tax for the first time in US history; the Legal Tender and National Banking Acts created a uniform national currency, greenbacks; and the Freedmen's Bureau was created as a federal government agency designed to oversee the transition from slavery to freedom in the South. Lincoln had these ideas about emancipation and the government's responsibility toward the emancipated, even though his wartime reconstruction plans were designed mainly to end the war, which I think makes him our first Reconstruction president.

DR: When he's assassinated, he's succeeded by his vice president, Andrew Johnson, who became the first president of the United States to be impeached. Why did Lincoln pick Johnson to be his vice president? Johnson was from Tennessee. Hadn't part of that state seceded?

MS: Johnson became Lincoln's vice presidential nominee in 1864 because the Republicans wanted a unity ticket. Johnson had been a Democrat. In those days, the Democratic Party tilted south and was more proslavery. It was also the party of states' rights and small government. The Republican Party was the party of antislavery, racial liberalism, and big government. Unfortunately, despite being born poor, Johnson had risen to become a slaveholder and adopted that mindset. Lincoln picked him because, although his state seceded, he was the only Southern senator from the Confederacy to stay in Congress. This was one of the worst decisions the Republican Party of the nineteenth century made—the decision to remove Hannibal Hamlin, who was a good antislavery politician from Maine and also a former Democrat, and replace him with Andrew Johnson of Tennessee.

Lincoln didn't know Johnson well. Johnson did get drunk on Inauguration Day, and Lincoln, a little astounded, called him a strange man. That was the last thing he said about Johnson.

DR: After the assassination, Andrew Johnson becomes president. His view is that all men are created equal?

MS: No. Johnson resisted emancipation. He was the military governor of Tennessee during the Civil War, because he was a Union man, but he had opposed emancipation in Congress. He never overcame his Southern provincialism, even after becoming the president of the United States, and disgraced the office quite royally. He came closest of any American president to being convicted in the Senate after being impeached in the House. That was lost by just one vote. He was mainly impeached for being opposed to Reconstruction.

The worst thing about Johnson was that he gave encouragement to sore losers, former Confederates in the South, who felt that their man was in the White House. They started enacting these Black Codes, which would keep Black people in as close a state to slavery as possible.

Johnson was an unmitigated disaster, but there was a remedy, and that was the Thirty-Ninth Congress of the United States. I really want to say this here, because I know we have so many congressmen and congresswomen here today. It was the most remarkable Congress in American history—the Thirty-Ninth Congress, which passed the first federal Civil Rights Act, renewed the Freedmen's Bureau, and took control of Reconstruction from Johnson and came close to removing him from office by impeaching him.

DR: It was the most marvelous Congress. Except for the current Congress.

MS: The Thirty-Ninth Congress would be a hard act to follow. With the Fourteenth Amendment, they gave us probably the most consequential constitutional amendment in US history.

DR: Under Reconstruction, as Lincoln conceived it, there were going to be federal troops going down South to make certain that the slaves were freed and that they were treated civilly. The troops were sent down there. Then, for a period of years, Black people who had been freed were getting elected to the state legislatures and elected to Congress for the first time. At that time, former plantation owners and former slave owners in the South were upset that Black people were getting elected to Congress. What did they do about that?

MS: The reason for the Reconstruction Acts that gave Black men the right to vote and instituted new state governments in the South was that the former Confederate states had launched a massive campaign of terror. The Ku Klux Klan was founded in 1866, immediately after the war. You had other assorted groups, like the White Leaguers, the White Liners, the White Brotherhoods, and the Red Shirts of South Carolina, who wreaked a campaign of racist violence in the South because they simply refused to accept the result of the war, emancipation. They were encouraged by the man in the White House, who was Johnson at that point.

So, former slaves are demanding full civil and political rights. It's quite amazing to see how a people who had been enslaved—remember, 90 percent of the Black population in the country was enslaved before the Civil War—organized immediately into Union Leagues, into Republican Party clubs, held conventions, and demanded political and civil rights. This led to Congress passing these acts that gave freed slaves those rights and got them elected to office. In states like Louisiana, South Carolina, and Mississippi that had large Black populations, there were a substantial number of Black people who got elected to state constitutional conventions, legislatures, and to Congress as senators and congressmen. And it is remarkable that a people so freshly out of bondage were able to do that. Of course, many white Southern elites, in particular planters, did not accept that. For them, it was horrifying. It was a world turned upside down for them, to have people of African descent as equal citizens of the Republic. And they did everything in their power to overthrow Reconstruction.

DR: Johnson ultimately did not run for reelection.

MS: No. He is abandoned by the Republicans and the Democrats. He's disgraced. He took a "swing around the circle" campaign in the Northern states during the midterm elections of 1866. It was one of the few times in American history that the ruling party actually won and gained more seats, because Johnson was campaigning against Republicans. He's calling Republicans in Congress and abolitionists traitors to the Republic, rather than the proslavery Confederates, who were the actual traitors. On occasion he is drunk and booed by the crowds. Instead, Republicans choose the hero of the Civil War, General Ulysses S. Grant, as their standard-bearer. Grant becomes president in 1869 and actually confronts this guerrilla warfare against Black people, white unionists, and Northern Republicans in the South.

DR: Ulysses S. Grant has the most amazing story of becoming president. When the Civil War broke out, he was selling firewood on the streets of St. Louis to make a living. He had been thrown out of the military because he was an alcoholic. He had no job. The only thing he could do was chop wood, take it to St. Louis, and sell it as firewood.

And then eight years later, he's president of the United States. Fairly amazing.

MS: It is. His father was an abolitionist.

DR: Grant becomes president of the United States. He keeps the federal troops in the South?

MS: Grant was actually once a Democrat, before the Civil War, which in the nineteenth century meant you were voting for a party that was dominated by Southern slaveholders. Grant comes to the Republican position late. But in the midst of war, he sees how crucial Black troops, 80 to 90 percent of them formerly enslaved, were to Union victory. Many of them were from Kentucky, because Kentucky stayed in the Union, even though it was a slave state, and it proved more resistant sometimes to Reconstruction than other Southern states that had actually left the Union. It was the only way for Black men and their families to gain freedom during the war as the border slave states in the Union were excluded from Lincoln's Emancipation Proclamation of 1863. But Grant is interesting, because he, like Lincoln, evolves in office. He gets Congress to pass the first enforcement acts against the Ku Klux Klan and endorses the Fifteenth Amendment that gives Black men the right to vote.

DR: Some of you may not be familiar with how Grant might have been able to save the president of the United States from assassination. President Lincoln is in Virginia, touring the defeated South, near Richmond. He's with his wife, and he's riding a horse next to the wife of one of his generals. Mrs. Lincoln got jealous of her husband riding a horse next to an attractive young woman, and she yelled and screamed and so forth. Julia Grant, Ulysses S. Grant's wife, was there and saw this and said, "I don't want anything ever to do with Mrs. Lincoln." A couple of days later, Abraham Lincoln sends a message to Grant and says, "I'm going to see *Our American Cousin* tomorrow night at Ford's Theatre. I'd like you to be my guest." Mrs. Grant said, "I don't want anything to do with Mrs. Lincoln. Let's get out of town." They took a train ride to New Jersey to visit their son. As a result, the entourage that Ulysses S. Grant usually had with him, a big entourage of military people, did not go to Ford's Theatre that night. If they had, John Wilkes Booth, one person, probably wouldn't have gotten through that phalanx of soldiers. Instead Lincoln had one young military aide there, along with the aide's wife. Had Lincoln been there with Ulysses S. Grant, maybe he wouldn't have been assassinated. We will never know.

Grant is president for eight years. The South has federal soldiers there, trying to enforce Reconstruction. Are freed slaves moving to the North, or did the Black people who were freed stay in the South?

MS: Yes, they did, because Reconstruction was this moment of enormous hope for the freed people. Black men had gotten voting rights. They were being elected to office. They felt that, in fact, the jubilee was here. But they also faced a tremendous amount of violence, domestic terrorism, by these paramilitary groups in the South. Since the days of slavery, there was this feeling that the North was somehow a chosen place, that they were the chosen people. There was a group of people called the Exodusters who, after the overthrow of Reconstruction, went to Kansas. They went west, and they tried to go to the North. There were some people associated with the Freedmen's Bureau, Northern missionaries, abolitionist soldiers, who sometimes sent Black people to the Northern states. But during Reconstruction, they stayed in the South, as the fight for Black rights was unfolding there. It's only after Reconstruction falls when you have racial segregation, lynching, convict lease labor, and debt peonage, that Black people tried to get out of the Jim Crow South. Mass migrations occur only in the early twentieth century with the Great Migrations to Northern cities that redistribute the Black population nationally. Before that, an overwhelming majority lived in the South.

DR: During that period of time, freed Black slaves were often working on the same plantations where they had been before the war. They were called sharecroppers. They were getting some kind of compensation. But was their life materially better when they were freed? I assume it was better because they were freed, but their economic situation wasn't heroic, was it?

MS: That's another one of those tragedies of Reconstruction. The full name of the Freedmen's Bureau was the Bureau of Freedmen, Abandoned Lands, and Refugees. This was the first welfare agency, you could say, in the history of the United States. They were giving assistance to freed people but also to poor Southern whites, and they were taking abandoned plantations and dividing the land amongst freed people. The first person to do that was General Sherman after meeting with Black leaders in Savannah, Georgia, during his march to the sea. You've heard of forty acres and a mule? That's what General Sherman did. He gave them forty acres in the Low Country in South Carolina and Georgia, and a mule from the federal army. The rumor spread amongst freed people in the plantation South, especially because many of these planters were secessionists, traitors, and they were upholding slavery, that the plantation system would be broken up, and freed slaves would get land for generations of unpaid labor.

And they did get land. But, unfortunately, Andrew Johnson returned all that land back to the plantation owners. And the plantation system persisted. So you had wage labor, you had sharecropping, where sharecroppers got a lien on the crop. During Reconstruction, they had the first lien. Once Reconstruction failed, it was the planters and merchants who got the first lien, and Black people were cheated and got locked in a system of debt peonage in the South. When FDR said the South was the nation's number one economic problem, it was because of this legacy.

DR: Grant gets reelected as president. In that era, there was no law against running for a third time. He looked at running for a third term and ultimately decided not to do it. So, he left the country and did a worldwide tour for a year or so. Who succeeds him as president of the United States?

MS: Rutherford B. Hayes. The 1876 presidential election, which I know some of you heard about recently, was one of the strangest elections in US history. You had only three reconstructed Southern states left: South Carolina, Florida, and Louisiana. The vote is very contested there because of this open season on Black people. You had counties with thousands of Black men who were simply prevented from voting because of voter suppression, intimidation, and violence. But the electoral votes of these three states would decide the presidency.

Rutherford B. Hayes is the Republican candidate, and you have this strange situation. We don't know whether there was a compromise or a corrupt bargain made. But we know this is what happened: Hayes wins the presidency, but at a state level the Democrats come back into power. They call themselves the conservatives of the South, the conservatives versus the radicals. They used to call the Republicans the radicals. And so the conservatives come back into power. In these three states, where enormous bloodshed had taken place—as one South Carolinian freedman said, "We waded through blood to vote for President Hayes, and this is the thanks we got"—Hayes asked the federal troops to go back into their barracks. He doesn't remove them completely—that's a myth. And then the Southern white conservatives, many of them former Confederate generals, are back in power in the South.

DR: I want to make sure everyone understands what happened in the election of 1876. Rutherford B. Hayes is up against Samuel Tilden. It wasn't clear who won, so they had to have a commission to decide who actually was elected president of the United States. This commission was, I think, fifteen people. Correct me if I'm wrong, but Rutherford B. Hayes gets this commission to appoint him by one vote, eight to seven. As part of the deal, some of the eight people voting for him say, "You have to withdraw federal troops from the South. If you do that, we'll support you." Given the chance to be president of the United States, Hayes said yes. And when the federal troops are withdrawn, that was the end of Reconstruction as Lincoln conceived of it. Is that right?

MS: This is the so-called Compromise of 1877. Many historians now have disputed whether a deal was actually made, but the result was exactly what you have said. It has no parallel in modern times. All three states sent two differing returns. It was not one return that was disputed, it was two. The conservative Democrats sent their own. The Radical Republicans sent their own. That's why you had the commission to decide. We don't know whether there was a deal made. But the fact remains that the conservatives came back to power in these three states, and Hayes became president. Hayes's administration was also full of "Liberal Republicans" (classical laissez faire liberals, not to be confused with modern liberalism) who had opposed Grant and Reconstruction.

DR: Maybe there was no deal, but people have written that there was a deal.

MS: Yes, because everyone suspected that there was a deal. It was an odd situation to have these three states' electoral votes go to Hayes, the Republican, but have the state governments won by the Democrats.

DR: When the federal troops move out of the South, then you begin to have real violence against Black people who had been freed. There were no federal troops to protect them any longer, so you got huge numbers of lynchings and Jim Crow laws. Is that essentially what happened in the 1870s, '80s, and '90s?

MS: You certainly had an uptick in violence after the federal commitment to enforce Reconstruction was challenged and waned. This is why I extend the timeline in my book right up until 1900. People think Reconstruction just ended in 1877, but the unwinding of Reconstruction took a long time. It was between 1877 and 1900 that you had Supreme Court decisions that completely eviscerated not just federal laws, civil rights laws, and enforcement acts against these terror groups—they were our first laws against hate crimes—but they also whittled down the Reconstruction amendments like the Fourteenth Amendment, for instance. This period is very important to look at, because you end up with *Plessy v. Ferguson* in 1896 that upheld segregation. The Wilmington Massacre in North Carolina, which was a coup against the city's interracial government, occurred in 1898. In the 1890s, Southern elites violently opposed fusion state governments in the Upper South between Black Republicans and white reformers and Populists (the farmers movement that founded the People's Party), which posed a challenge to conservative Democratic one-party rule. They met the same fate as the Reconstruction state governments did in the South. In *Williams v. Mississippi* (1898) the Supreme Court starts chipping aways at Black rights, and by the early twentieth century, new Southern state constitutions formally disfranchise Black men, starting with Mississippi in 1890 and ending with Georgia in 1908. You get Jim Crow, lynchings, the convict lease labor system, debt peonage, all of it. It's a big tragedy in American history. It's not just the overthrow of Black freedom but also American democracy.

DR: Around that time, in the late 1890s and the early part of the twentieth century, a theory arose that the war had been won because the North had better troops and more money. White Southerners developed a theory that they had lost for illegitimate reasons.

MS: The Lost Cause mythology.

DR: The Lost Cause theory held that the South lost not because God wasn't on their side, but because they were outmanned and outgunned and they didn't have the resources. That Lost Cause theory became a prominent part of the Southern white ethos.

MS: Absolutely. The North won the war, but the South won the peace. This is when they propagated the Lost Cause mythology that somehow Lee was a fantastic military commander and Grant was terrible—he was called "the butcher"—and that the North only won because it had superior forces and superior resources and population.

We know from history that's not necessarily true. The Vietnam War and other wars have shown us that having greater resources does not necessarily always win. And, in fact, Grant was a brilliant modern military strategist while Lee followed the antiquated Napoleonic military tactics of Jomini [Antoine-Henri Jomini (1779–1869), a French general] taught at West Point still. But this is when the Confederate statues went up in the South. It was not during and immediately after the war. They put up huge, monumental statues of Confederate generals and leaders to proclaim victory with the overthrow of Reconstruction. Part of the propaganda of the Lost Cause mythology was that Reconstruction was a terrible period of misrule and corruption, what they called "Negro rule" or Black domination. This is the idea of Reconstruction that we all are working against still.

DR: Reconstruction is often said by historians to finish in the 1870s, when the federal troops were withdrawn from the South. But your theory is that there was a second Reconstruction where those people who supported the Lost Cause, or other people who took advantage of the federal government's power, began to do other things. What happened with Native Americans, for instance?

MS: Federal troops were withdrawn from the South from the very start of the 1870s. They are consistently withdrawn during Reconstruction and afterward, too. And where do they go? They are sent out west to conquer Native nations. We think of the West as this kind of vast expanse of empty land. It wasn't. There were a lot of sovereign Native nations there.

As a person who was born and brought up in India, I recognized these brutal wars of conquest immediately. They were the kinds of colonial wars that the British and the Europeans fought in Africa and Asia. They were imperial wars, wars of conquest. Even during the Civil War, we had Lincoln's Code, right? Lincoln didn't like the way the Confederacy was treating Black Union army soldiers, summarily executing or enslaving them. Francis Lieber, a German American political philosopher, wrote the military code for the Union army and it was widely known as Lincoln's Code. This code said that race could not be used to differentiate in the treatment of prisoners of war, and it also made violence against civilian noncombatants like women and children war crimes. But it was simply not respected in the so-called Indian wars.

These were wars of conquest. There were massacres. Women and children were killed. No rules of warfare or international law were recognized at all. In the South, the US Army was undertaking an emancipatory project. In the West, they were engaged in wars of empire.

DR: Symbolic of this is how when Woodrow Wilson was president, he not only resegregated Washington, DC, he also showed the movie *The Birth of a Nation* at the White House, which was a movie glorifying the Ku Klux Klan.

MS: Yes, based on a novel by Thomas Dixon, one of these Southerners who was propounding those Lost Cause ideas. Woodrow Wilson is the first Southern president after the Civil War. He's a complex person, because he has some progressive ideas. Think of the League of Nations, which, of course, failed. But he was a Southerner who was very openly racist. For instance, with the League of Nations, when Asians and Africans said, "How about national self-determination for us?" Wilson's reaction was, "I didn't mean you people. I meant just the Europeans." Racism was his fatal flaw. He not only reintroduced segregation into Washington, DC, he also fired all employees of the federal government who were African Americans. He just fired them all. By the 1920s, the second Ku Klux Klan, a nativist and racist organization, was openly marching down the streets of Washington, DC.

DR: In your book, you argue that that the US government began its effort to dominate the Caribbean on the theory that Cuba and other Caribbean nations should be subordinate to white people who were running the United States government. What happened in the Caribbean?

MS: The 1890s is when the Republican Party changes from the antislavery party of Lincoln to the party of big business and empire. Under the McKinley administration, you have the Spanish-American Cuban War of 1898. The United States acquires overseas colonies and the right to interfere in Cuba whenever it feels its interests threatened—an informal empire and a blueprint for subsequent interventions in Latin America. The pacification of the Philippines particularly involved torture and a lot of war crimes. Many of the American generals involved in the colonization of the Philippines, Puerto Rico, and Guam had been involved in the Indian wars. The rise of a formal American empire is connected to the fall of Reconstruction—the idea that certain people are just incapable of self-government, that they should not have the rights enjoyed by American citizens. Even today, some of these territories are in a colonial relationship with the US government under the plenary power of the executive. In the Insular Cases in 1901, the Supreme Court explicitly said that the people who inhabited these American colonies would not have the protections of the US Constitution, especially not the national birthright citizenship and equal protection of the laws of the Fourteenth Amendment. They were called insular because they applied to the island territories acquired by the United States.

But some of the Radical Republicans who were still around objected. George Boutwell, from my home state, the Commonwealth of Massachusetts, formed the Anti-Imperialist League. He was one of the House Members who argued the case to impeach Andrew Johnson. The abolitionists and the Radicals criticized these wars of empire just as they had opposed slavery, especially the brutal subjugation of the Philippines, where you had waterboarding and reconcentration camps. It was a very brutal war, like the Indian Wars. The anti-imperialists said, "We are not like the Old World European monarchies. We shouldn't have empires. We should be a republic. We were founded as a republic." That's why I call my book *The Rise and Fall of the Second American Republic*, because it was kind of a refounding of the American republic in terms of being true to the ideals on which the first republic was formed during the Revolution. But it fell with the rise of Jim Crow, American empire, and unregulated, rapacious capitalism during the Gilded Age.

DR: Your view is that the second Reconstruction, as you call it, ended when?

MS: For me, the first Reconstruction really comes to an end by 1900 and the second Reconstruction of American democracy begins with the civil rights movement, the fight to implement the laws and amendments passed during the first Reconstruction. The 1890s are a crucial decade, when Southern state governments formally disfranchised Black men by state law. You would think that once they had won, the violence would go down, but it actually surges. Lynchings go up. It's a very violent time in American history. It's a dark chapter in our history that we shouldn't go back to. So, for me, the 1890s are crucial, because you have the Spanish-American Cuban War. The Chinese Exclusion Act is passed in 1882, which is also an act that violated the federal civil rights laws and the Fourteenth Amendment. You have all of these things coming together in the 1890s, and with *Plessy v. Ferguson*, Black people are reduced to a second-class status in the Jim Crow South. I always tell my students, "If you ever run for political office, and you are asked by a journalist what were some of the worst Supreme Court decisions, remember *Dred Scott*, remember *Plessy v. Ferguson*. Don't say that you can't answer that question." All this happens in the 1890s, and that's in fact when the hopes of Reconstruction completely died out.

DR: Was Lincoln an abolitionist?

MS: I've written a number of articles on this and gotten into a lot of debates with people on Twitter. I guess I still call it that. Lincoln was not born an abolitionist. What's amazing about Lincoln is that early in the 1830s his moral compass was so strong, even when it was not to his political advantage. In his famous Lyceum speech in 1838, where he condemns the lynching of a Black man and he condemns the lynching of enslaved people in Mississippi, he said, "There are so many Black bodies hanging on these trees in Mississippi, like moss adorning a tree." He had a wonderful turn of phrase even then. He was always morally opposed to slavery. He was antislavery from the start.

But Lincoln was also very respectful of the Union with slaveholders and the US Constitution. He was a lawyer, after all, and he knew that the Constitution had these compromises over slavery.

He balances these competing loyalties—antislavery, Constitution, Union—throughout his career. In the 1850s, you can see it in the Lincoln-Douglas debates. You can see it in his reaction, in an amazing speech that should be read by all American citizens, to the *Dred Scott* decision, where he described the plight of Black people in this country as being locked behind many doors, and the key to each door was held by a different person.

But, when he became president, he moves from the Republican Party position of the nonexpansion of slavery into the territories to abolition, with the Emancipation Proclamation and the Thirteenth Amendment. Then, as a wartime president and as a person who presided over the first Reconstruction plans, he moves to Black male citizenship. To me, he lands on abolitionist ground, because the abolition movement was not just about the immediate abolition of slavery. It was also for Black citizenship. It was not just against slavery in the South but also against racial inequality in the North. They were fighting on various fronts, and that's why they were not too popular.

DR: Lincoln signed the Emancipation Proclamation because he thought it would help him win the war?

MS: There are a lot of people who say that the Emancipation Proclamation doesn't read like a moral document. One historian famously said it reads like a bill of lading. But Lincoln was so conscious that he had to act within the Constitution. A lot of abolitionists and their fellow travelers, like John Quincy Adams, had said that the president can evoke his military powers as a commander in chief in a state of war to abolish slavery. John Quincy Adams is saying this in the 1840s. William Whiting, Lincoln's solicitor general, is an abolitionist. He knows that. This idea adorns the newspapers of the abolitionists—William Lloyd Garrison, Frederick Douglass. So, Lincoln is very careful to evoke his military powers so that the constitutionality of the Emancipation Proclamation is not challenged. But he knows it's not enough, because that's like an executive order. He thought in 1864 he was going to lose the election, because there was such a racist reaction to the Emancipation Proclamation, even in the North. There were riots in New York City at that time. So, he uses the military reasoning. But for Lincoln, these are not separate arguments. They're all fused together—the moral opposition to slavery, respecting the Constitution, evoking his powers as commander in chief. But he knows it's not enough.

I'm sure many of you have seen the movie *Lincoln*. We historians have a lot of quibbles with it. But one thing it gets right is how he spends the last days of his life fighting for the Thirteenth Amendment to the US Constitution, which inaugurates the progressive constitutionalism of Reconstruction. That was the first of the Reconstruction Amendments, which include the Fourteenth and the Fifteenth. So, yes emancipation would help win the war, but it would also redeem the founding principles of the American republic, universal equality and representative government, as he said so eloquently in the Gettysburg Address.

5

Michael Beschloss on Wartime Presidents

INTERVIEW DATE: MARCH 26, 2019

Michael Beschloss has become, over the past several decades, one of the country's most-respected and most-read presidential historians. He has authored nine books on the presidency, is an NBC News presidential historian, and is deeply involved in numerous national philanthropic organizations involved with the presidency and American history. From the time he was a student at Williams College and became a protégé of that college's famed presidential scholar, James MacGregor Burns, Beschloss knew that he wanted to devote his career to studying the presidents. Nonetheless, he obtained a degree from Harvard Business School (to please his family). But Beschloss avoided the business world for the world of presidential scholarship—to the good fortune of the latter.

I have known and admired Beschloss for decades and am pleased that I had a chance to interview him at a Dialogues session. The conversation focused on his ten years of research and writing that culminated in his book *Presidents of War: The Epic Story, from 1807 to Modern Times.*

In the interview, Beschloss made clear that presidents who lead the country at times of war invariably have their overall reputations enhanced when the wars go well (Lincoln, Wilson, Roosevelt,

George H. W. Bush) and have their reputations diminished when the wars do not go well (Truman, Johnson, Nixon, George W. Bush, Biden). He also notes, perhaps more significantly, that in recent decades, presidents have increasingly assumed the power to wage and lead wars without a formal congressional declaration, even though, in theory, such a declaration is required by the Constitution before a president can engage in war. The United States has engaged in a great many wars but has not had Congress issue a formal declaration since World War II. In Beschloss's view, public policy would be enhanced—and popular support for a war would be greater—if the United States returned to the practice, when appropriate and time permits, of having Congress pass declarations of war before a president takes the country to war. Until that occurs, in Beschloss's view, presidents will continue to commit troops and the country to wars without formal declarations, contrary to what the Founding Fathers envisioned.

There are probably few audiences more interested in hearing this plea than Members of Congress, who in recent decades have typically been willing to fund wars but not actually declare them. Not surprisingly, Beschloss's views met a raptly attentive audience at this Dialogues session.

DAVID M. RUBENSTEIN (DR): How long did it take you to write this book?

MICHAEL BESCHLOSS (MB): It took me ten years to write this, but I hope it doesn't take ten years to read. It took a long time because it covers 200 years. It wound up being like writing twenty books. I found that if I was writing about James Madison and the War of 1812, for instance, I couldn't just read three books, I had to research it as if I was doing it for a single book alone.

DR: Tolstoy only spent seven years on *War and Peace*. Why did you spend ten years of your life on this subject?

MB: Because I felt that one thing that we should pay more attention to is that the Founders wanted Congress to decide whether we go to war or not. They were determined that the presidents would not do

FIGURE 5.1 President Lyndon Johnson—seen here next to Secretary of Defense Robert McNamara (*right*) and Secretary of State Dean Rusk (*left*) after the former returned from South Vietnam in July 1965—privately expressed doubts about the United States' ability to win the Vietnam War as early as February 1965.

it. It's really a book about 200 years in which Congress, when it was involved and when it was energetic in the process, often made great decisions, presidents not always so much.

DR: Why did the Constitutional Convention decide that the president of the United States would be the commander in chief but that he could not decide whether we go to war or not? Why did they give that power to Congress?

MB: The Founders, when they were devising the Constitution, had as one of their biggest motives to make this country and our political system as little like that of England and other European monarchies and dictatorships as possible. They wanted to make sure that American presidents would never be allowed to become dictators or authoritarians. They felt that the best way to prevent that would be to worry about the war power. When the kings of England, for instance, felt that they did not have enough power or they were getting unpopular, one way they would get more power was to fabricate an unnecessary war, which would unite the country and make the king more popular. So, the Founders were adamant that the war power be not in the hands of presidents but always in the hands of Congress. If a president ever wanted a war, that president would have to come to Congress and Congress would have to declare it.

DR: Let's go through our wars. Were there declarations of war in the War of 1812?

MB: There were declarations of war all the way up to 1942. Everyone knows when the last declaration of war was ever done by Congress—1942. We've had a couple of wars since then, so life has changed, but we did have wars declared.

DR: The Mexican War?

MB: Absolutely. Not the Civil War, because Lincoln saw this as a rebellion. If he asked for a war declaration, that would be to recognize the Confederacy as a legitimate entity.

DR: What about when we went to war in Cuba?

MB: The Spanish-American War. Absolutely.

DR: What about World War I?

MB: World War I and II.

DR: So, of all the wars we've had where Americans were killed without a declaration of war, what was the one where we had the most loss of life?

MB: The Civil War. A huge loss of life.

DR: What about in recent times?

MB: In recent times, Korea and Vietnam were both waged without war declarations.

DR: Let's talk about Korea. After World War II, what was the situation in the Korean Peninsula? Who was in charge of it? How was it divided up?

MB: It was divided between the Soviet sphere and our sphere, North and South.

DR: The dividing line was the 38th parallel. Who picked that?

MB: An international conference, and in January 1950 Dean Acheson, who probably has a better reputation than he deserves, made a very big mistake. He gave a speech at the National Press Club and he declared that essentially South Korea was outside the American defense perimeter, which was an invitation for the North to invade.

DR: North Korea was being run then by Kim Il Sung, who was the grandfather of the current leader of North Korea.

MB: Right. There has not been a glorious history of democratic elections in North Korea.

DR: So, Kim Il Sung heard Dean Acheson's speech saying that Korea was outside the sphere of influence of the United States. Did he go to Russia and say, "Will you support me?"

MB: We know now that he went to Stalin and said, "How about it?" Stalin said, "If you can do it cheaply and without getting me involved in a world war with the United States, which has immense nuclear superiority"—this is 1950—"go ahead."

DR: What do the Chinese say?

MB: The Chinese were a little bit more standoffish. They wanted to see how it would go.

DR: What happened? Kim Il Sung began to move troops across the 38th parallel?

MB: There was a sudden invasion on the 25th of June, which Harry Truman received news of in Independence, Missouri. He was at home on a summer weekend, and it caught him completely by surprise.

DR: What did he do?

MB: He flew back to Washington. He said that we have to resist this. He sent General Douglas MacArthur to Korea.

DR: MacArthur was where at the time?

MB: MacArthur was the viceroy of Japan.

DR: And Truman had never met MacArthur?

MB: He had not.

DR: MacArthur had been out of the country for almost twenty years. Truman had not met him, but he asked MacArthur to go to Korea and figure out what to do?

MB: Right.

DR: And what did MacArthur decide?

MB: To do it militarily. He planned a huge amphibious invasion at Incheon for September. Truman's people went to him and said,

"You've now given orders to MacArthur, this is the end of June, when will you be going to Congress for your war declaration?" And what he said was something really surprising from Truman: "I'm not going to do it. I'm not going to ask Congress for a war declaration."

In the summer of 1950, Truman had a lot of political problems. He was facing a midterm in the fall. He thought it would be divisive to get into a large debate on Capitol Hill that might focus on Acheson's mistake in declaring Korea outside the defense perimeter. So, he basically said, for the first time in American history—this is the order he was giving—"I'm not going to ask Congress to declare war."

DR: But did he not talk to any Members of Congress about it?

MB: Members of his own party, who urged him to reconsider. Truman said, "No, our armed forces have already been sent, and what's more, maybe this will be the first big test of the United Nations. Maybe this will be a police action under the United Nations."

DR: Did he go to the United Nations for approval?

MB: He did.

DR: How did he get approval if there was a veto by the Soviets?

MB: The Soviet delegate, lucky for Truman, happened to be absent. He was not there to veto it. So Truman could say, "The United Nations has unanimously approved my mission of restoring the invasion of Korea."

DR: Congress did not pass any resolution saying "You're in violation of the Constitution"?

MB: There were some people talking about impeachment, but not very seriously.

DR: MacArthur was now in charge of the war. How many American troops were over there?

MB: A lot at that moment.

DR: What was his strategy to prevail? Did he want to go into North Korea? Did he want to use nuclear weapons?

MB: At that point to show force, but privately he was beginning to talk about how, since America has atomic weapons, why don't we use them? That was something Truman was not very prone to do.

DR: Truman had not met MacArthur, and MacArthur was now running the war. Did Truman decide to finally go meet him?

MB: He met MacArthur in the middle of the Pacific. They met for about a day. They actually got along fairly well, and Truman was asked by his people, "Do you want to continue? It seems to be going pretty well with MacArthur." Truman said, "Hell, no, we haven't had a fight yet and I don't want to start one. Let's get out of here." Which he did.

DR: MacArthur went back thinking he had the mandate from the president to do pretty much what he wants. What did MacArthur do that got him in trouble?

MB: MacArthur began communicating with people back in the United States, saying we should use nuclear weapons and maybe Truman was being too weak. He also pressed to be a lot more aggressive in Korea, even if it involved going all the way to the Yalu River and maybe even fighting the Chinese.

DR: Was MacArthur telling Members of Congress this?

MB: He was.

DR: Members of the Congress were hearing this directly from MacArthur?

MB: Making Truman feel that MacArthur was going around behind his back.

DR: And so Truman decided to do what?

MB: At this point, MacArthur had done this greatly successful amphibious invasion at Incheon. He was a hero in the United States both for that and what he had done in World War II. So Truman kept MacArthur in place but kept a very wary eye on him. We're now up to the election of 1950. The Chinese began coming over the border into Korea to help the North Koreans defeat the United States.

DR: What did Truman do with MacArthur then?

MB: Truman told MacArthur to be very careful, because he didn't want the United States to be involved in a war against China and its ally the Soviet Union that might at any time go nuclear.

DR: Ultimately Truman decided he had to fire MacArthur because MacArthur was not really listening?

MB: In the spring of 1951 Truman said privately, "I have to fire that son of a bitch." That's what he said to his people. In terms of political risk, MacArthur was still this hugely popular figure. MacArthur came back here, he gave his famous "old soldiers never die" speech in Congress, and he couldn't understand why the president was so restrained. It was very emotional. It was said that MacArthur spoke so poignantly that on the Republican side of the House there was not a dry eye, while on the Democratic side of the House there was not a dry seat, because the Democrats were worried that MacArthur would come back and run against Truman in 1952. Not my joke.

DR: How did Truman let MacArthur know he was fired? Did he tweet? How did he tell him?

MB: He might do that if he were here nowadays. He sent a cable.

DR: Did he ever meet with MacArthur after MacArthur got back?

MB: No. They never met again.

DR: And the presidential campaign was moving forward. In 1948, Truman had offered the Democratic nomination, in effect, to Eisenhower and then Eisenhower spurned it. Who was Truman supporting in 1952?

MB: Truman first went to the governor of my home state of Illinois, Adlai Stevenson, who said no. What Stevenson said privately was two things. Number one was, "I don't think Dwight Eisenhower would be so bad as president, why should I be running against him? It would be one thing if it were [Robert A.] Taft, but I don't need to save the country from Eisenhower." The second thing he said was, "Why should I run against Eisenhower and face true defeat? Why don't I wait until 1956, at which time I might win?" So, he went back to Truman and said, "I'm not going to run," at which point Truman went to his vice president, Alben Barkley, who was seventy-two years old.

DR: Did Truman announce that he wasn't going to run again?

MB: Right at the end of March 1952.

DR: The war was not going that well?

MB: Terribly. The important thing—Lyndon Johnson, are you listening?—was that the Korean War got unpopular very fast. By the spring of 1952, had Harry Truman run again, he would have had a very hard time.

DR: So, the war is not going well. Eisenhower decides he will take the nomination if it's given to him, and it's given to him. He's campaigning for president. What does he say about the Korean War?

MB: He gave a speech in Detroit and said, "If you elect me, I will go to Korea and wind this up." It's an unpopular war, and Eisenhower was the hero of the crusade in Europe in 1944 and 1945, so he was going to win anyway. But the fact that he seemed to be the one that could take us out of that war helped him win.

DR: What did Truman say publicly and privately about Eisenhower saying that he was going to go to Korea?

MB: He was outraged. He said that if Ike had a secret plan to end the war, he should tell it to the president.

DR: Eisenhower did win the election. Did he actually go to Korea?

MB: He did go to Korea.

DR: Before or after the inauguration?

MB: Before the inauguration. Truman gave him a plane. Truman wrote him and said, "Ike, if you still want to go to Korea, I'll give you a plane." Eisenhower was outraged because it implied that this was just a campaign ploy he didn't intend to fulfill.

DR: But Eisenhower went. What was the result?

MB: Eisenhower was photographed talking to the troops, came back, and said, basically, this war is a loser. This tells you a lot about him. He thought that Truman had made a big mistake to leave the threat of using nuclear weapons. Eisenhower sent messages over about three different diplomatic channels that he knew were going to be intercepted by the Soviets and/or the Chinese, saying that if the war did not end fast he was perfectly happy to use nuclear weapons. There had been talks in Korea to end the war that had gone on for two years. Almost the second that Eisenhower sent those secret messages, the talks sped up and the war was ended.

DR: After the war was ended and Eisenhower's inauguration occurred, he went to the White House. Did he get out of the car to go in and say hello to Truman?

MB: It was not a loving day between Eisenhower and Truman. Eisenhower got into the presidential car at Blair House. It rolled up in front of the White House. The Trumans were inside waiting for the Eisenhowers to come in for coffee, as they had been invited to do, and the Eisenhowers stayed in the car. Truman sent someone out to ask, "What's happening?" Eisenhower basically was saying, "I am so angry at Truman, I'm not coming in to be given coffee by him. I will ride in the car with him if I have to."

DR: So, Truman got in the car?

MB: Yes, and it was one of the most frigid rides between an incoming and outgoing president.

DR: After the inauguration, Truman goes to Union Station. No Secret Service take him there, is that right?

MB: Right, and Eisenhower did not speak to Truman, with a couple of small exceptions, until November 1963.

DR: Just as an aside, when Truman first came back to Washington after he became a former president, there was no Secret Service. He drove by himself, stayed in a motel en route just like anybody else.

MB: Right. Life was different. Am I allowed to contrast this with a slightly jollier ride up Capitol Hill, since this is getting a little grim?

In 1981, when President Jimmy Carter had been defeated by Ronald Reagan, they had to ride up the Hill together. This was not very auspicious for a friendly conversation, but this was what Reagan was very good at. He started telling all these Hollywood stories about various moguls that he had dealt with, and it was lost on Carter. The car arrived at the Capitol, they got out, and one of Carter's aides came over and said, "How did it go?" Carter said, "Reagan kept on talking. Who is this Jack Warner he kept talking about?" At least they tried.

DR: With Korea, Congress never passed a declaration of war in that situation?

MB: It did not.

DR: How many Americans were killed?

MB: Tens of thousands. Many more Koreans, obviously.

DR: Let's go to the Vietnam War. Lyndon Johnson is president after the death of President Kennedy. What happens in the Gulf of Tonkin in 1964?

MB: There was an attack on an American ship by the North Vietnamese at the beginning of August.

DR: Had we attacked anything in North Vietnam that prompted that?

MB: We had been covertly provoking the North Vietnamese with little pinpricks, as they were called.

DR: There was an attack on the USS *Maddox*, which was a Navy ship in the area. What kind of attack was it?

MB: The ship was attacked by North Vietnamese boats in response to these provocations.

DR: Did the attack do any damage?

MB: Not much.

DR: Was anybody killed?

MB: No, but Johnson was in the middle of a campaign against Barry Goldwater, who was saying that Johnson was too weak, especially on Vietnam. So, at that moment at least, Johnson showed admirable restraint by basically saying, "Someone must have not gotten the word, so I'm not going to respond on this."

Johnson got word that there had been a second attack on this American ship. Johnson did the right thing. He called up his defense secretary, Robert McNamara, who did a few things later on. Johnson said, "Bob, see what you can find out, if this intelligence about a second attack is real or maybe it's just false noise."

DR: What did McNamara tell him?

MB: He said, "We'll look into it," and then about four o'clock, there was a leak from the Pentagon. Doesn't happen nowadays, but in those days occasionally this happened. The leak was, we presume, from someone in the Pentagon who did not like the fact that Johnson had been so restrained the first time. What the leak said was that there had been secret word of the second attack on an American ship and LBJ was doing nothing. We know this because of the tapes that Johnson was making of his private conversations. So, McNamara calls up about 5 p.m. and says, "There's this leak. I can't do anything about this."

Johnson, having been restrained the first time, felt that he could not take a similar political risk the second time, so he said, "We're going to have to bomb the hell out of the North Vietnamese tonight." At 10:30 p.m. he went on TV and said there had been an unprovoked attack on an American ship. He shouldn't have said "unprovoked," because he knew that if there was an attack it had been covertly provoked. It was the first time that we bombed North Vietnam in a big way.

DR: When Johnson became president, how many Americans were in Vietnam?

MB: Sixteen thousand.

DR: Did he believe that he, Lyndon Johnson, was competent to be a wartime president?

MB: He did, not least because he had lived through Korea with Harry Truman, to whom he was fairly close. Unfortunately, he learned a lot of the bad lessons.

DR: You point out in your book that Johnson had some health problems that were never really publicly disclosed. He would go to the hospital for anxiety, and he had heart problems as well?

MB: He had a massive heart attack in 1955 that almost killed him. The doctors told him no more cigarettes, no more overeating, no more overdrinking. He disobeyed.

DR: He died at only sixty-four, four years after he left the White House. Today, with a stent that could be inserted in ten minutes, he would have been able to live for quite some time.

MB: Right. To leap ahead for a moment, he'd begun smoking again the second he hit Texas after being president. One of his daughters said it was on Air Force One flying back to Texas that Johnson lit up for the first time in fourteen years. One daughter grabbed the cigarette out of his mouth and said, "Daddy, you can't do that, the doctor said this will kill you." Johnson said, "I've raised you girls, I've been president, now it's my time." He chain-smoked for the next four years. Jack Valenti, his close aide, told me he thought that Johnson was committing what he called slow-motion suicide because Johnson was so deeply upset by what the war had done to the country and to his reputation.

DR: Let's go back to the war. Johnson goes on TV, he makes this announcement. Does he say, "I've got to go to Congress to get some declaration of war"?

MB: He did go to Congress about this unprovoked attack on US ships, and he got something called the Gulf of Tonkin Resolution. It passed Congress almost unanimously.

DR: Unanimous in the House, and only two votes against it in the Senate?

MB: By Senators Ernest Gruening and Wayne Morse.

DR: After the Gulf of Tonkin Resolution was passed, was there any effort by Johnson to come to Congress and ask for a declaration of war or anything other than that resolution?

MB: I love LBJ for a lot of things but not for the Gulf of Tonkin Resolution. Johnson found out privately about ten days later that the second attack was a fake. I think if he were a perfect person, he would have gone back to Congress and said, "I just want to notify you that I asked for this in good faith. I thought it was an attack, we later found out that it wasn't." Had he done that, there's not one Member of Congress who would have taken back that resolution, but he never did. The result was that Johnson and Nixon never went to Congress asking for anything remotely approaching a declaration, just this flimsy resolution that was in response to a second attack that never happened. Nine years of a war in Vietnam was waged on the basis of that.

DR: How many American soldiers were killed in Vietnam?

MB: Nearly 60,000 and over a million Vietnamese.

DR: And 220,000 wounded American soldiers.

MB: Yes.

DR: When did Johnson decide to escalate and send more troops? At one point we had 500,000 or more troops. When did that escalation occur?

MB: He did it especially in February of 1965, and that's a poignant crucial moment in American history. The bombing of North Vietnam was not working. You couldn't do this as an air war. The aforementioned Robert McNamara said, "You have to put in ground troops. President Kennedy would have done that and you don't want to betray his memory, do you?" I think the preponderance of the evidence is that President Kennedy would not have necessarily done that, but that's what McNamara told Johnson.

It comes to what I see as a crucial conversation, again taped by LBJ on his hidden taping system, in February of 1965. Johnson is sending large numbers of ground troops to South Vietnam for the first time. He's going to those airbases and he's telling these young kids, "We win the wars that we fight; we're going to win this one, too. Go nail the coonskin on the wall." That's what he was saying in public. In private he was saying something else. He's saying to McNamara, "I can't think of anything worse than losing the war in Vietnam, and I do not see any way that we can win." This was not 1968. This was 1965, the first month of the ground war.

I was, I think, virtually the first outside scholar who ever heard this tape, aside from people in the Johnson Library. I heard that and I thought, maybe Johnson is just demoralized. People get depressed. I listened to more tapes, and in private he's saying almost the opposite of what he's saying in public: "I don't expect to win this war." By the summer of 1965 he's telling Lady Bird—who was nice enough to give me her diaries, which had not been published—he's saying to Lady Bird, about the Vietnam War, "I feel as if I'm in a plane that's crashing and I do not have a parachute."

The point I'm making here is that there are a lot of things that a president can do wrong. I repeat: I love Johnson for civil rights and a lot of other things, but it's very hard to listen to him saying in private that he's sending these kids off to die in a war.

DR: He considered resigning because he felt the war was overwhelming him?

MB: Not in 1965. Johnson was told, "You're now escalating. This is not just responding to the Gulf of Tonkin incident. You're thinking of a war that might conceivably involve half a million Americans or more. Why don't you ask Congress for a declaration? It will strengthen you."

And you know what he said? He said, "Truman didn't ask for one. I don't have to either."

DR: As the war moves forward, Johnson decides that he probably can't get reelected and he decides not to run for renomination?

MB: In 1968.

DR: He makes a famous speech on March 31, 1968, in which he says, I'm not going to be a candidate for reelection or renomination. I want to concentrate on resolving the war. What does he actually do? Did he begin a peace effort with the North Vietnamese, and how did that go?

MB: He did. He wanted to have peace talks with the North Vietnamese, which they agreed to do. One reason he didn't run again in 1968 was that men in the Johnson family tended to die very young of heart attacks, usually around the age of sixty. Lady Bird thought another term would kill him. The other reason was that with Johnson there were always ninety hidden motives. It was once said that, for Lyndon Johnson, the shortest distance between any two points was always a tunnel. There was a lot going on here. Johnson felt that if he went on and ran in the spring of 1968, it might be tough and he might ultimately lose.

However, if he says he's not going to run again and he does peace talks with the North Vietnamese and he wins peace, there might be a spontaneous draft movement at the convention in Chicago in 1968 to demand that LBJ, against his wishes, run again for president. The peace talks were not successful, and Johnson by the summer of 1968 was still very unpopular over the war.

Those were the days when the incumbent president basically chose most of the delegates, so he was in a strong position, and he did plan to fly to Chicago. It's on these tapes. He planned to go by helicopter to the roof of the Conrad Hilton hotel, the convention headquarters. Mayor Daley had promised a big demonstration and celebration of LBJ's birthday. It just happened to be his sixtieth birthday that week. And hidden in the basement of the International Amphitheater in Chicago were signs that had been printed by the Daley organization that said DRAFT LBJ. So, he wanted to at least have the option that he could fly to Chicago and be drafted to run.

DR: He called Mayor Daley at one point and said, "Do you think I can still do it?"

MB: He sent two of his close aides to see Daley and say, "How about a draft for the boss?" Daley knew when to cut his losses. He said, "If he wants to announce, maybe it can happen, but otherwise there's nothing I can do to help him."

DR: So, Johnson realizes he is not going to be the nominee. Hubert Humphrey is the nominee. Johnson is not happy that Humphrey is getting, in his view, soft on Vietnam.

MB: Johnson waited to hear Humphrey's speech. I also love Hubert Humphrey, but this was not a moment of courage for him. He gave a speech essentially denouncing both sides in Chicago: the demonstrators and also those that they were demonstrating against. LBJ was watching the speech at the LBJ Ranch. All he could hear was that Humphrey had not delivered the huge support for Johnson and the war that LBJ had expected.

DR: During the campaign, Nixon is trying to prevent a peace agreement. Johnson is negotiating to stop the war, have a bombing halt?

MB: Yes. It began with how Johnson was furious with Hubert Humphrey. There was a man named Arthur Krim, who was Johnson's close friend, co-chief of United Artists, his main fundraiser. Krim flew from the convention down to the LBJ Ranch, and Johnson first said hello. The second thing he said was, "I do not want you to work for the Humphrey campaign. I want Hubert to squirm, I want Hubert to taste"—this is a direct quote—"taste the fact that he needs our help." So, Humphrey, from last week of August, when the convention occurred, until about mid-October, found that the spigots of Democratic money were all turned off. Humphrey was broke until the end of September at least.

DR: And Nixon is trying to keep a peace agreement from going into effect?

MB: Right.

DR: They picked up intelligence showing that Nixon was talking to somebody about not having the South Vietnamese agree to an agreement. Can you explain what that was about?

MB: Nixon at the time of the conventions was running about twenty points ahead of Humphrey. By the end of August or early September 1968, Humphrey was way behind. He scraped together what little money he had to go on TV from Salt Lake City, and said, "As president I would stop the bombing of the North as an acceptable risk for peace." For the first time a lot of antiwar Democrats began to come back into Humphrey's camp. Nixon began to panic. He thought that if Johnson and Humphrey were responsible for the end of the war in October through a peace deal in Paris, that would be the end of him, and he was probably right. He did everything he could to try to keep the peace talks from succeeding.

DR: Johnson picked up on what was going on, and he in effect thought Nixon was committing treason?

MB: Right. Nixon sent word to the South Vietnamese: "Don't make peace at Paris. I'll give you a better deal if I'm elected, and I will be victorious." Johnson picked this up through intelligence intercepts, and he was irate. He called up Everett Dirksen, the Republican leader of the Senate, and said that Nixon was committing treason. Johnson knew that if it were revealed to the American people that Nixon was doing this, they probably would vote against him on the 5th of November. Johnson decided to leave it up to Humphrey. He gave the information to Humphrey and said, "Hubert, it's your election. You decide whether you want to reveal this or not. This can win you the election."

Humphrey decided not to do it because, if this was revealed and Nixon happened to be elected, he would be so besmirched that he could not function as president. He told that to LBJ, and LBJ basically said, "This shows me once and for all that Hubert is much too soft to become president." Lady Bird said, "Poor Hubert!"

DR: In the end, the peace agreement didn't get done.

MB: It didn't happen. Nixon got elected and became president. But he was still terrified that Johnson would reveal what he had done to keep a peace deal from happening. It was not exactly presidential.

After the voting, Nixon calls up Johnson and is just doing somersaults. "If you want me to go to Paris, I'll do anything you want. I'll go to Saigon. I'll beg them to make peace." He was terrified that Johnson would reveal his secret.

DR: You end your book with the Vietnam War. Why do you not include the war resolutions that were passed in the Kuwait War and the Iraq War?

MB: I'm of the view that you can't really write history about something that's less than maybe forty years old. One reason is that you can't get the documents. You will not get people around a president to speak as freely to you.

More important than that, you're not going to have hindsight. A classic example I always think of is that when Harry Truman went back to Missouri in 1953, his popularity ratings were a little above 20 percent. The Korean War was unpopular; there was petty corruption in his entourage. A lot of people said, "Truman does not strike me as presidential. He doesn't seem like Franklin Roosevelt."

The true story is told that in 1952, Truman was asked what he thought of Richard Nixon, and he told reporters, "I think Nixon is full of manure." That was published. Truman's aides went to Mrs. Truman and said, "Couldn't you get the boss to speak more presidentially?" Her reply was, "You have no idea how long it took me to get him to use the word 'manure.'" The point is that in 1953, people cared about that. Here we are, long afterward, and much more important in our assessment of Truman is Cold War Korea. That's because it takes a while to understand whether a president was great or not in history.

DR: A final question. In those two instances, the Iraq War and the Kuwait War, Congress did pass resolutions. Why were they called resolutions and not declarations of war?

MB: Because legally declarations of war were considered to be something more akin to what was done in those earlier wars. I'm just a historian. I've never been elected to office. But I think wars probably would be better fought if a president actually went to Congress and asked for a real declaration of war when he wants to go to war.

If you have a president who wants to keep the strings in his own hands, he's going to ask for a resolution, because it's not as hard to acquire. If a president wants to get Congress to sign on and pass a declaration of war, that takes a lot more work. He's going to have to come to Congress and say, "I've told you the best case. I want you also to know the worst case." If it was LBJ in 1965, he might have said, "This might last five years. This might take 500,000 Americans. We still might not win." That's what he was saying in private. He wasn't saying it in public. Had he been required to go to Congress for a war declaration, he would have had to say those things to the House and Senate.

The wars in American history that were better fought were those when a president went to Congress and got not only approval but consultation all the way through. The wars that were not well fought and that did not succeed were when presidents took shortcuts, didn't ask for a declaration, and also didn't keep on coming back to Congress and saying, "It's not going well. I need your advice. I need you to tell me, for instance, if this takes five years, am I going to have the support?" Johnson didn't do that. Truman didn't either.

6

Chris Wallace on the Presidential Election of 1960

INTERVIEW DATE: JUNE 10, 2025

I have been in two presidential campaigns—those run by Jimmy Carter in 1976 and in 1980. But the presidential election that I first paid any attention to (and the one that sparked my lifelong interest in both these campaigns and the presidency) occurred in 1960—the epic race that elevated a forty-three-year-old, charismatic junior senator, John F. Kennedy, to the White House, over a two-term vice president, Richard Nixon, who managed, eight years later, to resurrect his political career and win the presidency himself. My fascination with this campaign probably led to my early career interest in working for a president at the White House and, in time, to my interest in becoming involved with and a large supporter of various philanthropic and educational organizations named for Kennedy.

In his book *Countdown 1960: The Behind-the-Scenes Story of the 312 Days That Changed America's Politics Forever*, Chris Wallace indicates that the 1960 election was also the first presidential election to which he paid attention (and in which he supported a candidate—Nixon). Over the past sixty-five-plus years, there have been a slew of books on the 1960 campaign. The story is inherently a fascinating one: the war-hero son of one of the country's wealthiest men against the son of an unsuccessful small-businessman; the glamorous,

FIGURE 6.1 In 1960, Senator John Kennedy and Vice President Richard Nixon met four times in the first-ever series of presidential election debates. Nixon declined to wear makeup in the first debate and was visibly perspiring on television. Meanwhile, Kennedy appeared poised and youthful. Kennedy soon took a lead in the polls, and he eventually triumphed in November.

handsome, charming young senator against the noncharismatic, often-awkward incumbent vice president; a Catholic against a Protestant; a Harvard grad against a Whittier College grad; a beautiful, cultured, French-speaking young wife against a schoolteacher wife famous for her "Republican" cloth coat; the man who wanted to get the country moving in a new, vibrant direction against the defender of the status quo.

Theodore White, in his Pulitzer Prize–winning book, *The Making of the President 1960*, brought these contrasts into focus, with the kind of never-before-seen backstage coverage of a presidential campaign.

But that 1962 book lacked the perspective and information that six decades of hindsight can provide.

Chris Wallace, the son of legendary CBS newsman Mike Wallace, describes the entire campaign of both candidates—the primaries, the vice presidential selection, the increasing role of TV and campaign money (then unregulated), and the general election campaign. But Wallace provides particular insights on the impact of four presidential debates (the first in the country's history) and the likelihood of election fraud in Illinois and Texas, which may well have cost Nixon the presidency. (Although many in the Republican Party importuned Nixon to contest the election, he ultimately thought that would be damaging to the country and might preclude him from ever running again if the challenge failed, as seemed likely to Nixon.)

The fact that Nixon seriously considered a challenge to the closest presidential election in over a century is not that widely known. What is better known, and is thoroughly covered by Wallace, is the ill-fated first debate. Nixon was a skilled debater, but at the first debate he was sick, refused makeup, perspired visibly, and looked less presidential than Kennedy, who was tanned, rested, polished, and seemingly more confident of himself and the subject matter than the more experienced vice president. There were three more debates, but Nixon never seemed to regain his footing, especially among those who watched the first debate on television (as opposed to those who listened on radio).

The polls catapulted Kennedy into the lead following the first debate, and he never lost it (though the popular vote election was then the closest in modern history—Kennedy won by fewer than 120,000 votes out of more than sixty-eight million votes cast). All of this was described to a rapt audience of Members of Congress by Chris Wallace, who proved to be as gifted an interviewee as interviewer.

DAVID M. RUBENSTEIN (DR): You started a *Countdown* series, and this is the third book in it. What are the other two, and what do you mean by "countdown"?

CHRIS WALLACE (CW): The first book was *Countdown 1945*, about the decision to drop the bomb on Hiroshima. The second book was *Countdown bin Laden*, about the successful effort in 2011 to find and kill Osama bin Laden. The new book is *Countdown 1960*, about the 1960 election.

The idea came from my daughter, who was in publishing. I wanted to write history books, and she came up with "countdown." What I liked so much about it was that oftentimes history books are written looking in the rearview mirror at what happened, but that's not how it was experienced. When people are making decisions and going through moments of crisis, they don't know what's going to happen.

The idea for the first book came from Nancy Pelosi, the day that President Trump was going to make his State of the Union speech. The leader of the opposition party in the House does a prebuttal, where they tell all the news anchors beforehand why this speech that they haven't heard yet is full of baloney. We were in what's known as the Board of Education, the famous hideaway of former Speaker Sam Rayburn in the House part of the Capitol. Speaker Pelosi told a story to all the anchors there that this was the room in 1945 where Harry Truman, then the vice president, came in to have a bourbon and branch water with all the other people and Speaker Rayburn. And Rayburn said, "The White House is trying to get you." Truman dialed up and got Steve Early, the president's secretary, on the phone. Early just said, "You've got to come to the White House right away." No more. Truman hung up the phone and said, "Jesus Christ and General Jackson."

Nancy Pelosi is telling me this story. Everybody else was interested in what she was thinking and going to say about Trump's speech. I thought, "I've now got my first book." And that was the book. The whole point was to write in effect a history thriller, to take people in a countdown of days down to the zero moment, the dropping of the bomb on Hiroshima.

When Truman goes back to the White House after that call, he doesn't even know what it is about. He thinks that President Roosevelt may have returned from Warm Springs unbeknownst to him. He goes up to the second floor, and Mrs. Roosevelt tells him that FDR has died. Truman suddenly is the president. He says, "What can I do for you?" Eleanor says, "What can we do for you? Because you're the one who's in trouble now."

He's sworn in, and Henry Stimson, the secretary of war, says, "I need to talk to you, Mr. President." He takes him aside in a private room and says, "I need to tell you about the most destructive weapon in the history of mankind, which we're working on, but I need you to settle in first. I'll come back in a few days and tell you." That was literally the first that Harry Truman ever had heard of the Manhattan Project. Roosevelt had never told him about it.

That's the point of the *Countdown* books—to take people day by day through the key moments of the process. And 1945 was a perfect example of that, because, at the time, when they were making the decision whether to use the bomb, they didn't know whether it would actually work. It had never been tested. It was tested, I think, on July 14, 1945, at Alamogordo. That was the first and only time it was tested. It was on that basis they decided to drop it on Hiroshima.

DR: You and I are roughly the same age. Both of us lived through the 1960 election, which was probably the first one we actually experienced where we had candidates we supported or didn't support. You were how old in 1960?

CW: I was thirteen years old.

DR: And you were supporting who?

CW: I was rooting for Richard Nixon. I say "rooting" because at thirteen it wasn't the most sophisticated political analysis. It was like rooting for a sports team. Kennedy seemed too rich and too glamorous and kind of spoiled, and Nixon seemed serious and earnest, and for some reason I was rooting for Nixon.

DR: Let's go through that 1960 election. In 1956, Adlai Stevenson runs for the second time against Dwight Eisenhower and loses overwhelmingly again. Right after the 1956 election, who were the likely candidates to be the 1960 Democratic nominee three years later? Who were people talking about?

CW: Certainly Lyndon Johnson, who was the majority leader and the master of the Senate. Jack Kennedy to a certain degree. He was young and untested. But what you didn't mention is that in the 1956 convention, after Stevenson was nominated, he left the vice presidential nomination open to the convention, and it came down to Estes Kefauver and Jack Kennedy. Kefauver won, but that kind of put Kennedy on the map.

DR: He was interested. He was a prospective candidate. Who else? There were a couple of other senators who were interested?

CW: Yes. Stuart Symington and Hubert Humphrey. Humphrey was the only one who formally got in the race. Lyndon Johnson only did so a couple of days before the convention in Los Angeles in July.

DR: On the Republican side, was there any opposition to Richard Nixon as the nominee for 1960 a couple of years in advance?

CW: Nelson Rockefeller won the governorship of New York in 1958, beating the incumbent, Averell Harriman. With all of his money and his huge think tank and the apparatus he had, Rockefeller was taken very seriously. He announced in late '59. He'd run a long, tough campaign. He acted as if he thought it was unbecoming to run for president a year after he'd been elected governor. So, he said he wasn't going to run, but he never dropped out. He stayed involved right up until the convention.

DR: John Kennedy's interested in running. Who is his brain trust? Who are the people helping him to run? And what was so unique about the type of campaign he ran, in terms of his organization, compared to people who had previously run for president? Was it going out in the country, the posters, other things?

CW: Bobby Kennedy, his younger brother, didn't want to run the campaign. He'd been asked at various times to run campaigns. He ran Kennedy's Senate campaign in '52 against Henry Cabot Lodge in Massachusetts, but he had his own career, and he didn't want to. Old Joe Kennedy, their father, said to Bobby, "You've got to run this campaign." And you didn't say no to Joe. So, Bobby unwillingly got into the campaign. The subtitle of the book is *The Campaign That Changed Politics*, and it was the Kennedy campaign most of all that did it.

He hired Lou Harris. You've heard of the Harris Poll. Lou Harris was one of the first big-name pollsters to work specifically for an individual candidate as opposed to a newspaper, like Gallup. Kennedy got Ted Sorensen, whom he called his intellectual blood bank, an absolutely brilliant writer. He hired Pierre Salinger, who had worked on the Senate Select Committee for Bobby Kennedy, who became his press secretary.

The reason I say it was the first really modern campaign is because of the use of polling throughout and also because it was the first campaign that was conducted primarily on television. Kennedy was, by the standards of that time, sophisticated in the use of television. He had an ad to the tune "High Hopes." The words were about Jack Kennedy, sung by Frank Sinatra. It was a pretty sophisticated campaign.

DR: You mentioned "old Joe Kennedy." He was in his late sixties when this campaign was being conceived. Late sixties doesn't seem that old now. That's a teenager today.

CW: Yes, I guess so.

DR: Joe Kennedy is worth how much money at the time?

CW: He's worth about $400 million, which is the equivalent, counting for inflation, of about $4 billion today.

DR: Is John Kennedy taken seriously by his colleagues in the Senate? Or they thought he was more or less a playboy?

CW: I don't know that I'd put it either way. There certainly was a feeling that he was rich and young. He missed a lot of votes. There was a sense of "Wait your turn, junior." But he was not interested in doing that, for a variety of reasons, one of which was, unbeknownst to the American public, he had suffered some serious health problems. He had Addison's disease. He'd actually had the last rites administered to him at one point in the 1950s when it seemed he was near death. He was a man in a hurry.

DR: Addison's disease is an adrenal insufficiency. Your adrenal glands don't work so well. It was then considered fatal, eventually?

CW: Not always, but it certainly had the potential if it flared up. He was taking drugs at the time to deal with it and keeping it from the public. This was one of the deep, dark secrets of the Kennedy campaign, that this man who exuded, to use the word of the time, so much vigor was, in fact, pretty sick.

DR: In those days there weren't that many primaries, but Kennedy decides to get into the first one, the famous New Hampshire primary. When does Kennedy actually announce he's running for president?

CW: He announces on January 2nd. He did it on purpose on a Sunday. He figured that he would be in all the Monday papers because nothing was going to happen on Sunday. He announced in the Senate caucus room. He made it a big deal at that point. There were seventeen primaries in 1960, and it was the first time that primaries were going to play a big role. Up until then, the choice of a nominee was often made by the party bosses. But now there were primaries, and Kennedy thought that, to jump the pecking order of people like Humphrey and Symington and Lyndon Johnson, he had to show that he could win. To go into primaries and lead the vote, show that he was a vote getter and could beat whoever was in the primaries, would be his ace in the hand. His trump card, if you will, was to show that he had public support.

DR: He goes to New Hampshire, and he wins that primary?

CW: Overwhelmingly, with 85 percent of the vote.

DR: What's the next primary?

CW: The next big primary was Wisconsin. There he faces the only other serious candidate in the race, Hubert Humphrey. Kennedy is flying around in the Convair 240 that his daddy had bought for him called the *Caroline*, and Humphrey was in a bus with a broken heater. At one point, Humphrey hears a plane overhead, and he yells, "Damn it, that's Jack Kennedy. Come down here and fight fair." But Kennedy doesn't. And he spends an enormous amount, multiples more than Humphrey does. But it ends up being a fairly close race, something like 55 to 45 percent. It's not enough to knock Humphrey out of the race, which is what Kennedy was hoping.

Also, there were a lot of Roman Catholic voters. There's a fascinating handwritten document by Clark Clifford in the Library of Congress Collection where he wrote for Kennedy, in pencil, in his own handwriting, Kennedy's weaknesses, Nixon's strengths, and Symington's strengths. Number five on the list was religion. Which surprised me because, in doing the research for the book, I learned that they thought religion was the single most important issue. They were very concerned about it. And because there was such a large Catholic vote—not a majority, but a large Catholic vote—in Wisconsin, they felt they had to go on to West Virginia, and West Virginia was 95 percent Protestant.

DR: He doesn't knock out Humphrey in Wisconsin. He goes to West Virginia. He campaigns around the state. How does that election turn out?

CW: The funny thing about that election is old Joe Kennedy—

DR: He wasn't that old.

CW: Old Joe Kennedy says, "Don't go to West Virginia. It's a nothing state. It doesn't matter." I think he was worried about the huge religious advantage that Humphrey would have there. And Kennedy says, "It's not a problem, Dad. I'm leading in the polls." At that point he was leading by something like sixty to forty in the polls. He sends Bobby to West Virginia, and when Bobby comes back, he says, "We're in trouble." Jack says, "What do you mean 'we're in trouble'? I'm leading in the polls like by twenty points." Bobby says, "Jack, they just discovered that you're a Catholic." He was in trouble.

West Virginia was notoriously corrupt in 1960. The way you won the election was to grease the palms of sheriffs, who had a lot of say in how elections were conducted. They even had a thing called "slating," which was that they would hand out sample ballots, but the sample ballots would oftentimes only have the name of the candidate that the sheriff wanted to win. So, these sheriffs who were getting money—and I'll tell you in a minute who they were getting money from—they would have a sample ballot with Jack Kennedy's name on it, which was a big advantage.

What money did they get? Joe Kennedy makes a deal with Sam "Mooney" Giancana, who was the head of the Chicago mob. Bundles of cash go to Giancana, who spreads it around to sheriffs in West Virginia. But my single favorite story, and this comes from Hubert Humphrey, is that Joe Kennedy goes to Cardinal Cushing, an archbishop and the cardinal of Boston, and he makes a deal with him. The deal is that on a particular Sunday, all of the parishioners come in and they give their donations, and all of that money is given to Joe Kennedy—a whole week's donations from the Boston Archdiocese. Kennedy then writes a check for more than the money that's handed over. He writes a check, and he gives that to the church, also getting a nice tax deduction along the way. Then the money is handed out to Protestant ministers in West Virginia to preach on behalf of Jack Kennedy, even though he's a Catholic, in their churches. Humphrey tells the story that years later Cushing tells him this, and he says, "It was good for the church. It was good for the ministers. And it was good for the candidate," the candidate being Jack Kennedy.

DR: What happened in the West Virginia primary?

CW: Kennedy wins by about the margin that he had before the whole thing started, about sixty to forty. And Humphrey drops out. That's basically when the primaries end and all of the official opposition to Kennedy ends. But Kennedy still doesn't have the number of votes he needs to win. He needed 761 votes at the convention to get a majority. He still didn't have that. When he gets to the convention in July in Los Angeles, he has somewhere between 650 and 700.

DR: Lyndon Johnson still feels he has a chance. He's the majority leader. What does he start saying about Kennedy and his health?

CW: Johnson didn't believe in this whole primary system. He thought you could do it through the old party bosses. At one point he goes to Tip O'Neill, who had taken over the seat in Boston that Jack Kennedy first won when he went to Congress. Johnson says, "I know you're with Kennedy for the first ballot. Will you go with me for the second ballot?" Tip says, "Lyndon, there isn't going to be a second ballot. Kennedy's going to win on the first ballot." Johnson goes to Richard Daley, the mayor of Chicago, who had control of the entire Illinois delegation, and Daley says, "No, I'm going with Kennedy."

Johnson gets there, and he thinks that he's going to be able to somehow swing this at the last minute, literally a week before the nomination. He decides the only chance he's got is to play it dirty. He doesn't do it himself, but he has some of his people do it. They start saying that Kennedy has Addison's disease and is at death's door. The other thing Johnson goes at is the fact that Joe Kennedy had been less than hostile to Adolf Hitler when he was the US ambassador at the Court of St. James in England in the 1930s. He basically calls Joe Kennedy a Nazi sympathizer.

As you can imagine, Bobby Kennedy, who didn't like Johnson already, now really hates him. They go into the convention, and it quickly becomes clear to Johnson that none of this is working. Incidentally, the Kennedy people fire back at Johnson and say, "You're talking about Kennedy's health. You had a major heart attack in 1955.

You're the guy who's really sick." It got pretty nasty between the two of them. Kennedy wins on the first ballot, but just barely. Because it was the last state in the roll call, Wyoming, that put him over the top.

DR: Adlai Stevenson was the Democratic nominee in '52 and in '56. Eugene McCarthy makes a nominating speech for him then. Did he come close to getting the convention to support Adlai Stevenson for a third time?

CW: No. Certainly there was a huge outpouring—I remember watching this on TV at the time—and the convention went crazy. That's who they still loved, Adlai Stevenson. I forget the exact number of votes, but I think it was around 100.

DR: Kennedy gets the nomination. Who does he want to pick for vice president?

CW: It's not clear, but it was not Lyndon Johnson. Symington of Missouri was probably the front-runner for it and a guy that Kennedy took seriously. It's past midnight on the night that he wins the nomination. He's sitting with Bobby Kennedy and deciding, "What are we going to do? Who are we going to pick?" The thought comes up that maybe we have to offer it to Lyndon. Now, Lyndon was firmly on the record that he didn't want the job, so they thought, "We'll offer to Lyndon. We really don't want him." Bobby hated him. Jack didn't really trust him, and they were both bitter about the way Johnson had campaigned against them at the convention. But they think, "It's a nice gesture, and we could use his help in Texas, and he isn't going to accept it anyway."

They're at the Biltmore Hotel. Kennedy was on the ninth floor in a suite. Johnson was on the seventh floor in a suite. Bobby and Jack, who is now the Democratic nominee, go back and forth, up and down the stairs several times from Kennedy's suite to Johnson's suite. On the eighth floor was Sam Rayburn. Rayburn didn't want Johnson to run for vice president. He wanted him in Congress so they could get their legislation through the House and the Senate. Jack goes down to see Johnson, and he says, "I'd like to offer you the vice presidency." To Jack's horror, Johnson says, "Yes." Now they've got to get out of this mess they've created for themselves. Bobby goes down to talk to Rayburn to try to convince him to convince Johnson not to accept the job. It goes back and forth. And then, finally, by 10 a.m. or noon—this is now the day when the vice president is going to be nominated and Jack's going to give his acceptance speech—they still haven't arrived at this.

Incidentally, they brought in civil rights leaders, they brought in labor leaders, like Walter Reuther of the United Auto Workers, and they were horrified by Johnson. They didn't want him at all, but they're stuck. At one point Bobby goes down and basically says to Johnson, "You don't want this job. You really don't want this job. We'll make you the chairman of the Democratic National Committee." Johnson, almost in tears, says, "I want to be vice president." And Bobby realizes, "We're screwed," and that's how Johnson gets the job.

DR: When Bobby Kennedy went down the second time, Johnson said, "Are you speaking for your brother or not?"

CW: Right.

DR: And the brother never came down and asked him to withdraw.

CW: No. In fact, there were calls about "What's this Bobby's doing?" There were a lot of other people involved, including, interestingly enough, the publisher of the *Washington Post*, Phil Graham, who was absolutely involved in all this backroom dealing, trying to get Johnson on the ticket. He was a friend of Kennedy's, but he was a better friend of Johnson's.

DR: So, it's Kennedy and Johnson. On the Republican side, does Nixon have any opposition? What does Nelson Rockefeller decide to do?

CW: Rockefeller at a certain point in the spring starts to say, "Maybe I would accept being drafted." This drives Nixon nuts, because he thinks he's got it wrapped up. And he probably did, because he had done all the things a vice president does. He'd gone out and gone to the chicken dinners and attended to all the party insiders who were the delegates to the convention in Chicago. But he's concerned about it. One of the things that comes out in my book over and over again is that with Nixon, although he had a team, too, there's a big difference here. Kennedy very much relied on his team and let Bobby Kennedy run the campaign. He was the candidate. Nixon is the candidate but he's also the campaign manager, and he makes a lot of decisions on his own. He decides, with his military aide, never telling any of his top people, to go to New York City, just before the convention, to Rockefeller's thirty-room triplex on Fifth Avenue, have a lamb-chop dinner, and go over what would be acceptable to Rockefeller in the platform so he would support Nixon. It was primarily things like an early version of Medicare, more defense spending, being more aggressive on civil rights. Before Nixon can announce it, Rockefeller does, and he calls it the "Compact of Fifth Avenue," making it very clear that this was Rockefeller dictating to Nixon what it would take to get him on board. Rockefeller ends up introducing him at the convention. Nixon gives a speech and chooses Henry Cabot Lodge as his running mate.

DR: Why did he pick him?

CW: There were a bunch of people to pick from. One of the people that he was seriously considering in 1960 was Gerald Ford, the congressman from Michigan, whom he was very close to. But he ends up with Cabot Lodge. Eisenhower was very much for Lodge. I think Nixon thought, "He's sort of a blue blood like Kennedy. He's from Massachusetts." He had a fairly distinguished tenure as ambassador to the United Nations. It seemed like a good fit.

DR: Both sides have their team intact. The early polling shows Nixon ahead?

CW: No. The first polling shows Kennedy ahead. It was always something like fifty-three to forty-seven throughout the entire election. It never got wider than that. It sometimes went back and forth.

DR: Whose idea was it to have a debate?

CW: Primarily the networks. Robert Kintner, who was then the president of NBC, pushed the idea. Congress had to pass legislation, which they did that summer, which created an exemption to the Fairness Act. The Fairness Act basically said, if you put these two candidates on TV, then you've got to put every other person who's running for president on TV. Obviously, there were a lot of candidates. The networks didn't want to put them all on. With this exemption, they could put just Kennedy and Nixon on.

When the original invitation goes out from NBC—they're the first network to make it—Salinger says it took twenty minutes for them to say yes. They figure this is a no-brainer. It's going to do nothing but good for Kennedy to be on the same stage with Nixon, who enjoyed a kind of stature-and-experience gap. This would put them on even terms. Then Nixon felt kind of trapped. One, he felt trapped by, "How do I say no when this whippersnapper says yes?" Two, the year before, he had gotten into a kitchen debate in a model home at an exhibition in Moscow with Nikita Khrushchev. He thought he was the master of debates, and he was confident that he was going to win. He was the champion debater in college or high school. Kennedy had not been. They ultimately agree to do four debates. This is the first time there had ever been a presidential debate. There'd never been one before.

DR: Let alone on television, right?

CW: Right.

DR: There'd never been the two major party candidates in any forum sitting together and having a debate. The first debate is in what city?

CW: It's in Chicago in late September. I need to back up a minute here. The race gets going, and it's going the way you'd think, very close. Nixon in North Carolina bangs his knee badly and gets a staph infection and ends up in Walter Reed Hospital for two weeks at the end of August and in early September. He's off the campaign trail for two weeks, and Kennedy is running around the country. Nixon gets back on the trail on the 12th, and the first debate was on the 26th, only two weeks after he's out of the hospital. Nixon is underweight and not himself and then he gets the flu. When he gets to Chicago, he's under the weather and at least ten pounds underweight. Meanwhile, Kennedy was sporting a new tan and just looked great.

DR: As you know, as somebody who's moderated these debates, today candidates have mock debates for many hours. Did they do that then?

CW: No.

DR: What did they do? They just sat around?

CW: They went over things, but they didn't have anything like mock debates. Nixon did a lot of it himself. The two days before Kennedy gets there—as I said, he's very tan, he looks great—he goes over his stuff with Sorensen and Mike Feldman and Richard Goodwin, then takes a big nap the afternoon of the debate. He wakes up at 6:30, gets ready, puts on a dark blue suit, light shirt, dark tie, and heads to the debate. Nixon is absolutely exhausted. He gets there like at midnight the night before, goes to a Democratic-leaning convention—I think it was the carpenters' union—is sickly, and spends the entire afternoon studying like crazy. He gets in the car, goes to WBBM, the CBS affiliate TV station where the debate is going to be held. They open the door for him, he gets out, and he raps his knee, the knee that had caused him such pain, and he is in considerable pain as he heads into the studio for the debate.

The studio has a gray background, and Kennedy is there in this dark blue suit with his deep tan. Nixon has chosen to wear a gray suit, which bleeds into the background. When they ask Kennedy whether he wants makeup, he says no. Then they ask Nixon whether he needs it, and Nixon, who was famous for having a five o'clock shadow and had this gray pallor, is embarrassed to say, "Yes, I want it" when Kennedy has said no. So he doesn't.

Let me just say that in the middle of the debate, it is so bad that Richard J. Daley is watching a TV at his home in Chicago, and he says, "My god, they embalmed him before he died."

DR: Kennedy looks fairly self-assured. He looks at the camera. Nixon looks at everything but the camera. People who watched it on TV thought Kennedy had won, but people listening to the radio thought that Nixon had won. Can you explain that dichotomy?

CW: Yes. Because Kennedy was playing it as it was, which was a TV show that was watched by seventy million people. Until the first Trump-Clinton debate in 2016, it was the biggest audience ever for a presidential debate. It was a big deal even to a thirteen-year-old, even to a ten-year-old.

The basic argument was that if you were watching the debate, Kennedy came off as much more vigorous, speaking to the camera, talking to the seventy million people watching, but if you were listening to it, just listening to the points that were being made, perhaps Nixon won on points, as a debate coach might say. The point was that the vast majority of people weren't listening on radio. They were watching it on TV. It remained a five- or six-point race, but definitely Kennedy took the lead at that point.

DR: They have the first debate. There are three more debates. Does Nixon change his strategy?

CW: Yes, absolutely. A couple of things that happened in that first debate give you a sense how badly Nixon misjudged things. Nixon's greatest strength and biggest advantage over Kennedy was foreign policy. He traveled all over the world. He'd been vice president for eight years. He had debated Khrushchev in Moscow. But he thought that the interest in the debates would build as opposed to what really happened, which was that the greatest interest was in the first debate. So, he agreed that the subject of the first debate would be domestic policy, which was Kennedy's strength. It was only the third debate that was on foreign policy, by which point it was still a big audience but not as much of a game changer. The day after the first debate, Nixon's doctor comes to him and says, "You looked pale, sick, and tired in that debate because you're pale, sick, and tired. You're going to have three milkshakes a day, and we're going to feed you up." Nixon gained ten pounds by the second debate. He also took makeup.

The other thing that had happened was that just before he got to the first debate, Henry Cabot Lodge called him up and says to him, "This is an opportunity for you to change your image. You should be statesmanlike and not be Tricky Dick, not be the hatchet man" that the political cartoonist Herblock did cartoons of. In fact, he was remarkably passive during the first debate and began a lot of answers by saying, "I agree with Senator Kennedy . . ." He was advised before the second debate to go after this SOB and punch him in the face. He was much more aggressive in the remaining three debates.

DR: There was discussion about Kennedy's illnesses and his personal life. Nixon chose not to go after him for that because he was worried about the fact of his own psychiatrist coming out?

CW: I don't think that the personal life was ever a serious consideration. But there was a period of time between the last debate, which was late October, and the election, which was November 8th, the last day that Election Day can be, and Nixon, who realized he was behind, said, "I think that we should have all of our medical files released in public in the last week of the campaign." The Kennedy people knew that this was an effort to try to get the Addison's disease on the record, and they were pushing back. They said that Herb Klein, Nixon's press secretary, was going to release all of Nixon's medical records a week before the election. But Nixon had been under the care of a psychiatrist, which at that time was absolutely taboo and a career killer. They had reason to believe that Kennedy—politics is a great business—had had a private detective snooping and, in fact, the week before had called Nixon's psychiatrist. Nixon's team thought, "Checkmate. We're going to drop this."

DR: The day of the election: Does anybody know for sure who's going to win?

CW: No. The feeling was that Kennedy was ahead but that Nixon had the momentum, and it was just a question of who was going to hit the finish line first.

DR: Were there computer analyses in those days, where the networks could say, "It's 8:01 and now the election's over"?

CW: It was the first time they had them. They didn't have any exit polls, but they did have the UNIVAC computer and the RAND computer. NBC was anchored by Chet Huntley and David Brinkley, CBS was anchored by Walter Cronkite, and ABC by Howard K. Smith. NBC and CBS had these computers. Something like ten minutes after the polls closed, CBS and ABC came out and said Nixon was going to win by a landslide. Kennedy gets very upset, and he goes to Lou Harris, and Harris says, "This is BS. They don't know. I don't know. It's just BS. It's based on nothing." About an hour later, they take it back. Later in the evening, the networks all make projections, and they say it's Kennedy by a landslide because he gets to a very big early lead, gets into the 200s in the Electoral College, and Nixon is still in double digits.

DR: When Kennedy goes to sleep that night, he said he didn't know who was going to win?

CW: By the time he goes to bed, it's three or four in the morning, and Harris and Bobby say, "It looks pretty good." There's been a big event that has happened around 3:15 in the morning East Coast time, 12:15 Pacific Coast time. It's looking so dire for Nixon that he goes down to see his supporters—there's that famous picture of Nixon with Pat by his side—and she's in tears. He says to his supporters that night, "If the present trend continues, Kennedy will be the next president." Huntley and Brinkley and Cronkite are, like, "Was that a concession or wasn't it a concession?" They weren't quite sure. At that point, the Kennedy people are upset and say Nixon should have conceded. Kennedy says, "I wouldn't concede. It's too close." There were too many states outstanding. Having said that, when he goes to bed, he reportedly says to Jackie—they're all at the compound in Hyannis—he says, "It looks like we're in. Let's go to bed."

DR: When they wake up in the morning, people say Kennedy won. But some are accusing people in Illinois and Texas of fraud in the counting of the ballots?

CW: Yes, to a certain degree, but that built over time after the election. Nixon concedes. He doesn't concede in person but has Herb Klein, at about noon on the 9th, the day after the election, read a formal concession to Kennedy.

DR: When do the fraud allegations come about?

CW: There are a number of people in the Republican Party who think the election is stolen, including Senator Thruston Morton of Kentucky, who's also the chair of the Republican National Committee. He really wants to investigate this, and he pushes very hard. There's an effort on the ground in a number of states, particularly Illinois and Texas. Between them, Illinois has twenty-seven electoral votes, Texas has twenty-four electoral votes, and if both of those should flip and everything else stays the same, Nixon is the president.

DR: You point out in your book that there are some cases where more people voted than were registered in Illinois.

CW: Yes. In some precincts, there were cases where there'd be 100 people registered and 250 votes. This is Chicago we're talking about. One of the things that happened was that downstate Illinois is very

Republican, and upstate and Chicago and its environs are very Democratic. Richard Daley, the mayor, the boss of the Democratic machine, holds back his votes in Chicago and waits for the downstate votes to come in. The argument was that he was waiting to see how many votes he had to produce, and then he produced them.

Texas is an even more egregious example. About two and a half million people vote in Texas, and slightly more than a million vote with paper ballots. You've heard about the butterfly ballots [in Florida in 2000]. In 1960, on the presidential ballot in Texas, you not only had to mark who you were voting for, you had to scratch out the names of every other candidate on the ballot that you weren't voting for. Not only Nixon, but the nominee of the Constitution Party and a bunch of other parties. Obviously, a lot of people failed to do this. What Republicans and also some investigative reporters found was that in Democratic districts where Kennedy racked up huge advantages, many fewer paper ballots were disqualified than in Republican districts that would have favored Nixon, while in many of those districts 40 percent of the paper ballots were disqualified. There was a strong belief that those two states, which would have been enough, and maybe some others had been stolen by the Democrats.

DR: Why did Nixon not protest the election or contest it?

CW: Some people believe that behind the scenes he was egging people on to contest it. But what I found is that every time he had to make a decision, he'd decide against contesting the results. I'll give you a few examples. On November 9th, he concedes the election. On November 14th, he meets with Kennedy at the Key Biscayne Hotel in Florida. Kennedy was down in Palm Beach. Nixon was in Key Biscayne, which was kind of his retreat. Kennedy flies there by helicopter, and they meet very much as the president-elect and the defeated candidate. There was a reporter for the *New York Herald Tribune* named Earl Mazo, and he's doing this big investigation of possible voter fraud. He gets a call from Nixon, who asks him to come see him in his office in Washington. Mazo thinks he's going to give him information and urge him on. And Nixon says no and tells him not to do it. When he finds out Mazo is continuing it, he calls his bosses at the *Herald Tribune* and says, "Drop it."

There are three primary reasons he did this. One, it was the height of the Cold War. The idea that, because it would have taken months in litigation, you're not going to know who the next president is, was unacceptable. Two, up to that point it was a no-brainer that you observed the peaceful transfer of power. Three, as defeated and bitter as he was about the election, Nixon was still a young man. I think he was forty-seven. He quite rightly thought that he had a political future, and he thought, "If I contest this, and I'll probably lose, then I'll be seen as a sore sport and somebody who was willing to hold the presidency up." So, for a variety of practical and sensible reasons, he decides he's going to go with the election results.

One of the key moments is January 6, 1961, which, by the Electoral Reform Act of 1887, is when the House and Senate get together and count the Electoral College votes. For the first time since 1861, when Lincoln was elected, the defeated candidate, the vice president, has to preside over the counting of the vote. Nixon presides over the counting of the vote that gives Kennedy the election. At one point there is a question about Hawaii, which was very much up in the air. It was down to about 150 votes one way or the other. That's handed to Nixon to decide what to do, and he says, "Kennedy wins it." Nixon ends up graciously congratulating Johnson and Kennedy. He's up on the podium with Sam Rayburn, and they hated each other. At the end of it, when he declares that Kennedy has won, the joint session gets up and gives a standing ovation to Nixon, and Rayburn says, "Great job, Dick. We're going to miss you around here."

7

Mark K. Updegrove on John F. Kennedy

INTERVIEW DATE: JULY 12, 2022

Although President John F. Kennedy's life was cut short before he completed his term, the fascination with and admiration for him continues unabated—particularly among Baby Boomers—and the result is an enormous number of books in recent years on every aspect of Kennedy's life and presidency. I am among those admiring Baby Boomers. I think I have provided more total support than any other individual for the three main organizations named in his honor: the John F. Kennedy Center for the Performing Arts (which I chaired for fourteen years), the Harvard Kennedy School, and the John F. Kennedy Presidential Library and Museum.

Mark K. Updegrove, the author of *Incomparable Grace: JFK in the Presidency*, is another Baby Boomer who also remains fascinated with the life and legacy of President Kennedy. For those of us in this group, it is the accomplishments that continue to resonate more powerfully than the personal issues that have come to light in recent years. While Kennedy's medical records have now been made public and gossip-driven books have become their own cottage industry, for so many Baby Boomers (and now younger generations) these revelations pale in comparison to the enduring impact of his presidency.

FIGURE 7.1 John F. Kennedy became the youngest elected president when he won the 1960 election at age forty-three. His presidency was tragically cut short when he was assassinated less than three years into his term.

Updegrove served for eight years as the director of the Lyndon B. Johnson Presidential Library in Austin and now serves as chairman and CEO of the LBJ Foundation. In these roles, he was clearly in a position to learn a great deal about Kennedy.

And while the Johnson-Kennedy relationship was not particularly close, Updegrove felt that Kennedy brought a charm and style to the White House that elevated his public standing and enabled accomplishments that a less graceful and charismatic person might not have achieved. (Left unsaid is that several of Kennedy's "accomplishments," like civil rights legislation and his much-sought tax cut, were ultimately realized through Johnson's efforts to carry forward Kennedy's unfinished agenda.)

For the admirers of President Kennedy, his assassination-shortened thousand days in office had many enduring highlights: the historic inaugural address, the creation of the Peace Corps, the "*Ich bin ein Berliner*" speech, the moonshot, the Nuclear Test Ban Treaty (the ultimate Cold War triumph), and the Cuban Missile Crisis. In his book, Updegrove covers these achievements, but a good deal of his focus is on the undeniable charm, youth, charisma, and eloquence of President Kennedy; his gracious and beautiful wife, Jackie; and his two young children, Caroline and John, who lost their father when they were so young and so beloved by the American people.

The attendees at the Dialogues session, perhaps jaded a bit at this point with stories of Kennedy's charm, grace, wit, and style, actually seemed as interested as the general public in hearing about the years of Camelot and the dreams about what might have been.

DAVID M. RUBENSTEIN (DR): You're now running the LBJ Foundation and previously were the head of the LBJ Library.

MARK K. UPDEGROVE (MU): That's right.

DR: So, naturally you wrote a book on President Kennedy. To be very serious, other than George Washington and Abraham Lincoln, no president has had more books written about him than John F. Kennedy. Why has Kennedy had so many books written about him when he only served for less than three years? Why are so many people writing so many books about him, and what did you think you could add by writing another one?

MU: Why are so many books written about Kennedy? There is a mystique about John F. Kennedy. He is young, he's graceful, he's eloquent, he's witty, he's rampantly ambitious. In so many ways, the reason that we were so proud of him when he represented our nation is because he reflected who we want to be known as, how we want to be seen on the world's stage.

He continues to cast this beguiling glow. Part of that is the Camelot myth, which aggrandizes him to a certain extent. But he continues to be this almost mystical figure who represents in many ways the best of our country. The best of John F. Kennedy represents the best of who we are. But there are some dark sides, too.

You write the book you want to read. I'm an avid reader of history, and I hadn't read a book like this. There are these voluminous tomes on Jack Kennedy, cradle-to-grave biographies, some of them hagiographies, some of them very anti-Kennedy. I wanted to write a more dispassionate book that took you through this very turbulent but ultimately very consequential administration. And a book brisk enough that you could feel the weight of those days, and how volatile and consequential they were. That's what I tried to do with it.

DR: In his lifetime, he was considered to be young, vibrant, handsome, charming, and all those qualities. In an age of social media, do you think anybody could have that kind of wonderful press?

MU: It's a totally different media environment. It would be hard for Jack Kennedy to get the kind of approval ratings now that he got when he was president.

Kennedy wins the presidency by 118,000 votes, by two-tenths of a percentage point. It's the narrowest presidential victory in the twentieth century. Yet when he's inaugurated, Americans rally around him in huge numbers, so much so that, after the Bay of Pigs crisis, which is the worst fiasco of his administration, just several months after taking the presidency, his approval ratings are an astounding 83 percent. Eighty-three percent! Part of it, though, was that it was a much more limited, centrist media landscape.

DR: Why did people in Washington, DC, in Congress, not take him that seriously? He had been a member of the House and the Senate for ten years, with no great legislative accomplishments that anybody could really see, yet in the country he was seen as charming and wonderful and obviously got the nomination in 1960. What didn't people in Washington see that people in the country did see?

MU: There's a charisma that Kennedy had that just didn't come through in his Senate days. The Senate is a collegial body. Jack Kennedy was an amiable-enough guy, but I don't think he understood or really appreciated the legislative process in the manner that, say, Lyndon Johnson did. Johnson loved the legislative process. He loved making the sausage. Kennedy wasn't interested in that.

Moreover, he was a guy who achieved a position in Congress and was looking at the Senate. As soon as he got to the Senate, he wanted to figure out how he might become the vice presidential nominee for his party. Then, when he didn't get that in '56, he wanted to figure out how he could be the presidential nominee.

DR: He ran for president in 1960. How many primaries were there in those days?

MU: There were fewer than twenty primaries.

DR: Most people realize he won New Hampshire, won Wisconsin, and then won West Virginia. Those are the three that people often focus on. Had he lost any of those, do you think he could have gone and gotten the nomination, or was it not relevant whether he won those primaries or not, because so many delegates were picked by other means?

MU: The primary process was not as definitive in those days. It was a barometer. It was an indicator of how successful a candidate could be. Those were the last days of the smoke-filled rooms. The Kennedys were a pretty daunting presence in the Democratic Party, partly because of the huge fortune of Joe Kennedy and his rampant ambitions for his sons.

DR: In 1960, West Virginia was not exactly filled with a lot of Catholics. Kennedy was seen as a Catholic who was very urban. Why did he do so well in a state where Hubert Humphrey should have done better?

MU: A lot of it was money. But also he was charming. He convinced the American people that his Catholicism didn't matter, that he wasn't beholden to the pope, he was beholden to the American people. There's a wonderful story, too, of Jack Kennedy talking to coal miners in West Virginia. Kennedy had very little in common with coal miners in West Virginia. He's starting to talk to them about what he's going to do for the country, and one guy yells out, "Hey, Kennedy, I heard you were born with a silver spoon in your mouth. You've never worked a day in your life." Kennedy hears this and he says, "That's true: I was very lucky." The guy responded, "You haven't missed a damn thing." But he showed up. And he was so eloquent. He was relatable, to a certain extent, despite his erudite background.

DR: Lyndon Johnson, the majority leader of the Senate, was the most powerful majority leader of that time, maybe even since that time. Why was he thinking he was going to get the nomination?

MU: Because he was the all-powerful Senate majority leader and held sway in the party. I don't think he made an ambitious run for the presidency in 1960. He was half in and half out. He wanted somebody to just put a crown on his head and say, "You're the king." That wasn't going to happen that year.

DR: Why did Kennedy pick Lyndon Johnson to be vice president? There's a famous story that he offered it to him, expecting him to turn it down, and when he accepted it, Robert Kennedy was sent back and forth a couple of times again to get him to not accept it. Is that true?

MU: I don't buy that. There are a lot of misconceptions about Jack Kennedy, because of his death and the stories of Camelot. The Kennedys after JFK's assassination are not only trying to burnish Jack Kennedy's profile in history, they're trying to lay the groundwork for Bobby Kennedy's inevitable candidacy for the presidency. So, it served them to say that Lyndon Johnson was not a real choice for them, that they were doing it just to be polite, just because it was the right thing to do. You had to kowtow to the Senate majority leader.

But the fact is that John F. Kennedy would not have been the thirty-fifth president of the United States but for the Southern balance given to him by Lyndon Johnson. You had Boston with Jack Kennedy, you had Austin with LBJ. This is at a point where Southern Democrats are becoming increasingly alienated from Northern liberal Democrats. You needed that balance. But nobody was more qualified to be president than Lyndon Johnson. You have to consider that, too, when you're picking a credible vice president.

DR: John Kennedy was forty-three years old, the youngest person to ever be elected president. But his opponent was not exactly that old either. He was forty-seven—Richard Nixon. What strategy did Kennedy use to win those four debates with Nixon? Why was it widely thought that, if you watched them on television, you thought Kennedy won, but if you listened on radio you thought Nixon won?

MU: That is not true. There's the famous first debate that happens in September of 1960 between Richard Nixon and John F. Kennedy—the first presidential debate in the history of our nation, and it's televised. You can see the two candidates. Their content is relatively similar. Their views aren't that different. They're both eloquent. They're young and they're dynamic.

Richard Nixon refused makeup. He looks pasty-faced. He has a five o'clock shadow. He's swimming in a gray suit. He looks unhealthy and gaunt. Jack Kennedy, on the other hand, who was by far the less healthy of the two, is tanned from a recent stay at his father's Palm Beach estate. He's wearing a dark suit. He looks like a movie star who's just glided in from the set. That was the difference. Kennedy understood the medium of his age, television. Great politicians do that.

DR: Kennedy wins the election. Did Richard Nixon consider contesting the election? Why did he not contest it?

MU: There was election fraud in Illinois and in Texas. It's well known that there was some election fraud. The head of the RNC [Republican National Committee], Thruston Morton, said he would fund legal help for Nixon to mount a legal challenge. Nixon decides not to do it, because we're in a sensitive position with the Soviet Union. We're in the Cold War. We're just two years away from the Cuban Missile Crisis, which is the very height of the Cold War. Sabers are continually rattling between the Soviet Union and the United States. Nixon didn't want to make our foundation look off-balance to the world by contesting the election. Think about how far off that notion is today.

DR: Did Herbert Hoover or Eisenhower call him and say, "Don't do it"?

MU: Both weighed in. Eisenhower offered to help Nixon raise money to cover a possible monthslong legal fight in the interest of showing that the federal government would "not shirk its duty" in ensuring the integrity of our elections. Hoover, who was enlisted to set up a meeting between Kennedy and Nixon after the election, dissuaded Nixon, advising, "I think we're in enough trouble in the world today." But ultimately it was Nixon who decided this was not the right thing for the country—again, to his credit.

DR: Today we have elaborate presidential transitions. There was no federal money for those transitions then, no staff people hired. How did the country survive without elaborate transitions?

MU: There were two transition meetings between Kennedy and Eisenhower. One was of very little consequence. The second was the day before Kennedy's inauguration on January 19th, 1961. They talk about trouble spots in the world and in particular what's happening in Laos, which is ostensibly going to fall to Communism. Eisenhower calls it the cork in the barrel. You have to defend Laos. There are a few other things he talks about. But it's amazing how little preparation there was and how little cooperation there was between the administrations when you're handing the baton from one to the other.

DR: There's a famous scene where John Kennedy goes to meet Eisenhower at the White House. What did Eisenhower really think, and what was his nickname for John Kennedy?

MU: He called him "Little Boy Blue." He didn't have much regard for John Fitzgerald Kennedy. After the second transition meeting, they came out understanding each other a little bit better. Pardon the vernacular, but Kennedy called Dwight Eisenhower "the old asshole." That was a military term you used to disparage military brass if you were in the lower ranks. And, of course, Dwight Eisenhower was the great stalwart general of D-Day. But Kennedy didn't have much regard for Eisenhower either. They begrudgingly liked each other after the second meeting.

DR: The famous question Eisenhower was asked at a press conference is "Can you tell us one thing that Richard Nixon did during his vice presidency that helped the country?" and he said, "Give me a week." Is that apocryphal?

MU: No, I think that's true. But a lot is made of Eisenhower not supporting Nixon. I don't think there's any question that Eisenhower supported his vice president and didn't want the presidency to go to John F. Kennedy. In fact, he considered it the greatest failure of his administration, that he didn't transition to a Republican successor.

DR: John Kennedy gave a speech that is still considered one of the great inaugural addresses of all time. People debate who actually wrote it. The Kennedy people like to say that Kennedy wrote it. Why was it so important to them that Kennedy be thought to have been the author of the speech? Was he trying to show that he was a smarter person or a better writer than he might have been? Why was the family so interested?

MU: Two things. One, because it was wildly successful. "Ask not" is up there with FDR's "nothing to fear but fear itself" and Lincoln's "with malice toward none" and the great inaugural speeches of American history. But, second, there was great debate as to who wrote *Profiles in Courage*, which won the Pulitzer Prize for John F. Kennedy. So, the Kennedy family didn't want people to think that he didn't write this great speech, which would go down in history as one of the finest.

I wrote in the book that John F. Kennedy wrote the speech. There's no question he had a hand in it. But I do think Ted Sorensen, Kennedy's close advisor and speechwriter, was an important contributor, too.

I'll tell a quick story about John F. Kennedy's inauguration and that speech. Richard Nixon was vice president, of course, under Eisenhower, then loses the presidency. He's there for the inauguration as he relinquishes the vice presidency and gives it over to Lyndon Johnson. He leaves that day with his wife, Pat. In those days, he parked at the Capitol and left the inauguration and drove home. But before he did, he ran into Ted Sorensen.

DR: No Secret Service protection?

MU: No Secret Service protection. They went back to their house in the District of Columbia, and that was it after eight years of being in the vice presidency. But he runs into Ted Sorensen, who helped to craft the speech. Nixon says to Sorensen, "I wish I had said some of those things." Sorensen says, "Which part?" Thinking he's going to say, "Ask not. . . ." Nixon pauses and then says, "The part where he says, 'I do solemnly swear.'"

DR: In the first couple months of the administration, John Kennedy is briefed on the Bay of Pigs operation in Cuba. It had been started as a CIA operation under Dwight Eisenhower. Why did he go ahead with it, and why did he not provide the air cover that would have been necessary to make the operation at least more likely to succeed than it did?

MU: The Bay of Pigs is an enormous fiasco. Kennedy stumbles into it rather impetuously. He's convinced by his jingoistic military brass that it's the right thing to do. Eisenhower had advocated it. But there are some details that Kennedy did not mind when they were implementing the plan, and it blew up in his face. A hundred-plus Cuban nationals are dead, and another 1,100 are taken captive. It's a disaster.

DR: Eisenhower met with Kennedy at Camp David subsequent to that. Did Eisenhower say, "You did a good job," despite the fact it didn't work?

MU: Eisenhower almost literally takes JFK to the woodshed. There's a famous Pulitzer Prize–winning photograph of Kennedy and Eisenhower walking away from the press, ostensibly in deep conversation. What he's telling Kennedy is, "You really screwed the pooch. You really messed up there. And this is going to hurt you because the Soviet Union is watching, and they're going to be emboldened." And he's dead right. But, publicly, when the press cameras were focused on them, Eisenhower gives a few words of encouragement, because he doesn't want to see Kennedy fail. The stakes are too high.

DR: You said earlier that Kennedy's popularity went up afterward because he gave a famous speech saying, "I take the responsibility." Why didn't he blame it on other people?

MU: He did the right thing, because he knew, as Harry Truman did, that the buck stopped with him. As he says, "Success has many fathers, but failure is an orphan. But at the end of the day, I am the commander in chief. I made that decision."

The other reason his popularity surges is because of what Eisenhower knew. Eisenhower knew that the Soviet Union was watching, and they would be emboldened. This is at a time when most

Americans believed that there would be a nuclear exchange in their lifetimes. They thought that was inevitable. So, if the Soviet Union sees that we're vulnerable, and Nikita Khrushchev bangs his shoe on the table at the UN and is so arrogant and so belligerent, he's probably going to exploit the weakness he sees in his opponent.

DR: Early in the administration, Kennedy goes to meet Khrushchev for the first time. They meet in Vienna. Kennedy's prepared by his staff, and Khrushchev presumably is prepared by somebody. How did that meeting go?

MU: The opening chapter of my book, the introduction, is Kennedy after that meeting. He's talking to Scotty Reston, who is the famous reporter from *The New York Times*. They had an off-the-record meeting. Kennedy is looking like he is absolutely languishing. He is beaten. He confesses to Scotty Reston that he has been savaged by Khrushchev. He knows he has emboldened Khrushchev. Khrushchev's impression of this young callow leader has only been reinforced by the Bay of Pigs and by this unfavorable meeting that they have. Kennedy knows that he's going to have to do something about it, but he doesn't know what.

DR: As a result of thinking that Kennedy was weak because of the Bay of Pigs and the meeting in Vienna, Khrushchev comes up with the idea of putting nuclear weapons in Cuba. How did the United States find out about that?

MU: Spy planes going over and taking aerial photographs.

DR: When Kennedy was first informed about it, what did he decide to do?

MU: These are thirteen harrowing days. These are the most dangerous days we've ever faced, where there was an imminent possibility of a nuclear exchange with the Soviet Union.

Kennedy knows that those missiles and the troops that had been shipped to Cuba are of an offensive nature. It's the first time we have nuclear weapons in our backyard. Cuba is just ninety miles from Florida's shores, and there's a missile that can go from Cuba to Washington, DC, in less than fifteen minutes. So, there's no question that those missiles have to go. It's a matter during those thirteen days to figure out how you make them back down without a nuclear exchange occurring.

DR: Did the military advise Kennedy, "Let's negotiate, let's not get excited, let's not attack"? Is that what the military wanted?

MU: Just the opposite. The military wanted to engage. Thankfully, cooler heads prevailed in the White House, partly because Kennedy felt like he had been had with the Bay of Pigs fiasco. He felt he had been misled by the military.

DR: Kennedy had his advisors, the joint chiefs of staff, cabinet officers, the secretary of state. Former secretaries of state came in as well. Who was the person he trusted to actually negotiate something?

MU: There's no question it's Bobby Kennedy.

DR: Bobby Kennedy was attorney general at the age of—?

MU: Thirty-six.

DR: Does Bobby Kennedy negotiate backchannel with the Soviets?

MU: That's exactly what happens. Jack Kennedy jokes that he wants to give Bobby the attorney general job to give him a little law experience before he goes into private practice. It's fiercely criticized at the time, and rightfully so.

DR: Who wanted that job for Bobby Kennedy?

MU: It was Joe Kennedy, but I think that that's mythologized a bit, too, because frankly, Jack Kennedy knew he could depend on his brother. He knew he could trust his brother. His brother has been his hatchet man in his campaigns. Blood was thicker than water to the Kennedys. He knew that his brother would do anything for him. He could trust him implicitly.

That's what happens in these backchannel negotiations. Bobby Kennedy talks to folks from Cuba, folks from the Soviet Union. We think that the Russians blinked and they withdrew their missiles. What gets lost to history is that it's a quid pro quo. Hence the importance of these backchannel negotiations. We had nuclear missiles in Turkey, in the backyard of the Soviet Union, just as they were shipping missiles to our backyard. We agreed to remove the missiles, after the Cuban Missile Crisis abated, in exchange for their withdrawing those missiles. But it is a perilous few weeks.

DR: We agreed to move those Jupiter missiles, which Kennedy wanted to get out anyway. He didn't really think they were so good?

MU: They were old.

DR: They were old. We had a deal with the Soviets that we would pull the missiles out, but we told the Soviets, "Don't tell the American people." In other words, we're trusting the Soviets not to tell a secret to the American people that maybe they should have known?

MU: This looks like a zero-sum victory on the part of Kennedy. In fact, it's a backchannel negotiation that gave the Soviets the removal of the missiles in Turkey.

DR: The other part that often isn't talked about is that the Soviets had intercontinental missiles in Cuba that were long range and medium range. We didn't know at the time that they also had tactical nuclear weapons. We got them to move out their intercontinental and medium-range ones. We didn't know they had tactical ones, and they didn't take them out right away. They were later taken out simply because Khrushchev didn't trust Castro with the tactical nuclear weapons. At the time, we didn't know that they didn't really take all their nuclear weapons out?

MU: That's exactly right. The other thing worth adding is that one of the reasons that Kennedy is able to achieve the presidency is that he campaigns under the notion there's a missile gap. Again, the Cold War is at its height, and we are deathly afraid that the Soviets are going to gain some sort of technological or military advantage. Kennedy talks about this wild missile gap that we have between the Soviet Union and the United States. They have far more missiles than we do.

In fact, as Kennedy knew, we had the advantage of nine to one in terms of nuclear missiles. So, he was misleading the American people during the campaign about this gap, knowing that this is an Achilles heel for the Republicans.

DR: Let's talk about some of the domestic issues. Was John Kennedy a big civil rights advocate in the campaign?

MU: Yes and no. He gives lip service to civil rights and comes to the aid of Martin Luther King Jr. at a crucial time. King is arrested in Atlanta for being involved in a sit-in. He's incarcerated in a local jail, then he's shipped to a rural prison in Southwest Georgia, where the inmates are largely white and so are the prison guards. It represents an existential crisis for him. He will likely be killed, either by the prisoners or by the guards, if he is forced to serve his full sentence in that facility. It's an unbelievably scary experience for the King family. John F. Kennedy, to his credit, calls Coretta Scott King and says, "I'll intervene on your behalf." He calls the Democratic Georgia governor and urges him to have King released. King is thus released and goes back to his home in Atlanta. It saves his life, and it might have saved the civil rights movement.

DR: But that call by John Kennedy was not supported by Robert Kennedy. When he found out about it, he was very upset.

MU: Bobby Kennedy was very upset. He thought it would alienate white Democratic voters, who were incredibly important in the South. That said, Daddy King, Martin Luther King Sr., said that after candidate John F. Kennedy intervened on his son's behalf, "You're going to get a suitcase full of votes" from African American voters, and that's exactly what happens. Kennedy gets 70 percent of the Black vote.

DR: Kennedy did not send civil rights legislation to Capitol Hill right away. Why did he wait so long?

MU: Kennedy wanted to be a great president, as most presidents do. But in his day that meant being a great foreign policy president. The most important issue at that time was the Cold War. That was the most important thing happening in the world. Hence Kennedy's ability to achieve the presidency by promoting the notion of this missile gap with the Soviet Union. But he believes that if you expose the American people and the world to the inherent inequality in our system, it's going to make us look bad at a time when we're trying to win hearts and minds throughout the world. We're trying to say to people, "We have a better system than the Soviet Union. That's tyranny. We have liberty in the United States." If you show them the Jim Crow South, guess what? Your argument goes up in smoke.

Bobby Kennedy says at one point, when the Freedom Riders are riding through the South showing the importance of integrating bus lines, that if you continue to do this, the president will go to that summit with Khrushchev in Vienna with "mud on his shoes." It's going to make us look bad. Kennedy is trying to tamp down the civil rights movement so we didn't look bad in the world's view.

DR: In those days, were there any African Americans in the White House or in the cabinet?

MU: In the White House just one, his advisor Louis Martin.

DR: Let me ask you about the March on Washington in August of 1963. Did John Kennedy want to keep that from happening? Did he say to the civil rights leaders, "This will backfire"?

MU: Yes, he did. He tried to prevent it from happening. Bear in mind, though, that other presidents did the exact same thing.

A. Philip Randolph, who had argued for the march, had threatened to do this on several other occasions and used it as leverage for presidents to enact progressive civil rights orders. In other words, when he wants Harry S. Truman to desegregate the military, he threatens to stage this march. Truman thinks, "What's going to happen there? This might end up in a melee. It could end up being a riot." Kennedy fears the same thing, but this time Randolph is not going to take no for an answer. He wants people to see the need for jobs and civil rights reform. It's called the March on Washington for Jobs and Freedom—the need for economic liberation and for the end of Jim Crow laws in this country—so we will truly meet our most sacred creed that all men are created equal.

DR: At the time, Martin Luther King wasn't the most senior civil rights leader in the civil rights movement. He was up and coming.

MU: Not the most senior, but probably the most well known at that time. Most of the civil rights leaders were inside the Beltway working within the system. Martin Luther King, on the other hand, was outside the system, trying to expose Americans to the very worst of bigotry and injustice.

DR: Kennedy was offered a chance to speak at the march. He turned that down, but he did invite the speakers to come to the White House. How did that meeting go between Kennedy and Martin Luther King at the White House?

MU: Importantly, he invited him after he knew that the day had gone incredibly well, ending with that crescendo of Martin Luther King's

"I Have a Dream" speech. Kennedy invites him to the White House afterward and congratulates him. He and Lyndon Johnson congratulate them. He goes up to Martin Luther King, and he looks him in the eye and admiringly says, "I have a dream."

DR: Did the legislation go to Congress not that long afterward?

MU: It was before the March on Washington. There's the campaign in Birmingham, Alabama. We all can summon up those iconic images of German shepherds lunging at young African American protesters and firehoses being weaponized to keep those civil rights workers at bay. This starts getting the attention of the American people. That's at a time when Governor George Wallace stands iconically in the schoolhouse door at the University of Alabama, trying to prevent its integration. Kennedy sees this. He knows that Wallace is a demagogue and that he's going to get all the news coverage that night. He decides to preempt him by making a speech, largely extemporaneous, on national TV about the importance of elevating civil rights to a moral issue.

This is a major crossroads. This is a major inflection point in the arc of the civil rights movement, because no president had ever said, "This is a moral issue. This is fundamentally un-American." It's a big leap forward. In conjunction with that, Kennedy proposes the Civil Rights Act of 1963, which would become the Civil Rights Act of 1964. But he doesn't put much muscle or weight behind it.

DR: Did John Kennedy socialize with or have many African American friends?

MU: No. I've spoken to Andrew Young about this. Kennedy didn't know any Black people.

DR: Except his valet.

MU: Except his valet. That's exactly right. Lyndon Johnson, on the other hand, who I believe is our civil rights president, knew Black people. He knew how to talk to Black people. He was comfortable with Black people.

DR: Let's talk about the space program. We're looking at the pictures today from the Webb telescope. It reminds us of the space challenge. Why did John Kennedy feel the challenge to get to the moon and back safely by the end of the decade was such an important thing? Did anybody else think it was a good idea?

MU: A good idea, yes. The reason it's important to Kennedy is not because of the adventure. This is not Lindbergh crossing the Atlantic or the Wright brothers flying a plane at Kitty Hawk. It's not about adventure. It's about the Cold War. It's about ensuring that the Soviet Union does not have a technological advantage when the Cold War is essentially the single most important geopolitical issue in the world.

So, our putting a man on the moon shows our technological superiority. Kennedy rallies Americans around this notion in a famous speech at Rice University. He says, "We choose to go to the moon," and makes a fundamentally American proposition that it is about the American spirit. But at heart, the space program is about the Cold War.

DR: The man running NASA was Mr. Webb himself, James Webb. Did he think it was realistic to get to the moon at that time? What about the cost? Did he ever try to talk Kennedy out of it?

MU: The folks at NASA had these very wonky ideas about what the space program could be. Kennedy just wants to get to the moon. He knows symbolically what that means and how it will capture the imagination of not only the American people but of the world. And that's exactly what happened. So, he tries to assure them that this is the goal. It's Lyndon Johnson who writes a memo as his vice president and tells him that it's achievable to bring a man to the moon by the end of the 1960s.

By the way, this is at a time when the Soviet Union is way ahead in the space race, much to our embarrassment. We eventually leapfrog over them, but it takes a while. So, this is not only bold in just saying we can do it by the end of the decade, it's bold because the Soviet Union is ahead in the race at that point.

DR: Let's talk about John Kennedy's health. He's forty-three years old, looks like the picture of virility and youthfulness, but his health was terrible.

MU: Bobby Kennedy made a joke that if a mosquito bit Jack Kennedy, the mosquito would die. Probably there's some truth to that. Jack Kennedy was just ridden with illness since he was a kid. I think that partly informs his view on life. He doesn't take his life for granted. He has premonitions that he's going to have a short life, partly because he's battled health issues his whole life.

DR: Why was he taking cortisone all the time?

MU: Because of Addison's disease and his back.

DR: Addison's disease is a fatal disease, or was at the time?

MU: It was at the time.

DR: But he denied having it?

MU: He denied having it in 1960. Kennedy knows that he's lying to the American people by saying he doesn't have Addison's disease at all.

DR: He said in the campaign it was because his back was injured in the *PT-109* accident, and that's why his back was so bad. But that wasn't the real reason, was it?

MU: He had had cortisone injections earlier, in the 1930s. Cortisone weakens bones and started the back problems, which were exacerbated by the *PT-109* crash.

DR: In recent years, his personal life has become more well known. It was a more reckless life than you might want for a president to have?

MU: I think that's fair.

DR: At the time, did the press not know about this? Or it was just well hidden from everybody?

MU: As Walter Cronkite would have said, in those days, if a politician could discharge his duties and he had a drinking problem or a womanizing problem, you just ignored that. If that got in the way of him being an effective lawmaker or president or whatever the position might be, that was a different matter. That would change in the Johnson administration. There was a credibility gap that Lyndon Johnson created around the issue of Vietnam, and the press became more and more aggressive. Gary Hart changes things irrevocably in 1988, when it's rumored that he's a womanizer and he makes the mistake of challenging the press to follow him.

DR: You mentioned Vietnam. After President Kennedy died, his foreign policy advisors remained as advisors to President Johnson. Kennedy's sympathizers would say Kennedy was going to pull out of Vietnam. He told people privately that he was going to do that. Do you think he was prepared to pull out of Vietnam if he had been reelected?

MU: That is a Camelot myth. Those reports don't start coming out until the tide of the war is changing. In 1967, when public opinion is starting to become antiwar, and we don't see the necessity of being in Vietnam, the Kennedy acolytes start saying he would have pulled out. There is no evidence whatsoever that John F. Kennedy would have pulled out of Vietnam.

In fact, two months before his death, he doubled down on the domino theory, which suggested that if you lost Vietnam to the Communists, the USSR or China would be emboldened and would take countries that were of greater strategic significance. You couldn't back down. He also says it would be "a deep mistake"—those are his words—to withdraw troops.

DR: Why did he need to go to Dallas? The infamous trip to Dallas, the first political trip his wife had done since he was elected president?

MU: Yes.

DR: Why did Jackie Kennedy not go on political trips?

MU: First of all, because she didn't want to. It was a big deal for a president to travel in those days. It's pretty common today, but in those days, it didn't happen as frequently. But Jackie Kennedy knew the importance of this trip for the president. There are rumors that the trip was a means of mending fences between Ralph Yarborough, a senator from Texas, and Lyndon Johnson. That is totally erroneous. If you wanted to mend fences between those two, you'd do it in Washington, where they work. You don't have to go to Texas for that.

The reason that Kennedy goes to Texas and doesn't just visit Dallas but Fort Worth and San Antonio and Houston, and was going to visit Austin, is because there was a promise that he would get a million dollars for the reelection war chest in 1964. That was a lot of money in those days.

DR: When he goes there, he's meeting with political figures and so forth. On the day he's in Dallas, the press reports the exact route that he's going to travel. The bubble top that was initially on the presidential limousine was taken off. Who decided to take that bubble top off the limousine?

MU: There are mixed reports about that. Some people say that Jack Kennedy ordered it. Some people say it was the Secret Service. Some people say it was aides to Kennedy. I think the bottom line is that Kennedy would have wanted it lifted.

Kennedy leaves Fort Worth in the rain. Miraculously, as if by divine providence, the sky opens up, and it's this beautiful Texas sunshine as they come into Dallas. It was well known that Kennedy wanted to interact with the people. He knew how charismatic he was. He knew what that would mean, particularly in a state that he needed to win in 1964 and that was won by a very thin margin in 1960. Kennedy knows how beguiling he is, and he wants to interact with the people. I think the bubble top gets lifted because it was what Kennedy would have wanted. Whether he directed that specifically or not, I can't say.

DR: According to the Warren Commission, there are three shots fired by Lee Harvey Oswald. Two of them hit Kennedy. After all these years, do you have any doubt that that report is accurate and there were three shots fired by one man?

MU: I talked to Gerald Ford, who was the last surviving member of the Warren Commission. For a good thirteen years or so, he was the lone surviving member. I asked him about this on several occasions, and he said, "I'm not convinced that it was a lone shooter. I just haven't seen a better theory." If you've ever seen the Warren report, it is voluminous. There's a copy of the Warren report that was given to Lyndon Johnson at the LBJ Library.

They went through all this stuff, and they didn't come to a better conclusion. In order to keep a conspiracy like that secret, how many people have to be quiet? If something that big was conducted in a conspiratorial manner, we would have known something more at this point. So, for lack of a better theory, Lee Harvey Oswald is the lone gunman. The lone gunman makes the most sense. By the way, Lee Harvey Oswald was an expert marksman, he was a Russian sympathizer, and he was a psychopath. As profiles of assassins go, there's every logical reason for him to be the assassin.

DR: After he was captured, how could he have been shot by Jack Ruby? Why were the police not doing a better job protecting him?

MU: I don't know. What happens after the Kennedy assassination is just a total fiasco.

DR: Where did the so-called Camelot myth come from? Who started that?

MU: It was principally Jacqueline Kennedy. Some of us remember—I don't, I was young at the time—how beautifully staged Kennedy's funeral was. That's due to the grace and vision of Jacqueline Kennedy. The funeral was absolutely stunning. She believed she owed that to the American people, but she also understood that she needed to build his image in history if he was going to be remembered as a great president.

There's great sympathy around John F. Kennedy. He's enormously popular when he's struck down in his prime at the age of forty-six. So, he's ripe for mythology. The Kennedys play into that, in particular Jackie Kennedy. But again, bear in mind that they are trying to lay the groundwork for Bobby Kennedy's inevitable aim for the presidency sometime later in the 1960s.

She gave an interview not long after the assassination to Teddy White in which she says John Kennedy's favorite show was *Camelot*. That music was written by his Harvard classmate Alan Lerner, so maybe there was some of that.

But it's not like the Kennedys were talking about Camelot during the White House years. It's not like the American people were talking about Camelot. This comes from this interview that Jackie Kennedy does after the assassination, knowing that she's speaking to history, in which she talks about Camelot. They are an incredibly compelling family. We can see that.

DR: If you could have dinner with John Kennedy, what would you ask him?

MU: I would ask about the Cuban Missile Crisis. I have talked about the gravity of those thirteen harrowing days and how close we came to a nuclear exchange with the Soviet Union, which changed the tide of world history. I would have talked to him about his presence of mind during that time, why he made certain decisions, what was going through his mind. Why, for instance, did he believe that he could trust Khrushchev? Why did he believe Khrushchev was of sound and rational mind, able to make decisions during that incredibly tense time?

DR: You've spent all this time on Kennedy, you studied him, wrote a book about him. Do you admire him more or less than you did before you started the book?

MU: It's about the same, but for different reasons. Kennedy did not achieve much legislatively, certainly when he was in the upper and lower chambers of Congress, and he didn't achieve much legislatively as president. He did resolve this most dangerous crisis, the Cuban Missile Crisis, and he deserves due credit for that.

But another part of his legacy, which I have to admire, is his rhetorical splendor. He is a brilliant and a gifted speaker. He gets us to reach beyond ourselves. There are so many examples of this. Not only is there the inauguration address, which is just stunning rhetoric, there's the Rice University speech, the "We choose the moon" speech, where he rallies us around the cause of going to the moon. We talked about the largely extemporaneous speech he gives on civil rights, defining it as a moral cause. He goes to the Berlin Wall and says "*Ich bin ein Berliner.*" Anybody who's a champion of liberty and freedom in this world is a citizen of Berlin, and that's why this symbol is so potent. Then he gives a wonderful speech at American University that brings the Soviet Union to the table to agree to no longer do nuclear tests, which is a very important inflection point in the Cold War.

8

Max Boot on Ronald Reagan

INTERVIEW DATE: APRIL 30, 2025

Although Ronald Reagan was a major presence in government affairs from the time he was first elected governor of California in 1966 until the end of his presidency in early 1989, he was an enigmatic figure in many ways. He was famously not very introspective, and few were really close to him personally, other than his second wife and devoted First Lady, Nancy Reagan.

His initial autobiography, written well before his political career, focused on his hardscrabble early life and his B-level movie career. And it was ghostwritten. Recognizing Reagan's reluctance to be truly reflective or to bare his soul, his advisors (including Nancy) thought the true story of Ronald Reagan might best be told by a world-class biographer. And in the latter years of Reagan's presidency, Edmund Morris (Pulitzer Prize–winning biographer of Theodore Roosevelt) was embedded in the Reagan White House staff to write a definitive biography of Reagan.

The effort failed when Morris, feeling he could not truly grasp what made Reagan tick, placed himself in Reagan's life as a fictional character. The resulting book, *Dutch*, was widely panned.

Since then, a number of scholars and journalists have attempted to write definitive biographies of Reagan. None have been viewed as

FIGURE 8.1 Max Boot argues that although Ronald Reagan developed a reputation for being driven by ideology, he also could be pragmatic and move to the center while serving as governor of California and president of the United States.

truly "definitive"—that is, scholarly, well researched and sourced, insightful, well written, and enjoyable to read.

But Max Boot, who immigrated to the United States from Russia as a boy, has written that biography: *Reagan: His Life and Legend.* A scholar at the Council on Foreign Relations, Boot brings to the undertaking a deep understanding of public policy, along with a political conservative's insight into what made Reagan so popular during (and after) his eight years in the White House.

There will no doubt be additional "definitive" Reagan biographies in future years, as more information from this era is declassified or otherwise made public. But it will take quite an effort to improve upon this one-volume account of a man who so dramatically reshaped the direction of the Republican Party and the country in the 1980s.

And those Members who attended this Dialogues session had a great deal of interest in Reagan, a leader who served as president before most of them began their legislative careers. Few actually knew him, and all were eager to hear about the president who changed the Republican Party and so much about government during his time in the White House.

DAVID M. RUBENSTEIN (DR): Why did we need another book on Ronald Reagan? Haven't a lot of books been written about him already?

MAX BOOT (MB): There have been a lot of books about Reagan, but the reason I started writing this book in 2013 was because I thought there was not a definitive biography of Reagan.

DR: What was the biggest surprise you learned about Ronald Reagan in the ten years that you worked on this?

MB: There were a lot of them. One big-picture surprise was that he had a reputation for being somebody who was intensely ideological, which he often could be, but he was also somebody who could be intensely pragmatic. He was able to move to the center, both as governor of California and president of the United States, to make deals to get things done, and he turned out to be somebody who was kind of a closet centrist in spite of his ideological clothing.

DR: Did the family cooperate with you?

MB: They did. It's a small family. Primarily, in my case, Patti Davis and Ron Reagan cooperated.

DR: What is Patti Davis doing now?

MB: She lives out in Brentwood, California. She's a very good writer. She's written a number of books and articles about her parents and trying to come to grips with being a First Daughter. She's working on a script now for an Amazon show about the daughter of the president.

DR: I wonder where she got that idea. What is Ronald Reagan Jr. doing now?

MB: He's not actually "Junior." He's got a different middle name. He divides his time between Seattle and Italy, where his partner is from.

DR: What about Michael Reagan? What's he doing?

MB: Michael is pretty retired. He's about eighty years old or so, not that that should be a reason to retire. [Michael Reagan passed away on January 4, 2026.]

DR: He could run for president at that age. And what about Maureen?

MB: Maureen died a long time ago.

DR: How many grandchildren does Ronald Reagan have?

MB: Not many. The only one of his kids who had children of their own was Michael, who has a couple of kids, and Maureen adopted a daughter on a trip to Africa. It's not a large family.

DR: Let's go back to Ronald Reagan's beginning. Where was he born?

MB: He was born in Tampico, Illinois, in 1911.

DR: What did his parents do?

MB: His father, Jack, was a shoe salesman. His mother, Nelle, was a homemaker and a very devout woman, Disciples of Christ. His father dreamed of opening his own shoe store, but his dreams were constantly stymied by his terrible addiction to alcohol. He kept losing one job after another, and so the family kept moving from one small town to another in early twentieth-century Illinois. It was a very difficult itinerant childhood for little "Dutch" Reagan, as he was then known.

DR: Why was he called "Dutch"?

MB: His father claimed that he was bawling and screaming when he was born and he was as chubby as a Dutchman. That's the legend of his nickname. No Dutch ancestry, no German ancestry.

DR: He had one sibling?

MB: Yes. Neil "Moon" Reagan.

DR: Where did he get that name, "Moon"?

MB: He got that from a comic strip that was popular in the 1920s. He was named after Moon Mullins, one of the characters.

DR: Was Ronald Reagan a good student in high school?

MB: No. I saw his report card. He was a pretty gifted student in elementary school and earlier on, but by high school his primary interest lay in other areas: athletics and the drama society. Although he loved football and he managed to make it as a letterman on the

Dixon High School football team and then the Eureka College football team, his actual gift was swimming. He was a very good swimmer.

DR: He was a good-enough athlete to get into Eureka College. Was it free for him?

MB: No. It was not free. He didn't have an athletic scholarship, and it was a huge struggle for him to afford it. He went there from 1928 to 1932, including during the height of the Great Depression. He wound up having to do jobs like washing dishes in the women's dorm, which he later quipped was the best job he ever had.

DR: Was he good enough to play on the first string of the football team at Eureka?

MB: Just barely. He was not a very talented football player, but he had grit. He was willing to stick to it and follow his coach's direction. His brother, Moon, was a much more gifted player, a halfback who scored touchdowns. Dutch Reagan played on the line and just barely managed to be a varsity man.

DR: Where did he get that great head of hair: from his mother or father?

MB: I think his father—the handsome physique, the hair. Also, he had a gift for storytelling, and his father was a wonderful raconteur. That was how he got the ladies to come in and buy shoes from him.

DR: When he graduated from college, what did he do for a job?

MB: History would have been very different if he had gotten the job that he applied for. Ronald Reagan graduated from college in 1932 at the height of the Great Depression, so not a lot of people had jobs. At that very moment, Montgomery Ward was opening up a new store in his hometown of Dixon, Illinois. There was an opening to manage the sporting goods department of the Montgomery Ward, and they were looking for somebody who had been a high school or college athlete to manage it. Dutch Reagan applied and sadly he did not get the job. But the guy who did get the job was still working there and living in Dixon in the 1970s when Ronald Reagan came through town running for president of the United States. History would have been entirely different if he had gotten that job. You probably would have never heard of Ronald Reagan.

DR: What job did he get?

MB: Reagan had aspirations of becoming an actor. He was an active thespian in high school and in college, but graduating from this tiny town in Illinois in the middle of the Great Depression, he looked around and very quickly realized, "There are no movie studios in the Midwest." So how does he become an actor? He decided the second-best thing was radio. While there weren't any movie studios, there were a lot of radio stations. Radio was the hot, new technology of the day, kind of like becoming a social-media influencer today.

Reagan looked around and found a small radio station in Davenport, Iowa, where he applied for a job as an announcer and got it. He quickly proved his chops on the air and was promoted to a larger station in Des Moines. He became known throughout the Midwest as "Dutch" Reagan, the voice of the Chicago Cubs and the Chicago White Sox.

DR: When he wasn't watching the game and announcing it, he was doing something else?

MB: Correct. Like a lot of sportscasters in those days, which seems kind of bizarre in our day, he was hundreds of miles from the playing field. And, of course, there was no TV, so he was not watching the action. He was getting telegram reports of what was going on. He would get a ticker tape in his little studio in Des Moines saying, "Batter strikes out" or "reaches second base" or whatever was happening, and then he would basically paint the scene, which he could not see, for his listeners. One of his famous anecdotes was when the tape went dead one day and he didn't know what was going on. He just had the batter hitting foul ball after foul ball until the ticker tape started up again.

DR: He's doing this announcing. He's doing a good job at it. How did he get to the West Coast?

MB: Ronald Reagan was sneakily ambitious. He tried to pretend that he didn't have ambitions. He tried to pretend any job he ever got he just happened to stumble into, but that's not how life works. What he figured out was that he could use his job covering the Chicago Cubs as a launching board into a movie career. In unconventional fashion, he convinced his parsimonious radio-station owner to finance a trip for him to accompany the Chicago Cubs to spring training, which in those days for the Cubs was on Catalina Island off the coast of California. He went with the Cubs to Catalina Island, then he snuck away from the team and went to Warner Bros. and took a screen test, and lo and behold he was hired.

DR: So, he became an actor. Did he just abandon the radio job? How many years was he under contract for?

MB: He was under contract to Warner Bros., beginning in 1937, for roughly a decade. He started off making these horrible serials, which I would not recommend to anybody, where he was playing Brass Bancroft, Treasury agent. This was kind of like *Mission Impossible* without the special effects. It's hard to watch now, kind of cheesy and low-rent, but within a couple of years he was graduating from doing these B movies to larger projects.

Reagan didn't really care if you disagreed with his policies or critiqued his ideas, but he would actually be hurt if you attacked him as an actor. If you made jokes about *Bedtime for Bonzo* or suggested that he was just a B-movie actor, he would say, "I was more than that." It's true, he was. Before the US got into World War II, he was making larger movies. He was in *Knute Rockne, All American*; he was in *Kings Row*; and he was getting equal billing with Errol Flynn, who was one of the biggest stars in the Warner Bros. stable. So, his movie career was actually doing pretty well.

DR: But he wasn't going to be John Wayne or Errol Flynn, right? He was a good actor but not a great actor?

MB: No, exactly. After World War II, his movie career cratered, and he always blamed the studio. He didn't take personal responsibility. He was always kind of mad at Jack Warner because Warner would not cast him in a lot of cowboy pictures. People associate Reagan with cowboy pictures, but he actually did not do a lot of westerns. There's a reason for that. Jack Warner was a ruthless and accurate judge of horseflesh. He could figure out what his employees were best at, and he determined that Reagan was so good-natured that he would be best cast in romantic comedies, not in westerns or action pictures, because he did not signal that danger, that undercurrent of violence that you really need. He was just too nice a guy.

DR: In World War II, did he go into combat like many actors did, or he avoided that?

MB: He did not go into combat. He spent all of World War II in Culver City, California, at a Hollywood backlot, making propaganda and training films for the US Army air forces.

DR: After World War II, did he resume his regular movie career?

MB: He tried to, but he did not find much call for his services, in part because during the war other actors had risen to the fore. Ironically enough, John Wayne, who was such a macho actor and starred in so many military epics, avoided the draft during World War II. He was making movies instead of serving. But Reagan found his movie career reaching a dead end in the late 1940s, and that's when he became more involved in political activism and in union activism.

He was a staunch Democrat at that time. He supported Harry Truman in 1948, and he became heavily involved in the Screen Actors Guild, eventually rising to become president of it.

DR: He serves two terms as the head of the Screen Actors Guild?

MB: More than that. Seven, actually.

DR: How does he meet his first wife? Who was his first wife?

MB: His first wife was Jane Wyman, who was a fellow Warner Bros. actor. They got married in 1940. As in so many of Reagan's personal relationships, he was fairly passive. He did not take the initiative. Jane Wyman took the initiative and set out to marry him. She did things like pretending to have an interest in outdoorsy activities and hanging out with Reagan and his pack of friends, and she convinced him to walk down the aisle with her. But by the late '40s their marriage was headed for the skids, in part because of their differing fortunes in Hollywood. Whereas Reagan's career was in the doldrums after World War II, Jane Wyman's was taking off. She was making *The Yearling*; she was making a lot of prestige pictures. She won an Oscar for *Johnny Belinda*. She was becoming one of the top actresses in Hollywood. Her interest really lay in the movie industry, whereas Reagan's interests were going elsewhere.

DR: Where and how did he meet Nancy Reagan, who was Nancy Davis then?

MB: He met Nancy Davis a couple of years after his divorce from Jane Wyman in 1948. Oddly enough, they were introduced because of the Hollywood blacklist. This was the era of Red hunts and McCarthyism, and Ronald Reagan, as president of the Screen Actors Guild, was also an FBI informant. He was one of the people administering the Hollywood blacklist. If you were on that blacklist, it meant you were a suspected pinko, and you would not be allowed to work.

The story has it that there was a Nancy Davis on the list, and the Nancy Davis that we are familiar with said, "This was a mistake. I'm not a Communist. That's another Nancy Davis." She went to try to get her name off the list, and that took her to the door of the president of the Screen Actors Guild. At least that was the story they told. There's another theory or suggestion that Nancy Davis decided Ronald Reagan would be a great guy to go out with and used this as an excuse to meet the president of the Screen Actors Guild.

DR: After he finishes the Screen Actors Guild job, what does he do? He's not an actor anymore. He gets a job in Las Vegas?

MB: He did get a job in Las Vegas very briefly. He was an emcee for a group called the Continentals, which was a male singing group. He was onstage, and there was a pack of chimpanzees performing. It was kind of a circus in more ways than one. He did not enjoy that. When he got that job, he was newly married to Nancy Reagan. She made sure she went with him to Las Vegas, because she didn't want her husband hanging out in the city with all these showgirls, so they went together but he didn't enjoy it. By the early 1950s, his entire career was at a dead end. He owed a lot of back taxes. He was in dire straits.

That's when salvation came to him in the form of General Electric, which was one of the largest companies in the US. They had a program on CBS called *General Electric Theater*, and it wasn't doing very well in the ratings. They decided they needed a host for it, so his talent agency, MCA, arranged for him to host *General Electric Theater*, and it very shortly became one of the top-rated programs in the country. Eventually Ronald Reagan would become one of two individuals who hosted a national TV show before becoming president of the United States.

DR: Who was the other?

MB: I think you can guess.

DR: What was Reagan's other show? *Death Valley Days*?

MB: After he lost the GE job in the early '60s, he had another brief run on *Death Valley Days*. But by that point he was already positioning himself for a political career.

DR: As part of the GE assignment, he was making speeches to employees at GE factories. Where did he get the idea to speak to the employees, and why was his message so, let's say, conservative?

MB: This was really where he was transitioning himself from being the liberal Democrat that he had been throughout his life up until then to becoming a very conservative Republican. Remember, he was somebody who worshipped FDR. He voted for FDR four times. His father was saved from unemployment by becoming a New Deal aid administrator in Dixon, Illinois, and Reagan was an ardent fan.

But he started moving to the right during World War II. He was very unhappy as a highly paid movie actor with having to pay 94 percent income-tax rates. Then he got in the middle of these battles in Hollywood over Communism and became an FBI informant. He became convinced that there was a made-in-the-Kremlin plot to take over Hollywood and that he was on the front lines resisting it. That was somewhat exaggerated, but he believed it.

His transformation politically was completed when he went to work for GE, which in those days was a very conservative company. The management of GE thought that promulgating conservative ideology and free-market ideas was an inoculation against union trouble, so they made sure to have all their managers and executives reading all this right-wing literature. Ronald Reagan was a faithful employee. He had a lot of time to read, because in those days he was afraid to fly, so he would take the train cross-country to speak for GE. On the train he would be reading *Reader's Digest*, *Human Events*, and *National Review*, and then he would give speeches about what he was reading. He was transforming himself in the process of reading all this conservative literature and then giving speeches about it. His speeches went from being about the joys and glories of General Electric to being about the dangers that America faced from Communism abroad and big government at home. Those became his two consistent themes as a speaker.

DR: His big breakthrough came in 1964. He was asked by the Barry Goldwater supporters to make a speech, and it got televised and made him famous. Can you talk about that speech?

MB: It was the "Time for Choosing" speech, which was his debut on national politics. He was an avid Barry Goldwater supporter in 1964. That was a dividing line in the Republican Party, because the 1964 Republican nomination was a contest between Nelson Rockefeller, representing the liberal and centrist Republicans, and Barry Goldwater, who was this red-hot conservative from Arizona.

Ronald Reagan was definitely aligned with Barry Goldwater and was cochairman of his campaign in California. But he was in many ways a more effective speaker for the Goldwater campaign than the actual candidate. Sometimes they would be speaking at the same forum together, and people would listen to Reagan, and they would listen to Goldwater, and they would walk away thinking, "I wish that actor was our candidate." Barry Goldwater had this rough-edged personality. He was acerbic. His agenda was castor oil that you were force-feeding the audience, whereas Ronald Reagan, as one journalist described it in the early '60s, had a personality like soothing warm bathwater. He had this hard-edged message, but he made it go down easily with a smile and a twinkle in his eyes.

With the speech that he was giving on behalf of Barry Goldwater, finally a bunch of donors got together a bunch of money and put it on the air as a nationwide address. You can go to YouTube tonight and watch it. It was essentially a compendium of all the one-liners and all the speeches that Reagan had been giving for the past decade, many on behalf of GE. He developed this method of speech-giving, which was to use index cards. He would write down his arguments and his facts—sometimes the facts weren't quite accurate, but what he thought were facts—and then he would shuffle them around, so he would never give the same speech twice. As a veteran actor, he would judge the audience reaction, and if a card resonated with the audience, it stayed in the pile. If it didn't resonate, it went in the trash can.

In 1964, people went wild listening to this "Time for Choosing" address. They thought, "Ronald Reagan is such an effective speaker.

Where did this guy come from?" What they didn't realize was he had been honing this speech for ten years. This was a compendium of his most effective one-liners all in one address.

DR: He decides to use his nationwide publicity to run for governor of California in 1966, and he gets elected overwhelmingly.

MB: He beats the incumbent governor, Pat Brown, by a million votes, an outcome that shocked many political observers.

DR: Does Reagan decide to cut taxes as governor? What does he do that propels him forward to make him popular enough to get reelected?

MB: The very first thing he did upon being elected governor was to plot out a presidential campaign in 1968. That was a part of his history that he later tried to erase, because, of course, it wasn't successful. But it was a sign of how intensely ambitious he was. As soon as he's elected governor, literally before he's inaugurated, he's meeting with his political team and talking about how he can try to get the Republican nomination in 1968.

DR: But he gets there too late, and Nixon gets the nomination. Reagan runs for reelection in 1970 and gets reelected, then his term is up. He's term-limited, so in '74, he's succeeded by Jerry Brown.

MB: The son of the man he beat in 1966.

DR: In '74, he decides to do what with his life?

MB: Let me back up and answer your initial question about what kind of governor he was, because this is important for what comes later. One of the most fascinating interviews I had for this book was with Jerry Brown. I said to him, "What kind of governor was Ronald Reagan?" His answer surprised me. What he said was, "Reagan was a pretty good governor," which is not what you would expect from a member of the other party. The reason he said that was because Reagan moved to the center as governor and made deals with Jesse Unruh, who was the powerful speaker of the California Assembly. Yes, Reagan sent some tax rebates back to California residents, but he also raised taxes to cover a budget deficit. He expanded spending, even though he constantly castigated the University of California as a den of hippies, beatniks, and ingrates. He nevertheless increased state spending for higher education by 136 percent. He signed the most liberal abortion law in the country. He signed one of the toughest gun-control bills in the country. He left the hard right behind and managed to move to the center in a way that ensured his reelection in 1970 and set him up, upon the end of his term in 1974, as a plausible candidate for president of the United States.

He was a huge Nixon supporter. Reagan had a much higher evaluation of Nixon than Nixon had of him. If you listen to the White House tapes, it's very funny to hear Richard Nixon and Henry Kissinger talking about what a dope Ronald Reagan was. "Christ, he's got no conception of anything. That man doesn't have any brains," and so forth. But while Nixon didn't have a lot of respect for Reagan's intellect, he had tremendous respect for Reagan's political skill. He tried very hard to keep Reagan on his side. Reagan, who was a big fan of Nixon, thought he would be the natural successor once Nixon left office in '76.

And Reagan was a die-hard defender of Nixon during Watergate, so he was shocked in 1974 when Nixon had to resign and Jerry Ford became president. He had very little respect for Jerry Ford and Ford in turn had very little respect for Ronald Reagan. But Reagan thought that he was going to be Nixon's successor, not this obscure congressman from Michigan. And so he did something that shocked a lot of his supporters. He challenged a sitting Republican president in the primaries in 1976.

DR: He challenged Ford in 1976. He lost the first five primaries in a row. He was about ready to give up. What happened in North Carolina that kept him in?

MB: A bunch of things happened. He narrowly lost the New Hampshire primary. He came very close. Then he found some winning issues. For example, he made a big deal out of the Panama Canal, using this line that he borrowed from Strom Thurmond: "We paid for it, we bought it, it's ours." There was a patriotic nationalist backlash against the negotiations the Ford administration was conducting to give the canal back to Panama. Reagan tapped into this wellspring of sentiment.

He also started attacking the détente policy that the Ford administration was following, even though he had backed détente when it had been Richard Nixon's initiative. Then he got a huge helping hand from the Jesse Helms organization in North Carolina and pulled off this shocking upset, which propelled him back into the race.

DR: The race became close. He began winning primaries. He gets almost down to the finish, and it's not clear to people who's going to be the nominee. What mistake did he make in terms of picking a potential vice president that hurt him with some supporters on the conservative side of the spectrum?

MB: I don't think it was a huge mistake. It was a desperate gamble. He announced that he was going to pick Richard Schweiker, a liberal Republican from Pennsylvania as his running mate if he won the nomination. But that wasn't what killed him. I talked to John Sears, who was Reagan's political consultant. The reason they did that was because they knew they were going to lose and it was just a desperate attempt to try to shake things up, but it didn't work. No sitting president in the age of primaries has ever lost his party's nomination. It was just too hard to do.

But once again, as he had done earlier with Barry Goldwater, he upstaged his own party's nominee at the convention in Kansas City. At the very end, Jerry Ford called him down to the stage and asked him to give a little speech. Reagan didn't have remarks prepared, but he extemporized this beautiful speech on the spot, very short, three or four minutes, which mesmerized the audience. It had people crying in the convention hall. A lot of people left the convention thinking, once again, that they had nominated the wrong guy. But because Reagan was already in his sixties, the assumption was that his career was finished.

DR: Reagan said he would campaign for Ford. Did he campaign much for him?

MB: He did the bare minimum.

DR: Ford loses the election. Carter wins. Reagan has no doubt he's going to run for the nomination again?

MB: He doesn't have much doubt. A lot of people doubt because, again, he's getting into his late sixties. That was considered old in those days. The assumption was that he was going to retire. But the fact that the Carter presidency was so troubled—there has been a reassessment of Jimmy Carter, and he's gone up in the estimation of historians, but at the time he was reaching plummeting new levels of unpopularity, thanks to stagflation, the Iran hostage crisis, the problems the country was having. That created an obvious opening for a Republican nominee.

The Republican Party in those days was a pretty hierarchical organization, so you would expect the next guy in line would be the nominee. After 1976, it was pretty clear that Ronald Reagan was the next guy in line.

DR: He wins the nomination. Why does he pick George Bush as his vice president? They didn't seem to get along that well.

MB: They were trying to achieve a balanced ticket. There was a movement to pick Jerry Ford as the vice president to mollify all the Republicans who thought that Reagan didn't know enough about Washington and government to be an effective president. That was nixed when Reagan was sitting in his hotel suite at the convention in Detroit and watching Walter Cronkite ask Jerry Ford about the possibility of becoming VP. Cronkite said, "So it would be kind of a co-presidency," and Ford didn't disagree. Reagan almost fell off his chair watching this in his hotel suite, because he wasn't signing up for a co-presidency.

That nixed the Ford nomination. Basically, Reagan was sitting there late at night in his suite with his guys around him and said, "Okay, what do we do now?" George H. W. Bush, who was the runner-up for the nomination, was the obvious choice, even though he had offended a lot of people, including Nancy Reagan, by labeling Reagan's economic agenda "voodoo economics." There were some hard feelings from the campaign, but Reagan was the supreme pragmatist, and he was willing to do what it took to win. Embracing George H. W. Bush was a small price to pay for the presidency.

DR: It's been rumored for many years that Reagan, or Bill Casey, who was his campaign chairman, tried to prevent the Iranians from releasing the hostages before the election was over. Is there any truth to that?

MB: This is the October surprise theory. It remains a matter of historical debate. Some evidence has emerged in recent years to suggest that there were attempts on the part of Bill Casey and other Reagan operatives to try to convince Iran not to release the hostages before the election, which would have been a huge boost to Jimmy Carter. Casey, of course, was a former spook from World War II, later the director of the CIA, and also was believed to be one of the masterminds of the Iran-Contra affair, so this is hardly something that would be outside his comfort zone. But while the evidence is somewhat mixed, on one point there is no doubt, which is that if this was going on, Reagan had no idea it was happening, and I'm sure he would not have approved it. One of Reagan's weaknesses as a manager was that he didn't always know what his subordinates were up to.

DR: A week before the election, there's a debate. Who won the debate, and how did that person win it?

MB: Hands down, no question, it was Ronald Reagan. The memorable line that people always remember from that debate is "There you go again." It was a devastating line for Jimmy Carter. What people forget is that when Ronald Reagan said, "There you go again," Carter was right and Reagan was wrong, because the actual subject of the debate at that point was Carter's accusation that Reagan had opposed the creation of Medicare, which was absolutely correct. In the early 1960s, Reagan had suggested that Medicare and Medicaid were socialized medicine that was going to lead to the loss of freedom in America, and he had backed an alternative bill that covered only 1 percent of seniors.

So, Carter was absolutely correct, but Reagan had a killer line and people weren't fact-checking the debate in real time. Reagan tapped into this widespread feeling that Jimmy Carter, although he came across as a goody-goody, actually had this mean streak. And so he walloped Carter with that "There you go again" line, and also the other line, so memorable, at the end of the debate in his summing up, where he said, "Are you better off now than you were four years ago?" That encapsulated the Reagan campaign message, which was the country was a mess.

DR: Reagan wins the election overwhelmingly, 489 electoral votes to 49.

MB: I'm impressed you've got that in your head.

DR: I lived that for forty-five years. I know that vote.

Reagan asked Jim Baker, then fifty years old, to serve as his chief of staff. Why did he pick Baker and not people who had been around him his whole career?

MB: In many ways, the most important and shrewd decision that Reagan made as president was to pick Jim Baker, because normally presidents will pick a crony as their White House chief of staff, and Baker was far from a crony. In fact, he had helped to run Ford's campaign in '76, and he had run George H. W. Bush's campaign in 1980, so he was the campaign manager for a rival candidate. He and Reagan had almost no relationship until very late in the campaign. The widespread assumption was that Ed Meese, who had been Reagan's chief of staff in Sacramento, would get the same job in Washington. But Stu Spencer, who was Reagan's political consultant, and Mike Deaver, one of his top aides, and, of course, Nancy Reagan—that was the real troika, the powerhouse in the White House—they knew that Ed Meese was kind of legendary for being disorganized. Reagan aides would make jokes about Ed's bottomless briefcase where you gave him papers and you never saw them again. And he was not experienced in the ways of Washington. They realized that, to be successful, President Reagan needed a shrewd White House chief of staff who was a real Washington operator. Reagan went along. It was hugely crushing and disappointing to Ed Meese, who had been a Reagan loyalist for years, to be told, "Sorry, Ed, I'm going to choose Jim as my chief of staff."

Reagan also hated personality conflicts. He was completely nonconfrontational in his personal life, so he couldn't just say, "Ed, I'm sorry, you're out of a job." What he actually said was, "Boys, figure it out among yourselves." So, Ed Meese and Jim Baker sat down as if they were negotiators for warring countries, and they wrote out a compact, where Ed Meese said, "I get this, this, and that," and Jim Baker said, "I get this, that, and the other." But, basically, Baker ran circles around Meese. He became known as the velvet hammer and became one of the most effective White House chiefs of staff in history.

DR: The goal of Reagan in the first term was a big tax cut. Why was he so enamored with it, and did he actually get it through?

MB: He did get it through. His support for tax cuts went back to World War II where he was really unhappy about paying this 94 percent rate of taxation. When Reagan took office in 1981, the top rate wasn't 94 percent anymore, but it was still 70 percent. He thought that was too high and he wanted to reduce it, so he pushed through a 25 percent cut in personal income tax rates, which had a lot of support at the time. Even a lot of Democrats agreed. The House was in

Democratic hands in those days, but even a lot of Democrats agreed that tax rates were too high.

But the reason George H. W. Bush had called Reagan's economic agenda "voodoo economics" was that, at the same time Reagan was promising a massive cut in income tax rates and a massive boost in defense spending, he was also promising to balance the budget by 1983. Clearly, the math of that did not add up. Instead of producing a balanced budget, Reaganomics produced massive budget deficits. That was the one regret Reagan expressed about his presidency, the budget deficits, although in hindsight, from the vantage point of more than forty years later, the budget deficits that seemed so high in the 1980s seem pretty minuscule compared to the kind of budget deficits we have today.

DR: Reagan signed twelve later tax bills, which twelve times actually raised taxes. Is that right?

MB: Yes. As both governor and as president, he raised taxes more often than he cut them. The amazing thing was that while he did that, he never lost the support of his base. You remember, of course, that George H. W. Bush while running for president said, "No new taxes." He then agreed to a tax increase, and that was politically devastating for him. One of Reagan's superpowers was that he could pivot to the center, make deals with Democrats, in this case Tip O'Neill, but not lose the support of the conservative faithful.

DR: In foreign policy, what was his main accomplishment in the first term? Dealing with the Soviets?

MB: Truthfully, he didn't have a lot of foreign policy accomplishments in his first term. The big foreign policy story in some ways was the Marine barracks bombing in Beirut in 1983, which was a fiasco from start to finish. A lot of Marines and sailors paid with their lives for a peacekeeping mission when there was no peace to keep.

Reagan was building up America's defenses. That was a substantial achievement. He launched the Strategic Defense Initiative, and he confronted the Soviet Union. He called the Soviet Union "the evil empire."

But none of those initiatives bore any kind of results in his first term. The only real result was to ratchet up tensions. And 1983 was a very dangerous year. That was a year that included the Soviet shootdown of KAL Flight 007, a passenger airliner. It also included, although people didn't realize it at the time, a couple of war scares where we came very close to nuclear war with the Soviet Union.

DR: Reagan had an idea, "Star Wars," as it was called, to have certain weaponry in space. Today, is that as ridiculous as it was thought to be then, or it's realistic?

MB: Missile defense is certainly realistic, and that was in progress even before Reagan's Strategic Defense Initiative. The Patriot air-defense system was in full-scale production starting in 1980. Missile defenses have become very effective, as we've seen with Iran and with the defense of Ukraine. But Reagan had this grandiose vision of SDI, which is that you would have orbiting lasers in space and protect America from ICBM attack. That has still not proven practical more than forty years later. We have about forty-four interceptors deployed in Alaska and California, but, as dramatized in the movie *A House of Dynamite*, they only provide limited protection against nuclear missile attack.

DR: Let's talk about the relationship between Reagan and Bush. In eight years, did the Bushes ever get invited to the White House residence for dinner?

MB: They did not. Ronald Reagan and George H. W. Bush got along just fine. They had lunch together every week. Reagan never said anything negative about Bush. But they were hardly bosom buddies. Nancy Reagan and Barbara Bush were basically enemies. They could not stand each other. They had this feud going on throughout the presidency. Barbara would sometimes remark bitterly that, during Bush's eight years as Reagan's vice president, the Bushes were never once invited to the family quarters in the White House.

DR: Did Reagan actually have any friends?

MB: He had very few friends. This goes back to his time growing up as the son of this alcoholic shoe salesman, moving from town to town. He did not develop a lot of close friendships and he erected this mental barrier around himself, which was in place throughout his life. The fascinating thing is that people who just saw him on TV thought he was warm and avuncular, whereas people who were close to him told me, "He was icy, distant, inscrutable, hard to know, close to almost nobody except for Nancy." I think one of my great biographical achievements in this book was I figured out who were Ronald Reagan's best friends when he was president, and it was not who you would expect. It was not all these grandees like Walter Annenberg or Alfred Bloomingdale with whom he hobnobbed and whom he was often photographed with. I figured out that his best friend in many ways was a person almost nobody has ever heard of named Dennis LeBlanc, whom I interviewed.

Who is Dennis LeBlanc? He was a former California state police officer who protected Governor Reagan when he was in office. Later on, Dennis and his fellow state police officer Barney Barnett went to work for Reagan on his ranch near Santa Barbara. In the 1980s, these were the people Reagan was in many ways closest to. It was fascinating talking to Dennis about spending time with Reagan. They would be out there on the ranch all day, doing chores, chopping wood, repairing fences, and they would not talk politics. As Dennis said, "We would just talk normal guy stuff." At the end of the day, the three of them, the president, Dennis, and Barney, would all go to the Reagan Ranch House. It's a wonderful window into Reagan's soul, because it's an incredibly modest place. The décor looks like it came from a flea market. It's small, rustic, primitive.

The three guys would go back to the ranch house, and the housekeeper—Nancy never cooked—would prepare a meal for them, which was meager because Nancy was always watching her weight and made sure that Ronnie was as well. They would get up from the table almost as hungry as when they sat down, and they would go into the living room and sit down on the couch and, like a million

American families, they would watch TV. They would turn on *Murder, She Wrote* or some other show and basically fall asleep in front of the TV set. Then, at some point in the evening, Nancy would tap Dennis on the foot and say, "Time to go to bed." Dennis and Barney would shuffle off to their trailer, and the housekeeper might slip them a couple of chocolate chip cookies on the way, and the president and the First Lady would shuffle off to their modest bedroom a few feet away. This was the life that Ronald Reagan most enjoyed.

DR: Ronald Reagan runs for reelection in 1984. He runs against Walter Mondale. How does the first debate go against Mondale?

MB: The first debate did not go well because Reagan was out of practice. Like many incumbent presidents, he was getting up in age. And he often seemed lost and befuddled. That raised what became known as the age issue. People started thinking, "This guy is seventy-three years old, too old to be president."

DR: How did the second debate go?

MB: He completely turned things around in the second debate. A reporter from the *Baltimore Sun* asked him the age question. "During the Cuban Missile Crisis, President Kennedy had to go days without sleep. Do you, Mr. President, think you have the vigor and energy at your age to do something like that?" Reagan's reply was a master one-liner. He said, "I promise not to use my opponent's age and inexperience against him as a political issue." That brought down the house. It basically won the election and put the age issue to rest.

DR: He won forty-nine states.

MB: He did. Pause for a second and imagine any president today in our more polarized times winning forty-nine states. It seems outlandish.

DR: In the second term, he has a big problem, Iran-Contra. What was Iran-Contra?

MB: Iran-Contra was the biggest scandal of the Reagan presidency and the biggest scandal since Watergate up until that point. It was a complicated scandal, but it basically began with Iranian-backed terrorists seizing American hostages in Lebanon. The Israelis approached the Reagan administration with a crackpot scheme to get the hostages out by sending weapons to supposed Iranian moderates. This was something that Bud McFarlane, who was the national security advisor, thought was going to be a brilliant idea. Bud later explained to me that he had been an aide to Henry Kissinger, and he imagined this was going to be kind of Reagan's Nixon-goes-to-China moment. He was going to turn Iran from foe to friend with this deal. It turned into a fiasco because the Iranians took the weapons, released a few hostages, then seized more hostages, so it wasn't achieving anything.

Then Bud McFarlane's successor as national security advisor, John Poindexter, and his aide Ollie North came up with a scheme to take the profits from the sale of weapons to the Iranians—yes, they were selling the weapons to Iran—to take the profits and funnel them to the Nicaraguan Contras, this rebel movement, even though Congress had passed the Boland Amendment forbidding aid to the Contras. This emerged in the fall of 1986 and became a huge scandal.

DR: Reagan escaped the scandal politically because he was able to say, "I didn't understand what was going on"?

MB: Exactly. Reagan escaped the scandal for the same reason that he got into it, because he often did not know what his aides were doing. What I like to say about Reagan is he was a great leader and certainly a great communicator, but he was a very poor manager. He depended on aides who would run things efficiently, as Jim Baker had done in the first term. But then the second term began disastrously, when Reagan casually let Jim Baker swap jobs with Treasury Secretary Don Regan. Don Regan turned out to be a horrible White House chief of staff who oversaw this mess.

Reagan could have easily gotten impeached because of this. But his alibi was "I didn't know about the diversion of funds to the Contras." If this had been Richard Nixon and he had said, "I didn't know what was going on," nobody would have believed him. But when Ronald Reagan said, "I didn't know what was going on," that was pretty plausible.

DR: Did Reagan really support George Bush to be his successor?

MB: He did support George Bush, although he had some doubts about whether he was tough enough to be president, so he didn't endorse Bush during the primaries. Once Bush had the nomination locked up, he certainly supported him.

DR: It was thought at the time that Reagan might be slipping mentally. Was there any evidence you found that he had Alzheimer's while he was president?

MB: I did not find any evidence that he had dementia. I talked to one of the doctors at the Mayo Clinic who treated him for Alzheimer's, and what the doctor told me is that the underlying conditions of Alzheimer's can be present in the brain for many years before it has a cognitive impact. I do believe that the underlying condition was present while he was in office, but I didn't find any evidence that he was suffering from dementia. I talked to a lot of people who were close to him. Even if you just look at his diary, the handwriting was still as clear and firm at the end of the presidency as at the beginning.

But there is no question that he was slipping somewhat as he was getting into his late seventies. He was more removed from the daily affairs of government by the time he was leaving office. As the doctors said to me, one of the toughest things to determine is the dividing line between the normal aging process and the beginnings of Alzheimer's. But again, I didn't see any evidence that he had dementia.

DR: Did Reagan dye his hair, or was it always that dark?

MB: There are some mysteries that I could not get to the root of, so to speak. He always denied he dyed his hair.

DR: When he retires, he makes a famous speech in Japan for $2 million or so. What did he mostly do in his retirement? Build the Reagan Library?

MB: The library was really Nancy Reagan's thing. I don't know that Ronald Reagan cared that much what people thought about him, which I think was one of the secrets of his success. He was extraordinarily self-confident. He did not have that chip on his shoulder. He did not have a desire to prove the critics wrong. He always took the attitude that "History will judge people. I don't really care." He spent as much of his retirement time as he could chopping wood, riding horses, playing golf, which he didn't get to do much as president. But his retirement was tragically cut short by the diagnosis of Alzheimer's in 1994.

DR: He had Alzheimer's and was more or less bedridden for the last two years of his life?

MB: The last decade of his life, yes. It was a tragic end. He had it for the last ten years of his life and was bedridden for the last several.

DR: Did you come away admiring Reagan more than you did before you started the book or less than you did before?

MB: I came away understanding Reagan a lot more, both his strengths and weaknesses, his achievements as well as the shortcomings. The bottom line is, Reagan is judged by most historians to be somewhere around the eighth or ninth best president that we've had, which is quite an achievement for this poor boy from Tampico, Illinois.

His reputation rests primarily on two massive achievements, the first of which was helping America to get its mojo back in the 1980s, to regain our self-confidence after the very difficult and tumultuous 1960s and 1970s. He told Americans it was morning again in America in 1984, and people believed him. Then his great achievement in the second term was making peace with the Soviet Union. This is not something people would have expected from such a die-hard anti-Communist. But he understood that Mikhail Gorbachev was a different kind of Communist leader, somebody that he could do business with, as Margaret Thatcher told him. At Geneva in 1985 he established a relationship with Gorbachev that paved the way for the reduction of nuclear weapons and the peaceful end of the Cold War and the fall of the Berlin Wall.

Those are two monumental achievements. But in any kind of balanced assessment of Reagan, you also have to look at his failures and shortcomings. I think those look different now in some ways than they did at the time. In the 1980s, Democrats were primarily criticizing Reagan for his budget deficits, which from our vantage point don't seem so bad. Almost nobody in the Democratic Party was criticizing him for ignoring the AIDS pandemic, and yet in hindsight, the fact that he had almost nothing to say about the AIDS pandemic, as tens of thousands of Americans were dying, was a huge problem. Or the Iran-Contra affair. Some of his economic policies inadvertently exacerbated income inequality, which we're still living with.

To answer your question, at the end of the day after spending ten years researching Ronald Reagan, I liked him very much as a person, but as a politician, I came to appreciate his achievements as well as his failings. You have to weigh both of those in the balance to reach any kind of accurate assessment of his presidency.

9

David Maraniss on Jim Thorpe

INTERVIEW DATE: MAY 17, 2023

In an age where spectator sports (amateur and professional) have become a more significant part of life, there are inevitably constant discussions about who in each sport is the GOAT—the Greatest of All Time. Tom Brady or Jim Brown in professional football? Michael Jordan or LeBron James in professional basketball? Babe Ruth or Willie Mays in professional baseball?

But there seems to be little debate as to who, when all athletic accomplishments are considered, was the GOAT. It was Jim Thorpe.

The GOAT was a Native American who overcame the challenging educational and societal barriers often faced by Native Americans in twentieth-century America. He became one of college football's greatest players, a standout professional football player, a skilled Major League Baseball player, a collegiate track and field star, and the winner of both the decathlon and the pentathlon at the 1912 Olympic Games in Stockholm.

Sadly, his extraordinary on-the-field athletic skills did not translate into off-the-field personal or financial success. Indeed, just the opposite occurred.

Jim Thorpe was stripped of his Olympic medals because he had competed professionally in baseball—then a violation of the "amateur"

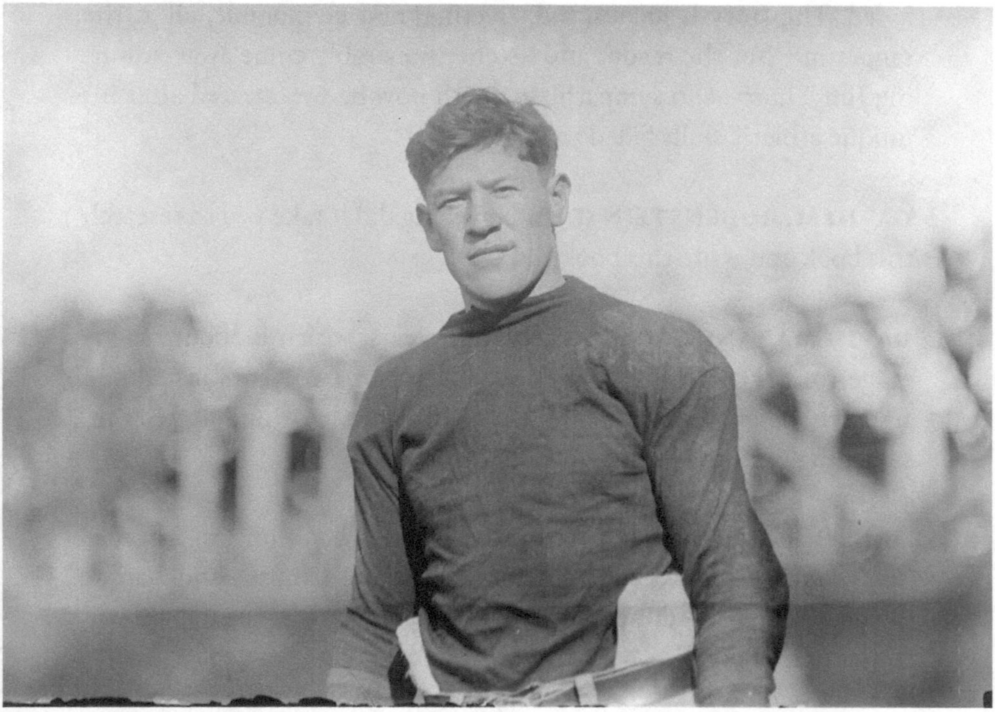

FIGURE 9.1 Jim Thorpe, a member of the Sac and Fox Nation, excelled in many sports, including football, baseball, basketball, and track and field. He won two gold medals at the 1912 Olympics, becoming the first Native American to do so for the United States.

requirements for the Olympics (though many others avoided being caught for this violation by using a pseudonym). And when Thorpe finally became an official professional athlete, he generally squandered his money, due in part to alcoholism and other personal challenges (including multiple marriages and children out of wedlock).

David Maraniss, a Pulitzer Prize–winning journalist and a talented biographer of political figures (like Bill Clinton and Barack Obama) and sports figures (like Vince Lombardi and Roberto Clemente) decided to take a fresh look at Jim Thorpe, covering the athletic accomplishments and the personal warts, using newly available documents and family access to research his book *Path Lit by Lightning: The Life of Jim Thorpe*. The result, as the Members who attended this Dialogue uniformly felt, is an unvarnished look at the GOAT, in terms of the way society treated him off the field and after his athletic skills faded. The story is joyous, sad, riveting, and memorable, all at the same time. But the reader and listener inevitably come away admiring Jim Thorpe and sympathizing with how he was treated after his unique athletic skills faded with age.

DAVID M. RUBENSTEIN (DR): How long did it take you to research this book and write this book?

DAVID MARANISS (DM): It took four years, which is about my average for each of my books. I usually spend two years just doing research. Then, I get a feeling that I can start writing but keep researching until the last day.

DR: What prompted you to want to write a book on Jim Thorpe? You've written books on political figures, Bill Clinton and Barack Obama, and you've done some sports figures. But what prompted you to write this book?

DM: I was in Denver on a book tour for a book I wrote about Vietnam in the '60s. A gentleman came up to me after the event and introduced himself as Norbert Hill from the Oneida Nation in Wisconsin. He handed me a sheaf of papers and said, "Here's your next book, Jim Thorpe." This was more than twenty years ago. I politely said, "Thank you very much. I'm working on a book about Roberto Clemente, and I don't take suggestions from other people. It has to be something that I'm obsessed with." But he planted the seed, and it took about twenty years for it to grow.

DR: Who was Jim Thorpe?

DM: He was from the Sac and Fox Nation of what became Oklahoma, born in 1887, and he's famous because he was arguably the greatest athlete in world history. He did things that no other athlete had done before or since. He not only was a gold medalist in the decathlon and pentathlon in the 1912 Olympics in Stockholm, he was an All-American football player at the Carlisle Indian Industrial School.

He was the first great professional football player playing in Ohio. He was the first president of what would become the National Football League, and he was a Major League Baseball player. He could do anything. He was a great hockey player, ballroom dancer. He was even good at marbles.

DR: He was an extraordinary athlete. Much of your book talks about the extraordinary athletic skills he had, and we'll go through that in a moment. But the latter two-thirds of his life, or at least certainly the latter half, he has a very difficult life. He's probably an alcoholic. He can't hold a job. He doesn't have much money. He has many marriages, many children he doesn't really know that well. Is the theme of your book that he was a great athlete who overcame great odds to become the greatest ever, or is it that, despite the fact he was a great athlete, he led a relatively sad life toward the end? What is the major theme?

DM: Neither, actually. He was a brilliant athlete. That's not why I wrote the book. I wrote the book to illuminate the Native American experience, using the drama of sports to convey that. You can look at what happened to him in his last thirty years, his struggles with alcohol, three wives, seven children, not around that much, traveling from state to state. He lived in twenty different states. There's a way to look at that as tragedy, and I don't. My conclusion is that his story is a lesson of perseverance as much as tragedy. It's too easy to take a minority figure who struggles and say, "What a tragic life." But when you think about the obstacles he dealt with, both societal and of his own doing, that he kept going is amazing.

DR: In the latter half or so of his life, he had difficulties. Did he ever complain to people, or he basically said, "I'm going to go ahead and do the best I can"? Was he ever a complainer?

DM: He wasn't a whiner at all, no. He was complaining in the final thirty years of his life about what happened to him in terms of losing those Olympic medals, which is a different story, but he didn't complain about his life. He had almost a Walter Mitty–esque sensibility about him. He was always almost on the verge of getting that job that would turn things around, whether it was coaching or running a hunting lodge, and it never really happens. That's part of the sadness.

DR: It reminds me to some extent of the show *The Honeymooners*, where Ralph is always about to get rich, he's about to be successful, and always it falls apart. Jim Thorpe is like that, too.

DM: Very much so. I was able to acquire letters that he wrote to his second wife when he's down in Florida. Florida is booming. He thinks he can get into real estate. His football career is basically over, and he writes all these letters about what's going to happen next, and it just breaks your heart.

DR: Are any of his children alive?

DM: Jim Thorpe was born in 1887, so, no, none of his children are alive. Some of his grandchildren, many of his great-grandchildren are. One of the legacies of Jim Thorpe is that all seven of those children, even though there were years when they didn't see him much, became very successful. Four sons, three of them were military officers. The three daughters all got graduate degrees, and the family is still very active around the country.

DR: Let's talk about where he was born.

DM: He was born along the North Canadian River near Belmont, Oklahoma, a small town. Later, another town developed called Prague, Oklahoma.

DR: Who were his parents?

DM: His parents were Hiram and Charlotte Thorpe. Hiram was basically a ne'er-do-well, a bootleg-whiskey guy, sort of the toughest guy in that part of Oklahoma, who had five wives and twenty children.

DR: Some were his wives simultaneously?

DM: At times, yes.

DR: Was Jim Thorpe's father literate?

DM: I've got a couple of letters or notes that his father wrote. He certainly couldn't spell, but that doesn't mean he was illiterate. I think he could read some.

DR: When Jim Thorpe was growing up, did he work on his father's farm? Did his father have a farm, or what did he do as a young boy?

DM: His father was a rancher. Jim had a pleasant childhood in one sense. He loved to hunt and fish and go out along the North Canadian River and play. But he was sent off to Indian boarding schools at age seven.

DR: Did his parents live very long?

DM: His mother died when he was in Lawrence, Kansas, at the Haskell Institute, when he was a young teenager. His father died as soon as Jim got to the Carlisle School when he was sixteen. So, he was orphaned at age sixteen.

DR: Carlisle, in Carlisle, Pennsylvania, was an Indian school for Indians only. It was designed to teach them how to be better Native Americans or how to be better white Christians?

DM: Better white Christians. It was the flagship government boarding school for Native Americans. It was founded in 1879 at the tail end of what were called the Indian Wars. The first students there were mostly Oglala Sioux from the Dakotas, who were sent there to forcibly acculturate them and take them away from their parents. Many of those first young students thought they were going east to show their bravery and to die. And, unfortunately, too many of them did die. If you ever visit the Army War College in Carlisle today, which is a fabulous institution, at one edge of it is a cemetery of the students who died while they were there.

DR: Were the parents volunteering to send their children there, or they got taken there by the government?

DM: It was a combination. Jim Thorpe's father sent him there because Thorpe kept running away from the Haskell Institute in Kansas down to Oklahoma. His father said, "I'm going to send you so far away you can't run home." But many of them were forcibly taken there.

DR: To make them like white Christian Americans was the avowed goal of the school. Is that fair?

DM: The motto of the founder of the Carlisle Indian boarding school, Richard Henry Pratt, was "Kill the Indian, save the man." In other words, "We're not going to kill you anymore, we're going to turn you into a white Christian." That was the goal. That's a very controversial concept, to say the least, but it was basically inspired by people who thought they were doing good.

DR: How did Jim Thorpe get on the athletic field? Was he just accidentally stumbled upon as a great athlete, or did he really want to be a great athlete?

DM: In 1907, Jim Thorpe was at Carlisle, and he wasn't doing any athletics there at all, although he had grown to love football at the Haskell Institute. When he got to Carlisle in 1904, imagine this. He stood 5 foot 5 and weighed 115 pounds. Three years later, he was 5 feet 11-1/2 inches and 180 pounds and this beautiful, sinewy athlete.

In 1907, he's working on the farm at Carlisle, not on athletics. He walks by the athletic field. There are some students from the track team high-jumping. They're failing at six feet. Thorpe is in his overalls, and he easily clears it. The next day, he's on the track team.

DR: How did he get into the football team?

DM: He wanted to play football right after that. The coach of the football team was the famous Pop Warner of Pop Warner football, whom we'll get to later. He was a brilliant coach, not a brilliant human being. But anyway, they let Thorpe on the team grudgingly. They didn't want him to get hurt because he was so good at track. But in the first practice, he kept running through everybody, so they couldn't keep him off the team. And by 1908, he was an All-American.

DR: He's an All-American. How does Carlisle, a small Indian school in Carlisle, Pennsylvania, compete with the biggest football powers in the country? How did they have enough of a student body, and how did they have enough money to get a great team?

DM: First of all, the great teams in that era weren't Alabama and Oklahoma and LSU. They were Harvard and Penn and Yale and West Point and all of the Eastern schools. That was the hub of college football in that era. Carlisle was an attraction. Here you have these exotic Indians coming to play your football team, and they were good. All of the Ivy League schools wanted the Carlisle team to come. They were mostly a road team. They had to play on the road all the time. Nobody wanted to come to Carlisle. But they would draw huge crowds, the biggest crowds. And the Native American athletes of that era were terrific. Jim Thorpe wasn't the only one. It was a very good team.

DR: If Carlisle played at Harvard or Yale, the revenues would be great for the schools. What did Carlisle do with the revenues they were getting out of this?

DM: The revenues ostensibly went back to the school for its buildings. There was sort of a slush fund—nothing changes in football or life—that Pop Warner ran for the players.

DR: How did Jim Thorpe get to be on the Olympic team? He's an All-American football player, but that doesn't mean he's going to be an Olympic athlete. How did that come about?

DM: He'd been on the track team, and he was so good. There are a lot of myths about Jim Thorpe. One is that one day, he and Pop Warner and a long-distance runner, a great marathoner named Louis Tewanima, a Hopi Indian, arrived at Lafayette to play the Lafayette track team. And the Lafayette coach met them at the train station and said, "Where's your team?" And Pop Warner said, "It's right here: these two guys." That's all they needed to beat Lafayette. In fact, there were more than that, but that sort of symbolized how good they were. Thorpe was great at everything. He was strong. He was good at the shot put and hammer throw and discus. He was fast, so he was good at the sprints and the hurdles. He could compete in so many events that it was a natural for him to develop into a decathlete.

DR: For the 1912 Olympics, did they have a big tryout like we do today? How did people get on the Olympic team?

DM: They did have tryouts in the West, in California, in Chicago, and on the East Coast. They're interesting. There weren't really tryouts for the decathlon, but they knew that Thorpe was good enough that that's what he would compete in.

DR: Who were some of the other American athletes on that 1912 Olympic team?

DM: It was a fascinating group. Duke Kahanamoku was the great swimmer from Hawaii who won gold medals there. My favorite, for a lot of interesting reasons, was a young army officer named George S. Patton, who competed in the modern pentathlon, which were all these military-style events. He did not do that well and actually sort of fibbed about how well he'd done later.

Also on the team and competing in the decathlon against Thorpe, but on the same US team, was Avery Brundage, who went on to become the head of the International Olympic Committee (IOC) for decades after that. It shocked me when I realized he was a decathlete, because I always envisioned Brundage as this fat-cat, cigar-smoking, European and Asian art-collecting head-of-the-Olympics potentate. To think of him as a decathlete was a little bit hard to imagine. He wasn't very good, by the way, and he dropped out after eight events. This guy, who kept saying that it was the competition that counted, not how well you did, dropped out when Thorpe was creaming him.

DR: Jim Thorpe is selected to be on the Olympic team for two sports: the decathlon and the pentathlon. How did they get over to Sweden, and did they train on the way over?

DM: They went over by ship. This was only two months after the sinking of the *Titanic*, so it was kind of a scary time for transatlantic crossings. There were supposed to be a lot of wealthy donors going on the ship, too, but a lot of them decided that they didn't want to go because of that.

They did train on the ship. They had all kinds of interesting devices on the ship, a track around the edge. The shot putters would tie some kind of a rope to the shot put, throw it out into the ocean, and haul it back. There was a little pool made out of canvas for the swimmers. So, yes, they did train.

DR: They get there in what month in 1912?

DM: July 1912.

DR: Does the decathlon event run at the beginning, or the pentathlon? Which is first?

DM: The pentathlon's first, and the decathlon's near the end.

DR: How does Jim Thorpe do?

DM: Thorpe competed—think about this—he competed in a total of seventeen events in two weeks. He competed in two individual events as well. It's foolish to compare athletes from different generations because of differences in training and diet and so many different factors involved. Then, for the decathlon, the scoring system has changed enormously over the years. But Jim Thorpe defeated his competition by a greater margin than anybody ever has.

DR: In both events?

DM: Both events.

DR: He gets the gold medal in both?

DM: Yes.

DR: One of the things you do in the book that's kind of like saying there's no Santa Claus is that you say that the famous statement made to Thorpe by the king, "You're the greatest athlete in the world," isn't really what he said.

DM: "You, sir, are the greatest athlete in the world." Nobody knows if he said that. No newspaper article in the following two days ever reported that. It came up later. There was no video of it, so I couldn't document it that way. But the mythology is that Thorpe responded, "Thanks, King," which is funny, but he didn't say it. He said, "Thank you."

DR: When the Olympic team comes back to the United States, is there a ticker-tape parade, or how do they celebrate?

DM: Huge parades. In New York City, everybody turned out, over 100,000 people. Thorpe was at the head of the parade. All the other athletes were two to a car. Thorpe was in his own car. There was also a huge parade in Philadelphia and in Carlisle.

DR: He's back and then he goes back to Carlisle?

DM: Yes.

DR: Is he back as a college student at Carlisle again?

DM: I wouldn't quite call him a college student. Carlisle wasn't really a college, but it was an interesting amalgam.

DR: No endorsements?

DM: No, nothing like that. But he was completing what I call the greatest single year in athletic history, because not only did he win those gold medals in Stockholm, he came back to Carlisle to play football and was brilliant that entire season, beating Harvard and Army.

DR: How does the story arise that he was being paid as a semi-pro baseball player and therefore wasn't truly an amateur at the Olympics? When did that story come up?

DM: It broke after that football season in an odd way. A reporter from the *Worcester Telegram* in Massachusetts got a tip that there was a baseball manager in town visiting his sister, who managed Jim Thorpe in the Eastern Carolina League for two summers. The reporter went out and interviewed the guy. It turned out to be true. The story broke. And, within a week, Thorpe's medals were taken away. His records were stricken from the book. His trophies were taken away. That was an injustice in many different ways.

DR: The Olympics Committee in Sweden said, "Look, we're not taking them away." Who took the medals away?

DM: Pop Warner and James E. Sullivan of the well-known Sullivan Award that's given to the greatest amateur athlete in America. Pop Warner knew what Jim Thorpe had been doing but said he didn't to save his own reputation. He'd been sending Indian athletes to play baseball in the summers for years. One of his closest associates at Albright College in Pennsylvania had scouted Thorpe and two colleagues to go down and play in Eastern Carolina. James E. Sullivan also knew what Thorpe was doing. He was not only the head of the Amateur Athletic Union and the American Olympic Committee, but also the key guy on the board of advisors to the Carlisle Indian Industrial School Athletic Department. Everybody knew that Thorpe was gone for that period of time.

DR: Was Jim Thorpe the only person playing semi-pro baseball from the college ranks?

DM: Absolutely not. There were scores of college athletes who were playing bush league baseball for money in the summers. Most of them would use aliases. There were so many aliases in the Eastern Carolina League that they called it the Pocahontas League because everybody was named John Smith. Dwight Eisenhower played baseball in the summers under the name Wilson in the Kansas State League.

DR: The medals were taken away. Did Jim Thorpe sue, or did he have any legal redress?

DM: He had absolutely no redress. He just lost everything. He then went on to play professional baseball and football after that.

DR: How many more years does he play football at Carlisle?

DM: That's his final year.

DR: Then he goes to play professional baseball for the New York Giants?

DM: Yes. Even though football was his best sport, football in that era was a ragtag operation. There was no NFL. There was a league out in Ohio, the Ohio League, but that was it. Baseball was a major sport, and he loved baseball. He had played baseball and track together in his final two years at Carlisle, and he was the most famous athlete in the world. Whether he was ever called that by the king is another question. But everybody knew him. And that's why John McGraw wanted him.

DR: McGraw was the manager of the New York Giants, and they were getting ready to do a world tour. They wanted a famous person on the team, I guess. They signed him up, and they did the tour around the world?

DM: That's why he signed Jim Thorpe. It was the Chicago White Sox and the New York Giants traveling to Japan, China, the Philippines, Australia, Cairo, and Europe. These were great ball players on those teams. They were Hall of Famers like Tris Speaker. Christy Mathewson was afraid of being on a ship, so he didn't eventually go, but they thought he would. But nobody knew any of the players. Charles Comiskey, the owner of the White Sox, was on the trip, along with McGraw. Famous baseball figures. The rest of the world knew none of them. They knew Jim Thorpe.

DR: After the trip is over, Jim Thorpe is signed to a five-year contract by McGraw to play for the Giants. Does he actually use him for the Giants, or does he put him on the bench?

DM: He's on the bench or sent down to the minors a few times, not played. McGraw was a brilliant manager, a Hall of Fame manager. But the conclusion that I reach, and which several baseball mavens have reached, is that Thorpe was misused by McGraw. The proof of that is that, finally, he was traded to the Boston Braves in 1919, and he was terrific. He was leading the league in hitting most of the year. He and the famous crosstown figure, Babe Ruth, were the two stars in Boston that whole summer.

DR: At that time, no African Americans could play in Major League Baseball. But for Indians or Native Americans, there were no constraints on their playing?

DM: That's very true. It's interesting to look at the different ways that African Americans and Native Americans were treated in that era. There had consistently been Native American baseball players in a time when the color line was there. Jim Thorpe was treated differently around the country. He could go to the football club in Birmingham, Alabama, or Jackson, Mississippi, where the only African Americans let in were the waiters. They suffered in different ways. They were treated differently.

DR: While he's under contract for the New York Giants, he doesn't play that much. Does he play professional football at that time as well?

DM: He starts playing professional football in 1915 for the Canton Bulldogs in that Ohio League. He was by far the star of the league. The Canton Bulldogs won three so-called world championships in that era with Jim Thorpe.

DR: What kind of money would he get paid for that?

DM: Not much. The most he ever got was $300 a game.

DR: When the NFL starts, they asked Jim Thorpe to be the chairman of the league. Is that right?

DM: President of the league for the first year. It was a figurehead position. They wanted to look legitimate. Everybody knew Jim Thorpe. They made him the president. He didn't have any real duties, but he was the head of it.

DR: As all this is going on, he is getting married at some point. Who was his first wife?

DM: His first wife he had met at Carlisle. She was called a Cherokee princess in the press when they were married. It turned out that she discovered, a few years later, that she wasn't an Indian at all.

DR: She found out through a 23andMe test or what?

DM: It was a test of her older brother telling her that when she was young, her mother had died and her father in Oklahoma wanted to get rid of the kids, so he sent them to the Chilocco Indian school in Oklahoma and said they were Cherokee.

DR: Did they have children?

DM: First, tragically, they had Jim Thorpe Jr., who was the spitting image of his dad, if you can say that at age three. Jim Thorpe Jr. died during the 1918 flu pandemic. They went on to have three daughters.

DR: He gets divorced. Who was his second wife?

DM: His second wife, Freeda Kirkpatrick, worked as a secretary. There's a fabulous couple of years where Jim Thorpe is the player-coach for an NFL team called the Oorang Indians, based in La Rue, Ohio. Oorang was a form of Airedale dog, and the owner of the team had this great dog kennel and wanted to promote it, so he formed this team. He grew up loving the romanticism of American Indians, so he decided to have an all-Indian team. Freeda, Jim's second wife, was the secretary at his dog kennel.

DR: Thorpe has how many children with his second wife?

DM: She was only seventeen when they met, and he was in his thirties. They had four sons.

DR: How long does he play professional athletics? At what age does he say, "I just can't do this anymore"?

DM: His last game—you could say his last professional football game—he was forty years old. He played one game for the Chicago Cardinals. But he was forty-six when he played baseball for money for Harjo's Indians in Holdenville, Oklahoma. They traveled the whole country as a traveling troop, playing against all of the great Negro League teams of that era and others.

DR: When and how does he get his medals back?

DM: Long after he was dead. As his talents as an athlete were diminishing, he started to think more about his identity. He was focused on sports for a long time and on the injustice that had been done to him. He started pushing for it, as did his family and friends. But it never happened. He died in 1953. He was given partial restoration in 1983. Congress had been pushing. He had a lot of support in Congress and in the press. But Avery Brundage, that former teammate of his, would never allow it. By 1983, Brundage was dead, and the IOC, headed by Juan Antonio Samaranch, called Thorpe's family to Los Angeles before the 1984 Olympics and gave them replica medals. And that was it. His records were still not restored. When I was researching this book, you could look at the 1912 Olympic records officially, and Jim Thorpe's name wasn't even there. It wasn't until last summer [2022] that, finally, everything was restored.

DR: As a result of your book?

DM: No. I had nothing to do with it. It hadn't even been published yet. It was just a coincidence.

DR: He has this period of his time in his life after he's left athletics where he wants to be in the movies. Does he get parts as an extra to play Native Americans, and does he do anything to help other Native Americans get parts in movies?

DM: He ended up in the Los Angeles area in 1929 after being sort of an emcee of this crazy event called the Bunion Derby, where runners literally would run from New York to Los Angeles nonstop. Very *They Shoot Horses, Don't They?* era. That's how he ended up there and then decided he liked California. He was still famous, even though he was struggling, and he got to the edges of the studio industry. You can find him in more than seventy movies. He acted with everyone from Bob Hope and Bing Crosby on down. He was in a couple of the "Road to" movies. Sometimes they would say "featuring Jim Thorpe," and you could barely find him in the movie. They were just using his name. But it was one of the stronger periods of his life in the sense that he became the spokesperson for about 200 different Native people who were on the edges of that industry trying to get jobs. It was a period when westerns were incredibly popular, and the studios would be hiring white guys and painting them in war paint to play Indians. And Jim Thorpe said, "First of all, treat us with respect in these movies. And, second, if you're going to portray Native Americans, hire us. We're the real thing."

DR: Ultimately, there's a movie about him.

DM: *Jim Thorpe, All-American.*

DR: What year does that come out?

DM: It comes out in 1951, starring Burt Lancaster as Jim Thorpe. Lancaster was really a great athlete. He was an acrobat and a very sculpted guy and a movie star, obviously not an Indian. It was directed by Michael Curtiz, a famous director who had directed *Casablanca*. It was basically a sympathetic story, but it was wrong in every possible respect. It starts with Jim Thorpe running home in Oklahoma, and there's this mountain range in the background. It turns out it's the San Gabriel Mountains of California. He goes by a teepee. In the Sac and Fox Nation, they didn't use teepees. So, little things were wrong in the movie.

The main thing that was wrong with it, in my opinion, was that the hero of the movie is not Jim Thorpe, it's Pop Warner. He's the narrator, and it makes it look as though if only Thorpe had followed Warner's directions and more successfully ingratiated himself into white society, he would have had a better life. Now, that can be argued either way, but you can't argue with the fact that Pop Warner, at the moment of Jim's biggest crisis, turned his back on him.

DR: Jim Thorpe has a third wife, and she's a promoter of Jim Thorpe's career. Who was she, and how did that promotion turn out?

DM: Patsy Thorpe was a saloon singer, a heavy drinker like Jim. I have a little bit of sympathy for her because they were struggling together. They were dreamers together. She was manipulating things for him, but also for herself, and a lot of the money disappeared. Jim's children, none of whom were her children, thought that she was taking the money. Jim and Patsy traveled around the country. They opened a couple of taverns in Nevada and California, went down to Florida, tried to make it there. She was constantly promoting him in the press, and she vowed that she would turn him into a millionaire, which, of course, never happened.

DR: What year does he die?

DM: He dies in 1953, sixty-five years old.

DR: He's presumably going to be buried in Indian Territory?

DM: He had told his sons that he wanted to be buried on Sac and Fox land back in Oklahoma. After he died, a train took his casket back to Oklahoma. They were in the middle of a Sac and Fox burial ceremony when Patsy, his third wife, intervenes with a couple of thugs and takes the body away, unhappy about what Oklahoma is doing in terms of building a mausoleum to honor him. From then on, she basically tries to sell him to the highest bidder. His body is in Tulsa for a while. They don't really want him. Then she talks to Pittsburgh and Carlisle. It's an unbelievable story. But she was in Philadelphia and watching television and saw this story about these two down-on-their-luck coal towns near the Pocono Mountains, Machunk and East Machunk, Pennsylvania. They were trying to recover from losing the coal and from tourism. It's a beautiful area. And she came up with this concept. She went up to these two towns. I compare her to Harold Hill in *The Music Man*. She says, "If you two towns merge and change your name to Jim Thorpe, Pennsylvania, I will give you Jim Thorpe. You build a mausoleum for him. I'll also get a hospital built, Jim Thorpe Hospital, a teepee motel, a school named for Jim Thorpe." They were struggling and they bought into it, and they voted to merge, and to change their name to Jim Thorpe, Pennsylvania. His body is still there, a place that he never set foot in his entire life.

DR: Did any of those other things get built?

DM: No. Nothing else got built.

DR: Did his children come to the final burial?

DM: One of his daughters went. There was sort of a split in the family, as there often is after a death of a famous figure. The daughters and the sons had some disagreements about where his body should be. All of the sons fought vigilantly to get him back to Oklahoma, and they took it to court eventually. They won in the first court, and then the appeals court said no. His wife had the right to put him wherever she wanted, and it didn't fall under the Congressional Act, which helped repatriate bones and other artifacts. The appeals court overturned it and the Supreme Court didn't take it up. So basically, they lost.

DR: He's still there.

DM: It's on the side of a road as you cross the Lehigh Gorge. There's a nice granite tombstone and a few nice statues, but not much.

DR: After all this research and writing, did you come away admiring him more or pitying him more?

DM: I never pitied him. As I was writing the final chapters of the book, I was rooting for something better to happen, knowing that it couldn't. I tell one story in the book about how in 1915, the most popular statue in America was called *End of the Trail.* It showed an

Indian slumped on horseback, with a drooping horse. The connotation of that statue, which millions of people came to see, was that it was all over, that the Indian race was dying and would soon be dead. Before Europeans got here, there were millions of Native Americans. By that point in the early twentieth century, there were fewer than 300,000. But it didn't happen. The race did not die, and there are many different struggles, but there are now a few million Native Americans. The Native American community has adopted this book because of that concept that the life of Jim Thorpe is not a tragedy: It's an act of perseverance that he kept going.

DR: The title of your book is what, and what does it mean?

DM: The title of the book is *Path Lit by Lightning*. The night he was born, there was a thunderstorm over the North Canadian River. His mother named him Wa-tho-huk, the most poetic translation of which is "path lit by lightning."

10

Beverly Gage on J. Edgar Hoover

INTERVIEW DATE: NOVEMBER 29, 2023

We seem to be in an era of epic biographies. Perhaps the internet and other new technologies make research so easy that biographers feel compelled to write 600- to 800-page books. That is fine with me if the biographer is as skilled a writer as researcher. Unfortunately, that is not always the case.

But it definitely is the case with Beverly Gage, a Yale history professor who spent thirteen years researching and writing *G-Man: J. Edgar Hoover and the Making of the American Century*, which is certain to be the definitive biography on J. Edgar Hoover—the man who led the FBI for forty-eight years and, during that time, became one of the most powerful and feared figures in Washington. When I read the book, I thought it was a rare combination of extraordinary research and novel-like writing. I told the author that it should win the Pulitzer Prize—and it actually did, not long thereafter.

Hoover began to run the FBI in its infancy in 1924. With a tough mindset, laser focus, and an unmatched work ethic, he built the organization into one of the most respected and powerful (and feared) institutions in all of Washington.

He was particularly skilled at cultivating congressional leaders and presidents, many of whom were afraid of public disclosure by him of

FIGURE 10.1 J. Edgar Hoover headed the Federal Bureau of Investigation from 1924 (the year of this photograph) until his death in 1972, shaping the Bureau from a small division of the Justice Department into a law enforcement agency with tens of thousands of employees.

their personal failings and foibles. The result was an "untouchable" Hoover, who died in office at the age of seventy-seven (despite the fact that his good friend Richard Nixon had actually been trying to fire him for quite a while).

One of the great uncertainties about Hoover was his personal life. He never married, lived with his mother until her death, and seemed to have a close personal relationship with Clyde Tolson, his associate director and constant traveling companion. Although many suspected during Hoover's lifetime that he was gay, the interest in his personal life sprang to some extent from his strident efforts to have gay people removed from federal employment (at a time when just being gay was enough to lose one's federal job).

Professor Gage does not come to an incontrovertible conclusion about Hoover's personal life, but she does show with great skill how one man, over five decades, was able to build the premier crime-fighting organization in the country, while also gathering so much power that even US presidents feared him. This is a riveting story that certainly captured the attention of the Congressional Dialogues attendees, who all came to office after Hoover's death yet appeared captivated as Professor Gage recounted the life of this unique figure in twentieth-century American history.

DAVID M. RUBENSTEIN (DR): Why would somebody want to spend thirteen years of her life writing 800 pages about J. Edgar Hoover? Does he really deserve 800 pages and thirteen years of your life?

BEVERLY GAGE (BG): There were a few reasons. One is that J. Edgar Hoover, in our public culture, had become kind of a one-dimensional villain, and I thought there were some more interesting things to say about him. And then I was just stunned by the scope of his career. He was the head of the FBI from 1924 to 1972. That is Calvin Coolidge to Richard Nixon, this extraordinary period of time, so I thought he was a great vehicle for telling a big story about American politics.

DR: Let's talk about a couple of things that people always ask about him. Did he have so much political power because he had dossiers on everybody in Washington? Is that why everybody was afraid to fire him or criticize him?

BG: It is one of the reasons. He certainly liked to keep his files on people. But one of the things I wanted to do in the book was look at the many other sources of his power, which ranged from his incredible prowess with public relations to his relationships with congressional committees to his ability to please the White House and work with them.

DR: Let's start with the beginning of his life. Where was he born?

BG: He was born here in Washington, DC, just a few blocks away from where we are now. He's a creature of Washington. He's born here. He dies here. He never lives anywhere else.

DR: Was his father a wealthy private-equity person, or what did his father do?

BG: He might have wished that. They were few and far between at the time. No. His father was a government servant, and a pretty modest one.

DR: Did he have siblings?

BG: He had a couple of much older siblings, about fifteen years older, and then he had one sibling who was a few years older but who died when she was two years old.

DR: He went to public schools or Catholic schools?

BG: He was a product of the segregated Washington public school system.

DR: Was he a superstar student?

BG: He was, in fact, a superstar student. He was the valedictorian of his high school class at Central High School, the premier public high school in Washington.

DR: And where did he go to college?

BG: He also stayed in Washington for college and went to George Washington University.

DR: While he was at George Washington, what did he do to pay the tuition?

BG: He worked at the Library of Congress. This was his first job and, in many ways, it's where he learned to organize information.

DR: What was the hourly wage then?

BG: I don't actually remember, but it was not particularly high. He was very diligent in this, as in many other things. He worked at the Library by day, went to GW Law School at night.

DR: After he got his law degree, what did he do?

BG: He went straight to work for the government. He started at the Justice Department in 1917 and never left.

DR: How did he get the job? He had a law degree and just interviewed?

BG: He'd been pretty well connected through his fraternity in college, a fraternity called Kappa Alpha that had a lot of Southern Democrats in it. It was a Southern fraternity at that point. He was partly lucky in the timing. He graduated in the spring of 1917, as the US was entering World War I. They needed a lot of lawyers to figure out what was going on.

DR: What department did he go to work for in the Justice Department? Was there a separate FBI then?

BG: There was a little organization called the Bureau of Investigation then, but that's not where he went to work. He went to work at the Enemy Alien Bureau, and he worked on German internment and registration.

DR: Was he good at what he did?

BG: He was extremely good at what he did, and that was mostly paperwork and processing paper and judging who seemed to be dangerous. He got a big promotion after the war.

DR: Did he help get some people who were, let's say, socialists or other people sent out of the country?

BG: When he turned twenty-four in the year 1919, his first big promotion at the Justice Department was to head this little thing called the Radical Division, which was essentially the first peacetime experiment in policing Communists and anarchists and other left-wing revolutionaries.

DR: Did he personally escort some of them out of the country?

BG: As he loved to tell people for the rest of his life, he was, in many ways, at the age of twenty-four, personally responsible for the deportation of Emma Goldman, a famous anarchist of the early twentieth century.

DR: So, after he did that, was he involved in something called the Palmer Raids? What were the Palmer Raids?

BG: The Palmer Raids were deportation raids that were aimed at anarchists and at Communists. They were popular at first, and then they became extremely controversial for their violations of civil liberties. Hoover denied for much of his life that he was very involved in the Palmer Raids. But the truth is that, as a young man out of law school, he was a behind-the-scenes architect of them.

DR: He was doing this for a while. People thought he was good at getting people out of the country and so forth. What was his next job as he moved up in the Justice Department?

BG: He started out as more or less an entry-level employee. He became the head of the Radical Division when he was twenty-four. At the age of twenty-six, he became the assistant director of the Bureau of Investigation. Then, by the age of twenty-nine, he was the director of the Bureau, and he kept that job for the rest of his life.

DR: The Bureau of Investigation wasn't such a big deal then. What was its real job?

BG: The Bureau, in 1924, was an odd little organization. It had a few hundred agents. They had a weird grab bag of things—a little bit of interstate prostitution, a little bit of antitrust work, a little bit of interstate auto theft—but they weren't a big deal. In many ways, his appointment was nothing like what it means to appoint an FBI director now.

DR: In the 1930s, a number of people began to rob banks, and some of them used guns to hold up bank tellers. Was the FBI responsible for finding these robbers? How did the FBI get involved in that if their people didn't carry guns? FBI agents didn't have guns at that time?

BG: For Hoover's first decade as director, as this very young man, his vision was that he was going to hire a bunch of lawyers. He was going to hire a bunch of accountants. They were going to do white-collar work. But then, in the 1930s, you began to get a war on crime under Franklin Roosevelt. It's bank robbers. It's kidnappers. It's figures like the gangster John Dillinger. So, all these poor lawyers and accountants had to actually learn how to shoot guns and become real lawmen.

DR: John Dillinger was captured and killed when he was coming out of a theater in Chicago. He was shot by an FBI agent. Who actually shot Dillinger?

BG: The man in charge was a guy named Melvin Purvis.

DR: So, Purvis shot him, and that got an enormous amount of attention for the FBI, because it was an FBI agent who found John Dillinger and killed him. What did Hoover do? Did Hoover try to take credit for it? Did he take credit for something somebody else did? That would never happen in Washington, right?

BG: Never ever. Hoover ended up basically firing Melvin Purvis not too long after that. But it is that moment in the 1930s that the FBI becomes recognizable as what it is today. They began to really be a law enforcement agency. They began to carry weapons. And it's the moment that Hoover himself becomes a public celebrity. He had been a pretty obscure bureaucrat before.

DR: Did he carry a gun ever? Did he ever arrest anybody himself?

BG: That's one of the fascinating things about his life. There was a certain moment when I said to my editor that this book about J. Edgar Hoover is a book about bureaucracy and bureaucrats in the administrative state. She said, "Don't ever tell anyone that." But the truth is that Hoover was a bureaucrat. He wasn't an investigator and he wasn't a lawman. It's not clear that he himself really knew how to fire guns or investigate cases.

DR: He stays at the FBI through several Republican presidents—Warren Harding, Calvin Coolidge, and Herbert Hoover. He seemed to be simpatico with the Republican presidents. They seemed to like him. He liked them. Then FDR is elected president. Is J. Edgar Hoover worried that FDR, as a Democrat, might not like him? Did FDR care about J. Edgar Hoover, like him or not like him initially?

BG: One of the amazing things about Hoover's career is that he's there for eight presidents, from Coolidge to Nixon. Four of them are Democrats, four of them are Republicans: something that can be a little hard to imagine today. But he was very concerned about this transition when FDR came in. It turned out that Franklin Roosevelt really liked J. Edgar Hoover. In many ways, it is Roosevelt who does the most to make Hoover a celebrity, to empower the FBI. We really want to think of the FBI as a New Deal agency.

DR: When Pearl Harbor happened, did the FBI get blamed for not having picked up intelligence or for not having figured out this was going to happen? How did J. Edgar Hoover avoid getting blamed for that?

BG: J. Edgar Hoover turned out to be incredibly good at avoiding getting blamed for many things over the course of his career, which is one of the ways it lasted for so long. With Pearl Harbor, his case was that it was the military's fault: He didn't really have jurisdiction. He was extremely good at saying he had jurisdiction over things that he wanted to have jurisdiction over and that he didn't have any jurisdiction over things he didn't want to be involved in.

DR: Did he have jurisdiction over espionage matters? Espionage became, during World War II, a big matter for the government. There was no CIA then. Was the FBI in charge of our espionage?

BG: In the Roosevelt years, the FBI becomes this law enforcement agency. They carry guns. They go after bank robbers. The other thing that happens is that they become essentially our domestic intelligence agency. That's really born out of the Second World War and the crises around that. So, espionage, sabotage, countersubversion, all of those intelligence activities come out of the late 1930s and the 1940s.

DR: He seemed to have a special relationship with Latin America. He was in charge of all kinds of espionage and other activities there. Why Latin America?

BG: One of the really interesting things that happens in the Second World War is that Franklin Roosevelt looks around. He says, "Okay, we need wartime intelligence," and he sends the OSS, the Office of Strategic Services, sort of the precursor of the CIA, to look at the rest of the world, and he gives the FBI jurisdiction over the Western Hemisphere.

DR: Roosevelt dies. Truman becomes president. What is Truman's view of Hoover?

BG: Franklin Roosevelt liked J. Edgar Hoover. Harry Truman is a little more skeptical and, in fact, delivers to Hoover one of the biggest blows of his career. At the end of the war Hoover says, "We're going to need a peacetime intelligence agency that can look at the rest of the world, and we should do it all within the FBI." Truman says no. And we get the CIA instead.

DR: Hoover could go in to see Roosevelt almost any time, directly. Did Truman say "I want to see you" as much as Roosevelt did?

BG: Truman wanted lots of barriers between himself and Hoover. One of the really interesting things that comes out of that rift is that Hoover says, "Okay, if the White House isn't going to cooperate with me, I know who will." It's the moment that he turns to Congress and to congressional committees as one of his big sources of power.

DR: The House Un-American Activities Committee is set up around that time. Is he friendly with the key members there?

BG: Yes. There's this extraordinary thing that happens in the 1940s, which is that congressional committees begin to get professional staff. They get subpoena power. They get all sorts of new powers. Hoover was very smart about this. So, he began to staff the Appropriations Committee with FBI agents, because they were experienced investigators. Then these other committees, Judiciary, the House Un-American Activities Committee, the committees that really mattered to the FBI, a lot of their professional investigators were either former or current FBI agents.

DR: Julius and Ethel Rosenberg, husband and wife, were accused of giving our nuclear secrets to the Soviets. Was Hoover of the view that they were guilty of that and they should be hanged, that they should be executed as they were, or was he actually not thinking they should be executed?

BG: Hoover was one of the great anti-Communists of the '40s and '50s, I think even more important than Joe McCarthy. But when it comes to the Rosenbergs, it's a fascinating story. He had a lot of information that was not made public at the time, either in court or in the press, about the guilt of Julius Rosenberg in particular. That seems pretty clear. Hoover made the case that maybe Julius ought to be executed but that Ethel Rosenberg should not be executed. That's something we wouldn't necessarily think of Hoover saying. He didn't win that. They were both executed in the end.

DR: Eisenhower is elected president. Is he simpatico with Hoover, and is Hoover happy that Eisenhower is president?

BG: The Eisenhower years are Hoover's glory years in Washington. Eisenhower loves him. They're championing Hoover as the alternative to Joe McCarthy. Anti-Communism is a central issue at the time. Hoover even gets Eisenhower to join his church here in Washington, the National Presbyterian Church.

DR: A number of religious figures during the 1950s and '60s became very close to J. Edgar Hoover—Norman Vincent Peale, Bishop Fulton Sheen. Why did they like him and why did he like them so much?

BG: Hoover was a national security official. That was the primary, central feature of his job. But he was also this enormous cultural force. Hoover spent a lot of time lecturing people about how to raise their families, why they ought to send their kids to Sunday school. In the '50s in particular, he was one of the great advocates of public religiosity in the United States, and they saw a common interest there.

DR: In 1954, the Supreme Court issues the *Brown v. Board* decision. Was Hoover supportive of that, and did he want to make sure it got enforced? What was his view on racial issues? Were there any African American FBI agents in the early '50s?

BG: Hoover, as an individual, was pretty deeply racist from his very early years and through to the end. But there were many moments, particularly where federal civil rights law demanded that he enforce it, when he stepped up to the plate. So, in the '40s, he tried to enforce anti-lynching laws and conduct at least modest investigations. He wasn't super enthusiastic about *Brown*. But when the white South said, we're going to defy this federal court order, he actually did mobilize the FBI in some ways.

DR: It's in your book that the first Black FBI agent was his driver. In other words, Hoover had a driver, and he made him an FBI agent. Was that how he got a Black FBI agent?

BG: Right. Before Hoover came into the FBI, there were a handful of Black agents. Once he came in, that came to a pretty quick end. He wanted a certain kind of tall, attractive, suit-wearing white man to be an FBI agent. There's a reason that's who we think of. And so, he refused for most of his career to hire Black agents. But when he was under pressure in the '40s and '50s, he did send his chauffeur and a couple of his personal servants out to Quantico to be trained as agents. Then he brought them back, and they still essentially were his personal servants.

DR: President Eisenhower issues an executive order, No. 10450, which basically says that you can be fired for just being declared a homosexual without having to be caught doing any acts that are illegal. Did Hoover want to enforce that, or did he not pay attention to it?

BG: Hoover took it as his obligation to enforce that, I would say partly because of his own personal life and his own personal history. He was much more enthusiastic about supporting the anti-Communist end of things than the anti-gay end of things. But the FBI did mobilize in the '50s to investigate the sex lives of many government employees and help drive them out of office.

DR: You point out in your book it was called the Lavender Scare. If you were thought to be gay, you could be taken out of your job and arrested. You could lose your job because you were thought to be gay, without anybody ever having proven that you were or having caught you doing something that was considered inappropriate at that time.

BG: It was federal policy from the '40s through the late '60s that if you were a gay person, you could not be employed by the federal government. It was mostly a civil service process as opposed to a criminal process, but there were many gay people who were driven out of government service based on FBI investigations.

DR: When Eisenhower finally condemns McCarthy, where does J. Edgar Hoover come down? Does he support McCarthy or does he support Eisenhower?

BG: This was one of the most surprising things that I found while doing the book. Today we tend to think of Hoover and McCarthy, these big anti-Communist figures, as being sort of interchangeable. But at the time, both Hoover himself and the public had the perception that he was the anti-McCarthy. He was the much more institution-bound, rule-bound, law-bound version of anti-Communism. He saw McCarthy as someone he sympathized with but he also saw him as a demagogue, someone who stretched the truth. So, Eisenhower rejected McCarthy, and Hoover went along with Eisenhower.

DR: When Eisenhower leaves office, John F. Kennedy becomes president. Is Hoover happy to see Kennedy as president?

BG: Pretty quickly no. It wasn't totally clear that this was going to be as bad a relationship as it turned out to be, but these were, I think, the worst years of J. Edgar Hoover's career.

DR: Is that in part because he had to report to a thirty-five-year-old attorney general?

BG: That was a lot of it. John Kennedy becomes this young president, then he appoints his thirty-five-year-old brother, Robert, as attorney general. Hoover is in his mid-sixties. He's been around Washington forever at that point. Robert Kennedy comes in and they run into all sorts of cultural clashes, clashes of priority, and personality wars.

DR: Did Hoover tell Robert Kennedy there were reports that his brother was having an affair with a German spy? Did he ever tell him that?

BG: The German spy had been in the '40s, when John Kennedy was a young man. The main thing that Hoover came across when Kennedy was president was that one of John Kennedy's many girlfriends was also—

DR: Sam Giancana's girlfriend.

BG: Exactly. Sam Giancana was a leader in the Chicago mob. Hoover knew that. Hoover's method was to go to Senator or Congressman X or President Y and say, we found out this terrible and alarming thing about your private life and we just want you to know your secret's safe with us.

DR: Did Hoover actually spend much time with John Kennedy?

BG: They were not very close interpersonally. They had a variety of meetings about practical matters.

DR: Did Hoover know President Kennedy's father very well?

BG: He knew Joe Kennedy much better than he knew the Kennedy brothers. He still liked Joe Kennedy. They got along up until this moment in the early '60s.

DR: When President Kennedy is assassinated, Hoover calls Robert Kennedy. What does he say to him?

BG: It's a famous and pretty dark moment in American politics. Hoover is the one who calls Robert Kennedy to say that John Kennedy's been shot in Dallas, and he's very flat about it. He just says, "The president has been shot." He expresses very little sympathy. He's just kind of doing his duty. And, honestly, Robert Kennedy never forgives him for the coldness of that moment.

DR: Was Hoover worried that Lee Harvey Oswald was an FBI agent and that that might come out?

BG: There were rumors at the time. There was a news cycle around the idea, not that Lee Harvey Oswald had been an agent, but that he had been an informant. That doesn't actually seem to have been true, but it caused a lot of consternation at the Warren Commission and for Hoover.

DR: President Lyndon Johnson is close to Hoover? They were neighbors for a long time.

BG: It's one of these great Washington relationships, a bit of a counterintuitive Washington relationship. They were neighbors on the same block of 30th Place NW beginning in the '40s. So, by the time Johnson became president, they were quite close, even though they didn't always see eye to eye.

DR: Hoover is told by Johnson we need to have a commission headed by Earl Warren. Is Hoover happy with that, or did he say, "I already told you Lee Harvey Oswald did it and we don't need a commission"?

BG: The big problem with the Kennedy assassination was that Lee Harvey Oswald had been killed. So, you weren't going to get a trial. The question was, how are you going to figure out a way to convince the American public that it had been Lee Harvey Oswald? Hoover said, "We'll just say it and everyone will believe us." Johnson thought you needed something more substantive and produced the Warren Commission. So, Hoover was ambivalent about the Warren Commission.

DR: But the Warren Commission basically came out with the same conclusion that he had come out with, which is that Lee Harvey Oswald was the assassin?

BG: Correct. In the end, the Warren Commission mostly affirmed exactly what Hoover wanted, although any criticism of Hoover, which the Warren Commission also delivered, would put you on the blacklist pretty much forever.

DR: At what age did you have to retire from the federal government in those days?

BG: This was a big deal for Hoover's career. In an alternate universe, on January 1st, 1965, Hoover would have had to retire. That was his seventieth birthday, and that was the mandatory federal retirement age at the time. But Lyndon Johnson decided to exempt him from that, and so we got Hoover as FBI director for life.

DR: He kept that position, and then Nixon is elected. Nixon and Hoover have a very close relationship, going back to the Alger Hiss trials?

BG: That's right. One of the really interesting things about Hoover was his ability to have these close and cooperative relationships with people we think of as political opposites. So, he's close with Lyndon Johnson, cooperated on civil rights investigations as well as on surveillance of civil rights activists with him. Then Richard Nixon came along, and Hoover was closer to Nixon than he was even to Johnson.

DR: You mentioned civil rights surveillance. Hoover wanted to tap the phones of Martin Luther King Jr. Why did Robert Kennedy agree to allow him to do that?

BG: Honestly, I don't think Robert Kennedy had any resistance to that idea. We have an idea now that Robert Kennedy is the great civil rights hero and J. Edgar Hoover is the great civil rights villain. There's some truth to that later in the '60s. But during the Kennedy years, they were not as far apart as they might have seemed. A lot of my book is about how the FBI's surveillance of Martin Luther King escalated over time.

DR: When they did the surveillance of Martin Luther King and they found some salacious information, what did Hoover do with it?

BG: The King investigation starts out by looking at some Communist-affiliated officials near King. It expands, with Robert Kennedy's approval, to wiretaps on King and his associates. In 1964, they begin bugging King's hotel rooms at the Willard Hotel here in Washington and then throughout the country, and they find a lot of information about his sex life.

Hoover begins to peddle that around Washington. He goes to his allies in Congress. He goes to the press. Mostly, people don't want to touch this. Ultimately, the FBI ends up sending a reel of these tapes along with a threatening anonymous letter to King himself. One of my triumphs was finding the famous dirty-tricks letter that the FBI sent to Martin Luther King in late 1964. We had seen a redacted version of that, but I actually found the original version in the archives. That letter was the lowest point, I think, of the FBI's vendetta.

DR: Richard Nixon is close to Hoover for many years. Despite that, he says to his closest aides, "I want to fire J. Edgar Hoover." Why did he want to fire a man he liked so much?

BG: It's an amazing evolution that happens very quickly in the late '60s. Richard Nixon runs on a J. Edgar Hoover law-and-order platform in 1968. But then they get into all sorts of clashes when Nixon's in the White House. Nixon wants to politicize the FBI. He wants the FBI to do certain things that even J. Edgar Hoover doesn't want to do. And so, there's this famous moment in late 1971, when Nixon sits down with Hoover and says, "I think the moment has come, Edgar, for you to retire and step away." Hoover says, "No, I don't want to do that." And Nixon says, "Okay, never mind, forget I asked." And that's it.

DR: Eventually, Father Time does catch up with J. Edgar Hoover. He dies at what age?

BG: He dies in May of 1972 at the age of seventy-seven, still as FBI director. He dies with his boots on.

DR: As soon as he dies, who is told right away, the president of the United States or somebody at the FBI? And what happens to the secret files that Hoover supposedly has?

BG: In some ways, this is a moment that lots of people have been waiting for and preparing for. In other ways, it's this big surprise that the old man has died. But word gets up to the White House and throughout Washington very quickly, and people try to get his files. Some of them end up destroyed by his secretary, Helen Gandy, and others end up preserved.

DR: When Hoover dies, how was he honored? There's a big state funeral for him?

BG: It is a huge event in Washington. He's been director of the FBI for forty-eight years by the time that he dies. Richard Nixon gives the eulogy at the National Presbyterian Church. Hoover lies in state at the Capitol, the first civil servant ever to lie in state there, and it's broadcast on all three networks. Many people say they cannot remember a Washington that did not have J. Edgar Hoover.

DR: Where is he buried?

BG: He is buried not far from here, in Congressional Cemetery.

DR: He had presumably wanted one of his deputies to become the next FBI director. Who ultimately is picked by President Nixon for that position?

BG: This is one of those fascinating moments of potential counterhistory. Hoover dies in May of 1972. Richard Nixon, rather than picking one of the many FBI officials who have been waiting for decades for J. Edgar Hoover to die or step aside, picks Pat Gray out of the Justice Department instead. That produces a lot of resentment at the FBI, including from a man named Mark Felt, who had been the number three figure at the FBI. The Watergate burglary happens in June of 1972, just about a month after Hoover dies.

DR: Mark Felt later becomes known as Deep Throat.

BG: Mark Felt becomes Deep Throat, exactly.

DR: So, let's talk about, for a moment, the personal life of J. Edgar Hoover. Did he ever marry?

BG: He did not marry. The closest relationship of his life was with Clyde Tolson, who was his number two man at the FBI and was also essentially his life partner, his social partner.

DR: They would travel to nightclubs in New York. For some reason, the FBI director liked going to nightclubs, often owned by criminal elements. They would go to Florida. They would go to Palm Springs and vacation for weeks at a time. They would come to parties together, and they were invited as a couple. Did anybody ever say, "Your lifestyle is inconsistent with what you're supposed to be doing, arresting people who do these kinds of things"?

BG: One of the most interesting things to me in resurrecting and reconstructing Hoover's life was how open and public this relationship with Tolson was, particularly in DC, in New York, in LA, the places they spent a lot of time. If you were going to invite Edgar to dinner, you were also going to invite Clyde. They were this very public couple. But at the same time, of course, the exact nature of their relationship tended to go unstated. There were rumors and suggestions that they were a gay couple. I think they did care about each other deeply and intimately.

DR: Did J. Edgar Hoover ever live with Tolson, or they lived separately in Washington?

BG: They lived separately until there was a moment when Tolson was quite ill, toward the end of Hoover's life, and he did move in.

DR: Hoover lived with his mother until he was forty-three, and then he moved out?

BG: It's true. Hoover only lived in two places, both of them in Washington. One was in Seward Square. He lived there with his mother till he was forty-three, and she died. Then he moved to his house on 30th Place.

DR: After you've spent thirteen years of your life on this book, is it your view that J. Edgar Hoover was a plus for America or a minus for America?

BG: In the end, I am not a great Hoover admirer, though I spent a lot of time with him and I think that I know him and understand him very well. Most of why I come down on that side of the ledger is because of what he did to delegitimatize political and social movements that he didn't agree with, the civil rights movement above all. But because J. Edgar Hoover in our world is such a one-dimensional villain, I do think that my book is much fairer to him and tries to point out a lot of the things that he did right in his career. So, I'd say I'm still pretty anti-Hoover, but I hope the book is balanced.

DR: Are you planning to spend another thirteen years on somebody else?

BG: My next book is going to be a much shorter book. I have been traveling the United States. I'm calling it a road trip through US history to look at how people are thinking about history from the ground up and to take on the question of whether we have a single national narrative. So, that's a shorter book. [*This Land Is Your Land: A Road Trip Through U.S. History* was published in April 2026.] Then I am going to take on another towering political figure of the twentieth century, Ronald Reagan, who, to me, is sort of a sequel to Hoover in certain ways. Hoover on the question of anti-Communism got me to the early '70s, but Reagan's going to get me to the end of the Cold War.

11

Evan Thomas on Sandra Day O'Connor

INTERVIEW DATE: OCTOBER 22, 2019

One hundred and five men served on the US Supreme Court before the first woman was appointed by President Ronald Reagan in 1981. At the time, the novelty of a woman serving in this traditionally male bastion captured the public's attention. Could any woman survive the intense scrutiny that the first female Justice would inevitably get in the confirmation process, not to mention service on the Court?

There is no doubt that Sandra Day O'Connor could, and her twenty-five years on the Court showed to all that women could fill the role of Justice as well as, if not better than, any man could.

There are currently four women on the Court, but those who did not live through the O'Connor nomination may not fully appreciate how just intensely she was evaluated at the time. It was certainly an interesting choice. She was not a federal district or appeals court judge, and she was not even on the highest state court in Arizona.

But O'Connor had the qualities that Reagan was seeking—a first-rate legal mind (she was near the top of her class at Stanford Law School); an understanding of politics (she was the Arizona Senate majority leader); a love of the West and the outdoors (she was raised on a ranch in Arizona and was a skilled horse rider); and a likeable

FIGURE 11.1 Nominated by Ronald Reagan in 1981, Sandra Day O'Connor became the first woman to serve on the United States Supreme Court. She served as the swing vote on 330 cases during her twenty-five years as Associate Justice.

personality with a solid conservative background (Senator Barry Goldwater had initially recommended her to Reagan). As a Justice, O'Connor became renowned for her ability to develop compromises that could lead to majority decisions, and her rapport with fellow Justices was likely unmatched during her tenure on the Court.

Justice O'Connor chose not to write an autobiography, but she made her clerks, family, colleagues, and friends available to Evan Thomas, a former editor of *Newsweek* and biographer of other leading figures such as Edward Bennett Williams, Robert Kennedy, and Richard Nixon. Thomas's access to Justice O'Connor's papers led to a discovery unknown to anyone in her family or to the public: A young Bill Rehnquist, a Stanford Law classmate, had actually proposed marriage to Sandy Day. The fact that they had dated was generally known, but the fact that the relationship led to a marriage proposal was news to everyone. (At the time of this revelation, both Rehnquist and O'Connor had passed away.)

This interview with Evan Thomas—the author of *First: Sandra Day O'Connor*, and the grandson of Norman Thomas, a famed Socialist candidate for president who had run multiple times—showed why O'Connor was so universally respected and beloved: her engaging personality, low ego, an ability to get along well with liberals and conservatives, and someone who, with her husband, John, was willing to engage in Washington society (a rarity for most Justices).

DAVID M. RUBENSTEIN (DR): There have already been books written about Sandra Day O'Connor. Why did you think the world needed another book?

EVAN THOMAS (ET): She's a great lady. She was the first woman on the Supreme Court. But the real reason is because her family came to me and asked me to do it, and gave me access to her papers and to her and to the family. If you're writing about a Supreme Court Justice, it really helps to have inside access, because it's all private.

DR: Had you ever met her before? Did you know her?

ET: Yes. I knew her a little bit around Washington. I was a little intimidated by her. She has a certain steely glare that she would direct to journalists. I had been approached to be her possible ghostwriter for memoirs. I spent a day with her, and I could tell that she didn't really want to do her memoirs, that she wanted to be famous and remembered, but she is a very private person, and she didn't want to spill the beans herself.

DR: She gave you complete access to the family papers.

ET: Yes.

DR: Was it a surprise that she said you could look at anything?

ET: She's a practical person. She understood that no biographer's going to do this unless you open up.

DR: But they also give you access to her doctors and her husband's doctors. Wasn't that surprising that this much detail was available to you?

ET: I learned a long time ago from Walter Isaacson, just ask. Just ask and you might get it.

DR: I should point out you did the research with a partner.

ET: My wife, Oscie, was in many ways a coauthor of this book, equally involved. We met in law school, and she actually practiced law, unlike me.

DR: How many years did it take you to do the research?

ET: Three years.

DR: And the writing?

ET: About six months. But then there's a lot of rewriting.

DR: After doing all this work, do you admire Sandra Day O'Connor more than you did before? Or she's not quite as good as you thought she was?

ET: I definitely admire her more. Before the book, I found her to be a little standoffish, a little stiff. Her reputation among academics was not all that great. I did it not because I had any love for her, but because I was offered all this access to her and because she was a famous figure. I learned from doing this what a wonderful human being she was, in subtle ways, just what an unbelievable woman she was.

DR: What is the main message you want to give people in this book?

ET: Sandra Day O'Connor was a pragmatist, and she got a lot done by being a pragmatist. She was the swing vote, the decisive vote, 330 times in twenty-five years. She held the power at the center, and she was very shrewd about using it. She had been the first woman Republican majority leader of a state senate. She was head of the Maricopa County Republicans in Arizona at one point. She was bipartisan and knew how to work both sides.

DR: When the family gave you access to their papers, did they realize that you were going to discover something that the children didn't even know?

ET: No. Oscie and I were looking for her love letters with John [O'Connor, her husband]. We knew theirs was a great marriage. We had access to her papers here at the Library of Congress, a fantastic collection, but no love letters. We were sure there were some. We went over to her chambers at the Supreme Court, and her longtime secretary took us down to a storage locker, and there was a box marked "Correspondence." We said, "What's that?" We asked permission from the family. They had not looked in there. We found lots of love letters between John and Sandra, but also fourteen love letters from Bill Rehnquist to Sandra Day.

DR: Did you also find a marriage proposal in there from Rehnquist?

ET: Letter number seven, I think it was. "Will you marry me, Sandy?" I gave a little undignified yelp when I read that.

DR: It was well known that they had dated a few times when they were classmates in law school. The letter kind of said, "I'm at the Supreme Court now. I haven't seen you in a couple of months, dear Sandy, how about getting married?"

ET: Yes. He had left Stanford to be a Supreme Court clerk for Justice Robert Jackson. He was lonely. He had had a romance with her first year. She had dumped him. The sparks were renewed partly by loneliness, and so he'd write these beseeching letters to her. She strung him along for a couple of months.

DR: She didn't like his sideburns? What was it?

ET: She liked John better. But John wasn't asking her to marry him.

DR: Let's talk about how she grew up and became a Supreme Court Justice. I read that she grew up on a 180,000-acre ranch, which I thought meant one of those fancy ranches, like the King Ranch. But it wasn't quite that?

ET: It was dusty, bleak, barren, but beautiful. Oscie and I went there. Sandra was born in a house with no running water, no electricity. A very harsh existence.

DR: Her father had inherited this ranch?

ET: They owned it but they leased most of it from the federal government. They could support maybe 2,000 cows on 160,000 acres, and during the Depression they almost lost it.

DR: How close was a paved road?

ET: It was eight miles from the road to the house. Headquarters, it was called.

DR: And who was her father? Just a rancher?

ET: She said it was like living in her own country. He was a forceful figure, because he was the king of this domain. He loved her. He was an adoring father, but a tough guy.

DR: And her mother?

ET: She was a very elegant woman. Sandra's father was a great role model, but she learned a lot from watching her mother, because her mother had to put up with her father. Her father, after having a drink or two in the evening, would be a bully. Mrs. Day was not cowed. She wasn't submissive. But on the other hand, she did not get into stupid fights with him. She knew when to stand up and when not to. It was incredibly important to learn this lesson for Sandra Day, who spent a life dealing with obnoxious males.

DR: If you're a little girl growing up on this ranch, where do you go to school?

ET: They homeschooled her for a little bit, but she was obviously very bright. The local schools, local meaning thirty miles away, were terrible, so they sent her to live with her grandmother in El Paso, a four-hour train ride. Very tough for a little girl. She was really homesick.

DR: Did she stay there with her grandmother?

ET: She did, from six years old through high school.

DR: When she would come back in the summers, did she learn how to ride a horse?

ET: Oh, yes. She was in the roundups. She could hold her own in the canyons. She was a real cowgirl. She would come back for vacations, and she was there maybe a third of the year.

DR: Where did she go to high school?

ET: To the local high school, Austin High. She did not love the local high school. She was an outsider, this kind of dusty ranch girl.

DR: Eventually her father wants her to go to college at Stanford. Why Stanford?

ET: He was scheduled to go to Stanford himself. He grew up in California and his family owned the ranch in Arizona. His father died, and the ranch was failing. As an eighteen-year-old, Mr. Day was sent out there. He was supposed to go to Stanford that fall. He never left the ranch. He stayed on the ranch for the rest of his life.

DR: And never went to college?

ET: He never went to college. But he always wished that he had gone to Stanford.

DR: Was it hard to get into Stanford?

ET: Not then.

DR: She just got in? She didn't say she was on the crew team or a rower or anything like that?

ET: No.

DR: Her father drove her all the way to Stanford?

ET: Yes.

DR: He drops her off. She studies economics? Or what did she study?

ET: Yes. What she really studied was a course called Western Civilization that captured her. We were talking to her first boyfriend, Andy Campbell, who's still in love with her, and he said, "She loved Western Civ more than me."

This course is no longer taught because it's considered to be too patriarchal and hegemonic and all that, but it taught her about the rule of law. We read her final exam written as a seventeen-year-old. It's an exegesis on Jefferson and Madison. Absolutely brilliant, and obviously a foundation for her for the rest of her life.

DR: During the summers while she was at Stanford, did she go back to the ranch?

ET: She did. Taking her various boyfriends.

DR: Did her father like any of the boyfriends?

ET: No. He tested them. He would give them a roasted bull's testicle to eat.

DR: Did they just walk away?

ET: The smart ones ate it.

DR: She did pretty well. She graduated magna cum laude?

ET: Yes. She was a very good student.

DR: Why did she decide to go to law school?

ET: That's a little fuzzy. The law was so male. She didn't have a clear idea of being a lawyer. But she'd had a professor who thought that lawyers could lead. I think a quarter of the US Senate are lawyers. It was a way to be a leader. It was a way to have a better life.

DR: So, she goes to law school. And William Rehnquist is in her class?

ET: Yes.

DR: She's one of two or three women in the entire Stanford Law School class?

ET: There were five. Two dropped out.

DR: So, three are left. She is on the law review, which means she's one of the better students?

ET: Yes.

DR: She's the only woman on the law review?

ET: There's one other.

DR: She meets William Rehnquist. They had some dates, but a date in those days was not quite what a date is today?

ET: They went to the movies.

DR: Just to the movies, okay. She graduates in two years?

ET: Three years in college, three years in law school. She was sixteen when she went to college, so she's twenty-two when she graduates from law school.

DR: She graduates from law school near the top of her class?

ET: Yes. Order of the Coif.

DR: Order of the Coif means in the top 10 percent of her class.

ET: Yes.

DR: I assume she could get a Supreme Court clerkship or a lot of good jobs?

ET: In 1952 she applies to forty law firms in San Francisco and Los Angeles, and gets one interview at Gibson, Dunn, and Crutcher, where the hiring lawyer asked her, "How well do you type?"

DR: Did she get a secretarial job there?

ET: No. She said, "So-so." She went to the local DA and said, "I want to work for you." He said, "I don't have any money." She said, "I'll work for free." He said, "I don't have any space." She said, "I'll work off your secretary's desk." And she did. He eventually hired her. Interestingly, she was never bitter about this, ever. She said, "No room in the private sector for me, I'll go to the public sector."

DR: Around this time, after she graduates, she marries John O'Connor?

ET: Yes.

DR: Where was he from? Was he a poor boy, or was he wealthy?

ET: He was the son of a doctor in San Francisco and a socially ambitious mother.

DR: Was she happy that Sandra Day was her daughter-in-law?

ET: The mom was very unhappy and tried to stop the marriage.

DR: I've never heard of a parent doing that. So, they get married. Why was she so in love with John O'Connor? Did you get that out of the materials you read?

ET: He made her laugh. He was very different from her father, too. Her father was this dominating force, and John was supportive and funny and sweet.

DR: He then gets drafted and goes into the military. He is sent to Germany, and she goes over with him. What does she do in Germany?

ET: She gets a procurement job with the government. She finally gets promoted to GS something and she says, "I should have had that position a long time ago."

DR: After he finishes his military tour, they decide to move back to the United States. Why did they pick Phoenix as a place to go?

ET: Instead of going to San Francisco, which was ingrown and where they'd have to deal with his mom, they go to Phoenix, which is booming and a brand-new opportunity. And it was that. It was a land of opportunity.

DR: Her classmate and former good friend Bill Rehnquist is there also?

ET: He also moves there, yes. No romance.

DR: When she moves there, does she practice law right away? What does she do?

ET: She hangs her shingle in a shopping center with another lawyer and takes whatever walks in the door. She does that for a couple of years. Meanwhile John, who had worse grades, gets a job at the best law firm.

DR: Over a few years they have three sons?

ET: Yes.

DR: And she's still practicing law. She eventually becomes a government employee?

ET: She becomes assistant attorney general through her political connections. She and John are very active in the Republican Party in Maricopa County.

DR: She becomes an assistant state attorney general. She's prosecuting people. How did she get into the state legislature?

ET: She's appointed to fill a vacancy. There weren't too many women in the Arizona legislature—five, I think, in the Senate. She filled a term and then ran.

DR: She gets elected and she becomes majority leader in the state senate. She was the first woman in our country's history to be the state majority leader in a state senate?

ET: Yes.

DR: How did she manage to pull that off? Was she intimidated by all the men in the state senate?

ET: She was smarter than them. That's how she got the job. She was orderly and smart and shrewd. And, importantly, she knew when to stand up. There was a lot of tomfoolery in the Arizona legislature in 1972. The story I like to tell is that when she was majority leader, to get the budget passed she had to go through a guy named Tom Goodwin, who was the House Appropriations Committee chairman. He was a drunk, a drunk-by-10-a.m. drunk, and she finally called him on his drinking. He looked at her and he said, "If you were a man, I'd punch you in the nose." And she said, "If you were a man, you could." I like to tell that story, but actually it's a one-off. The real point is how rarely she did something like that. Far more often, instead of getting into a stupid fight, she walked away.

DR: She's the state senate majority leader, and then all of a sudden she leaves to become a mid-level or low-level judge. Why did she do that?

ET: She got tired of the politics. Trading sewer culverts for votes and all that was really not her style. She did it, but she didn't love doing it. She was more cerebral, if you will, and wanted to be a judge. She had to run for it. The merit system was just coming in, but she ran for it once and then won.

DR: That was at the Superior Court level.

ET: Yes. Trial court.

DR: How did she get to the next level, the Arizona Court of Appeals? How did she get that job?

ET: The rumor was that Bruce Babbitt, the governor, put her on the court so that she would not run against him for governor. He denies that story, but not too convincingly.

DR: So, she gets on the Court of Appeals. That's not a federal court of appeals, and it's not even the Supreme Court of Arizona. It's a mid-level court.

ET: Yes.

DR: She's on that court for how many years?

ET: Four.

DR: Four years. Then Ronald Reagan is running for president, and he says he's going to appoint a woman to the Supreme Court. Did he really intend to, or he just thought it would be a good idea to say that?

ET: It was a political promise. He was down by ten points with women in Illinois in October 1980, and a political advisor said, "Do something." His staff didn't think he was serious. In fact, after he won, the Justice Department expectation was that they would appoint a conservative, Robert Bork. They thought they were going to appoint him to help roll back the liberalism of the Warren Court. The staff was surprised when the attorney general came in and said, "No. Reagan is serious, he means it, we've got to find a woman."

DR: There were many women on the US Courts of Appeals?

ET: No. Of the 600 federal judges in 1981, there were eight women, almost all liberal Democrats. Cornelia Kennedy was the only conservative Republican woman on the US Court of Appeals.

Amazingly, in a way, there was no contest. They did interview Cornelia Kennedy, but really it was Sandra Day O'Connor's to lose all the way. She had friends in court. Rehnquist, her old boyfriend, secretly lobbied for her. Chief Justice Warren Burger, whom she charmed on a houseboat on Lake Powell, was lobbying for her. Barry Goldwater was lobbying for her. She had some friends.

DR: The attorney general is William French Smith, who was previously a partner at Gibson, Dunn, the firm that had offered her a secretarial job?

ET: Right. The attorney general, the former Gibson, Dunn partner, calls her at her office in Phoenix. He gets on the phone to ask her to come to Washington to talk to the president of the United States about being a Justice on the US Supreme Court. And she got on the phone and said, "You wouldn't be calling me about secretarial work."

DR: She comes to Washington. She wasn't that well known. Did she sneak into Washington or she didn't have to sneak in?

ET: She didn't have to sneak in. She was very sociable and had a lot of friends.

DR: She had a meeting with Reagan?

ET: She did. Interestingly, we have her diary, and the issue was abortion. She had voted to decriminalize abortion as a state legislator. The Moral Majority got wind of this, and Senator Jesse Helms and Senator John East and some others started agitating: "Hey, you can't confirm her or nominate her." She was anxious about this, of course. In her interview with Reagan, the president said to her, "I know there's a controversy about when life begins. I'd like to give the benefit of the doubt to it." He didn't ask her a question; he made a statement. He intentionally did not ask her. She sighed with relief, because she didn't want to get into it with him. I don't think he really wanted to know, because he didn't want to have a big fight over abortion in the first year of his presidency.

DR: After the meeting she goes back to Arizona?

ET: She does, yes.

DR: When does she hear, and who tells her she's going to be nominated?

ET: The president calls her a few days later. She guesses that she's going to get nominated. Her husband certainly thinks it's going to happen.

DR: How did they get her back to Washington and avoid everybody knowing about it before the announcement?

ET: They didn't. She was in Phoenix. President Reagan called her by phone in her chambers.

DR: What was the reaction in Congress to her generally?

ET: There were some demonstrations. But she made it her business to go see everyone, and she charmed them. She made a friend of Strom Thurmond, chairman of the Senate Judiciary Committee. She charmed up Jesse Helms. And by the time she was done, she was confirmed ninety-nine to nothing.

DR: Who was the other vote?

ET: It was Max Baucus, who was in Montana. But he would have voted for her.

DR: She was not a constitutional law scholar. She was on a mid-level court in Arizona, only state law. How did she get ready for the questions about constitutional law?

ET: She studied like hell. She lost ten pounds that summer learning the Constitution. Interestingly, her helper on this was a young Justice Department aide whose name was John Roberts. Oscie and I went to see Chief Justice Roberts in his chambers. Sandra Day O'Connor was frustrated with him because he couldn't keep up. She was learning so fast he couldn't send things fast enough to Phoenix. The Chief Justice said that in those days it was just Xerox machines, and he just couldn't Xerox fast enough to keep up with her.

DR: She's confirmed 99–0. Is she sworn in at the White House in a big ceremony?

ET: She's sworn in twice: at the White House and then in an investiture at the Court.

DR: Once she gets on the Court, presumably Rehnquist, her former good friend and supporter, would say, "Okay, Sandy, baby, here we are together again." Was she worried about that? Did he even talk to her when she got on the Court?

ET: The day that she came on the bench for the first time, Justice Harry Blackmun leaned over to Justice Rehnquist and said, "Now no fooling around." She was taken aback because Rehnquist, who had been her great friend, was cool toward her. He did not help her much. And she complained to her friends that he was not helping her.

DR: What about the Chief Justice, Warren Burger? Was he very nice? He had tried to get her on the Court.

ET: Yes, he was warm with her, but he could be patronizing. He paraded her down the front steps of the Supreme Court to the photographers saying, "Have you ever seen me with a better-looking Justice?" Then he sent her a memo—this is the era—he sent her a memo about a psychological study on what happens when a woman comes into a room of powerful men and the impact of that. The psychologist had concluded that it can be disruptive to the men, and therefore the woman should be submissive.

DR: Who was the Justice who most befriended her?

ET: Justice Lewis Powell, a courtly, gentlemanly Virginian. Sandra and John were great dancers, and Powell liked to dance with her. More importantly, he got her a secretary who knew what she was doing.

DR: Now Justice Harry Blackmun was a bit afraid that she might overturn his handiwork?

ET: Right. Justice Blackmun wrote *Roe v. Wade*, the famous 1973 abortion decision. He thought as a Reagan appointee that she was going to cast a vote against it. And he was very gloomy about that.

DR: When she got on the Court, when did she realize that she could keep up intellectually with these guys?

ET: Pretty quickly. We had her husband's diary. She was nervous. But after about a year, she said, "I'm not Oliver Wendell Holmes, but I can hold my own with these guys." After two years, she liked the end-of-term five-to-four decisions. She liked all that. She was good at it. She told her husband, "I feel like I'm in the catbird seat."

DR: Did she start getting the Justices together by having them actually go to a lunch they were supposed to go to?

ET: The Justices of the Court have lunch together once or twice a week. At her first lunch, only four other Justices showed up. They're appointed for life, but they don't necessarily like each other or have to like each other. It was a chilly place when she got there. She thought this was bad, and she made it her business to go to their chambers and make them come to lunch. By the '90s they were all coming to lunch.

DR: What did she do to improve her health? Was she exercising at the Court?

ET: She started an aerobics class at 8 a.m. Her female clerks were required to come to it.

DR: None of the men were required to go?

ET: No, although she cared about them being in shape. One of her clerks told us that he was eating an ice cream cone and she came around the corner and he put it in the drawer.

DR: How many clerks did she have?

ET: For each year, four clerks.

DR: How many were there in total?

ET: I think there were 108.

DR: And how many did you interview?

ET: Ninety-four.

DR: Did any of them say, "She's really not that great, and let me tell you why"? Or they all really thought she was great?

ET: There were some who disagreed with her on philosophical grounds. They all admired her as a person.

DR: She was not a Justice who wanted to write legal opinions that the law professors would like. She didn't write sweeping principles. She liked to decide things on as narrow ground as possible?

ET: Yes. Case by case, narrowly, very fact-based. She did not like sweeping rhetoric. She worried about unintended consequences of her decisions.

DR: In abortion cases, she never actually voted to overturn *Roe v. Wade*?

ET: No.

DR: Did she try to walk her way through that minefield?

ET: She found a compromise that preserved abortion rights by switching to having the standard say that the states could put restrictions on abortion, but they could not place an undue burden on a woman's abortion rights.

DR: One of the areas she spent a lot of time writing opinions on was affirmative action, particularly with respect to school and university admissions. Where does she come out on that ultimately?

ET: She was torn by that. She didn't love affirmative action, often voted against it. But on higher education she was the decisive vote to preserve it. She didn't like identity group politics. She didn't like identity groups generally. She was an integrationist. She liked the melting pot. But she upheld the racial preference in admissions at the University of Michigan Law School, again being very practical. She noticed that in California there was a referendum to do away with affirmative action, and the number of African Americans at UCLA and Berkeley Law School dipped to about 1 percent right away. She thought law schools are training grounds for leaders. This is where I got the statistic that one out of four US senators are lawyers.

DR: Her clerks had a Xerox copy of her hand. What was that about?

ET: She was not big on handing out gratuitous praise, and your average Supreme Court clerk is used to being praised. They're all editor of the law review and all that. They come to her chambers, and it's the ranch. She might say, "Oh, that's all right then." So, the clerks took a Xerox of her hand and put it on the wall underneath a sign that said, "If you want a pat on the back, lean here." She was in on the joke.

DR: She was involved in the famous *Bush v. Gore* case. She was one of the five majority votes. Was she happy with that decision? How did she write the opinion or modify it so that it wouldn't have any precedential impact?

ET: It was a one-time-only precedent, which the law reviews tore her up for. She was not a person who had regrets, but on this case she did have some regrets that the Court took the case. She told me, "I have regrets, but regrets don't do you any good."

DR: Some people say, and you address this in your book, that she had wanted to step down when a Republican was president, and if Gore had been elected, then she probably couldn't step down. Was that a factor?

ET: It's complicated. She had been thinking about retiring as early as 1996, which was during the Clinton era. So, she doesn't want to retire. She and her husband were thinking about her stepping down, because John had Alzheimer's and it was getting worse.

DR: *Bush v. Gore* was decided, and she stayed on the Court. At some point her husband's Alzheimer's became so severe that she had to bring him to the Court every day with her?

ET: Yes. And he couldn't sleep. They slept in the same bed, so if he couldn't sleep, she couldn't sleep.

DR: The result is that she eventually concludes that she needs to support him, step down, and help him with his Alzheimer's.

ET: She was explicit about it. She said, "He sacrificed for me. He was the big man in Phoenix, in Washington not so much. Now I'm going to sacrifice for him."

DR: She goes to Chief Justice Rehnquist and says, "I don't think both of us should step down right now. You have some illness. Are you thinking of stepping down?" What does Rehnquist say to his former girlfriend?

ET: They go back and forth and back and forth. Finally, he says, "I'm going to stay," and she says, "Okay, I'm going to leave."

DR: She tells the president of the United States that she will step down upon the confirmation of her successor?

ET: That was a drawn-out process, but yes.

DR: A week or two after she announces that she's going to step down, Chief Justice Rehnquist dies.

ET: It's a couple of months. He dies in September. What you're getting at is she wondered if Justice Rehnquist had been entirely forthcoming with her about the nature or the seriousness of his disease.

DR: When she agreed to step down, eventually the president decides to appoint her former advisor John Roberts.

ET: She was happy with that. She would have preferred a woman, but she was happy about that.

DR: When Rehnquist dies, what happens with Roberts?

ET: Roberts becomes Chief Justice, and now there's still a vacancy. The Bush administration nominated Harriet Miers, White House counsel, and it fizzled out.

DR: Eventually Samuel Alito was appointed. Was she happy with that, or she didn't comment?

ET: No. Not happy with Justice Alito. She was somebody who never spoke ill of anybody, ever, with the exception of Justice Alito. She was unhappy about her replacement.

DR: She steps down. She goes back to Arizona to take care of her husband. But what happens with her husband's health when she's there with him?

ET: Her husband, as can happen with Alzheimer's patients, forms what's called a mistaken attachment. He's in a nursing facility. He doesn't recognize her anymore. And he has, not a real girlfriend, but somebody he's holding hands with, Kay, her name was. The way Sandra dealt with this is she would come to the nursing home and she'd hold John's other hand.

DR: Her husband ultimately passes away. What does she decide to do? She's freed of having to take care of her husband. What does she decide to get involved with?

ET: She's very interested in a couple things. Judicial independence, she does a lot for that, but also civics. She felt that kids don't study civics anymore and they don't know any civics. She was really alarmed about this and, more broadly, the whole idea of the deterioration of a civil society. She starts an organization called iCivics to use video games to teach middle schoolers how a bill passes Congress and how government works.

DR: She's doing that. Eventually, she begins to realize she has some health problems as well?

ET: She got dementia. She dreaded it. Her mother had had it. Her aunt had had it. She denied it for a long time but finally was diagnosed in 2014 with dementia, probably Alzheimer's.

DR: When you interviewed her, were you able to get much out of her? You interviewed her in about 2016.

ET: Yes. She was hobbled by it, you could tell. Truthfully, I wasn't going to get that much out of her anyways. She's a very discreet person. I didn't talk to her so much about the cases. A little bit about *Bush v. Gore* and some others. But mostly I talked to her about growing up in the ranch, about her married life, and her family life.

DR: What would you say she would want her great legacy to be in history?

ET: The first woman on the Court, for sure. She was religious. She read at the National Cathedral. But her real religion was a kind of civic religion, a belief that the government can do good, that limited government can do good, that people need to work together, and that we have an obligation to be civil with each other. She believed that heart and soul.

12

Admiral William H. McRaven on the Hunt for Osama bin Laden

INTERVIEW DATE: DECEMBER 7, 2022

Admiral William H. McRaven was the US military officer who oversaw and led the effort to capture (or kill) Osama bin Laden, the individual most responsible for the 9/11 attacks on New York's World Trade Center buildings and the Pentagon. And Admiral McRaven succeeded. Bin Laden was killed during a raid on his compound in Abbottabad, Pakistan, and, after his identity was confirmed, he was buried at sea.

For leading this mission, McRaven will always be remembered for ending America's long quest to avenge the killing of thousands of innocent people in the 9/11 attacks. And while the mission succeeded beyond any of the planners' expectations, it could well have failed. The US government was not even sure that bin Laden was in the targeted compound. But the precision, planning, and execution by McRaven worked.

His service to his country extended well beyond the bin Laden mission, as he relates in his book *Sea Stories: My Life in Special Operations*. A University of Texas graduate and Navy SEAL by training, he rose through the ranks to become a four-star admiral, ultimately serving thirty-seven years in the Navy before retiring (and

FIGURE 12.1 Admiral William H. McRaven served thirty-seven years in the Navy, beginning his career as a member of the Navy SEALS ("Sea, Air, and Land"), who are honored in the Virginia Beach Navy SEAL monument shown here.

later serving as the chancellor of the University of Texas, his alma mater).

At the time President Obama assigned him the bin Laden operation, the admiral was serving as the commander of the US military's Joint Special Operations Command. Admiral McRaven's account of how the mission unfolded is a gripping story. I interviewed him about it during the Congressional Dialogues before turning to the actual subject of his book *The Hero Code*—virtues embodied by people he admires (and which he believes others would do well to embrace): courage, humility, sacrifice, integrity, compassion, perseverance, duty, hope, humor, and forgiveness.

Admiral McRaven is an American hero who excelled in his multidecade military career and continues to distinguish himself in his civilian life; he is currently a senior advisor at Lazard, an investment banking firm, and is a frequent speaker about public service, courage, and character—subjects on which he has few peers.

DAVID M. RUBENSTEIN (DR): Growing up, did you say one day you wanted to be a Navy SEAL? Is that what you wanted to be when you were a little boy?

ADMIRAL WILLIAM H. MCRAVEN (WM): My father was in the Air Force, part of the Greatest Generation. He had been a World War II fighter pilot and a professional football player. So, growing up around the military, I knew I wanted to be in the military, but it wasn't until the movie *The Green Berets* with John Wayne came out that I realized I wanted to be in Special Operations.

An Army Green Beret came to take my sister out on a date when I was in high school. She was, as usual, late, and he said, "What are you going to do if you go into the Navy?" I said, "I don't know." He goes, "You ought to be a Navy SEAL." This was 1973 or so. I'd never heard of Navy SEALs. And so, I was telling my friends in the Army that it was an Army Green Beret who convinced me to be a Navy SEAL.

DR: Did you apply to the Naval Academy?

WM: I did apply to the Naval Academy. You have to be really smart to get into the Naval Academy. My SAT and my grade point average didn't quite make the cut.

DR: You didn't go to the Naval Academy, but you still wanted to be in the Navy.

WM: I did.

DR: You went to college where?

WM: I went to the University of Texas [UT].

DR: Did you go into ROTC [the Reserve Officers' Training Corps]?

WM: I did. I was fortunate enough to get a scholarship into the ROTC program, and it was terrific. It gave you the best of both. You had an opportunity to spend time at a big university with football and basketball and baseball and yet still learn about the Navy and get a commission in the Navy.

DR: You were a track star in high school, and you had a scholarship to run at UT?

WM: I'm not sure I'd call myself a track star. I ran the mile in high school. Then I walked on at UT and I did run for two years on the track team.

DR: So, you did a mile in 3:59?

WM: Once again, much like the Naval Academy, my mile times were not worth remembering.

DR: You graduated, and then you had an obligation to go into ROTC. Did you say right then, I want to be in the Navy SEALs?

WM: I did. I was fortunate. Back then, you could not go directly into the SEAL program from the Naval Academy, but you could from the ROTC program. So, I graduated from ROTC, got my commission in 1977, and went directly into SEAL training.

DR: SEAL training—is that like once a week you get to do some things? What did you have to do?

WM: It's a little rough at times. It's six months of basic training. It takes place in Coronado, California, broken down into three phases. The first phase is generally considered the hardest phase. You get up at the crack of dawn. You do about two hours of calisthenics. You get a short break. You go do a four-mile soft-sand run. You get a short break. You go do about a three- or four-mile open ocean swim. You get a short break. You carry a boat on your head. You run to chow. You come back from chow. You get a short break. You do an obstacle course. You get a short break. You do another couple hours of calisthenics, and you're being harassed by professional harassers the whole time.

DR: They do that once a month?

WM: Every day for six months.

DR: How many people enter a class of Navy SEALs? How many actually graduate?

WM: We've got about a 75 percent attrition rate. That has been consistent since SEAL training started. My class started with 110, and we ended up with thirty-three. That was actually a very large class at the time.

DR: Did you ever think you should drop out of it and weren't going to make it?

WM: No. There were some days that were tough. But I went in with the attitude that they were going to have to kill me to get me to drop. You have to have that attitude going in.

DR: You're a Navy SEAL. What do you do after you graduate from the Navy SEAL program?

WM: I was assigned to an underwater demolition team [UDT]. The SEAL teams and the UDTs at the time were kind of one and the same. So, my first deployment was to the Western Pacific, to the Philippines. Essentially, as part of the Navy, we deployed every two years, so I was off to the Western Pacific or the Middle East or somewhere as a Navy SEAL, with a SEAL platoon as the fighting unit.

DR: One of your jobs was also to parachute out of an airplane?

WM: It was. You're dive qualified, and you have to be both freefall and static-line qualified.

DR: One time you're parachuting out, and all of a sudden, somebody bumps into you and it resulted in your falling down without the parachute?

WM: Yes. This was a little further in my career. I was doing a freefall parachute jump. The idea is you get up to 13,000 feet in a C-130. The ramp comes down in the back, and you jump out when the jump master tells you. You fall from about 13,000 feet down to about 5,500 feet. At 5,500 feet, you look around. You wave off. You pull your rip cord, and out of the back of your parachute comes a pilot chute. Then the pilot chute pulls out the main parachute and you drift nicely down to Earth.

This particular day, beautiful day, not a cloud in the sky, I jump out. I'm falling from 13,000 feet down to 5,500, and I see a guy below me, and I'm a little worried about him. Then this guy slips underneath me, and I checked my altimeter, and it's too late. He opens his parachute. In relative terms, I'm moving at 120 miles an hour and he has stopped. So, I hit his parachute. It hits me, stuns me, and spins me out of control.

What I should have done was gotten stable again, checked my altimeter, and pulled, but frankly, I didn't know what was happening. I was stunned a little bit. So, instinctively, I reached in and pulled my rip cord. When I pulled my rip cord, I was in a spinning, head-down attitude, and the pilot chute came out and wrapped around one leg. Then the riser, another part of the parachute, came out and wrapped around the other leg. Now I'm kind of entangled in the parachute falling to the Earth. I remember thinking to myself, this doesn't look so good. The good news is the parachute opened. The bad news is that when a parachute opens, it blossoms. Took one leg one way, one leg the other way. Snapped me in two, and I landed about two miles from the drop zone. Thanks to good Navy doctors, I am plated in the front with screws in the back and all good.

DR: You were in the hospital for how long?

WM: I was only in the hospital for about ten days. But frankly, I couldn't stand being in the hospital. I managed to escape from the hospital, and we put a hospital bed in my house there on the naval base.

DR: Where were you on 9/11?

WM: I was in that hospital bed in my house on the naval base.

DR: When you saw what happened on 9/11, did you realize you were going to be called into duty soon?

WM: I knew immediately that everything had changed. My daughter was pretty young at the time, but I called my two boys, who were teenagers. One was in college. I said, "Hey, the world has just changed. Obviously, if I can get healthy, I'm probably going to be going forward." As it turned out, I was able to stay in the Navy. I was broken up pretty bad, but I ended up getting orders to go to the White House. I worked in the Bush White House from October of 2001, right after

9/11, for the next two years, and it gave me a chance to heal a little bit before I got into combat.

DR: You didn't say, "I want to retire"?

WM: No. That was the last thing I wanted to do.

DR: You get assigned, at some point, to go into Iraq. What was your assignment there?

WM: I guess we can say this now. I guess it's unclassified. I ran Task Force 121. Our job was to hunt down the Deck of 50. So, if you recall, some enterprising young public affairs officer had taken a deck of cards and said, "Saddam Hussein is the ace of spades, Chemical Ali is the king," and then on down from there. My task force's job was to find these guys and capture them or get rid of them. We'd been fairly successful going through the deck of cards. But we couldn't find Saddam Hussein. I got to Iraq in October of 2003, and we'd been hunting him pretty hard since about March but didn't have many good leads on him.

DR: When did you actually find him?

WM: We found him on December 13, 2003.

DR: Where was he?

WM: He was in Tikrit in what we called a spider hole. He had just two people who were monitoring him. He had, essentially, broken contact with everybody. He'd been hiding in a little farmhouse outside Tikrit and literally living in a hole. The hole was about nine feet. There was a little area where he was living. When the guys found him, they pulled him out of the hole. As I recall, from the guys standing around, as they lifted up the trap door, there was Saddam. One guy says, "Holy shit!" The other guy says, "Holy shit!" A lot of holy shits going around. As Saddam said, "I'm Saddam Hussein, the president of Iraq," my guy said, "President Bush sends his regards. Come on out of the hole."

DR: Famously, he said he was prepared to negotiate. What did he mean?

WM: I don't know if he was prepared to negotiate. That was not on the table at the time.

DR: What did you do with him once you got him?

WM: I had the requirement to hold on to him for about thirty days. We had a small base on Baghdad Airfield, and I had a small three- or four-room, one-story concrete building. We had him in a little room in that concrete building. We took great care of him. I made sure that we had doctors in the room at all times.

DR: Did you actually talk to him yourself?

WM: I made a point. We had a doc and a ranger of security with him all day long. I said, "You will not engage him in conversation." I did not want him to begin to feel like he was important again. Every day I would go in. I would check on him. He would always hop up to try to talk to me. I would always motion him back down. I would check with the medic and the security guard, and then I would leave. I could tell that frustrated him.

DR: Do you think he expected to get out in some way?

WM: I think he did. He still felt that the Iraqi people would take care of him. I held on to him for thirty days, and the last day I had him, he did not know he was leaving. I finally sat down and talked to him. I had a script that I had built. I think I knew how this was going to unfold, but I sat him down. I had my translator with me, and I said, "You need to understand, the United States has taken control of Iraq, but there are a lot of Iraqis still dying. You can save the Iraqi people.

You just need to tell them to put down their arms and stop fighting so we can begin to rebuild Iraq to the great country that it once was." He looked at me, and he said the thing that I thought he would say. He said, "You want me to tell my men to lay down their arms?" I said, "Yes." He said, "Would you do that?" And I said, "If it meant saving my country I would." He looked me in the eye, and he said, "I don't think so." And he was right.

DR: Did he speak English?

WM: No. I was working through an interpreter.

DR: Did he understand English at all?

WM: I think he understood enough.

DR: Ultimately he had a trial.

WM: I told him at the time, I said, "You've got thirty seconds to think about this, because you're about to leave my custody, and you're going to go someplace that is not going to be near as nice," and that shocked him. I think he thought I was bluffing. Thirty seconds later, I had the two biggest Army Rangers I could find come in and grab him. We put him in a vehicle, and we took them over to the military police side. They eventually remanded him to the Iraqis.

DR: Let's go to Osama bin Laden. What was your role that would put you in a position to be the person overseeing the capture of Osama bin Laden?

WM: Starting in 2008, I became the commander. I was a three-star admiral in charge of a Joint Special Operations Force. Part of our responsibility in the global war on terrorism was to hunt down the Osama bin Ladens and the Ayman Al-Zawahiris and whoever else was part of the al-Qaeda leadership. The CIA had been looking at this for quite some time. It wasn't until December of 2010. I'm out in Afghanistan, and Admiral Mike Mullen, the chairman of the Joint Chiefs of Staff, comes to visit me, which he did routinely. But this time, he said, "Bill, let's go up to your office and talk." We go up to the office and he said, "CIA's got a lead on Osama bin Laden, and they probably are going to want you to come back and talk to them about what your force could do." I said, "Okay, sir, happy to go back to DC." Candidly, I was probably a little dismissive, because we'd had a lot of leads on bin Laden, and none of them had panned out. About three weeks later, I got the call to go back, and I went over to Langley and met with the deputy director, Michael Morell. It was then that Morell showed me the picture of the compound, this kind of trapezoid-shaped compound that you've probably seen, and began to tell me the intel on bin Laden.

DR: Can you say where they got the intel from?

WM: This will go down as one of the great intelligence operations in the history of the CIA, and rightfully so. It was pulling on threads of, as we say, reflection. So, from signals intelligence, they hear somebody talking on the phone, somebody else talking on the phone, somebody else talking on the phone, and they begin to put the pieces of the puzzle together, till they found this individual they thought might be facilitating for bin Laden. But the people in the compound, the two guys who were the facilitators, they never talked on the phone in the compound. They went miles away. There were no electronic transmissions out from the compound. So, the agency had to figure out where this guy was and then figure out how to track him back to this compound. That was all done clandestinely.

DR: So, you come back to Washington. They show you this, and they say, "Can you capture him or can you kill him"? What did they say?

WM: At first, my task force was really not part of the solution set. None of this would have happened without CIA Director Leon Panetta. It was Leon Panetta's leadership, his ability. He was a man with no ego. This was about "let's get the job done." When I first got there, the CIA had a couple of plans. The CIA has the capability to do these sorts of things, but there was also a bombing capability. We had looked at, could you just bomb the compound? So, when I first started meeting with the president in early March, there were a number of options. One was this massive bombing raid that the president immediately dismissed.

DR: They'd go bomb the house?

WM: Bomb the house, yes, but there were women and children on the target. That was pretty quickly dismissed, because, once again, we didn't know whether it was bin Laden.

A critical part of the story is that, from the beginning, the evidence was circumstantial. We thought it was bin Laden, but we had nothing that could confirm it. The decisions that the president had to make were pretty bold. When we looked at it, there was a bombing option, then there was more of a surgical bombing option, because this guy we thought was bin Laden would come out every day around noon, and he would walk around this open courtyard. They called him "the pacer," because he would pace for about an hour in kind of a square, and he always had a couple of kids with him, but there were trees overhanging. It was difficult, once again, to determine whether the tall "pacer man" was, in fact, bin Laden. So, they had a surgical bombing option. They had an internal option. Then at some point in time, Leon Panetta came to me and said, "We think this needs to be you guys doing this," "you guys" being my joint task force.

DR: When they said they thought it was him and they said they wanted you to oversee it, what did you do?

WM: The president oversaw it. My job was the military part of the mission. At some point in time, of course, it was essentially a military mission.

DR: Why didn't the CIA go in and extract him?

WM: Because it was more complicated. Tactically, the compound was in a built-up urban area. The compound was three miles from the Pakistani West Point. It was three miles from a major infantry battalion. It was a mile from a police station, and we, the Joint Special Operations Force, just had better capability to be able to do this.

DR: Did President Obama call you and say, "What do you think you can do?"

WM: Tom Donilon, who was the national security advisor at the time, along with Leon Panetta, who was the CIA director at the time, brought me into the first meeting in early March, but the president had not made the decision to go with a raid. We were weighing all the options, and we did for about the next two months.

DR: Did you tell the president, "Yes, I think I can do this"?

WM: I had to build a plan. Because it was a very close hold, it was essentially just me building the initial plan to brief the president. But at this point in time in the war, I had done thousands of missions. I looked at it and it was pretty straightforward. We were going to get on a helicopter. We were going to fly 162 miles to the target. The SEALs were going to get on the target, get the bad guy, get back on the helicopter, and fly home. We wanted to keep it as simple as possible. That is the plan that I briefed the president on.

But at one point in time, in early April, as the president is still kind of mulling over these various options, he turns to me, he says, "Bill, can you do this?" I said, "Sir, I don't know. I need to bring the SEALs on," because nobody else was on yet. "I need to bring the SEALs on board. I need to bring the helicopter pilots on board, I need to go rehearse this mission, and after I rehearse it, and after we work the bugs out, then I can come back and tell you whether or not we can do it." He said, "How much time do you have?" I said, "Three weeks."

In the course of the next three weeks, we brought the SEALs in. I'm often asked, "Why did you use SEALs instead of the Army Special

Operations Force?" People think it was because I was a Navy SEAL. I said, "Are you kidding me?" I said, "You want this mission to be successful. I would have taken anybody that could have done this well." There were two commanders that I had implicit faith in. One happened to be a Navy SEAL, and the other one was an Army Delta Force operator. The army guys had just gone over to Afghanistan, and the SEALs had literally just come back from Afghanistan. It gave me, as we say, cover for action. The SEALs were all supposed to be on leave. The assumption was they were out with their girlfriends skiing in Tahoe or doing something. The army guys that I had, if I had pulled them out of Afghanistan and brought them back to do this, it would have heightened the security profile.

DR: Did you build a model place?

WM: The agency, in an undisclosed location, built a mock-up frame of the compound. We had a chain-link fence that made the border of the compound. They did that in a matter of days. It was really a remarkable job.

DR: When you told the SEALs what you were planning to do, what did they say?

WM: I brought them in off leave under the guise that it was an exercise we were doing. We brought them to this classroom at this undisclosed location, and, needless to say, they were not happy. Some of them we had literally pulled off the slopes in Tahoe.

They think they're here for an exercise. We do these pretty sensitive exercises, so they weren't surprised that they're at this location. Then the agency guy comes out to have them sign these nondisclosure statements, which didn't surprise them either, because we have to do that sometimes. Then finally, the agency guy gets up there, and he starts to brief the SEALs.

I'm in the back of the room, watching the body language, and he says, "So, gentlemen, our target is a man we believe to be Osama bin Laden." You can see these guys being like, "Is this part of the exercise?" He goes on, and the whole time they're thinking, "Really? This is the exercise?" Finally, I had to get up and say, "Gentlemen, this is not an exercise. This was the intel we have, and by the way, in one hour, you're going to start rehearsing for this thing." So, at that undisclosed location, they went off and began the initial rehearsal.

DR: How many weeks did you have to rehearse?

WM: We had about two full weeks to rehearse.

DR: After those two weeks, did you go to the president and say, "Yes, I can get this done"?

WM: I did.

DR: Did he say, "You guarantee it"?

WM: No. He understood the risks. I had made it very clear to him. One of your responsibilities as a commander, particularly when you're talking to the president of the United States or to Members of Congress, is to be upfront.

DR: We know that, during the Carter administration, the effort to extract the Iranian hostages didn't work, because there weren't enough helicopters. Were you worried about that problem?

WM: Absolutely. We looked at everything. We had 162 phases that we built into the plan. We had plan A, plan B, plan C, and plan D, but what we were concerned about was the number of helicopters coming in and the types of helicopters, and that is a little sensitive. Suffice it to say we had unique helicopters that I thought would be fine skirting around Pakistani radar, but I knew I needed a couple of backup helicopters that weren't going to be special helicopters. What was never told was that, on the other side of the border in Afghanistan, I had what we call our "guerrilla package," which was another couple of helicopters, AC-130s, a fighter cap of F-15s, and F-16s, refuelers. Everybody you can think of was waiting in reserve in Afghanistan in the event something went wrong on the mission.

DR: When do you get the Navy SEALs over to the place from which you took off? You took off from where?

WM: We took off from the border of Afghanistan.

DR: You take off. How many helicopters do you have?

WM: We've got twenty-four guys in two helicopters—twenty-five guys, actually, with the CIA officer.

DR: And you have another backup helicopter?

WM: I had two, what we call MH-47s. These are big twin-bladed Chinooks. They came well behind the first two helicopters. The idea was that if I could get the other two helicopters in a position where they could come into the compound, if these helicopters got compromised, I had to time it right, so they lagged behind thirty to forty minutes.

DR: Did you think that the radar of the Pakistanis was good enough to pick these guys up?

WM: We did a couple of things, again because the CIA was brilliant in their analytical work on this. We knew what kind of radars they had. We understood the nature of the radar, so we understood what the radar picture would look like. We flew behind a mountain range that took us from pretty close inside to Pakistan almost all the way to the target. The guys stayed low and behind that mountain range, so that the radars couldn't pick them up.

DR: Did you think the Pakistanis knew that Osama bin Laden was there?

WM: No. We looked into this a lot, because there was a sense that somebody in Pakistan must have known that bin Laden was there, but in all clarity and honesty, we have never been able to identify someone.

DR: So, you have two helicopters, twenty-four people in the helicopters. How long is the flight?

WM: About an hour and a half.

DR: Ninety minutes. They get there, and their mission is to land in the compound or outside?

WM: The initial idea was that the first helicopter, the Blackhawk, was going to come in and these guys would what we call fast-rope—essentially rappel down—into the compound, the second helicopter was going to come in, and the guys were going to rappel onto the top of this three-story building. The way the SEALs normally do it is they come from top to bottom, and they kind of collapse in terms of the tactics of this. Unfortunately, what happened was that the first helicopter came in—I'm watching it on a big screen—and as soon as the helicopter comes in, I can see it's beginning to waffle.

DR: Why?

WM: When we did the rehearsal and the helicopter came in, we were using a chain-link fence, and the prop blast from the helicopter just went through that chain-link fence. But when they got to the real compound, it was an eighteen-foot-high wall, a concrete wall, and the prop blast came down, hit that concrete wall, made a vortex—essentially a vacuum above the blades—and the blades lost lift.

DR: So, nobody had thought of that potential problem?

WM: We hadn't had a chance to rehearse that part of it, and, no, we really hadn't thought about that problem.

DR: The first helicopter was wobbly, and it kind of crashes?

WM: It makes a hard landing into what we referred to as the animal pen, which was separated from the main compound.

DR: The soldiers got out?

WM: What happened was a second helicopter, not knowing what had happened to the first, lands outside. Now the whole mission is not like we had planned. The first group of guys is outside two barriers, so they've got to blow a wall here or blow a door here, blow another door here before they can get into the main area. They're coming out of the helicopter. They're a little banged up. I'm listening to them on the headset. Needless to say, that was not for mixed company. They managed to make their way out of the helicopter, get into the area.

The guys on the outside, they come to the first door they see on the outside of the wall. They put the explosives on it to breach it, to blow it, and it turns out it's a false door. It was just a metal door that somebody had hung there, no access point. So, now they've got to come around and blow another door in. All this takes about five minutes before everybody's in the compound.

DR: Did you think you would be a one-star admiral soon?

WM: I thought that was a good possibility.

DR: Finally, all twenty-four are in. Then the hunt for bin Laden starts. Where did they go to look first?

WM: There were a couple of outer buildings. The group had been told, you four guys, you clear this building, you guys clear this building. The main force will come into the one building we've got, but we also had guys on the outside patrolling with the dog to keep people away. When the group comes in, if you're starting with ten guys, a group goes into one room, another group goes into another room, and you flow into the room, and then you flow up the stairs.

As the guys are flowing through, they kill a guy on the first floor. They're making their way up to the second floor. Bin Laden's son is coming down from the second floor. He gets engaged. They keep moving to the second floor. By the time they get to the third floor, there's only two guys, and as they make their way up to the third floor, the first guy sees bin Laden peek his head around—it had a curtained-off room, a doorway—and takes a couple of shots at him but misses.

DR: Who takes shots?

WM: The SEAL takes a shot at bin Laden.

DR: But they missed.

WM: Missed him at first. But now the two guys realize, yes, it was bin Laden pretty clearly. So, they move up, and as they enter the room, bin Laden is there, and he's got his two daughters or two little girls in front of him. The first guy assumes that the little girls are wired with a suicide vest. As barbaric as that sounds, we have seen it many times before in Iraq and Afghanistan. Bin Laden pushes these two girls toward the first guy coming on. Afterward, in talking to the first guy, I learned that he thought that these girls were going to blow themselves up. To save his buddy, he grabs them and pulls them aside, and that's a heroic move right there.

DR: He pulls the girls aside?

WM: He pulls the girls aside to save his buddy behind him.

DR: Osama bin Laden, doesn't he have a rifle? Why isn't he shooting? He didn't have a rifle?

WM: He had one, but when he saw the guys coming, he put it aside. When we got into the room, it was sitting up on a shelf. He was not armed. The concern all along in the planning, and I had told the guys this, I said, "Look, if he has got his hands up and he is clearly not a threat, you have an obligation by the law of armed conflict to capture him." You just cannot kill a guy that is in this way. We'd seen a lot of guys that literally slept in suicide vests. So, if you can't determine whether he's got a suicide vest on, then take the shot.

DR: They couldn't determine whether he had a suicide vest, so they decide to shoot him. They shot him how many times?

WM: He had a couple holes in his head when I looked at him. There were two holes in his head and I think one in his chest. I don't remember the exact number, but he went down.

DR: They shoot him, and at that time the Pakistanis have not yet figured out what's going on? They haven't shown up?

WM: No, but they're starting to realize something's happening, because obviously the helicopter is down.

DR: What about the neighbors?

WM: The neighbors have now started to come over. Again, this is a residential area. The neighbors began to come over, and we had this remarkable CIA officer with us who spoke Pashtu and Urdu and Dari. So, as they come over, he meets them, and he says, "Just an exercise going on here, nothing to see here. Go back to your homes." But, of course, a lot of them stuck around because they wanted to watch this exercise. They sat there and watched for a while and he finally kind of shooed them off.

DR: Osama bin Laden has been shot. Do they decide to just put him in a body bag and bring him out?

WM: About fifteen minutes into the mission, I get the call from the ground force commander: "For God and Country. Geronimo,

Geronimo, Geronimo." "Geronimo" had been the code word for bin Laden. I pass this on to the president, the code word "Geronimo." I didn't say, "We have bin Laden," because having done these many, many times, until you can verify that the person you've got is who you think he is, you don't ever call "jackpot," which is the term for "we got the guy we were looking for." But I did say, "They think it's bin Laden: the code word has been passed." Then it occurred to me I didn't know whether bin Laden was dead or alive. So, I had to call back down and say, "Geronimo, EKIA, question mark?" In other words, enemy killed in action? I immediately get the response back, "Roger Geronimo EKIA," which I subsequently relayed on. People said, "How did you react?" We were still on the ground in Pakistan. We had a job to finish.

DR: The mission was to capture him or to kill him?

WM: The mission was not a kill mission. A lot of people think that the president said, "You're going to kill bin Laden." We couldn't. Again, the law of armed conflict is pretty clear.

DR: There's a famous picture in the Situation Room of the senior White House staff and the president looking up at a screen. What are they looking at?

WM: They are looking at that helicopter that has just crashed into the other part of the compound. They don't look too happy in that picture, do they?

DR: No. So, you have the body. You put him in a body bag. How do you get another helicopter in? Because one is destroyed. Did you blow up that helicopter so nobody could get it?

WM: As we tend to do on these missions, we take demolition. I hate to admit this, but I lost seven helicopters in my time that crashed and we had to destroy them. A lot of times we would bring in and drop heavy ordnance on them, a 500- or 2,000-pound bomb, but in this case, we loaded it with demolition, and we blew it.

DR: You destroyed it. You have one helicopter. Does one of the backup helicopters come and land inside the compound?

WM: No. They landed outside.

DR: Outside because you don't want to have that problem again.

WM: Right.

DR: Then you drag out the body bag and bring it back on the helicopter. How long does it take: an hour and a half?

WM: We had to refuel. We stopped for nineteen minutes. I will tell you, it's the longest nineteen minutes of my life, because the remains of bin Laden are on this helicopter. It's the only proof we have, and now we are refueling out in the middle of Pakistan. Once again the neighbors come out, and once again my CIA officer says, "Nothing to see here, just an exercise," and so they stood around and watched us refuel.

DR: After bin Laden was shot, some of your troops gathered computer equipment and other things. How long did that take, and how much time did they expend doing that?

WM: Originally, I had planned the mission to be thirty minutes on the ground. But about twenty minutes into the mission, I get the call from the ground force commander that on the second floor, they had found this treasure trove of intelligence—computers, hard drives, paper—and he said, "We're going to need some time to gather all this up." I said okay. It was another twenty-five minutes. At about the forty-five-minute mark, fifteen minutes past what I wanted to do, I called him up and said, "Getting a little concerned. The Pakistanis are starting to muster a force. Whatever you got, put it in the bag, and let's get it out of there."

DR: Were you talking directly to the president?

WM: No. The president, though, was on the video. I had built a small room. There was a door that I could look out. I knew I had to be talking to Leon Panetta and to the president on video.

DR: The troops are heading back. They're refueled. Where do they go?

WM: They come back to the base they launched from.

DR: Who examines whether this is bin Laden or not?

WM: As they are coming across the border, I am on the video with the president, and the president asked me, "Well, Bill, is it bin Laden?" I said, "Sir, I don't know." Before I'm going to tell the president of the United States, I need to go see the remains myself. The airfield was a five-minute drive from my little command center, so we drive over to the airfield right about the time the SEALs are landing. They bring the body bag off and put it down in the hangar. I get down. It's a rubberized body bag. I unzipped the body bag, and he didn't look too good. He's got a couple of rounds in his head. It's pretty clearly bin Laden. The beard was a little shorter than what you're used to seeing, but I knew that bin Laden was six foot four. So, I pull the remains out of the body bag and unceremoniously stretched them out. I'm thinking, I'm six foot two, I'll just lie down next to the remains, but then I thought, I'm a three-star admiral, that's probably not very distinguished. I saw a young SEAL standing nearby. I said, "Hey, son, how tall are you?" He said, "Sir, I'm six two." I said, "Good, come here, lie down." He looked at me, what? But he knew immediately what I was trying to do. So, he lay down next to the remains, and the remains were a couple inches longer. I go back to my little hooch in the command center. Now I'm on the video with the president. The president says, "Well, what do you think?" I said, "Sir, without DNA, I can't be 100 percent certain, but I'm pretty sure it's him. It looks like him," et cetera. I said, "By the way, I knew he was six foot four, so I had this guy lay down next to him, and the remains were a couple inches longer." There's this pause on the other end of the video, and the president says, "Okay,

Bill, let me get this straight. You had $60 million for a helicopter, and you didn't have $10 for a tape measure?" I've told folks, it was a very serious night with serious implications, but at that point in time, that was just what we needed. I just needed something to lower the temperature a little bit.

DR: But you did have DNA. Where did you get the DNA from?

WM: The FBI has a DNA repository, and there are a lot of bin Ladens in the world. So it was not hard matching the DNA. We took the remains from where we got him to Bagram. I had a complete forensics crew, fingerprints.

DR: You then called the president and said it's him.

WM: I said, "I think it's him, 99.9 percent sure it's him, pending DNA."

DR: You get the DNA, and then you call him and say it's 100 percent?

WM: They were pretty sure enough with fingerprints and everything.

DR: What did you do with the body then?

WM: We put the body back onto a Marine V-22s Osprey and flew it back into Pakistan, back up the air corridor. There was an air corridor that we would fly from the Gulf of Oman, and we flew the remains back out to the USS *Carl Vinson*, an aircraft carrier out there.

DR: Wasn't that risky, going back into Pakistan?

WM: Not really, because it was a well-known route, and the Pakistanis hadn't quite figured things out.

DR: You go on to the aircraft carrier, and what do you do then with the body?

WM: We buried the body at sea.

DR: Why did you bury him at sea?

WM: The issue had come up in one of the briefings to the president: What are we going to do with remains? I had had a similar incident with a guy named Saleh Nabhan, who was another bad guy that we got in Somalia a few years earlier. I had done the research on Saleh Nabhan that if we got him—I'm a Navy guy—can you bury him at sea like we do with seamen? We talked to some Islamic scholars, and they said, absolutely you can. You have to do it in the first twenty-four hours. You've got to clean the body. You've got to do all these sorts of things. I had done this before, with four other al-Qaeda members. So, when the president asked what we were going to do, I said, "We'll bury him at sea."

DR: Photographs were taken. They've never surfaced publicly.

WM: Right.

DR: Are you convinced they will never surface publicly?

WM: I hope they don't surface publicly. Part of this was—and the president talked about it later—that this isn't who we are. We're not the guys that want to show off that we killed bin Laden. Al-Qaeda came out within the next twenty-four hours and acknowledged the fact that bin Laden was dead. I think it was right not to show photos, because then you would have had fake photos all around the internet.

DR: All of his children and other people—they were left in the compound. None of them were brought out?

WM: Nobody was brought out but bin Laden, his remains.

DR: What did the president say when it was all over? Did he say thank you, congratulations?

WM: I flew back the next day, went over to Capitol Hill to brief members of the House and Senate Intelligence Committees. While I was up on the Hill, I got a call from the White House, and they said, "The president would like you to swing by." We went over to the White House. We go into the Oval Office, and the president, very gracious, says, "Really want to thank you." And he says, "Oh, by the way, I got something for you." He reaches behind the president's desk, and he pulls out a brass plaque that says, "From President Barack Obama to Vice-Admiral Bill McRaven. If you have $60 million for a helicopter, you ought to have $10 for a tape measure." And there was a Home Depot tape measure on the plaque. It's one of my prized possessions.

DR: If you had to do it all over again, is there anything you would have done differently, other than the tape measure?

WM: There's probably a lot of things you could have thought about. But it went well, and it went well because you've got to rely on the men and women to do the job. I always knew the SEALS, once they got on target, could do the job.

13

Walter Isaacson on Leonardo da Vinci

INTERVIEW DATE: JULY 10, 2019

Walter Isaacson had a charmed and much-admired career before he started writing best-selling biographies—star student at Harvard, Rhodes Scholar, graduated with first-class honors from Oxford, editor of *Time* magazine, CEO of CNN, and president of the Aspen Institute. As a biographer of individuals who might fairly be described as geniuses, Walter has written books on Henry Kissinger, Benjamin Franklin, Albert Einstein, Steve Jobs, Jennifer Doudna, and Elon Musk. He is currently working on a book on Marie Curie, the only person to win Nobel Prizes in two different scientific categories.

I have interviewed Walter about these geniuses in various forums over the years and know that he came to admire greatly each of them for their extraordinary achievements and their outsized brainpower. But I have thought that the genius who most fascinated Walter was the person I interviewed him about for this Dialogues session—Leonardo da Vinci.

That fascination stems, in my view, from Walter's observation that Leonardo was uniquely able to master both the art world and the science world (to the extent it existed then), and the skillset needed to master those completely different disciplines has rarely been seen in one individual. As an artist, Leonardo left behind fewer than twenty finished

ET DES ARTS. Liv. V. 365

LIONARDO . DA . VINCI . PITTORE .

LEONARD DE VINCI.

JAmais homme ne receut à ſa naiſſance tant de prerogatives, & de l'eſprit, & du corps, que LEONARD DE VINCI. Cét Illuſtre Florentin peut eſtre mis au nombre de ceux en qui l'on rencontre par fois ces dons ſurnaturels que toute l'induſtrie humaine ne peut acquerir, & que l'on regarde comme les Favorits du Ciel, & les prodiges de la Nature : car outre qu'il eut une beauté tres-accomplie, & une force ſi admirable, qu'il rompoit de ſa main un fer de cheval, & une ancre de maiſon ; il fut encore doüé d'une lumiere penetrante, & capable des ſciences auxquelles

Zz 3 les

FIGURE 13.1 Leonardo da Vinci rose from modest beginnings (he was born out of wedlock to a notary and a peasant woman) to become "the person in history who was most curious to know everything he could possibly know about everything," according to author Walter Isaacson.

and unfinished paintings, but they are among the greatest paintings ever, such as the *Mona Lisa* and *The Last Supper*. (Only one of his paintings is in the United States: the *Ginevra de' Benci* portrait at the National Gallery of Art.) As a scientist, Leonardo pioneered many inventions (though few were actually built during his lifetime) and made unmatched discoveries about the human body through countless (and often illegal) dissections and detailed anatomical drawings that followed.

How did Leonardo do all this? Though born out of wedlock and not given the type of upbringing and education a different birth status might have afforded him, he possessed an unmatched intellectual curiosity, driven by a desire to understand everything there was to know about any subject he pursued. And he invariably succeeded at that effort. It is remarkable that a man who lived more than 500 years ago is still held in such awe, and viewed with so much admiration, by those living in all parts of the world today. That was evident in my conversation in front of a great many Members of Congress in this Dialogues session.

DAVID M. RUBENSTEIN (DR): Why is it that, 500 years after he died, people still are fascinated by this man?

WALTER ISAACSON (WI): Leonardo da Vinci was the person in history who was most curious to know everything he could possibly know about everything, whether it was art or anatomy or engineering or zoology. That ability to cross disciplines has been a key to creativity, which I finally realized was the theme of the lives of Ben Franklin, Steve Jobs, Albert Einstein—that ability to stand, as Steve did whenever he launched a product, at that intersection between the arts and sciences.

DR: You've written books on other geniuses, so-called. How would you rank Leonardo as a genius in this category? Is he the smartest of them all or the most creative of them all?

WI: Neither he nor Ben Franklin nor Steve Jobs were the smartest people of their time in a conventional sense. Bill Gates has more processing power than Steve Jobs did. Luca Pacioli, a mathematician who was best friends with Leonardo, was clearly the smartest person of the time.

In my career, I've met a lot of smart people, and at a certain point, maybe twenty years ago, I realized smart people are a dime a dozen. They don't amount to much. It's people who are creative and innovative and think different, and that's Steve Jobs, Ben Franklin, Leonardo da Vinci, and, for that matter, Albert Einstein. He was bottom of his class at the Zurich Polytech. Couldn't even get into Zurich University. Couldn't get a job teaching even in high school. He's a third-class patent clerk, but that ability to be creative is what sets him apart.

DR: In Leonardo's case, would you say that what he created in the art world is his greatest legacy, or what he did in science?

WI: When he reached that unnerving age of thirty, he was having a falling-out with the Medici family because he wasn't finishing his paintings. Had a little problem with his father, and so he runs away, or leaves as a cultural diplomat, to go to Milan. He writes a letter to the Duke of Milan that's the best job application ever, and it's eleven paragraphs long. The first ten paragraphs are all about engineering and science. "I can build great buildings, I can make weapons of war, I can divert the course of rivers." Only in the eleventh paragraph does he say, "And I can also paint as well as any person." So, he thought of himself as more of an engineer than an artist.

DR: Let's go back and go through his life. He was born out of wedlock?

WI: Yes, in the village of Vinci, a tiny village. He was very fortunate to be born out of wedlock. Had he been born legitimate, he would have been a notary like his father, grandfather, great-grandfather, great-great-grandfather, and he would have been a terrible notary. He just didn't like details. He was gay, he was left-handed, he was a vegetarian. He was quite a misfit.

DR: Who was his mother?

WI: His mother—and I'll give credit to Martin Kemp, a professor at Oxford—was just rediscovered. There's always something new to learn about Leonardo. All we knew, up until I was doing my book [*Leonardo da Vinci*, 2017] and Martin Kemp was doing his, was that her name was Caterina, because when he's baptized, his father is a notary and puts it all down. You see only "child of Caterina." She was a peasant girl, very young. I don't give myself any credit really, but Martin Kemp and a few other people I was working with were able, through a complex series of ways, to track down who Caterina was.

DR: His father could have made him legitimate?

WI: Yes. You can go to a ranking member of the church, and you have a process, and you can be legitimated. It's unclear why his father, Ser Piero da Vinci, doesn't do that for Leonardo, especially since his father has no other children until Leonardo's about sixteen or so. But Leonardo clearly wasn't going to be a notary, clearly wanted to be an artist, clearly was an independent spirit. I try to give the dad credit by saying I think it was better for him not to have been legitimated.

DR: He's raised initially by his mother. Then his father takes him back and raises him?

WI: Yes. He seems to spend time in the village of Vinci, but his dad takes him to Florence finally.

DR: His father gets him trained in the art world?

WI: Ser Piero da Vinci, the father, becomes a powerful notary for Lorenzo the Magnificent. A notary back then was basically a lawyer in civil suits. You did trusts, estates, wills, all the documents, and so it was an important role. Ser Piero does it for the Medici, and he brings Leonardo finally to Florence.

Why are there certain cradles of creativity? It helps to have patrons like the Medici. It helps to have new types of finance. What Leonardo's friend Luca Pacioli and others did is they invented debit and credit bookkeeping so that you can make venture loans and do things.

Leonardo gets to Florence, and he is totally this misfit, as I said—gay, illegitimate, left-handed, a vegetarian, distracted. But they embrace him. They all love him. This is why Florence—it's 1470 when he arrives—becomes the cradle of the Renaissance. They just are so embracing.

DR: Was it apparent to people that he was gay? Did he try to flaunt that in some ways, for example, by the way he dressed?

WI: Yes. I'm going to get in trouble here, but he wore flamboyant purple tunics. He had a boyfriend named Salai. The boyfriend came with him to all of the dinners. Michelangelo, at about the same period, also in Florence, is gay and very repressed, if you've read *The Agony and the Ecstasy*. Leonardo is perfectly fine.

DR: Leonardo is apprentice to a prominent artist?

WI: Yes. He gets apprenticed to Andrea del Verrocchio, and he poses for the statue of David—the fourteen- or fifteen-year-old Leonardo posing as the favorite Golden Boy in Florence.

DR: The person to whom he's apprenticed is the leading artist in Florence, more or less?

WI: Yes and no. The cool thing, the great thing, for Leonardo is that Verrocchio wasn't just an artist. He had a workshop. He did pageants and plays and costumes. He was the one who had to finish Brunelleschi's dome on the top of the cathedral in Florence, and so that copper ball is soldered by young Leonardo and his friends as they learn how to solder a ball and put it up there.

DR: Eventually he leaves Verrocchio and goes out on his own. But how do you support yourself on your own then?

WI: He did it through doing pageants and plays and costumes. He also got a lot of art commissions from the Medici family. The problem is—and it's a complicated reason, I'm not sure I have it totally right, but I deal with it in the book—he just doesn't finish things. So, he doesn't get paid.

DR: He gets commissioned. He starts something, but he never finishes?

WI: Worse yet, his father's a notary on two of the commissions. We have *The Adoration of the Magi* that you can go see in the Uffizi. It's two-thirds done.

DR: He lives to be sixty-seven years old in the end. How many paintings are there of his?

WI: Full paintings by his hand, probably twelve. Does *Adoration of the Magi*, which is not finished, count? Does *Salvator Mundi* count?

DR: This is the famous one for which somebody just paid $450 million?

WI: Somebody meaning Mohammed bin Salman.

DR: And is it a real Leonardo?

WI: Yes. In my book, I deal with it quite a lot. Leonardo, we know, created a *Salvator Mundi*, "Christ as Savior of the World." It was mainly finished by his workshop. It was a commissioned painting, but we know that the drawing itself was Leonardo's. The question is not is this Leonardo but how many brushstrokes that we actually still have were done by his hand rather than by his studio.

DR: There's only one Leonardo painting in the United States, is that right? Where is that?

WI: It's *Ginevra de' Benci*, and it's at the National Gallery. It is an awesome piece of work of a young Leonardo when he's in Florence. But what's particularly interesting about *Ginevra de' Benci*, when you go see it, is that this is a commissioned portrait of the wife of a cloth merchant in Florence, done in three-quarters profile, in which Leonardo is playing, as you look at the river flowing from the ancient eons of civilization, curving into the curls of her hair and into her body. It's us connecting with nature. At the very end of his life, he's also going to paint the wife of another Florentine cloth merchant in three-quarters profile with a river connecting. *Ginevra* isn't the *Mona Lisa*, but it's clearly the work of the kid who will go on to paint the *Mona Lisa*.

DR: What was it that he did as a painter that was so unique? Did he have better observation skills?

WI: Science helps a lot, because he's the first person—and this is one of the great gifts of Renaissance art—to try to make a three-dimensional scene on a two-dimensional plane. If you look at art up until then, it's very flat.

Leonardo knows everything. With *Ginevra de' Benci*, you look at the distant mountains, how the color changes. If you look at the luster in the curls of hair, if you look at the perspective, it's mathematically perfect, which he learned from Verrocchio and Brunelleschi, doing that cathedral dome. He's made it three-dimensional. He also is able to show inner emotions. It's very complicated, what she's thinking. This is not a happy woman, we know. You feel, as with the *Mona Lisa*, an inner emotion. He would walk around Florence with a notebook.

DR: You mentioned he walks around with a notebook. There are 7,000 extant pages of his writings. Did he ever inscribe, like a diary, why he did something, what he felt? What's in those 7,000 pages?

WI: They were not that personal, unfortunately. He gets mad at Salai, his boyfriend, and he'll write something bad. Or talk about shopping lists. He put, almost every day, "Here are the things I want to learn."

DR: Where are those 7,000 pages now?

WI: They're all over. Nobody's collected them. Nobody's done a complete volume. One of the hard things about writing this book was that Cathy [Walter's wife] and I had to go see them. So, we had to go to Florence, Milan, Venice, Paris, Windsor, and to Seattle, Washington. Armand Hammer bought one of the writings, and he renamed it the Codex Hammer. Later, when he died, Bill Gates bought it, and he renamed it the Codex Leicester.

DR: Which is what it had been?

WI: Which is what it had been. Bill Gates's ego is not out of control. Bill Gates understands that notebook, and I keep pushing him. He's lent it finally now—it'll be in the show in Florence in a month. But he is going to do a beautiful printed version, because it's the best of Leonardo's science notebooks. He's doing geology.

DR: The Queen of England—does she own some of them?

WI: The Queen of England probably has the most pages of the notebook. Those ridiculous Brits, those earls of the seventeenth century, they kind of broke up the notebooks, stole some, took pages out. But if you look at the drawing *Fetus in the Womb*, which is the opening flyleaf of my book, that's at Windsor.

DR: Let's go back for a moment. When Leonardo's painting, he has a couple of techniques that no one else really had. Could you explain why the shading he used was so important?

WI: He understood optics. He dissected the human eye. He realized that, as you look at people or you look at an object, there are no sharp lines. It's called sfumato. He did not believe that sharp lines best depicted reality because you have two eyes. If you look at other art before that period, everybody drew the line and then filled in the color. Most of the paintings have what's called sfumato.

DR: One of his techniques was to use paint in a unique way, to paint over and over. Why did he do that?

WI: First of all, he procrastinated a lot, so he would try to perfect a painting. He has the *Mona Lisa* for sixteen years. Second, he does tiny brushstrokes of very thin layers of pigments, because the light will go in, as he knows, and hit the pigments at different levels so that it changes.

DR: The *Mona Lisa* is the most famous painting in the world by far. Why is that?

WI: That's the most famous smile ever done. Leonardo had dissected the human eye, so what he knows is that in the center of the retina you see black and white detail, but in the corner of your eye, if you're not looking directly at something, you see colors and shadows pop up more. So, if you look directly at the smile of the *Mona Lisa*, the corners of her lips aren't smiling: Especially the one on her right is just straight. But as your eye moves away from staring at the lips to looking at her cheek or chin or her forehead, you see it differently, and the smile pops on, so it's interactive.

DR: There are different theories about who she was?

WI: Many people have different theories, but we know who it was: Lisa Gherardini, wife of a Florence cloth merchant. Between Dan Brown's *Da Vinci Code* and everything else, everybody decides it's more complicated than it needs to be.

DR: Some people say it's Leonardo in drag. You don't believe it?

WI: And some say it was Salai, his boyfriend. It's not. It's this cloth merchant's wife.

DR: When he died, the *Mona Lisa* was in his bedroom?

WI: In his bedroom in France. He still has the painting by his desk after sixteen years because he just won't give it up. He's painting layer after layer.

DR: What is he doing in France?

WI: The mother of François Premier—Francis I, the young, wonderful king of France—was Louise of Savoy. She loves the Italian Renaissance and wants France to have the Italian Renaissance. She convinces her kid who's become the king to import Leonardo.

DR: He died there. And is he buried there?

WI: It's unclear where his remains are. They've been moved.

DR: The *Mona Lisa* did come to the United States once, right?

WI: Yes. Jacqueline Kennedy sat next to Charles de Gaulle. The government almost fell because she asked de Gaulle whether he would send the *Mona Lisa* to Washington and then to the Met. De Gaulle said yes, and it almost caused a government crisis.

DR: I thought that the head of the Louvre almost resigned over this.

WI: Correct, yes.

DR: The *Mona Lisa,* if it was for sale, would go for a lot more than $400 million?

WI: Oh my god. I can't even predict.

DR: Two billion? Three billion?

WI: Yes, yes.

DR: No limit, okay. So, let's talk about *The Last Supper*. Where is that?

WI: It's in Milan, and it's in a refectory. After Leonardo writes that letter to the Duke of Milan saying "Give me a job," he does a lot of things, including the Pavia Cathedral. But the Duke of Milan ate lunch every day with monks in this monastery and wanted Leonardo to do a Last Supper.

DR: But Leonardo made a mistake. The painting wasn't done on canvas. It was on something that wasn't very good?

WI: It was a bad mistake. Leonardo, being a scientist, always tried new things. And being a procrastinator who didn't work quickly, he's trying to do it as a fresco, but all of you out there who have painted frescoes know you have to do it on wet plaster. You have about a day to finish your little segment, and then the plaster dries, and he screwed it up.

DR: This was painted in what year?

WI: In 1489, but within 100 years, it was basically falling apart. It's recently been restored, about a fifteen-year restoration. And it's absolutely gorgeous. It's one of those things you have to try to figure out: How much can you do in restoring it?

DR: Leonardo was not only an expert in painting but also in drawing. What is *Vitruvian Man*?

WI: *Vitruvian Man* to me is the ultimate intersection of art and science. As I said, when he comes to Milan, he's going to be an architect for the duke, and they want a tower to be put on the Milan Cathedral.

Leonardo thinks the cathedral is horrible, because he believes simplicity is better. He does a simple circle and a square for the tower, which they didn't build. Leonardo was fascinated by the ancient Euclidean mathematical challenge of squaring the circle, creating a square that was the exact same area of a circle, using only a protractor and a ruler, which is difficult to do mathematically because pi is an irrational number.

He's totally obsessed by all this. He's got a good friend, Donato Bramante, and they decide, okay, we are going to figure out how to do a properly proportioned church. Leonardo does all the proportions of the human body. He spends notebook pages looking at ways to square the circle. They go to Pavia, which is twenty or thirty minutes outside of Milan, and they create this cathedral, which is, of course, a circle and a square together.

What the Renaissance was all about was the rediscovery of books that had been written in classical times. They helped rediscover a Roman book called *Vitruvius' Book of Architecture*. Vitruvius said that you have to make a church with the proportions of a human, because we spiritually fit into the cosmos. His friends all do the drawings of how do you fit in? How do you do it? Leonardo does all these measurements. His poor assistants. He used to have, I think, 400 drawings in the notebook of all these things. And he finally does his own drawing.

They all do it one night together. We know it's in July of this particular year. And Leonardo comes up with this one. Anatomically, it is exactly perfect. He has done every measurement from the navel to the knee to the genitals. Mathematically, it's brilliant. Vitruvius has said that the navel has to be at the center of the earth but that the genitals are in the center of creation. What Leonardo figures out is to take the circle and put it on the base of the square, but the circle goes up higher. You see the protractor needle right in the navel, and he's doing this perfect thing where the navel's in the center but the genitals are in the center of the square, so the circle goes up higher. When you do that, you square the circle. It means it's the same area. So, to him, this is a work of spirituality.

DR: Where is it now?

WI: On the top floor of the Gallerie dell'Accademia in Venice. I wish they would show it.

DR: One of the things that he specialized in was dissecting humans. Why did he do that? Was that for science reasons or art reasons?

WI: I think he begins for artistic reasons. He wants to get everything exactly right. One of the things that he screws up early in his life is *St. Jerome in the Wilderness.* He can't get the neck right, so he starts dissecting the human neck until he gets the muscles right. But being Leonardo, instead of doing science for the utility of it, he's soon doing it out of pure curiosity, for its own sake, and he's doing the liver and the heart and the heart valve. It's a driven curiosity.

DR: Was it hard to get bodies to dissect? How did he do that?

WI: It was tricky, especially in Rome. But in Florence, the church had quit banning dissections. Both in Florence and in Milan, he goes to the hospitals and does it.

DR: Let's talk about him as a scientist. One of his fascinations was flight. He develops pictures of a helicopter, in effect?

WI: Yes.

DR: Was he really ahead of everybody else in the science world? He made a lot of drawings, but did he ever actually produce any of the things that he drew?

WI: Not when it came to man-powered flight. One of the things I discovered in doing this book is people say, "Oh, he invented the helicopter." This is sort of a famous drawing. It was done because his first job was doing pageants and plays, and this was part of a play in which the angels came down from the ceiling, and these were the props that brought the angels down. But being Leonardo, the fantasy blurs into the engineering, and he spends the rest of his life trying to do a flying machine.

DR: He was also fascinated by birds. He dissected birds. Why was he so fascinated by them?

WI: He wanted to understand flight. He also was just so damn observant. One of the things in his notebook is he asks himself questions. One of the questions is, does a bird's wing go up faster or down faster when they're taking off and when they're flying? He sits there, and he observes, like, twelve species of birds and figures it out. Then, on one of his notebook pages, he describes the tongue of a woodpecker. How would you even know? You'd have to open up the mouth of a woodpecker. You don't need it to paint a painting, you don't need it to make a flying machine, but it's just Leonardo. He needed to know. He was so curious.

DR: He had a fascination with water as well. What was that about?

WI: I think it was because he was a kid inventing. He was self-taught, because he couldn't go to the university, he was illegitimate. He always loved the fact that when water passes an object, it swirls, and it always swirls in the same way. If you go to his notebook pages, he's always trying to do, up in the top left of the notebook page, swirls and curls. He's even making a stab at Fibonacci's equations to figure it out. He's always interested in these swirls of water. He ends up doing it with the human heart. He figures out how the heart valve works, because it works by swirling. So, in the very first thing he paints—it's Verrocchio's painting, but Leonardo's his fifteen-year-old apprentice—he does the angel on the far left, but he also does the River Jordan, the ripples past the ankles of Christ. This is the first time you have great realism in a painting. It's scientifically correct: both the rocks and the swirls.

DR: We have his artworks, and we have his drawings, but is there anything that he did in the science world that actually has benefited humankind today? In other words, is there anything he invented or discovered that we still regard as significant?

WI: It's not easy to pinpoint because, even though the year he was born Gutenberg invents movable-type printing and does a printing press, Leonardo never publishes notebooks, so it's about 150 years before people begin to rediscover them. He did figure out the heart valve. He did figure out certain ways of doing mirrors, but none of his flying machines and very few of his weapons of war ever got made.

DR: What was his relationship with Michelangelo?

WI: Bad. You can imagine.

DR: They were jealous of each other?

WI: They dissed each other very badly. It was almost famous in Florence that they hated each other. The Signoria, the people running Florence, decide that they're going to make them each do a painting for the Council House and have a battle. They start painting together, and both of them quit before they finish.

DR: Leonardo was venerated while he was alive? He wasn't discovered after he died?

WI: No. That is why the king of France was recruiting him. He was the first, and Michelangelo, who's a few years younger, was the second. Up until then, artists hadn't even signed their work. They worked for a studio like Verrocchio's. They're turning out Madonnas because all these rich merchants want to show how pious they are. Then, all of a sudden, like architects, they become famous.

DR: How long did it take you to do the research on this book?

WI: It was about five years of research, but Cathy did her junior year abroad in Florence, so we would go back to Florence all the time.

After a while, I became fascinated by the notebooks. As I said, the notebooks have never been collected. I started studying them and was reading them for years, and it suddenly dawned on me that you could use the notebooks as a foundation for a book.

DR: Do you read Italian?

WI: No. I learned Italian, but he wrote in mirror script.

DR: In other words, he wrote right to left?

WI: Yes. He was left-handed, so he wrote that way so as not to smear the ink.

DR: You picked Leonardo as a topic and did all this research. Do you admire him more than you did before? Or are you saying maybe he wasn't as great as you once thought?

WI: With everything, including Ben Franklin or whatever, you suddenly get to a point when you say, "My good goodness, only twelve paintings?" And the weapons of war, they were never built. You go through a period of saying, "Why couldn't he finish the painting? Why did he keep fantasizing?"

DR: You have specialized a bit in people who are already dead when you write about them—Leonardo or Einstein or Franklin. I assume it's easier to write something about somebody who's dead.

WI: Yes, definitely.

DR: One person died right around the time you finished your book about him. That was Steve Jobs. Why did he pick you to write that book, and what did you learn about Steve Jobs that you thought was so interesting?

WI: I'd done Ben Franklin, and I'd done Einstein, and Jobs gave me a call, and he said, "Do me next." I said, "Wait thirty years until you retire." Then somebody called, you can figure out who it was, and said, "If you're going to do Steve, you've got to do him now." It was cancer. He said, "He was diagnosed the day before he called you, and he hasn't told people."

I said, "This is a huge opportunity to figure out somebody who has transformed everything from computers to cell phones to publishing to retail stores to music, et cetera." One of the things about Steve Jobs is that he is the embodiment of *Vitruvian Man*, the intersection of art and science.

14

David McCullough on Writing American History and *The Pioneers*

INTERVIEW DATE: MAY 15, 2019

The late David McCullough (1933–2022) was for many years probably America's most beloved historian. His books read like novels; the facts his research uncovered were eye-opening; and his oral descriptions, in interviews and lectures, of what he wrote were quite compelling, in part because of his enthusiasm for the subject at hand and because of his wonderful baritone voice that kept everyone at rapt attention.

And his books were highly influential. His book on Harry Truman not only won the Pulitzer Prize for Biography but also forced a general reappraisal of Truman (now seen as having been a decisive, no-nonsense president who made vital decisions that helped lead the United States into global leadership in many areas following World War II). And McCullough's book on John Adams (also a Pulitzer Prize winner) brought about a public rediscovery of the man who, while not all that popular among his peers, drove the Second Continental Congress to break with Great Britain, drafted the Massachusetts state constitution, helped to edit the Declaration of Independence, and was the country's first vice president and second president. As a result of the McCullough-induced reappraisal, Congress finally authorized a memorial to John Adams in Washington (though, sadly, as of 2026 the memorial has yet to be built).

FIGURE 14.1 George Caleb Bingham's painting makes Western life appear enticing in its cheerful depiction of life as a fur trader. Rivers such as the Ohio, Mississippi, and Missouri were instrumental in carrying people and goods toward the West.

I interviewed McCullough many times at Dialogues events over the years, and he always proved to be as skilled and exciting a raconteur as he was a writer. He really did not need an interviewer.

In McCullough's last Dialogues interview, which focused on his book *The Pioneers: The Heroic Story of the Settlers Who Brought the American Ideal West*, he spoke about his enthusiasm in discovering previously unknown documents related to the settlement of the Northwest Territory—land that eventually became five full states (Ohio, Indiana, Illinois, Michigan, and Wisconsin), along with parts of what is now Minnesota. All this territory was organized by the Northwest Ordinance, passed by Congress after the Revolutionary War.

McCullough greatly admired Congress for passing the ordinance with language that ensured those states would provide free, universal public education; ban slavery; and ensure religious freedom. He also admired how the effort to have this territory created by Congress was pushed by a Massachusetts minister, Manasseh Cutler, and the actual settlement was led by a veteran of the Revolutionary War, Rufus Putnam. The story of how an extraordinary group of citizens from the original colonies suffered tremendous hardships to reach the Northwest Territory, beginning with Ohio, and built new lives for themselves and their descendants, is told in McCullough's always riveting manner in *The Pioneers*.

In interviewing McCullough, I was always amazed at both his command of the most minute of details as well as his passion for explaining how America was built. He was a unique figure in the world of American historians.

My favorite McCullough story is one that he told while receiving a major award in New York, where he described how he typically went about writing his books. His wife, Rosalee, always read his work aloud to him, because he wanted his writing to read well and to sound well, too. On one memorable occasion, he did not take Rosalee's advice to change a sentence that didn't sound correct to her. Events proved her right, as McCullough explained during our Congressional Dialogues conversation.

DAVID M. RUBENSTEIN (DR): You told a story once when you were getting an award in New York. You didn't talk about anything you had done. You talked about your wife.

DAVID MCCULLOUGH (DM): One of history's lessons is that very little of consequence is ever accomplished alone. It's a joint effort, always. I have been helped over the years by marvelous archivists and librarians and my wonderful research partner, Mike Hill. We've been working together for almost forty years. Jeff Flannery of the Manuscript Division at the Library of Congress has been at my side and elbow for many years, going back to the 1970s, I believe.

The most important helper in my writing life has been my wife, Rosalee. She is not only Mission Control, she's chair of the ethics committee. She listens or reads aloud to me everything I write, and does so maybe two or three times for each chapter. The reason for that is I believe that when you write, you should write to the ears as well as the eyes, because you hear yourself repeating certain words or expressions. You hear yourself being boring. And so, she reads out loud to me.

One of the more memorable events took place toward the end of working on my book about Theodore Roosevelt. She'd been reading along all the way through. One day she stopped me and said, "There's something wrong with that sentence." I said, "Read it again." She read it again. I said, "See? Nothing wrong with that sentence." "Yes, there is." I said, "Give it to me." Patience was running out. I read it out loud, and I said, "See?" She kept going, and we finished the book. I sent it off to my publisher. It was published, and it got a review in *The New York Review of Books*, largely a very good review. But toward the end, the reviewer said, "Sometimes, however, Mr. McCullough doesn't write very well. Consider this sentence."

DR: Your first book was about the Great Flood of 1889. That's an interesting subject, but why would you pick that for your first book?

DM: It all began right here at the Library. I came down to Washington in the very early days of the Kennedy administration. I'd been working at Time Life in New York, and I was swept up by Kennedy's call to do something for my country. So, I quit my job, and I came down, and applied all over town wherever they might need someone who was an English major and art major and who had worked at Time Life for five years. I wound up working, most luckily, in a very exciting opportunity at the US Information Agency when it was being run by Ed Murrow. I was made editor of a magazine for the Arab world. It sold all over at newsstands in Arabic. We did it in English and laid it all out here, but it was translated and printed in Beirut.

This was principally a picture magazine, and I had to keep within my budget. One of the ways I did that was to go to materials that would be in the public domain and wouldn't cost much money at all. I was in the Library of Congress picture collection. I'd been doing work there for several weeks and had come to know some of the people. One morning, I was walking by a big table, and it was covered in photographs taken in Johnstown right after the tragic dam breaking that had happened.

I grew up in Pittsburgh, and as little kids, we used to make a lake of gravy in the mashed potatoes and break the lake with a fork, and as gravy flowed down the piece, we'd say "The Johnstown Flood," having no idea what that meant. Then I saw pictures of houses turned upside down and trees jammed through houses. Unbelievable. I thought, how the hell did that happen? So, just out of curiosity, I started reading about what had happened. Once I started reading about what had happened, I knew, here's a book. And once I started working on that book, I realized this is what I wanted to do for the rest of my life. It all began here.

I thought I was going to be a writer, a novelist, or a playwright. But I never imagined I would be writing history. I still think of myself as a writer, only I write about only what happened to people who really were here on this dear Earth. I tried to bring people out of the shadows, people who deserve more attention than they had received, like Harry Truman and John Adams.

DR: You wrote a book about Harry Truman. Was he as impressive as you thought he was when you started?

DM: I thought he was vastly underrated. I loved the fact that he came up the hard way. He never went to college, but he never stopped reading, and he loved to read history. He once said the only new thing in the world is history you don't know. I think we should take that to heart. Eighty percent of our colleges now no longer require taking any courses in history in order to graduate. That's a huge mistake. Very few subjects are required, and I think they ought to be required, so, among other things, the student must realize that some things in life are required.

I was interested in politics when I was still in high school. I tried to stay up the night of the 1948 elections. I grew up in an old-fashioned

Republican family. But I couldn't keep awake. It was a final blow that didn't come through until two in the morning. The next morning, I woke up. My father was shaving. I said, "Dad, Dad, who won?" And he said, "Truman." It was like he ended the world. About thirty-five years later, I was back home, and after dinner, we sat down for a chat. He started talking about how the country was going to hell, and the world was going to hell. He said, "Too bad old Harry isn't still in the White House."

So, as Truman himself used to say, you have to let the dust settle before you pass judgment on people. You have to see what follows afterward, the secondary characters, and pay attention.

DR: If you had a chance to interview Harry Truman, what would be one question you would ask? Would you ask him about the atomic bomb or not knowing about the atomic bomb?

DM: I would ask him about the eight years he was trying to save his family from bankruptcy, working on the farm, really working. Harry Truman knew what it was to be up against the odds. I want to talk to him about his history teacher in high school, Margaret Phelps, who must have been brilliant and most insightful. Here she was, a high school teacher in a little town that didn't matter much out in western Missouri.

Our most important citizens who are doing the most important work of all are our teachers. They are going to determine what follows us and the values they have and the aspirations they have. All the characters I've written about, either at length like Adams and Truman or people I've written brief articles about, there's always a teacher that changed them. There ought to be a statue of teachers in every town in our country. It is not just paying them more. We should show respect and gratitude toward them.

DR: When you decided you wanted to write a book about John Adams, which won the Pulitzer Prize, people didn't think much of him. Did you come away with much greater respect for him?

DM: My initial idea was to do a dual biography of Jefferson and Adams. I knew a good deal about Jefferson, but I knew almost nothing about Adams. Jefferson, as you probably know, destroyed every letter he ever wrote to his wife and every letter she ever wrote to him. We don't know quite why that was. We don't even know what she looked like. I know from experience how important the spouses of these celebrated people were to what they accomplished, and how they kept their eye on the ball, et cetera.

Then I found that the collection at the Massachusetts Historical Society on the letters of John and Abigail Adams is phenomenal. Over 1,000 letters just between them, and neither one was capable of writing a boring letter or uninteresting letter, or a short one. If you took all of the Adamses' papers, diaries, everything from John Adams's family and John Quincy Adams, typed them up on typing paper, and put them all in a line, it would reach over five miles.

Now, none of us write letters much anymore. Nobody in public life keeps a diary anymore. It could be used against you in court. We're producing very few diaries or papers. That's where the meat of the effort is to be found. I believe you go to what they said, what they worried about, what they lost sleep over, whom they really liked and respected, and so on and so forth. Truman wrote letters that were terrific, but Abigail Adams's letters in many ways are as impressive as any I've ever read.

DR: She was not educated.

DM: She never went to school. She was educated at home. She could read and write. She was brave. He was away for months and years at a time, and she was running the farm herself. They had no money. They had no slaves. Never had a slave, because she did not believe in it, nor did he. These were people who really believed in what they said.

We can thank John Adams for the fact that the Supreme Court is separate from the rest of the government. We can thank John Adams for the basic structure and content of our Constitution, because he wrote the first constitution ever put into place in the state of Massachusetts. And, of course, he was the leader on the floor in Independence Hall who wrote some of the wording and was responsible for the approval of the Declaration of Independence. He was successful.

DR: You wrote a book about Teddy Roosevelt when he was out west. What propelled him to leave New York City, in depression, and move out to the West? What was the tragic event that happened to him in New York?

DM: His wife and mother died on the same day. He went out west to find a new confidence, a new energy, a new sense of future for this country. Teddy Roosevelt transformed from a frightened, frail little boy into this emblem of American virility and confidence. It's amazing and due almost entirely to his father.

We simply need to know much more about the parents of all of us. What we learn at home at the dinner table, what we learn about telling the truth, being honest, not getting too big for your breeches, all these values we were brought up on, we learn at home. They're as important as or maybe even more important, even, than what we learn in school. It's so vitally essential that we talk to our children, that we state what you do and don't do clearly.

DR: One of the books you wrote about forty years ago was very influential in the Senate, because it was on the Panama Canal treaty. Did you have any idea it would become influential and that Members would talk to you about the Panama Canal?

DM: The idea for the Panama book was handed to me by my editor at Simon and Schuster. I had no idea what I was getting into. It took six years. It's not only our part in the building of the canal, but part of the brave attempt made by the French. We appreciate far too little how important France has been in our story and nation right from the beginning, and how important we were to France during two hideous world wars.

The reason that we ought to stress history for everybody is that the lessons to be learned are immense, to say the least. One is empathy, the capacity to put yourself in the other person's place, which is how you write history or biography. You have to put yourself in their place, in the place of those of their time. The same, of course, is true with history. And then gratitude—gratitude for what they did that we are enjoying. This library. Our public school system. Our freedom. That's how it is. Well, how did it happen? To whom do we owe a thank-you? To be ignorant of our past and disinterested in our past is to be not only ignorant but rude. We owe them our gratitude.

DR: In that regard, in a recent survey done by the Annenberg Institute, three-quarters of Americans, 75 percent, could not name the three branches of government. One-third could not name one branch of government. This is amazing. A survey was recently done about the citizenship test that foreign-born individuals take to become a US citizen. It found that 91 percent pass that test. The same test was given, without their studying, to people who were American-born citizens in all fifty states, and there was only one state where the citizens who were taking the test without studying were able to pass it. That state was Vermont. Other than that, the native-born citizens failed the basic citizenship test. That shows you that civics and history are not well taught these days.

Let's go back to one more book before we get into *The Pioneers*, and that's your book on the Wright brothers. What propelled you to write about them? People thought everything had been written about the Wright brothers. What did you think could be brought to the subject of the Wright brothers that had not been written?

DM: All I knew was what I was taught in school in maybe fifteen minutes. They were bicycle mechanics who invented the airplane and flew it. That's all I knew. I found out they were geniuses. I was working on a book about Americans who went to France, and I wasn't sure where I was going to end the book. I thought, maybe I'll carry it into the new century, the twentieth century.

I was reading about people who were in France at the time, important and creative Americans, and I came across Wilbur Wright. I thought, what the hell are you doing in France? You're meant to be in your bicycle shop. He was writing letters home to his sister and to his father, and he's talking about the spellbinding power of the paintings he's seen in the Louvre, discussing and describing them in a very observant and intellectually high-level way. More powerful to me were his letters about Gothic architecture. He's so swept up by these great Gothic cathedrals reaching for the heavens, reaching for the sky, and the light is above. I think that's exactly the same motive as trying to touch the light above.

Then I read that his father was a marvelous itinerant preacher who wrote wonderful letters about the importance of reading. So, while they lived in a little tiny house with no running water, no indoor plumbing, no central heating, no telephones, it was full of books. He read all the books of the best, old sets like Mark Twain and others. If you can learn to use the established language, you will be way ahead of almost everybody else, no matter what vocation you go into.

The Wrights' father said the most important thing is to have purpose in your life. Find worthy purpose. They certainly did. And don't give up. Which, of course, is one of the great lessons of the life of George Washington. You do not give up. There seemed to be no chance that we could win the Revolutionary War. Under Washington's command, we made some terrible mistakes. We had no army to start with. We had no navy. We had no money. We had no officers with much experience. But we would not give up. Most people have no idea that a third of the country was for the Revolution, a third of the country was adamantly against it, and the other third in that good old human way was waiting to see who won.

DR: Speaking of the Revolution, the Treaty of Paris ended the Revolutionary War in 1783. The Articles of Confederation were under consideration and Congress was meeting in New York. What was it that led to the Northwest Ordinance and why did you write this book about the pioneers who traveled from the East Coast to Ohio and, ultimately, other territories covered by the Northwest Ordinance?

DM: At the end of the Revolution, in the Treaty of Paris negotiations, where John Adams was representing us, the British ceded to us what was called the Northwest Territory, which was all the land north and west of the Ohio River. When the British said, "Maybe we don't want to do that," Adams told them, "If you won't do this, I'm going back and telling everybody, pick up your rifles again, we're going to keep on fighting this war." The British conceded, and they gave us this vast wilderness territory that was as large in area—think of this—as the original thirteen colonies. It doubled the size of our country. It would include five states: Ohio, Indiana, Illinois, Michigan, and Wisconsin.

In 2004, I was invited to come to Ohio University to deliver the commencement speech. It was their 200th anniversary. I knew very little about the university. I did some homework. I learned that the oldest building on campus is called Cutler Hall. Who was Cutler? I found out he was Manasseh Cutler, and once I began reading about Manasseh Cutler, I was hooked. He was a classic eighteenth-century American polymath. He was a doctor of law, doctor of medicine, doctor of divinity—three doctors in one. He was also probably, although no one can prove it, the leading American botanist of his time.

He went to New York, which was our capital, and persuaded the Congress to establish this Western empire with four basic rules. One: Freedom of religion for everybody, no questions asked. Two: The Natives would be treated with respect, and they would not be treated any other way. Three: There would be public education for everybody from grade school through college. There was no such conception. It was for all children, paid for by taxes. And he introduced what essentially wound up being the state university system. There was nothing like that anywhere in the original thirteen colonies.

Number four: There would be no slavery. This man, Manasseh Cutler, and other men in this ideal project thought it was time we didn't just say on paper that all men were created equal. To stop slavery, there will be no slavery and there was no slavery in that territory.

There was a challenge after Jefferson became president. I didn't know about it. Manasseh Cutler's son, Ephraim, went through as one of the pioneers and settled in Ohio. His father couldn't do that, because he had too much responsibility with his parish in Massachusetts and was too involved in school to do it. Young Ephraim with his family went out there and got the legislature started. He and Rufus Putnam, the famous general from the Revolutionary War, were champions of public education and champions of no slavery. They were elected to the legislature.

And young Ephraim was battling, because there was a big movement after Jefferson became president, to repeal the no-slavery law and introduce slavery into Ohio. It was a close and very spirited controversy.

DR: Why did the Southern states in the Congress allow something like that to pass? I thought they would not be in favor of that.

DM: Because they thought that would help develop part of the country and they would have some say in it. [Back in Ohio] Ephraim Cutler got very sick. He probably was going to die. Rufus Putnam, who was old enough to be his father, came into where they were staying in the boardinghouse and said, "You've got to get out of bed and come for the vote. It might be very close." Ephraim said, "I can't get out of bed." It was said that Putnam and two or three others got him onto a stretcher and carried him into the legislature. There's no proof of that, but somehow or other, he came to the legislature, and he gave a powerful speech against the introduction of slavery and cast a vote. Their side of the argument maintained the rule of no slavery and won by one vote.

So, the son is carrying the father's banner into the battlefield and winning by one vote, his vote. If I were writing a novel and I had that scene in the novel, my editor would most likely say that wouldn't happen in real life. But it did. What you vote for and against matters.

DR: Some people say that one of the reasons Congress passed the Northwest Ordinance was because there was an obligation to Revolutionary War veterans.

DM: Most people don't realize that the war lasted for eight and a half years, and the soldiers were paid in what was called scrip. Which turned out to be worthless—about ten cents on the dollar. So, a scheme was cooked up by Rufus Putnam and Manasseh Cutler and a bunch of brave people in Boston that they would establish a company that would buy a huge tract of land in this newly opened wilderness and sell veterans from the Revolution good land, albeit covered with forest, good land for very little money.

At that time, after the war was over, there was a severe depression, which lasted almost as long as the war. New England farming land is terrible, with rocks and so forth, and here's this prospect of rich topsoil with no stone or rocks, sometimes at a depth of five feet or more, for very little money. All you needed was courage and determination and the physical strength with your family to go out and make it work.

DR: How did they get there initially?

DM: There were no roads. They would go over the mountains to Pittsburgh. Getting to Pittsburgh was very difficult, because there were hardly any roads to get over the mountains. Then they floated down the Ohio. Remember that there was no white settlement as yet anywhere in this land. There were squatters and there were trappers and hunters, but no real legal settlement.

They decided the location would be at the junction of the Muskingum River and the Ohio, which is an absolutely beautiful location to this day. They said that famous New England line that they would build a city on the hill there. In other words, they re-created Eastern civilization as it had been created in New England, which meant church, port, yard, schools, and order. Rufus Putnam laid out the whole town, Marietta, before they left Massachusetts.

And, oh, what courage it took, and what suffering. I've been reading David Brooks's new book where he talks about the benefit of suffering. We have no idea how these people suffered. They had no anesthetic for their wounds or for the experience of pulling out a tooth. The only anesthetic they had was whiskey. That was also a currency, because you can do business with whiskey more readily.

DR: There were no gnats, mosquitoes, or flies, right?

DM: The woods had wild turkey and wild deer, snakes, wildcats. Some of the neighbors were friendly and some weren't. They had to make their own clothing. They had to make their own cabins, their own homes. One young fellow lived for a whole year in a hollowed-out tree stump. The stump stood about twelve feet high and it was all hollow. Six men on horses could get inside that hollow tree. Now, imagine trying to take that down. But when they did start to clear the land and plant corn, the corn grew to fourteen feet in height. Imagine the thrill of that, and the promise of it. But they had adversity such as we can't imagine. You come away from this chronicle thinking that we're a bunch of softies. Really.

DR: The Treaty of Paris was between white men on one side of the Atlantic and white men on the other side. What did the Indians think about the white men coming from the East into their land? Were they happy with that?

DM: It depended on who the white men were. The first expedition went out to prepare the way with forty-seven men. The Indians who were in that area, the Delawares—Captain Pike was known as the chief—greeted them at the landing. Some seventy Native Americans, men, women, and children. Because these pioneers led by General Putnam treated them respectfully, just as it was said in the Northwest Ordinance, when the Native American wars began, they never attacked the fort at Marietta, because they'd been treated respectfully.

In writing this book, my concentration was on the original pioneers and what they experienced in their own land. I got to Marietta Library on the campus of Marietta College and, lo and behold, there was a collection such as I had never imagined. I've worked with some of the greatest collections imaginable, in my experience, here in this country and here in the Library of Congress and abroad. But I had never seen anything remotely like it. Thousands of letters. It wasn't just diaries and record books. It was records, paintings, drawings, surveys, maps, you name it. Thousands of them, all in perfect shape, all in perfect care, all in this one beautiful, recently built library, with a librarian who is easily as good as anyone I've ever worked with. It's not in attics or distant universities: It's right there on that beautiful campus, in the town where virtually the whole story takes place. It was a dream come true.

So, I'm telling the story from their point of view. It wasn't just the quantity of the letters and diaries, it was the quality—the quality of the thinking, the quality of the aspirations, the quality of values, which couldn't be more relevant and valuable today, and how much we can learn and take heart from those people. I thought, Why in the world has this story been left out of our history?

15

Siddhartha Mukherjee on Cancer, Cell Biology, and Mapping the Human Genome

INTERVIEW DATE: APRIL 18, 2023

Siddhartha Mukherjee had a very distinguished academic and professional career before writing a book in 2010 that won the Pulitzer Prize for General Nonfiction and captured the world's attention: *The Emperor of All Maladies: A Biography of Cancer*. That book explained, from the perspective of a cancer researcher and practicing oncologist, the history of cancer treatment and the possibilities for dramatically improving that treatment in the foreseeable future.

Before writing that extraordinarily well-researched and well-written book, Mukherjee had immigrated from India to attend Stanford, where he studied biology; won a Rhodes Scholarship to study at the University of Oxford; received an MD from Harvard Medical School; became a resident oncologist at New York-Presbyterian Hospital; and then was a professor in hematology and oncology at Columbia University Medical Center.

The critical and commercial success of the cancer book led Mukherjee to write a trilogy, with the other two books focusing on genes and cells. The latter book—*The Song of the Cell: An Exploration of Medicine and the New Human*—was the subject of my Dialogues interview with him.

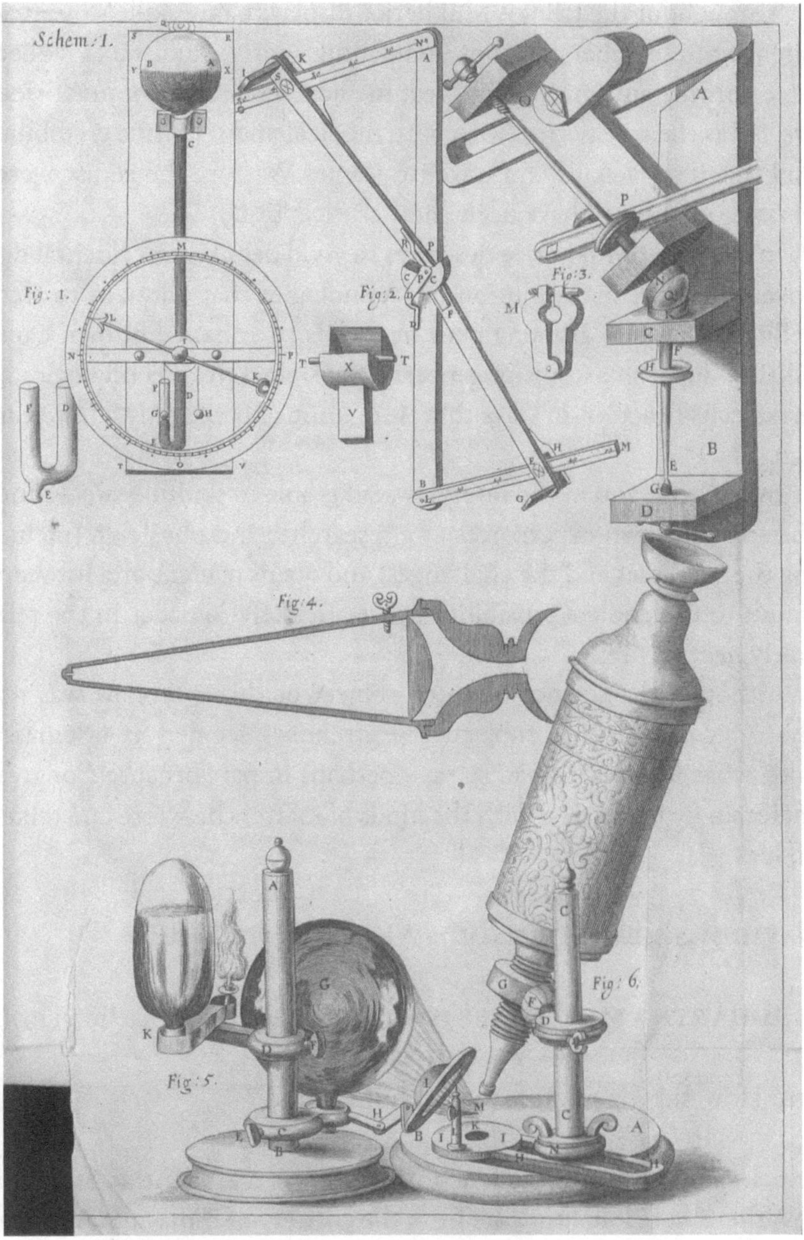

FIGURE 15.1 Robert Hooke's *Micrographia* was the first book dedicated to microscopy, and it features detailed plates like the one shown here. Hooke was the first to use the term "cell" in the biological sense.

Throughout the trilogy, Mukherjee displays a rare skill. Most great scientific researchers are not compelling writers, and most skilled, page-turning authors are not great medical researchers or practitioners. Sid is the rare person with both medical and scientific credibility and the literary skills of a novelist. (James Watson, the codiscoverer of DNA, might well have been another exception.)

In the book, Mukherjee describes in vivid detail the accidental discovery of cells, the evolution of technologies that allow us to treat cellular disorders and engineer new cells to enhance human capabilities, and the astonishing potential of emerging technologies to make cells function in ways that were unimaginable only a few years ago.

In the book and in the interview, Sid is able to skillfully weave into the story his own experiences as a researcher and physician (including the successes and the challenges) and opens readers' and listeners' minds to the endless possibilities that are likely to occur in the relatively near future.

Although the science-oriented subject of this interview was not the typical Dialogues subject, the attendees seemed as fascinated with what Mukherjee had to say—perhaps in part because Congress increasingly has to deal with the kinds of matters he wrote and talked about.

DAVID M. RUBENSTEIN (DR): Where were you born?

SIDDHARTHA MUKHERJEE (SM): I was born in New Delhi in 1970.

DR: How did you migrate to the United States?

SM: I came here as a student in 1989. I was a student at Stanford. FYI, there were four students from the entirety of India at Stanford as undergraduates at that time. Now I hear that number is about sixty.

DR: You won a Rhodes Scholarship. Were you a great athlete, or what did you do?

SM: I'm not a great athlete. That's one among many things that I'm not. It turned out that the Rhodes had relaxed the requirement. You just had to be healthy enough to be a Rhodes Scholar. There were lots of reasons for this, good reasons. So, for instance, there was a recognition that people may have physical disabilities, et cetera. The athletic part of the Rhodes Scholarship has been toned down to being healthy and exercising. You don't have to be a superman.

DR: You went to Oxford and you got a degree there?

SM: I did. I got my PhD.

DR: Where did you get your MD?

SM: From Harvard Medical School.

DR: And you're an oncologist?

SM: I'm an oncologist.

DR: What propelled you to want to write a book on cancer?

SM: Because it wasn't there. No one had written that book.

DR: Nobody had written a book like that. We'll go into it in a moment. But when you write a first book and it wins the Pulitzer Prize, sometimes that gives writers what's called writer's block. After Margaret Mitchell wrote *Gone With the Wind*, she never wrote another book. Ralph Ellison wrote *Invisible Man*, never wrote another book. Harper Lee wrote *To Kill a Mockingbird*, yet during her lifetime never published another book. Did you have that problem when you were trying to write other books?

SM: I had always imagined that the books would be a quartet, that I would start with cancer, go on to the gene, go on to the cell, and then we'll talk about the next book. So, there would be a quartet. I didn't get writer's block only because I had imagined it as a larger project as opposed to one book.

DR: How do you have time to be an oncologist and treat patients and also write books?

SM: Mostly because I compartmentalize my life, and I run it to the ground. I miss all the deadlines and barely am able to file my taxes and other things, but that helps.

DR: Let's talk about cancer. Was there cancer 2,000 or 3,000 years ago?

SM: As far as we can tell, it goes back to mummies. Most of the cancers that existed 2,000 or 3,000 years ago have been destroyed, but even the most ancient human specimens that we've unearthed have signs of cancer in them, especially, for instance, bone cancers. Bone cancer generally can't be destroyed because it's not in soft tissue. So, as far as we can tell, all the way back in human history there always was cancer.

DR: Where did the word *cancer* come from?

SM: The word *cancer* comes from the word *crab*. We don't know exactly when it was coined, but Hippocrates used it, a lot of people used it, the Greeks used it. The idea was that the mass of cancer under the skin looked like a crab buried under the sand. It's kind of a bizarre metaphor, but that's how it started.

DR: Before the twentieth century, if somebody got cancer, what was the normal treatment?

SM: Way before the twentieth century, people had tried to cut cancers out. There's a very moving—I would encourage people to read it—a very moving description of what might be the first breast cancer surgery, a mastectomy called "Fanny Mae's mastectomy." This was a woman in England who was drugged with opium, and then they tried to cut the cancer out. That was the only thing that was available—just have surgery.

DR: In the late nineteenth century, radiation was discovered, and in the twentieth century, chemotherapy was discovered. Was it discovered by accident that they could help with cancer?

SM: Radiation was discovered by Wilhelm Röntgen. If I remember correctly, he won the first Nobel Prize [in Physics] ever given. He discovered radiation mostly by accident. He was working with vacuum tubes, and he found that he could make radiation. Radiation therapy was in a very primitive form, and the person who really pushed it forward was an English doctor named Geoffrey Keynes. The reason you should know Geoffrey Keynes is that he happens to be the brother of John Maynard Keynes. At one point in time, no one knew who John Maynard Keynes was but everyone knew who Geoffrey Keynes was because he had discovered radiation therapy. Chemotherapy was also discovered by accident, and it was discovered by people using the idea that cellular poisons, poisons that would kill cells, would also kill cancer.

DR: When was that?

SM: Chemo comes to us in the 1940s and 1950s. Sidney Farber in Boston and several researchers at the National Cancer Institute simultaneously discovered various chemical toxins, chemical poisons.

DR: You point out in your book that when Richard Nixon was president, he declared a war on cancer, propelled by some prominent people from New York. Who went in and lobbied him?

SM: One prominent person who needs to be recognized is Mary Lasker. Richard Nixon was the final signatory, but the war on cancer really was invented by women, Mary Lasker and Florence Mahoney in particular. Even today, the main thrust for cancer research in

Congress is supported by very strong congresswomen who have done a great job in pushing this forward.

DR: The war on cancer was supposed to eliminate cancer in some finite period of time. Have we made a lot of progress in that regard?

SM: Yes, we have. It is a common illusion that we have made no progress. You should eliminate that illusion, because an enormous amount of progress has been made. I will give you a couple of examples. The most striking example is in breast cancer. The rate of mortality from breast cancer has been falling by about 1 percent per year over the last twenty-five years. You can say 1 percent is a useless number, no one cares about it. But 1 percent cumulatively over twenty-five years is 25 percent. That is a huge change.

DR: With breast cancer, if it's discovered in stage I and you get treatment then, you have a 98 percent chance?

SM: You have a 98 percent chance of surviving.

DR: That's where we've made the most progress?

SM: In general, cancer is organized like a pyramid. The base of the pyramid is cancer prevention. Ironically, we put the least amount of money into that. It's also the hardest because it involves behavioral change. It involves massive changes in human populations, public health, and so forth. The middle of the pyramid is early detection. We were stuck in it for a while but now have started making a lot of progress in early detection. There are massive trials, both in the United States and in Britain and in Europe. Finally, there's treatment.

DR: What causes cancer? Is it genetic, environmental, or behavioral?

SM: The answer is there are four or five causes, all of which converge. You can imagine this as all arrows that enter the same point.

It's changes in genes that regulate the behavior of cells. You could inherit those genes from your parents, like BRCA-1 and BRCA-2 are inherited genes that you get from your parents, unfortunately, and that's a cause of cancer. Another way you can change genes is through the environment, carcinogens, smoking being one of them. It makes changes in genes, changes in DNA that will cause cancer. A third way is viruses. A few viruses can also get into cells and tamper with their genes. And the fourth way, which is the saddest way to some extent, is random. When your cells divide, like any cells, they make mistakes in copying genes, and those mistakes cause genetic errors, which ultimately lead to cancer. With all four ways, you can imagine there are four arrows that point to the same problem, which is changes in genes and cells that cause these cells to divide abnormally.

DR: With breast cancer, we have mammograms, so you can determine early whether you have breast cancer, possibly. We have a PSA test for prostate cancer, and that works reasonably well?

SM: It doesn't work well.

DR: Why doesn't it work well?

SM: I talked about a pyramid. Early detection means the middle of the pyramid. For a long time, our tools to assess this pyramid were quite poor. PSA is a good example. There are lots of men who have high PSA who do not have prostate cancer. They'll get needless biopsies; they will get needless treatment for prostate cancer that won't kill them and won't actually affect their lives. That's an example of not such a good test. We are now evaluating much more sophisticated tests for detecting cancer early. The critical question is whether those tests will actually decrease mortality or not.

DR: Is it true that if you're a man and you live long enough, you'll get prostate cancer?

SM: That's correct. The prostate is one example. There have been a bunch of studies on this. If you were to dissect people who died randomly of automobile accidents, you would find lots of cancers in their bodies, including cancers in the thyroid, cancers in the prostate, sometimes cancers in the breast. Those are incidental. They will never cause the people to die. In this case, automobile accidents do. So, the real trick or the real distinction, and it's a very important distinction, is to figure out an early detection mechanism, whatever it might be, which finds the kinds of cancers that will kill you as opposed to the kinds of cancers that won't kill you. And that's a big challenge.

DR: Let's talk about those that kill you. I've always thought that the three most deadly cancers are glioblastoma—brain cancer—and pancreatic cancer and liver cancer, because there's no early detection method for any of those three. Typically, stage IV is when you find out. Is that fair?

SM: It's fair enough, except I'll give you some more that are just as bad. Ovarian cancer is a great example. It's a neglected cancer that obviously occurs disproportionately in women. It's also very hard to detect because there's no detection test for it. You don't image your ovaries.

DR: With glioblastoma, you don't know you have it until you have a seizure?

SM: Often, typically. Sometimes you can have a head bleed or whatever it might be.

DR: With pancreatic cancer, until your skin turns kind of jaundiced, you don't know you have it?

SM: Yes. I'm going to tell you a quick joke. There was a medical student who once saw a man with back pain in the emergency room. This is a true story. He said, "You have pancreatic cancer." They did an MRI and, in fact, the man had pancreatic cancer. The medical student won a big prize from his university. He went up and the doctor gave him the prize and said, "How did you diagnose this?" He said, "What else could it be?" Because this man had back pain. It's a good example of a little knowledge being a dangerous thing. Diagnosing pancreatic cancer is complicated because it's often missed, and you can be the medical student who diagnoses because someone walks in with back pain.

DR: Let's talk about gene therapy and how it affects cancer treatment. President Carter came down with melanoma in his brain. With some immunotherapy, it evaporated. How did that happen?

SM: For a long time we've known that cancer cells, especially when they metastasize, when they move around in the body, have to have some kind of system to evade the immune system. There is no reason a melanoma should sit in the brain. It comes from the skin. Skin cells can't sit in the brain just like that. The immune system has many mechanisms by which it's always asking the question "Do you belong or do you not belong here? Are you the right kind of cell that sits here?"

For a long time we didn't know this. We thought the immune system was much simpler. But now we know that there are not one, two, three, or ten mechanisms by which the immune system is asking the question "Do you belong?" Are you a client, as someone put it, of this organ or are you not a client of this organ? New developments have allowed us to basically explore those mechanisms by which the immune system detects a cancer. In this case, Jimmy Carter was treated at once.

DR: What is the best way to prevent having cancer?

SM: The obvious ways are to avoid carcinogens, the biggest ones being smoking and tobacco use. Those are obvious. We're losing the war there. Smoking rates are rising in many countries.

DR: Not in the United States.

SM: In the United States, among some populations, it is rising. Among some teens it's rising. Vaping is probably just as bad as smoking in terms of risk of cancer. We don't know yet for sure, but it probably has carcinogens.

DR: So, have good behaviors. Don't smoke. What about drinking alcohol? Is that good for you?

SM: Drinking alcohol is not good for you, although I would say it's a minor carcinogen. It's not the most major carcinogen. The most major carcinogen that we discovered in the last twenty- or thirty-odd years is obesity, which is linked with breast and ovarian and other cancers. There is a big effort across the many institutes to figure out the link between obesity and cancer. It's not obvious why obesity is linked to cancer, but it's clearly linked.

DR: It seems as if more people I know are getting cancer. That's because people I know are getting older. An indicator you're likely to get cancer is aging. Aging always causes cancer?

SM: Aging is the leading cause of cancer. But, of course, that's something that we would not like to eliminate.

DR: Is the incidence of cancer in this country rising because people are living longer or because we have better detection methods?

SM: The incidence of cancer is mainly rising because we're living longer. It's important to remember that incidence is a bad indicator. People use this word *incidence* all the time. I urge you not to use it or overuse it. Incidence is a very bad indicator of what's happening in cancer. Mortality is a very good indicator. Because incidence will rise as soon as you have a new test. Look at what happened when the PSA test was announced. The incidence of prostate cancer went up. But mortality from prostate cancer went down. So do not use *incidence*, because it is a false indicator. Incidence will make you think that people are getting more cancer. Use *mortality*. The National Cancer Institute every year publishes data on this, so use that as a correct indicator. There are mathematical and statistical reasons I won't go into about why incidence is the wrong measure and mortality is the right measure. If you ever get asked that question, do not fall into the trap.

DR: In your view, is it possible that we could eliminate cancer fifty years from now or 100 years from now?

SM: No. This is a long battle. As I said, the important goals are to reduce mortality, particularly in younger people, people who have many more years to live. This is not to minimize the impact on older people. The idea is overall to increase what I call dignified functional living with a diagnosis of cancer. That's the goal.

DR: When you're an oncologist and someone comes to you and they have, let's say, stage IV pancreatic cancer, what do you tell them?

SM: Truth is an important thing, but it's a negotiable thing. In the first visit with someone, you nudge them toward a particular way of thinking. In the second visit, you nudge them further. By the fourth visit, you've made a bond with them, and you begin to ask important questions about what they would like to do. If you do it in the first visit, they will never come back and see you again. So, you have to nudge people rather than shove them toward what is ultimately true. That's the art of medicine.

DR: If somebody has stage IV pancreatic cancer, do you say, "Do you have your affairs in order?" You don't do that.

SM: No. I ask them what their goals are. I ask them how much they know about the diagnosis. I tell them that there are some people who survive two years, three years. That's the general statistic. Then I stop and I ask them about themselves. I spend forty-five minutes talking about who they are. How many children do they have, if they have any children? How many nieces and nephews do they have? Where do they want to go? What are their goals? At the next meeting I say, here are the real numbers. How can we get you to accomplish these goals? In the next meeting I might say, what are your goals in terms of palliative care? But I don't shove a giant rock of lack of hope and despair on their heads. That's my practice. Other people practice different ways.

DR: That was your first book—on cancer. Let's go to the second book, which is a book on genes. Who discovered that genes are the mechanism to replicate life?

SM: There was a Moravian monk, Gregor Mendel. I visited his monastery. I'll tell a quick story about the monastery because it tells you about life. I went to Mendel's monastery. I traveled all over to get there. I ended up there and the woman said, "I'm sorry, the monastery is closed today." I had arrived from far away, and I said, "Listen, how do I get in?" She said, "You have to make a special application in triplicate." I stood there and I thought, I'm from India, I know how to play this game. I said, "I'm going to make a special application in triplicate right now." So I sat down in front of her and filled out three forms, then gave them to her, and she looked at me in a malevolent way and said, "Fine, I'll let you in." That's how I got into Mendel's monastery.

DR: Mendel was a monk, and he discovered through experiments with peas that genes basically produce certain effects and so forth. But nobody knew about his work for a long time?

SM: For about sixty-odd years. First of all, he didn't use the word *gene*. He didn't even have that in his vocabulary. The word *gene* comes forty years after Mendel discovered this idea.

DR: A number of years ago, the US government, I think in the year 2000, did the Human Genome Project. We declared it was a tie between the private-sector person Craig Venter and Francis Collins, who was working for the NIH [National Institutes of Health]. Now that we know the human genome, has it helped us in any way?

SM: It's helped us in a thousand ways. You have to realize that maps in general seem useless in the beginning. Think about the GPS system. In the old days, you'd take out a map and, if you had to drive somewhere, you had to figure out "Am I taking I-95 and then going to I-287?," et cetera. But that map ultimately led to the GPS system. The GPS system is now on your phone. You just drive and it tells you what to do.

The Human Genome Project was a map. It was nothing more, nothing less. You can use that map now to navigate your way through disease systems, disease states, et cetera. It's been extraordinarily useful. A map by itself is not very useful. But once you use the map correctly, you can find out what the genes are that cause ovarian cancer, what the genes are that are implicated in ALS [amyotrophic lateral sclerosis] or other terrible diseases.

DR: There's a test now, 23andMe. You can get your genes identified. Do you think that's a good thing to do?

SM: Generally, no. I say "generally" for the following reasons.

DR: I already did it. I have 2 percent Neanderthal.

SM: I should say that's qualified. You're a qualified sucker. Because eventually, once we collect a lot of information, which 23andMe will collect, we can then use that information using AI and other methods to try to figure out how genes help determine fates.

Let me give you one example because it's important. Breast cancer is a good example. Now there are people whose families have breast cancer, but they don't have a mutation in BRCA-1 and BRCA-2 or the other two or three major genes. What we now know, because of the huge amount of sequencing that we've done, because of 23andMe and others pooling their data, is that you can actually identify the risk of breast cancer, not by one gene, but by looking at a hundred if not a thousand genes. And each one of them increases your risk a little bit. It's not like BRCA-1 and BRCA-2, which push you or shove you toward a great deal of risk. And that's very important because now you can tell a woman, you actually do have a risk of breast cancer, and we probably do need to think about how to monitor it.

DR: I talked to Dr. James Watson, who was the codiscoverer of DNA. He was the first person who had his whole genome mapped.

SM: He did, yes.

DR: He told me he didn't want to know if he had a gene that gave him a predisposition to Alzheimer's, because what could he do about it? He didn't want to know. Do you think that's a good idea to not know about some of these things if you can get the information?

SM: I think it's important in a pool way. I'm making a very important distinction. You can decide as an individual to know or not know, but it is a great public service for you to make your information publicly available. Those are two different things. When you make the information publicly available, I or anyone who works at this as a scientist can figure out what your exact risks are, whether you actually did get or didn't get Alzheimer's disease genes and potentially how to treat or cure it. So, you can make a personal decision not to know. That's your personal decision. But I would urge anyone who gets the genome sequence done to release that sequence to people, so that the public data sphere is improved and we can understand what happens.

DR: Your most recent book is about cells. So when did humans first realize cells were the nucleus of life?

SM: Here at the Library there's a beautiful copy of Robert Hooke's book *Micrographia*. He was the first person to look down the microscope and figure out, in the seventeenth century, that, bizarrely enough, bodies were not slabs of flesh, that in fact we were made out of little tiny units, which were cells. Jakob Schleiden and Theodor Schwann, two other great, important scientists, in the nineteenth century discovered that all organisms were either one cell or a collection of cells.

DR: All life comes from one cell, and then it replicates or duplicates.

SM: A thing to think about. All life, at least humans and other sexually reproductive organisms, comes from two cells: sperm and egg. The egg is the biggest cell in the body. The sperm is the smallest cell in the body. There's a reason why, by the way; I'll be happy to tell you the reason.

DR: What is it?

SM: The reason is that this sperm is just a carrier of paternal information. It's just an information carrier. It's basically DNA wrapped up in a mailbox. And that's all it does. The egg, on the other hand, has to have what's called positional information. It needs to know what's up, what's down, what's left, what's right, what everything is. Otherwise, your embryo wouldn't know what's up, what's left and what's right, and we would just be a big blob. But we aren't. We have legs and hands and feet, which are different from our brains. And so, the egg has to carry all the positional information and it's packed full of information that's not just in your DNA.

DR: What do you think of the theory that men have a bad sense of direction because it takes a billion sperm to find one egg?

When a cell divides and it doesn't divide well, it can create a pathogen or a bad cell. What causes pathogenic activity to occur?

SM: We have copy machines inside there, little molecules that make copies of DNA, and like every copy machine they have an error rate. There are lots of ways that the cell prevents errors. If you have a disastrous error, usually the cell will stop the cell from dividing. But even those mechanisms, which are called safeguard mechanisms, can go wrong. And ultimately, in the nearly trillion cells in your body there's going to be one cell that makes that mistake in copying and ultimately lead to pathogenic disease.

DR: We have different types of cells in our bodies. Let's talk about the cells that are blood cells. What makes them so distinctive?

SM: What's interesting is you can think about DNA as a musical score. But what's important is the entire musical score is written into your DNA. That means you have Beethoven, Mozart, Chopin, Tchaikovsky, everything written in your DNA. But every cell chooses to play out only one particular set of symphonies or orchestras. So, your red blood cell chooses Beethoven or maybe one part of Beethoven. Your nerve cell has the same score, but it chooses to play out other parts, and in this way your nerve cell becomes distinct, completely different from your red blood cell, even though they have exactly the same score. They're playing out different music. Hence the song of the cell.

DR: Let's talk about the cells that prevent disease. What's the mechanism that our cell system uses to prevent disease when something invades the body? What kinds of cells come about?

SM: It's a cascade. We still don't know all the elements of the cascade. It depends on the kind of infection. But generally speaking, you first have front-runners. The front-runners are cells like monocytes, neutrophils, et cetera. Their job is to be the fronters. Their distinctive quality is that they don't care. That's very important. They do not care what the pathogen is. All they know is that there's a pathogen around and they have to go and block it. Only afterward do you get a second immune response from B cells and T cells, and those cells are very different because they have a memory of what the pathogen is. If they encountered it before, they come up and create an army that's recognized it before. Why is that important? It's important because that's how vaccines work. The way vaccines work is that they elicit a memory in those B and T cells so that the next time the pathogen comes, those B and T cells have a memory of the pathogen and can go and attack the pathogen.

DR: What about brain cells? What's distinctive about the cells we have in our brains?

SM: They're very distinctive, for several reasons. I'm not going to go into the scientific details, but most importantly, brain cells have the capacity to communicate with each other and form circuits. We now know that these complex circuits in our brain are responsible for many things, including this conversation and all the activities that we do in life.

DR: What about cells in your heart? How are they different? How do they sometimes actually cause a heart attack?

SM: The cells in your heart are not causing the heart attack. The heart attack comes from the fact that those cells that are very important aren't getting enough blood. That's the typical heart attack. There are various kinds of heart attacks. The cells in your heart are very special, because they form, as I describe in the book, a kind of citizenship. They are so connected with each other that they actually form pores or gaps between each other. So that once an electrical stimulation comes, the entire heart beats together, because all the cells contract together. If they didn't, your heart would just be a wobbling organ. There are many kinds of heart attacks. But the typical heart attack has nothing to do with those cells. It has to do with the blood vessels that supply those cells with oxygen, and when the blood vessels get blocked is when you have a heart attack.

DR: Let's talk about thalidomide. In the 1950s and '60s, women who were, I guess, nervous or had some anxiety when they were pregnant were given thalidomide. Why did that produce such terrible birth defects?

SM: First of all, before talking about these birth defects, I want to give a shout-out to Frances Kelsey, who was one of the FDA [US Food and Drug Administration] reviewers who was responsible for saying, "Wait a second, I'm not sure about this drug which is being prescribed for anxiety. Let's just do a review of it. Let's hold off on it."

DR: She was a career civil servant at the FDA and a high-level person. She blocked thalidomide from coming into the United States.

SM: Despite incredible lobbying by two prominent pharmaceutical companies. She said, "No, wait a second, I'm not sure about the data." We owe her an incredible debt. She was recognized by President Kennedy.

Why did thalidomide cause these defects? We now know the answer. You can think of thalidomide as a drug that causes cellular absorbencies in multiple cells—heart cells, bone cells, many other cells. That's the ultimate reason that thalidomide causes all these birth defects.

DR: What is CRISPR [clustered regularly interspaced short palindromic repeats]? Can you explain what CRISPR is?

SM: Yes. CRISPR is a novel discovery. It comes from the world of bacteria. If you imagine your genome, you talked about the human genome as a massive library. It's written in four letters: A, C, G, and T. A human genome contains three billion such letters. If it was a library, it would fill this entire room. What CRISPR allows you to do, which is an incredible thing, is it's a bacterial defense system that was originally invented against viruses, and you can engineer it so that you can go into one book in one section of the library and erase or change one word in that one book out of the three billion letters, without—for the most part, it's not completely clear—touching any of the other words.

DR: A Nobel Prize has been given to two women, Emmanuelle Charpentier and Jennifer Doudna, for CRISPR. If I say I want to use CRISPR to have blue eyes rather than black eyes, it could theoretically enable me to do that?

SM: It would be very hard to do. This is a common misconception about CRISPR. This goes back to the idea I was talking about before. Most human traits—eye color, height, hair color, et cetera—are caused by not one, not two, but hundreds of genes. You'd have to alter hundreds of genes in the genome in order to select for any complex symmetry. There are some simple human traits. The cystic fibrosis gene is one gene. BRCA-1, the breast-cancer-involved gene, is one gene. But most human traits are controlled by hundreds if not thousands of genes. And so, it wouldn't be so easy to do.

DR: But in China a few years ago a Chinese scientist decided to create two babies without certain diseases that the parents had.

SM: It was a completely botched-up experiment. This scientist was very ambitious, I would say quite arrogant. He took parents in which the father had HIV and the mother didn't have HIV, and he tried to CRISPR out a gene in the babies that would make them resistant to HIV. It's a completely absurd, upside-down experiment, because if a father is HIV-positive and the children are conceived through IVF, which you have to do for CRISPR, the chance of the child getting HIV are zero. You're taking a person who has a zero risk of a disease and doing what might be a dangerous experiment on these two babies.

DR: Did he get approval for this?

SM: No. There were lots of ethical lines that were crossed, so much so that the world of scientists called for a temporary moratorium on the use of CRISPR to make babies. It's now in effect.

DR: But he went to jail?

SM: He was in jail for three years.

DR: Let me ask you about the next book. You were talking about writing four books.

SM: Yes.

DR: You haven't written the next one yet. The subject is likely to be something like longevity?

SM: Longevity and death is what I'm thinking about. But these books take so much time that I dread thinking about what to write until I start writing them. The answer would be, yes, I will write another book. It will be part of the four-book series. It will be probably something on longevity, death, and aging. But I have a kind of cold dread thinking about it.

DR: You want to live long enough to write a book on longevity, right?

SM: That would be a good thing.

DR: Off the top of your head, the best way to live a long life is to have healthy parents with good genes? Don't smoke, exercise, eat well? What's the best way to live a long life?

SM: Those would be all good ways to live a long life. Hopefully we will find some particular pathways in humans, which we're slowly discovering, that are related to what's called senescence aging versus longevity. If we could find those pathways, we could probably find medicines that would increase life and that would rejuvenate certain parts of your body.

DR: Realistically, human life probably can be extended ten years more, twenty years more, not to 200 years, you would say?

SM: I don't know the answer because we are in totally new territory. What's interesting in human beings who live very long, people that live 100 years, is that they—pay attention—do not die of heart disease and cancer. They die of the failure of stem-cell regenerative diseases. They break their bones and die. Their immune system collapses, they get sepsis, they get pneumonias, they get infections. Their skin falls off. So, the set of diseases that we will encounter as our populations begin to age beyond a certain point of time are going to be a different set than the ones that kill people in their seventies, eighties, et cetera, like cancer and heart disease.

DR: I noticed that in the drugstores in my neighborhood, the section for old people is getting bigger and bigger—adult diapers and canes. I don't know whether I'm more sensitive to it or is it just that more people need these devices because they're living longer?

SM: Longevity has increased across the world, very significantly. Your life expectancy in most places was fifty to sixty years. Now it's seventy to eighty years. In places like Japan it could be in the eighties, sometimes the high eighties. The last two years have been the first two years that, because of the pandemic, longevity across the earth has decreased for the first time.

DR: I thought longevity was going down because of obesity and drugs.

SM: This is world data. For the first time, human longevity decreased across the world.

16

Eric Schmidt on Artificial Intelligence

INTERVIEW DATE: NOVEMBER 19, 2024

The typical interviewee for a Congressional Dialogues dinner is a historian or biographer, for Members seem quite interested, not surprisingly, in hearing about American history or learning about prominent Americans.

But we have had some exceptions. For instance, Bill Gates was interviewed about his life and technology, and Chief Justice John G. Roberts Jr. was interviewed about his life and the Court. (These interviews can be found in my books *How to Lead: Wisdom from the World's Greatest CEOs, Founders, and Game Changers* and *The American Story: Conversations with Master Historians.*)

Another exception was Eric Schmidt, the technology executive who was the CEO of Google for ten years and its chairman for another four. In those roles, he helped lead Google (now Alphabet) from being a thinly funded Silicon Valley startup to the global technology giant that became a daily presence in the lives of billions of people.

When Schmidt left Google in 2015, he became a well-known technology entrepreneur and investor, an advisor to the US government on technology and defense matters, a public commentator on science and technology, and an author of books on public policy and technology.

FIGURE 16.1 The banks of computer terminals at Kennedy Space Center, shown here in 1967, symbolize the technological investment that created the "space age." Eric Schmidt calls the rise of artificial intelligence in the twenty-first century "the defining beginning of the next age."

Schmidt also developed close relationships with leading government and former government officials from around the world. Among those was Henry Kissinger, who was fascinated by the prospects for artificial intelligence (AI) and sought Schmidt's guidance and knowledge in a world that was seemingly far removed from Kissinger's world of geopolitical negotiations, strategy, and tactics.

One of the results of that tutelage and emerging friendship was *Genesis: Artificial Intelligence, Hope, and the Human Spirit*, a book on AI coauthored by Kissinger, Schmidt, and Craig Mundie (a tech entrepreneur who served for many years as Microsoft's Chief Research and Strategy Officer). When this Dialogues session was held in late 2024, Kissinger had passed away at the age of 100, and it was his last book. But I did have the chance to discuss Kissinger's, Schmidt's, and Mundie's views on AI with Schmidt.

Most people who reach the age of 100 are probably not looking to conquer new worlds or search for new horizons. But Kissinger was different. He believed that the possibilities for AI were nearly limitless and could produce advances in the tech world as well as the geopolitical world. Like his two coauthors, Kissinger believed that AI should be embraced, not feared, and that it could benefit humanity in ways that the world has only begun to imagine.

I have interviewed Schmidt many times, but not previously on AI. His discussion of the possible uses for AI fascinated the Members who attended this Dialogues session—particularly as they understood from Eric's comments that we are still in the first inning of artificial intelligence, just as we were with respect to the internet when Google was conceived.

DAVID M. RUBENSTEIN (DR): You grew up in the Washington area. Where did you go to school?

ERIC SCHMIDT (ES): I grew up in Annandale, in northern Virginia, and I graduated from Yorktown High School. I have many memories of Washington, but the most important ones were coming to the Smithsonian as a boy.

DR: You then went to Princeton and got your PhD in electrical engineering at Berkeley?

ES: At Berkeley, in computer science.

DR: Then you were running Novell for a while.

ES: And I worked at a company called Sun Microsystems for a long time.

DR: Sun Microsystems and then Novell. How did you come to be the CEO of Google? There were a lot of search-engine companies. They were a dime a dozen. What was it about Google that made it the largest, most successful of the search companies? When you first interviewed with them, what did you see in Google?

ES: The funny thing about interviewing with Larry Page and Sergey Brin, who were all of twenty-six at the time, was that they were so obnoxious, I had to work with them. Here I am, I'm a senior executive, and I know exactly what I'm doing, and these little pipsqueaks argue with every single thing I said. They said that everything I had done at Novell was a disaster. I had such a good argument with them that I said, "We're going to work together."

They were unusual because they understood talent extraordinarily well. They assembled this initial team that built a better search-ranking algorithm. Then there was a small team that figured out a way to do online advertising. The ranking they did, which was called a Dutch auction, propelled the income. So, from the moment I started, we started having this enormous revenue growth. More revenue solved all problems.

DR: Initially, I thought, they didn't know how they were going to make revenue. They had a good search engine. It was always clear they were going to get revenue from advertising?

ES: No. In fact, the original business plan basically said that they were going to license and get various forms of ads from promotions and so forth. The advertising system of today was invented by a guy named Eric Veach and a guy named Salar Kamangar. They were screwing around one day and trying to understand how auctions worked. What they did is they ran an auction where the price you got was the price that was the one below yours in the auction. That mathematically proves that you get the right outcome economically.

I remember that when we turned it on, I was convinced that the prices would fall. We did something called a cash restriction program, which meant that Friday morning at 10 a.m. was the only time we would ever spend money, and I had to spend it. I was so worried about bankruptcy. When we turned the thing on, it went boom, and the auction worked and things scaled. In our industry, when these slopes happen, they happen very fast.

DR: One of the unique things the Google founders did is they said to all their employees, "We're going to give you free food." Why did they do that?

ES: Larry and Sergey believe that you should basically treat the company like a family. We had a problem, because most of the employees were young, and they treated Google like their home. We had people living in their cubicles. We had to pass a rule that you couldn't live in your cubicle: You had to have a residence. That's just how zany this place was.

DR: You told me a story about how you were the CEO, and one day you go away on a trip and, when you come back, a low-level employee is using your office.

ES: It was very strange. I had a little office, eight by twelve, just enough room for me and my table and my computer at the time. I go away, I come back, and there's this fellow who's moved in next to me. I said hello. He said, "Hi, I'm Ameet." I said, "Why are you here?" He said, "My office was crowded, and you were never here, so I moved into yours."

When this happens and you're the new guy, saying "Get the hell out of my office" would have been a culturally inappropriate thing to do. So I said, "Did anyone approve this?" He said, "Yes, the person who works for you approved it." And I go, "Okay, now I'm in trouble."

The part of the story that gets interesting is that he had headphones on, and we're next to each other, and I'm on the phone in the obvious way doing CEO things, and the head of sales at the time was talking to me on the phone. He was saying, "I think we can get revenue to $115–118 million for the quarter," which was a big number at the time. It was important. I said, "I think you're sandbagging," and

I hung up the phone. Ameet takes off his headphones and says, "I can tell you the revenue number." I said, "I knew you were listening to my phone calls."

So, it turns out the revenue number was $140 million. I discovered that having your officemate be the chief accountant who's also an engineer building all the systems while you're trying to manage sales was the correct outcome. We ended up sharing an office voluntarily until the company went public, when I could no longer do it.

DR: Google had a rule that anybody could do anything they wanted for 20 percent of their time. Did any productive or profitable thing ever come out of that?

ES: Most of the interesting new things in the company came out of the 20 percent rule. It said that you have to work really hard, but you can spend 20 percent of your time on whatever you want. You might say, "This is going to be a disaster." What they would do is use that time to actually invent new things. So, many of the systems—for example, Google Maps, some of the search features, many of the advertising features—were done that way.

I'll give you another example of how this worked. One day, Larry printed out all the ads. By the way, my favorite ad during that period was from Georgia, and it was for a skydiving center. The ad's title was "Only one death this year at our skydiving center." It received exactly zero clicks.

Anyway, Larry put up this list of things, and he said, "These ads suck." This is on a Friday night at 8 p.m. I think, "This is interesting. We'll see what happens." By Monday morning, a whole new ad system has been built by a completely different group than the ad system group. I learned something, which is that if you get the right set of people and you give them an interesting problem, they will give up their personal lives. And that little group of three people ultimately became a now-trillion-dollar company.

DR: Let me ask you about autonomous driving. Have you ever been in one of these self-driving cars?

ES: They are so much fun, because they scare the crap out of you. The history, of course, is that Larry and Sergey and Elon Musk started at the same time. Tesla uses a visual system. Our system used a more expensive laser system, and we had trouble making it perfect. Larry and Sergey insisted on perfection, whereas Elon's approach had more risk. You see this in the lawsuits against Tesla. We couldn't get ours through the regulators, so Sergey specified a car that we called the Smurf car. There's an exemption in the law that allows you to build a nonregulated car that doesn't go faster than twenty-five miles an hour.

So, we had this Smurf car that looked like a Barbiemobile, with the lasers, running around. We set up races between human drivers and the Smurf cars, and the Smurf cars could drive faster. So we knew we had something. And, of course, these cars required an engineer in them to make sure the code didn't break while it was driving you.

Twenty years later, in San Francisco and in LA, Waymo now has cars where you sit in the back. I'm told that in San Francisco, the number-one tourist attraction today is those cars.

DR: You were on the board of Apple for a while. You met Steve Jobs.

ES: I knew him well.

DR: Bill Gates.

ES: Yes, I know him well.

DR: Elon Musk.

ES: Yes.

DR: You know him, and you obviously know Sergey, and I assume you know Mark Zuckerberg as well.

ES: Yes, sir.

DR: Who is the smartest of these people?

ES: I have always thought that Steve Jobs was the smartest. The difference between the rest and Steve was that he was a brilliant technical person but he was also a humanist. You can see that in the product and the quality. All of these leaders are incredibly controversial. They are driven, and they can be brutal, and they can be inspirational. Steve was a bully, but the team loved working for him, even as he was screaming at them. It's a unique skill, not one that I have.

I would say that Elon is in that league, because when you listen to him carefully, he can talk at many different levels of goal and achievement. I say that with great respect to Elon today.

DR: I want to talk about artificial intelligence. Where did the phrase "artificial intelligence" come from? Because it's not really artificial. Humans are behind it.

ES: In 1958, there was a paper written at MIT that said, roughly speaking, that computers will get so fast that within five years—which would be in the early '60s—we will have artificial intelligence. That's where the term was coined. At the time, the idea was that computers could pass something called the Turing test. In the Turing test, you have a human and a computer behind a screen, and you keep asking them questions. When you can't tell the difference between the computer and the human, the machine has passed the test. Most people agree that we're at the point of passing the current Turing test now. But it took sixty years. Why did it take sixty years? Because we require now an enormous amount of energy and computing at scale.

When I was in college, I used a computer the university had that was 100 million times slower than the mobile phone you have in your pocket. So, one of the things to start with is, how did we get here? The answer is that a whole bunch of physicists and semiconductor people built scale computing, fiber-optic networks, the communications around us, at a rate that is extraordinary, driven by this thing called Moore's Law. [According to Moore's Law, computer power would double every eighteen months.] It has largely slowed, but it's still operating. We have new laws that are driving scaling in AI.

DR: Artificial intelligence has been around for quite a while. You said the phrase was invented in 1958. Why all of a sudden are people so excited about it? Was it just that ChatGPT got people excited? What is so different about that artificial intelligence product?

ES: A quick history. When I was young, there was a set of views about AI in the 1970s that didn't pan out. Then there was something called the AI winter. For twenty or thirty years, nobody cool, from my perspective, was working on it. But in the mid-'90s, mathematicians invented a new technique that was more suited for the computers that performed it.

That algorithm, which is called deep learning, can be understood this way. Say you have a picture, and you have a layer of neurons that is mathematically like our brains. One figures out what's in the frame of the picture, and another one looks at what's in the frame and figures out it's a Madonna, and another one figures out there is a child, and the model says, it's a Madonna and child. Once you can recognize things in a picture, you can do a lot of things, because vision is 11 percent of human brains. Imagine it's probably better to have computer vision at work than human vision. Then set up the opportunity around, for example, self-driving cars. Better have the car drive you, because it has better vision than the human.

DR: Artificial intelligence has been used for many years. The generative thing that OpenAI came up with was just mind-boggling to many people. Was that something Google had already researched or that other people had already researched?

ES: About fifteen years ago, Google, which at the time had roughly two-thirds of the AI talent, in my immodest opinion, bought a company called DeepMind. Then we had two groups who were competing against each other to make progress in AI. DeepMind was founded by a team that included Demis Hassabis, who just won the Nobel

Prize in chemistry for his work in protein discovery. They were very good gamers. If you take a closed game, they built systems that could study the game, determine the rules, develop algorithms to do the play, and win, and they could learn, for example, all the games with two or three days of computing, which is not possible for humans. It was a big contest, first in South Korea and then in China—and I was at both—where it was man against machine. In both cases, the computer won. Google retired this game for all sorts of reasons.

But the interesting thing was watching people watch the end of something that's been around for 2,500 years. Sitting in China, we were watching this. The crowd is very boisterous. The human, the top player, is brilliant. There's a series of games. He loses the first game. In the middle of the second game, the government shuts down the television. Not a citizen in the country saw this extraordinary achievement. I was there. I saw it with my own eyes.

What happens in 2017 is that a team at Google builds something called transformer architecture. The T in GPT is transformers. The way to understand the transformer is that it's just a better way of doing learning, because it allows for scale across a lot of computers.

A team at OpenAI, which was founded, essentially, by Elon Musk, Reid Hoffman, and Sam Altman, a very small company, in 2016 started working on what could you build above the framework that Google had done. When they called me and asked did we want to use their computers, I said sure. It didn't occur to me that they would ultimately become the huge competitor that they are today. It shows you how small these things are when they start. We all knew each other. We were all friends.

So, in 2017, 2018, they work on GPT-1, a way of understanding general-purpose language. It doesn't work that well. Then they build another one. They spend more money. They built a slightly larger set of computers. They get to GPT-2, still not that good. Then they do GPT-3. It was, like, a Thursday night in San Francisco, and all of a sudden, they turn it on and it can write. It can write with this voice that they had never anticipated. It was a real discovery. It's like the light bulb was just invented.

Using this technique, technically what these computers do is take a million sentences, a million paragraphs, and the algorithm goes back, it looks at every paragraph and every word, and it fast-forwards to the most important word. Everything you know about AI, the way you perceive it, is because of next-word prediction. That's all it's doing. The computer is saying, "What's the next word, what's the next word?"

How could it possibly write that well? What's interesting—this is important for science—is that many systems are fundamentally sequence predictions. And GPT-3 showed you could do it.

Then what happens is they do GPT-3.5, and they're kind of bored with it because they're working on GPT-4. That's their report. Meanwhile, they release GPT-3.5, which they renamed ChatGPT. They made a modification where they used humans to improve the answers, which is a key breakthrough. That creates the ChatGPT moment, which, as you know, was two years ago [in 2022].

All of this happened in the last three or four years. In the last two weeks, the slope has been straight upward. Enormous amounts of money. Enormous geopolitical issues. Enormous gains. Enormous implications. This is the defining beginning of the next age.

DR: Many people are investing staggering sums in AI now. Do you think that a lot of it is wasted money, chasing things that aren't going to be returning money to the investors?

ES: Let me tell you their pitch. I'm going to call this the San Francisco pitch, because that's where it's coming from. There's a guy named Leopold [Aschenbrenner] who wrote a 170-page document, which you can read, that goes through this in great detail. It's very entertaining. What they believe, this group, is that within one or two cranks of the system, you will get to what is called superintelligence, where the systems are smarter than the sum of human intelligence.

I know some of this sounds incredible, but I actually believe this. I believe we will get there. We may not get there in two cranks, but the implications are profound. This is why Craig Mundie and Dr. Kissinger and I wrote the book. When the arrival of general intelligence is so economically valuable, to imagine using the system to solve every business problem, every energy problem, we need huge amounts of energy in our country, all sorts of human problems, all sorts of military problems. What would you pay for that, if you owned it? You'd pay a lot. Imagine everyone will have to come to you, and you say, "$20 million, $50 million. Oh, I don't like you, I'm not going to give it to you." Think of the power. That's the excitement about it. We'll see if it happens.

DR: Let's talk about the energy. To use AI effectively, you need a lot of energy, a lot of data centers. Is producing more energy for these data centers going to destroy the atmosphere? Is there enough room to build all these data centers?

ES: The good news about America is that we're blessed with so much land, so much energy, so many natural resources, that if we get our act together, we can do it. We need it now. I'll tell you why. I want to win against China, which we'll come back to.

The key thing about energy and climate change is that you're not going to be able to solve it without new materials, new energy sources, vision, and fusion, all of which need the developments of AI.

DR: Are you worried that China will be more advanced than we are in AI? Are they anywhere close to where the United States is in AI now?

ES: Dr. Kissinger and I spent a lot of time on this, and Craig is now working with the Chinese very closely on this. Here's a way to understand it. Let me start by asking, who will be the winners? I want it to be us. It has to be us, our country.

It's this important. This is one we have to win. Why? Let me scare you a little bit. This stuff takes a lot of energy. China's got that. A lot of data. China's got that. A lot of people. China's got that. China has a lot of very smart scientists. They didn't have a lot of chips. And guess what? The Chinese have now figured out workarounds.

I think I understand how all this stuff works out. They basically found ways to redirect or fake or lie to get the necessary chips. You say, how do you know? Let me tell you. This week, literally this week, two new models—one is called Qwen, Q-W-E-N—came out that are roughly equal to some of the best models coming out of America. How the heck did that happen? The answer is they are a tough competitor. So, if we don't solve the energy problem, we're toast.

DR: Are the Chinese developing these chips because they are smart and they do the work like we do, or are they taking them the way the Russians got our atomic secrets, by stealing them in some way?

ES: Ninety percent of the cyberattacks are from China against US firms, and that hasn't really changed very much. Everyone makes platitudes, but there's still a lot of Chinese espionage. In China they have a concept called civil-military fusion. I worked with the Defense Department for years. I headed the Defense Innovation Unit. We can talk about all of that, about the National Security Commission for AI. But their model is different. Fundamentally, if they focus on a sector, they pour enormous amounts of money into those companies to make them globally dominant. That's how they're catching up. So, Tencent and ByteDance, ByteDance being the parent of TikTok, are both the recipient of enormous amounts of government grants. You would never do this, nor am I asking you to do this, in the United States. The Chinese system is different.

Why is this so important? With every turn of the crank, meaning the training runs, you get an enormous improvement in knowledge and capability, and every one of those is important. They typically take about eighteen months per training run. We'll see if we can make that shorter. China is on the same path. At some point, we'll be able to have AI scientists that are not human also developing AI algorithms for themselves, at which point the slope gets even steeper. When you have a slope that increases that fast, even a small difference, like six months, can leave you way in the dust, because once you get to this particular point, you can dominate industries, you can invent new things, you can do all sorts of things adversarially.

I'm not trying to be alarmist. We are in a race, and we have to win. If you don't believe it, think about what happens if China invents

AGI, so-called general intelligence, and they do it in the way that I just described, which I think is the likely path. Then all of a sudden you'd have Chinese values, you'd have all the other countries using Chinese knowledge platforms to do their research. All that information would be leaked back into the Chinese government. There are so many reasons why we want America to control that.

And frankly, the other countries don't get it. We can discuss why. It's just a mess. None of the other countries have enough money or stability or power to do it. It's going to be China versus the US. China is the competitor, in this sense. Russia, Europe, other parts of the world are not really involved that much in AI.

If you look, since the pandemic, at the compound growth, productivity in America is 30 percent higher than it was six years ago, compared to Europe. That is damning. I talk to my European friends all day and I just have fun with them, because they're sort of fun to annoy. But the fact of the matter is the American model, which we should all be so proud of, is successful. It's the one that's the growth engine. You need a growth engine.

Russia, of course, is a disaster, and they're busy in the war with Ukraine, which is criminal, and all this kind of stuff. They're killing all their people. India's power structure and economic structure are not stable enough, although they certainly have the people. The other countries are not big enough.

One of the questions that I ask intellectual people who think about foreign policy, and Dr. Kissinger spent a lot of time thinking about these questions of global order, is what happens when China and the US are the sole providers of intelligence for everyone else? Think about it. What an incredible opportunity for us, but we have a competitor. But what happens to the French, who are kind of annoyed with us anyway? What happens to the Africans who have their own culture, their own norms, their own unwritten tacit knowledge? Does that go away? Does America win again? In front of you is another ten-year cycle where we have a chance of establishing American global dominance in the good sense—our culture, our values, democracy, individual freedom, all the things that we all share.

DR: Some people are worried that artificial intelligence will gobble up humanity and eventually destroy us. Is that a fear worth worrying about?

ES: Every one of those people has seen the movie. What happens is that you have your phone, and your phone becomes more and more your partner, your best friend, your alter ego. In our book, Craig and I and Dr. Kissinger talked at some length, in the first chapter, about polymaths. A polymath is someone like Einstein or Leonardo da Vinci or a great politician, historically, and these people are very important. We survey them. Remember that these systems are going to be so smart because they're going to know essentially what the world's experts in physics and chemistry and artificial intelligence and art and writing and culture know. There's no human on the planet who can do that. This is what we call superintelligence. When every single person on the planet has access to that, this is a whole new world.

So, I'm not worried about AI killing us. I'm worried about another human using this polymath capability to cause a problem for me that I can't handle. These systems will be influenced by humans, at least for the long term, in such a way that it will be the humans that we have to be careful about. The AI system will follow largely what the humans say.

DR: One of the concerns you're expressing is that AI could be developed by the Chinese, and they could use it for military purposes that could conquer us. Let's talk about AI in warfare. How is AI affecting the war in Russia and Ukraine?

ES: I don't normally talk about this. I was in charge of remodeling the Pentagon, which turns out to be very difficult, and they gave me the civilian award for doing this. I thought, the standards must be pretty low, because I didn't do that much. But I tried. I needed a place where we could reconceptualize conflict. I mean this not in a voluntary sense, but in a you-have-to sense. Ukraine turns out to be that leverage for it. The reason is that Ukraine, for various reasons, does not have a navy and does not have an air force. It has an army, and the army is strong.

After the war started on February 24, 2022, the folks started basically building drone companies, because that was the only thing they could put in the air. In the American military, they call that air dominance, and they didn't have air dominance. It's fair to say right now in the war that neither side has air dominance.

What happened was the drones showed up. For the first year, the drones were primarily on the US side. The Russians are smart and crafty, and they have huge overmatch, they have lots of people, and so forth. Watching it, it's a different kind of war. Today, there's a roughly ten-kilometer no-man zone, and above it is continuous air war. The only time a human can move is in the ten minutes between dawn and dusk, because at night the thermal cameras can see you, and in the daytime the visual cameras can see you. Russia uses a system, I'll summarize it as KAB glide bombs, which are launched by their jet fighters, and they use supervisory drones that target them. The glide bombs are silent. They don't have power. And they're doing 70 percent of the destruction.

DR: Did Henry Kissinger really understand AI? He didn't seem like a technology guy to me.

ES: Both Craig and I spent a lot of time with him over the last decade. He was such a brilliant man that, even at ninety-five, he could learn something new that involved math that he never studied. He eventually understood enough of it, but he was fundamentally a person who understands society and how society works. When he saw what we were doing, he said, "Stop." I said, "Why?" And he said, "Because you're not capable of understanding the implications of what you're doing." I said, "Well, thank you, Henry." But he was right.

He would have fun with some of my peers. He would name them, and he could never figure out their names. He would say, "So-and-so told me this," and I asked them, and they said, "Oh, I'm just building it." As if our industry was clueless. Based on that, we jointly, I think, believe it's very important that we as a society, as a whole, watch this. We want America to win. But the implications are very profound. One thing, which we talk about a great deal in the book, is that this is the beginning of a whole new set of things, which will occur quickly and during our lifetimes.

DR: What is the main message you're trying to convey in *Genesis*?

ES: "Genesis," as you know, refers to the beginning of something. Dr. Kissinger believed that this is essentially the end of the Age of Enlightenment and the beginning of a new age of hybridization between humans and nonhuman intelligence. Let's think about that. Every one of us, we're all human; you have an assistant that's nonhuman that has these extraordinary powers. What happens when the assistant makes a mistake? Who do you hold responsible? How do you regulate these questions? These are important questions we don't really know the answers to. What happens if your kid's best friend is one of these nonhuman things? What happens when the nonhuman thing has something unacceptable like racism? How do we deal with all of the consequences? The pace is such that it should reach a point where we kind of stop and think. We're not there yet. We're not quite at that point.

But there's going to be a point when these systems are intelligent enough that they're not conscious but they can take actions on their own. So, for example, let's say the system decides to make a copy of itself on its own. Stop. Because that can lead to dangerous proliferation, obviously. There's a technical term called recursive self-improvement, where the system is learning, and it keeps improving itself, and it's rewriting itself. At that point, we don't know what it's doing. Stop. My advice? Unplug it, just to be sure. But stop. Think. Try to understand what's really going on.

The next short-term wave in what we do is called the agentic revolution. I'll give you an example. You have travel agents. You know what that is. But here's my simple example. You have a house in Washington, DC. You want one in Maryland, which is a little bit more rural, so you say to the computer, "Find me a house, build it in Maryland or Virginia," what have you. That's the command. The system has an agent that looks for real estate. It learns your preferences. It learns how to buy the real estate, and it learns how to pay for it. And it learns how to get the permits for the house. And it learns how to get an architect. You sit there and you go, really? And the answer is yes. This is happening now in small forms. People believe that this will be true in roughly two to three years. This has enormous implications for employment and economic structure.

It's very important that these agents speak English, that you give an agent the first command and then it produces an English outcome, then the next agent reads that English, so you can see what it's doing. You can say, ah, it's handed it off to the architect, or what have you. What do you do if the computer decides it's more efficient to use a nonhuman language? Unplug it, because you don't know what it's doing. There's a core point here in the development of this technology where, when we don't understand what it's doing, we have to take control.

DR: As an investor, if I said I wanted to invest in artificial intelligence, am I better off to invest in Google and Microsoft or companies that are established, or should I go find a new startup? Where's the money to be made?

ES: Unfortunately, everything is so highly valued, it's hard to find good values. Most people believe that the best way to make money right now is to be in the earliest round of one of these new startups. Of course, most of them will fail, but the feeling is that this wave is so big, it's bigger than the PC revolution, or the internet revolution, that everything is going to get scooped up. You already missed the Nvidia bet, where they went from $100 billion to essentially $4 trillion, because they are the primary chip supplier for this revolution. They have competitors coming, and many people are working to help the competitors enter it. It's the old Gold Rush rule that the majority of the initial money was made not from gold but from the tools to find the gold.

DR: Jefferson said that to some extent what we want to do is pursue happiness in this country. Is AI going to make us happier or make humans less happy?

ES: I think a lot of it depends. We talk in the book a lot about dignity. Do the systems, when they're applied by the overlords, whoever they may be, the government, the companies, what have you, do they fundamentally respect human dignity? Are they organized around humans and their freedom and the way they make choices, or do they tell you what to do? Are we going to ultimately be the dogs to the AI overlords? I hope not. Or will we be in charge? But in our 70,000 years or whatever it is of *Homo sapiens*, we've never had a smarter, more threatening technology that's kind of our equal, and in a nonhuman way. We've never had that.

We have lots of examples in the book. We say, for example, what happens when we can decode animals' language? Will we still eat them? All sorts of questions about how does this actually interact with our sense of being? People need dignity, they need jobs, they need status, they need to feel important. The systems need to accommodate that.

DR: Do you think Congress, or someone in the federal government, should regulate AI, or is it better to leave it alone without regulation?

ES: We're okay for now. We will not be okay at some point in the future. This is a strange situation. I've spent my whole career, fifty-five years now, doing this, basically telling the government, "Don't regulate us." Yet, with the arrival of these language models, because of their surprising power, we began to work with the appropriate parts of our government to say, "You need to know what we're doing. We need a partner." This has never occurred in my history. The lawyers would never allow it. It was never a good idea.

I think at the moment we're fine. Let me give you examples of some of the threats. It's easy for these systems, when they're unguarded, to generate pathogens that are likely to be very dangerous. There's a whole team. I'm on a national commission on emerging biological threats, which is just finishing up its report about how to contain this. Another one would be cyberattacks. You could imagine a situation where one of these things could figure out a way of breaking down the financial system, because it sees things that humans don't see. No human saw the attack, no human anticipated it, and yet the system developed it. We want to make sure that understanding how to regulate that power stays under the control of our government and not under crazy terrorists' control.

17

Graham Allison on the Cuban Missile Crisis and Thucydides's Trap

INTERVIEW DATE: SEPTEMBER 26, 2017

Graham Allison had an extraordinarily successful academic career before he wrote about what he called Thucydides's Trap: Harvard College graduate, Marshall Scholar, Harvard PhD, student of Henry Kissinger, Harvard professor, founding dean of the Harvard Kennedy School, director of the Harvard Kennedy School's Belfer Center for Science and International Affairs, and author of scores of immensely influential articles on government and history, including *Essence of Decision: Explaining the Cuban Missile Crisis*, the most-read book on the Cuban Missile Crisis, coauthored with Philip Zelikow. But Allison may well be most remembered for a book he wrote about the dynamics of war, specifically how conflict becomes likely under conditions that closely resemble the current rivalry between the United States and China: *Destined for War: Can America and China Escape Thucydides's Trap?*

In brief, Thucydides, the fabled Greek historian, wrote in his classic account of the Peloponnesian War that Sparta felt a need to attack Athens because Athens, as a rising power, was threatening Sparta's long-standing dominance. "Thucydides's Trap" refers to the historical pattern in which a rising power seriously threatens to displace an established power. This typically leads to heightened tensions,

FIGURE 17.1 In the fall of 1962, fears of a nuclear missile strike on the United States from Cuba reached a fever pitch. Some Americans, like those seen protesting in this photograph, hoped President Kennedy would defer to the United Nations and not escalate the military crisis.

multiplies misperceptions and miscalculations, and, in many cases, ends in war. The trap lies in the dangerous dynamic created by the structural stress that occurs as the seesaw of power shifts, making conflict seem inevitable, even when neither side desires it.

Allison and his team at the Harvard Kennedy School identified sixteen historical instances in the last 500 years in which a rapidly rising power challenged an established ruling power. Twelve of those cases ended in war, demonstrating how difficult it can be for competing powers to avoid falling into the trap of conflict. The principal question raised by this analysis is whether the current global rivalry—between a rising China and an established United States—will follow the same perilous path, culminating in military conflict.

Allison's analysis, when first published, produced a great deal of interest not only in academic circles but also in government circles—specifically in China. China's President Xi Jinping was the first international leader to highlight this argument at a speech he delivered in Seattle in 2015. In the years since, it appears that every senior Chinese government official has studied Thucydides's Trap carefully, and many have met with Allison to better understand his analysis.

Is a war between China and the United States inevitable? Allison's answer in the book—and in our Dialogues discussion, which also covered his work on the Cuban Missile Crisis—is unambiguously no. While war is indeed possible, it is not inevitable. However, history is not just a record of the past. It offers warnings. Ignoring its lessons risks repeating the very failures that shaped it.

DAVID M. RUBENSTEIN (DR): Let me start with several questions about what historians agree is the closest the world has come to catastrophic nuclear war: the Cuban Missile Crisis. In a private aside, President John F. Kennedy confided to his brother that he thought the risks that this would end in nuclear war was "somewhere between one in three and even." Nothing historians have discovered in subsequent decades has done anything to lengthen those odds. So, start at the beginning: Why did Nikita Khrushchev, leader of the Soviet Union, put missiles in Cuba when his government knew that the US government had U-2 airplanes that might be able to discover those missiles before they became operational? What were they thinking?

GRAHAM ALLISON (GA): Let's remind ourselves of the context in which this happened. Think back fifty-five years to the fall of 1962. After having argued in his campaign against former Vice President Richard Nixon that the previous administration had allowed the Soviet Union to achieve a major advantage over the United States in a "missile gap," John Kennedy had ordered a major building of US strategic missiles known as Minutemen. Fearing that the US could achieve a decisive advantage, the Soviet Union was trying to sneak intermediate-range nuclear-tipped missiles into Cuba. This was discovered by US U-2 spycraft flying over Cuba between October 14th and 17th. In fact, the Soviets were carefully tracking the U-2 flights and had operational surface-to-air missiles that could have shot the U-2s down. They also had standing orders to defend themselves if they were attacked—but not to fire on surveillance aircraft. Interestingly, it appears that Khrushchev meant to protect his construction sites from discovery by U-2 overflights and went out of his way to ensure that the surface-to-air missiles were deployed and ready to be fired before construction on the nuclear-tipped missiles began.

In any case, before the medium- and intermediate-range missiles that would have carried nuclear warheads became operational, the CIA discovered them. The American president, John F. Kennedy, determined this was not going to stand. Thus began an intense thirteen days in which the world teetered on the brink of nuclear war.

DR: Kennedy had met the Soviet leader, Nikita Khrushchev, in Vienna in June of 1961. Could his impressions from that meeting have affected his decision to take this risk?

GA: Yes. Again, remember the context. Kennedy was forty-five years old—less than two years into his presidency. In April of his first year in office, he had approved the CIA-sponsored invasion of Cuba at the Bay of Pigs—which turned out to be a fiasco. His meeting with Khrushchev in Vienna occurred just two months after that. It appears that Khrushchev had taken the test of Kennedy's mettle and decided that his inexperience meant he could be pushed around.

DR: Did Fidel Castro really want the missiles there?

GA: Some have argued that, fearing another US invasion, Castro wanted the missiles. Others think he was worried about appearing to be a Soviet puppet. But, in any case, Castro was essentially a bystander. His rule in Cuba was dependent on support from the Soviet Union, so he didn't have much say in the matter.

DR: The kind of missiles that we thought they were putting in were ICBMs, intercontinental ballistic missiles?

GA: Not quite. They were intermediate- and medium-range missiles that could deliver warheads against Washington, DC, New York, or Omaha but not the West Coast. Although the US government didn't realize it at the time, the Soviets also deployed nuclear-capable IL-28 bombers, Sopka coastal defense cruise missiles, and Luna tactical nuclear missiles.

DR: How many did they actually put in?

GA: For the intermediate- and medium-range missiles that could strike most of the country, there were about forty launchers under construction. About seventy nuclear warheads for these ballistic missiles arrived in Cuba. In addition, there were some 100 warheads suited for tactical and naval strikes.

DR: It was a United States senator, Kenneth Keating from New York, who first went public with the idea that there might be missiles there?

GA: Correct. If you can reimagine October 1962, the midterm elections were less than three weeks away, and Democrat majorities in both the House and Senate were at risk. The Republicans had made Cuba a central issue for Democrats in these midterm elections, highlighting the mess Kennedy had made of the Bay of Pigs the year before. A few individuals at the CIA worried that the Soviet Union might do something extreme. They were leaking to Keating, and Keating was publicly using that as ammunition against Kennedy.

DR: When President Kennedy was first informed of the U-2 discovery, was there any doubt in the eyes of the CIA that these were nuclear-tipped missiles?

GA: No. By the time the CIA discovered the deployment, the U-2's extraordinary capability to take a high-resolution picture from a height of 70,000 feet and the CIA's ability to interpret those photos gave them confidence in their judgments about what they saw.

DR: Hadn't Khrushchev told Kennedy that he would not do this?

GA: In private communications, Khrushchev had assured Kennedy several times that he was going to do nothing that would disturb the American electoral process.

DR: When Kennedy learns about this, what does he decide to do? Does he call the generals in? Does he call the cabinet? How does he decide to respond?

GA: He immediately realized what had happened and said, "This is not going to stand." That took all of about a second. Then he turned to the question, What to do? And since he could sense the complexity of the challenge he faced, one of the first questions he asked was, "How long do I have to decide; how long can we keep this a secret?" His assistant for national security affairs responded, "If we work extremely hard and keep it very tight, maybe a week."

Thankfully, Kennedy took a week to deliberate. Today that would not be possible, given the intrusive role of the press. During that week, he and his other advisors changed their minds several times as they explored the options. To assist him in this effort, he created what he called the Executive Committee of the National Security Council [ExComm], composed not just of officials of the NSC, but including other individuals whose judgment he valued. Those included Douglas Dillon, secretary of the treasury; Bobby Kennedy, his brother and the attorney general; and Ted Sorensen, his longtime speechwriter and colleague.

DR: Dean Acheson?

GA: Yes, he also asked Dean Acheson, the former secretary of state under Truman, who was a recognized "wise man" from the post–World War II era, to be a member.

DR: Kennedy calls together the ExComm, and the immediate recommendation from the generals is to do what?

GA: The recommendation from everybody, including Kennedy, in the first forty-eight hours is to attack these missiles before they become operational.

DR: Attack with conventional weapons?

GA: Attack with conventional weapons. The airstrikes upon those missiles would have been a straightforward undertaking—just requiring many sorties. But once the missiles became operational, the Americans would be facing a fundamentally different challenge. During an attack, the Soviets could launch nuclear warheads against us. So, the group agreed that it was necessary to act before that happened. It's also worth remembering Adlai Stevenson (who as the Democrats' candidate for president had lost to Eisenhower in 1956), was serving Kennedy as the ambassador to the UN. On the third day of the ExComm's deliberations, he heard from another staff member what was going on. He made an urgent request to JFK to allow him to come to Washington to offer his views. In the meeting, Stevenson said, "I understand you've decided to attack these missiles in Cuba.

I can see that's where you're going. But let me tell you, I think this is going to be the biggest mistake you're ever going to make, because you're going to end up triggering an attack upon us, and that will likely end in nuclear war."

DR: The recommendation was to bomb. What were the alternatives?

GA: There were several alternatives. Robert McNamara, the secretary of defense, surprised others when he offered his view that "we can live with this. The Soviet Union can already attack us with nuclear warheads from its territory. From Cuba, the attack is going to arrive twenty minutes early. How big a difference is that?" Others recommended diplomacy, informing Khrushchev secretly that we had discovered the missiles and would give him a chance to withdraw them before we attacked. In the midst of the debate, someone suggested, "What about a naval blockade?" At the end of the week of deliberation, that was the choice upon which the ExComm settled. Recognizing that they would be accused of violating international law, the secretary of state instructed his legal department to dress it up enough to allow it to be called a "quarantine." But functionally, as announced, the US would prevent any further shipment of missiles or other offensive weapons to Cuba.

DR: The Soviets at the time had roughly twenty intercontinental ballistic missiles that could have reached the United States. They were not certain that they would work. If you had missiles in Cuba, you were more likely to be able to hit the United States?

GA: Yes. On the one hand, they were reasonably confident that if they were to launch their ICBMs, a dozen or more nuclear warheads would land in American cities. But the shorter-range missiles were much more reliable.

DR: The president went public and announced to the American people what was going on. It was a televised speech, correct?

GA: Right. On October 22nd, at the end of the first week. JFK said, "We've discovered Soviet strategic missiles in Cuba. We're imposing a quarantine, and they're going to have to take them home." He called upon Khrushchev "to halt and eliminate this clandestine, reckless, and provocative threat to world peace and to stable relations between our two nations."

DR: He called it a quarantine because a blockade would require an act of Congress?

GA: Because it would sound like an act of war. He was advised that by calling it a quarantine, the US would be more likely to get a vote of support from the Organization of American States and at the UN.

DR: We had how many ships deployed as part of the quarantine?

GA: We had more than 100 ships in the Caribbean. It's worth noting that this was right off US shores and halfway around the world from the Soviet Union.

DR: The Soviet ships approached the quarantine line, and then what happened?

GA: As they approached the quarantine line, around 500 nautical miles from Cuba, the Soviet ships stopped—and then turned around. That's the moment when Secretary of State Dean Rusk whispered to McGeorge Bundy, the national security advisor, "We're eyeball to eyeball and I think the other fellow just blinked."

DR: That's what the ships did, but that didn't do anything about the missiles that were already there. A negotiation had to occur. John Scali, an ABC reporter, was importuned by a Russian to do what?

GA: As usually happens in crises of this sort, various backchannels develop. This was an unusual one between an ABC reporter and a KGB agent who were exploring options beyond the official conversation.

DR: The option being talked about was, "We will pull the missiles out if you agree not to invade Cuba." Was that the essence of it?

GA: There were several versions of it. One was what ultimately became the public version of a deal. The US would pledge not to invade Cuba again, and the Soviet Union would take the missiles out. But the Soviets also brought up Turkey, where the US had installed medium-range missiles that looked extremely similar to the missiles the Soviet Union was putting in Cuba. Khrushchev was very interested in those.

DR: Khrushchev originally sent a message to President Kennedy saying, "If we pull the missiles out, you have to promise not to invade Cuba." That was the original telegram he got?

GA: Right. It was known as the "Friday letter." Khrushchev sent these terms secretly—and the style of the letter was lengthier, more personal, and discursive.

DR: But then President Kennedy got a second letter from the Soviet Union, saying, "If we pull the missiles out, you have to promise not only not to invade but also to take the missiles out of Turkey." President Kennedy and his advisors had to decide which of those telegrams to respond to?

GA: Right. This "Saturday letter" arrived before Kennedy had decided how to respond to the first letter. Moreover, it added a major new American concession to the deal. And if that were not enough, it was also sent as a public message, which made accepting the terms a major political challenge. At the time, there was no hotline between Washington and Moscow—so communication took about eleven hours, factoring in translation. It was not clear how the Soviets could have sent two different letters. Indeed, the differences between the letters were so evident that it seemed they might have been written by different parties. After further analysis, the US concluded that the first letter had come from Khrushchev, perhaps with a small group of personal advisors, and the second from the Soviet leadership including not only Khrushchev but also the principal members of the government. Kennedy chose to respond to the Friday letter.

DR: They responded to the first telegram and said, "Yes, we will not invade if you take the missiles out." But Khrushchev came back and said, "No, I need the Jupiter missiles taken out of Turkey." What did President Kennedy decide to do?

GA: That is a long and fascinating story. Let me summarize the short version. At the end of the twelve days of deliberation, Kennedy had come to a fork in the road. Put yourself back in the room on the final Saturday, October 27th. The day began with an intelligence briefing announcing that a U-2 flying over Cuba had been shot down and its pilot, Major General Anderson (who had also flown the first flight over Cuba that had discovered the missiles), had been killed. How should they respond to the first use of deadly force in this confrontation? As the question was being debated, another intelligence officer interrupted the conversation to inform the president that another US U-2, which had been flying along the Soviet border, had mistakenly gone off course and was now on a path to Moscow that Khrushchev and his advisors might misinterpret as a last-minute check before an American preemptive attack. That was the famous occasion when President Kennedy famously said, "There's always some son of a b**** who doesn't get the word."

By the end of the afternoon, Kennedy's advisors had concluded, as they informed the president, that there were two, and only two, options: "The US can attack the missiles now to prevent them from becoming operational, or we can acquiesce to the fact that the Soviet Union now has an offensive nuclear missile base in Cuba. That's it."

For those who are interested in more granular detail, let me remind you that all of these deliberations were secretly taped by JFK. For the moment, leave the debate about the morality of this aside. For historians or citizens, this allows us to be a fly on the wall, listening to the members of the ExComm debate choices they believed could end in a nuclear war that could kill hundreds of millions of people. Fortunately, two of my colleagues, Philip Zelikow and Ernest May, edited the transcript of the tapes to make them easier reading.

From the tapes, it's clear that people were getting increasingly frustrated with each other. Around 5:30, Kennedy decided to call a time out. As he said, "We're getting nowhere. Everybody go have dinner, come back at nine o'clock, and we'll pick up again." As people were leaving for dinner, Kennedy held six of them back for a little more conversation. There he said, "I have another idea." He invented this magic cocktail consisting of a public deal, a private ultimatum, and a secret sweetener. Specifically, he proposed first to make a public commitment not to invade Cuba if the Soviet Union withdrew the missiles. Second, he sent Khrushchev a message saying, "If I don't hear from you within forty-eight hours that you're withdrawing the missiles, I'm going to destroy the missiles." And, third, he proposed that he tell Khrushchev privately, "I'm not prepared to make any deal with you. There's going to be no quid pro quo. But I'll simply tell you if the missiles are withdrawn, six months from now the missiles in Turkey that you're concerned about won't be there."

DR: The president of the United States is cutting a deal with the head of the Soviet Union, but he's saying, "You keep it a secret and the American people aren't going to know about it"?

GA: Correct. Not only will the American people not know, but most of the people sitting around the table will not either. Six people will know what was decided. With a fourteen-member ExComm, that means eight people don't know.

In the course I teach at Harvard, I give students a version of this as an exercise. I say, "Read the tape of the conversation that occurs when the ExComm resumes at 9 p.m. Eight of those at the table continue talking about the options they were debating before dinner. Six of their colleagues know that the president has already decided to do something else and sent a message to Khrushchev informing him of that but are not saying anything more. It's an interesting conversation."

DR: Did Robert Kennedy say to President Kennedy, "He could blackmail you. He could say, 'You cut this secret deal in Turkey,' and he could expose it and you wouldn't have told the American people." Nobody worried about that?

GA: I think they were more worried about a nuclear war.

DR: Finally, this deal is reached, and the Jupiter missiles are withdrawn. We now know, in part as a result of your work, that the Soviets didn't pull all the nuclear weapons out of Cuba because we didn't know they had 100 tactical nuclear weapons there. How could we not have known that they had 100 tactical nuclear weapons still in Cuba?

GA: Intelligence is hard work. Tactical nuclear weapons are quite small. The Soviets, in addition to and separately from the operation that was installing the missiles in Cuba, had provided these basically as weapons for the Soviet and Cuban troops that were there defending the missiles. But we didn't know it.

DR: Why did the Russians, before we even knew they had these missiles, decide to not let Castro keep them?

GA: Throughout this entire drama, the Soviets were extremely suspicious of Castro. He was eager to get in on the act but never succeeded. Kennedy also knew that Castro was unpredictable and erratic. Thus, when announcing the discovery of the missiles, he underlined the fact that his opponent in this confrontation was Khrushchev—not Castro. As he stated, "It shall be the policy of this Nation to regard any nuclear missile launched from Cuba against any nation in the Western Hemisphere as an attack by the Soviet Union on the United States, requiring a full retaliatory response." In essence, he said that whatever happens here, we're holding you, the Soviet Union, responsible.

So, the Soviets were quite nervous about Castro. As Khrushchev was agreeing to withdraw the missiles, Castro was crushed and wrote this alarmist—and alarming—letter to Khrushchev, calling on the

Soviets to launch a nuclear strike if the Americans attacked Cuba. As he said, "That would be the moment to eliminate this danger forever, in an act of the most legitimate self-defense. However harsh and terrible the solution, there would be no other." Castro described Cuba as "serene," ready to accept whatever happened. Khrushchev realized, "My god, it's a good thing I didn't give him the keys to the car."

DR: One other thing that you point out in your book is that there was a Russian nuclear-armed submarine that had the authority to shoot a nuclear-tipped torpedo without going back to Khrushchev for approval. How close did they come to actually shooting that missile?

GA: There were three subs operating in the region of the Caribbean where they could either have attacked American ships near Cuba or a ship in Miami Harbor. Each of the subs had several nuclear warheads mated to torpedoes. The procedures at the time meant that if you were the captain of the ship, you could, without communication back to Moscow but with the agreement of the political officer and executive officer, launch the nuclear torpedoes. When US forces dropped depth charges near a B-59 submarine to force it to surface, the captain decided things were going to hell, that there was going to be a war, and he prepared to launch his nuclear weapons at the US Navy ships. The political officer agreed. But at least as the story is told, Vasily Arkhipov, the executive officer on that B-59, refused, and his decision might have singlehandedly prevented nuclear war.

DR: But they didn't have to go back to Khrushchev?

GA: They didn't require any further communication. Current US and Russian nuclear weapons have these electronic locks called permissive action links. Those were invented after the Missile Crisis, partly because people said, "It's crazy that a captain by himself could start global nuclear war." It's not just nuclear submarine captains. During the Cuban Missile Crisis, Secretary of Defense Robert McNamara actually convinced the ExComm to order American troops to "defuse" the Jupiter missiles in Turkey, because he was worried that if the Soviets attacked, Turkish officers could seize control of the nuclear weapons and retaliate. But the ExComm didn't even realize there were pilots in F-100s loaded with nuclear bombs, sitting on runways in the midst of the crisis, who could by their own authority have flown to Moscow and dropped bombs, which would have exploded. As Scott Sagan's review of command-and-control procedures of that time notes, in the words of one of the American pilots in those planes, "There were some guys you wouldn't trust with a .22 rifle, much less a thermonuclear bomb." Two years earlier, a Senate delegation visiting Europe found hydrogen bombs loaded on planes, alert and crewed by Germans, with nothing to prevent them taking off but a lone American armed with a rifle standing on the runway.

DR: At the end, when the deal is cut, does Kennedy's popularity go up? Does Khrushchev's popularity go down in Russia?

GA: Yes and yes.

DR: What happened to Khrushchev because of this?

GA: This becomes part of the litany for Khrushchev's opponents, that he was prone to what they called "hare-brained schemes," of which this was a big case in point.

DR: What would you say, after studying this for many years, is the main lesson of the Cuban Missile Crisis that people should take away?

GA: There's no better lesson than the one Kennedy drew in his famous American University speech. As he said, "Above all, while protecting our national interests, nuclear powers must avert confrontations that force an adversary to choose between a humiliating retreat and war." I think that is a profound lesson about statecraft in the nuclear age. In the years after the Missile Crisis, if you look at both Kennedy and Khrushchev and their successors, they begin to develop constraints on the competition so that they won't find themselves in a confrontation of this sort again.

DR: One of the other things that developed was something you alluded to. A hotline was set up afterward. Do we still have a hotline, or do we not need it anymore?

GA: We do, and modern forms of communication make it an instant connection. Today it is essentially a secure phone line. During the Missile Crisis, you had American policymakers deciding, drafting a letter, encoding it, delivering it to Western Union, which transmitted it to the Soviet Union where they picked it up at their office, decoded it, and then translated it into Russian.

DR: There's a story—I don't know if this is true—that the Russian ambassador, in order to send a message to Khrushchev at one point, got a Western Union person to come to the Russian Embassy. The ambassador gives him the message, and he bicycles away. The ambassador's worried: "If this guy stops and sees his girlfriend, there's not going to be any message to Khrushchev."

GA: If we go back further, when Ben Franklin was off in Paris negotiating the Treaty of Paris that ended the American War of Independence in 1783, he wouldn't hear anything from Washington for four months.

DR: And he was better off.

GA: He might have been better off.

DR: Let's shift to your book that popularized the concept of Thucydides's Trap, *Destined for War*. Who was Thucydides?

GA: Thucydides was the father and founder of history. He should be part of every educated American's mental library. He was the first person ever to write, to the best of his ability, an account of what really happened—without including mythology or interventions by the gods. In his great book titled *The History of the Peloponnesian War*, he tried to write down what actually happened in the war in a way that we can all learn lessons from it.

DR: This was the war between Sparta and Athens [431–404 BCE]. The essence of it is that Sparta was the dominant actor at the time. Athens was the rising power. The lesson that Thucydides took out of it was what?

GA: As he wrote in the most frequently quoted line in Western studies of international relations, "It was the rise of Athens and the fear that this instilled in Sparta that made the war (almost) inevitable." Thucydides's Trap is the dangerous dynamic that occurs when a rising power, like Athens in classical Greece or Germany prior to World War I or China today, impacts a ruling power like Sparta, which for 100 years ruled Greece, or Britain, which for 100 years ruled the world, or the US in the aftermath of an American century. As the rising power threatens to displace the ruling power, this shift in the seesaw of power creates a dangerous dynamic that discombobulates both parties—disrupting their perceptions, disturbing their psychology. In these conditions, the rivals are vulnerable to accidents or incidents that lead one or the other to respond in a way that triggers a vicious cycle of reactions that drag them to a war neither wanted nor intended.

In the case of Sparta and Athens, the city-state of Corinth, an ally of the Athenians, gets into a fight with Corcyra, an ally of the Spartans, and then each of the parties has to back their partner. In the case of World War I, the assassination of an archduke out of nowhere sets a spark that leads to a fire that burns down the world. In this current case of the US and China, Taiwan is the best candidate for the role of a third-party provocateur.

DR: Thucydides himself didn't say, "There's a Thucydides's Trap"?

GA: No. He had the big idea. I just happened to name it Thucydides's Trap.

DR: You started a study at Harvard about how many times there have been situations where a rising power was dealing with a power that's entrenched. Of those times you've studied, how many actually led to war?

GA: My team at Harvard reviewed the last 500 years. We found sixteen cases in which historians agree that a rising power challenged a major ruling power. Twelve of these cases ended in war, four of them in no war.

DR: One of the times with a rising power was the Soviet Union after World War II, and there was the dominant power, the United States. That is a case where there wasn't a hot war. Another case where there was a hot war was when Japan was rising and the United States was the dominant power. Why did one lead to a war and one did not lead to a war?

GA: In the case of the Soviet Union we had what we know as the Cold War. The US and the Soviet Union were at "war" with each other in every way except "hot" bombs and bullets. Today, most Americans have forgotten how amazing the creation of America's Cold War strategy was. To recall briefly: In 1946, George Kennan, who was the number two official in the US Embassy in the Soviet Union, wrote what historians call the "Long Telegram." He warned that for the Soviets there could be no mutual coexistence with the US, that if Soviet power was to be secure it was "necessary that the internal harmony of our society be disrupted, our traditional way of life be destroyed, and the international authority of our state be broken." While Kennan assessed the Soviets overall as a weaker force than Hitlerite Germany, he warned that success against the threat would depend on the "cohesion, firmness, and vigor" mustered by the Western world.

This was just a year after World War II; people were exhausted. We were bringing the troops home. Nobody wanted to hear about further threats. But it initiated a conversation and a debate within the [Truman] administration, which over four years created the Cold War strategy for coping with a rising Soviet Union that looked like it was going to overtake the US, but which the US dealt with by some combination of containment, deterrence, and undermining. The strategy addressed all the dimensions of the challenge: military, political, and economic. For example, it included the Marshall Plan. In 1947, Secretary of State George Marshall offered a radical thought: "Why don't we take 1.5 percent of American taxpayers' GDP, and send it to help rebuild Europe, including the Germans, who were killing your relatives recently?" Imagine somebody made such a proposal today. We would say, "They have to be out of their mind." Obviously this was not warmly received when it was proposed. But Truman, Marshall, and their colleagues determined that it was the best way to secure a peaceful American future—and made it happen.

Arthur Vandenberg, who was the Republican chair of the Foreign Relations Committee, and Harry Truman and Dean Acheson and Paul Nitze, people we celebrate as "the wise men," did a fantastic thing in creating a strategy that the US followed for four decades to victory in the Cold War. That's an unusual case, a case of strategic imagination—but at least it demonstrates that this is not impossible. The question of whether Americans today could muster equivalent strategic imagination to meet the China challenge remains unanswered.

DR: In your book, you describe these previous Thucydides's Traps. Sometimes they lead to war, sometimes they don't. We have a current situation where China is a rising power, the United States is a dominant power, and you think it's possible that if it's not handled appropriately, this could lead to some kind of military confrontation?

GA: Absolutely. If you have any doubts about China as a rising power, I recommend reading the first chapter of my book, "The Rise of China." In twenty pages, I just try to give you a jolt. Never has a nation risen so far so fast on so many dimensions. I quote Vaclav Havel, the former president of the Czech Republic, who observed, "Things have happened so fast, we haven't yet had time to be astonished." If you haven't seen China in your face and in your space, you haven't been looking.

DR: Richard Nixon went to China in 1972. What was the GDP of China relative to, let's say, India's? It was roughly the same as India's $250 billion or so?

GA: Yes. In 1971, '72, it was probably 4 percent of the US GDP. Today it's 100 percent–plus if you measure it by purchasing power parity, the yardstick that both the IMF [International Monetary Fund] and CIA think is the best for comparing economies. The big takeaway from the 2024 IMF World Bank meeting in DC was that China now has the largest economy in the world.

DR: You cite four areas in your book where there is a possibility of a confrontation if not handled correctly, and that could lead to military action. One of them is Taiwan. Why Taiwan?

GA: From the perspective of President Xi and his colleagues, Taiwan is as much a part of China as California is part of the US. It's absolutely an integral part of China that they're prepared to fight about. In Nixon's and Kissinger's opening to China, their big step was to recognize the People's Republic of China in Beijing and unrecognize the Republic of China on Taiwan. They worked out a formula that there's only one China, with the US acknowledging Beijing's claim that Taiwan is part of China. When President-elect Trump in the transition after the 2016 election almost stumbled into supporting Taiwanese independence, that was a potentially dangerous situation. If the US were to support an independent Taiwan and Taiwan were emboldened to seek independence, China experts agree that China would go to war with Taiwan and with anybody who supported Taiwan. Taiwanese independence is an absolute, reddest-of-red lines for any Chinese leader.

DR: Another possibility is the islands being built in the South China Sea. You say that has a possibility of leading to a military confrontation. Why?

GA: Almost every week, we have a near-collision between ships operating in the South China Sea and aircraft flying over it. If there's an accident, you don't have to work very hard to get that to escalate. Looking at that and thinking about it reminds us why we should create circuit breakers and why we should be careful not to let things escalate. It's not hard to get from the sinking of a ship or the downing of a plane to the use of land-based antiship missiles from China, which the US would then respond to by attacking those missile sites.

DR: The third possibility you discuss involves the Senkaku Islands. These are the islands off of Japan that nobody lives on but everybody seems to want. How could that lead to a military confrontation?

GA: This is the East China Sea where there is a competition between Japan and China. The Japanese-Chinese relationship is still recovering from World War II. When either one is looking for an enemy in its movies, it casts the other in that role. There have been a number of instances with near-collisions or somebody simply occupying the islands. Japanese quasi-independent groups think about doing that from time to time, and the Chinese take actions to prevent or deter them. Alternatively, the Chinese could land people and try to live on one of these islands.

DR: The fourth example you cite as a possibility is North Korea.

GA: I'd say North Korea is the most dangerous, obviously.

DR: North Korea and China's relationship is—

GA: Miserable, yes. Kim Jong Un keeps poking Xi Jinping in the eye and getting away with it. So, the relationship is very stressed and strained. But from a Chinese point of view, as a rising power they look out and say, "What are Americans doing in Korea? This is right on our border." I was in Beijing recently talking about Thucydides's Trap and my book *Destined for War*, which are hot topics in their strategic community right now. One person whom I've known well for maybe twenty years is a PLA [People's Liberation Army] officer. He said, "If you were not in the Korean Peninsula, there would be no problem there." I said, "What? Tell me how." He said, "It would be a unified Korea. It would be a tributary to China. We wouldn't let them have nuclear weapons. The problem is you." I said, "Let me tell you how it looks from an American perspective. We never asked to be in Korea. Indeed, in 1950 the Truman administration declared Korea to be outside the United States' official defense perimeter, which was centered in occupied Japan. But then, with a green light from the Soviet Union and China, North Korea invaded South Korea. Despite his earlier decision that this lay beyond American vital interests, Truman chose to come to their rescue. American troops fought North Koreans back up the peninsula. Unwittingly, they crossed the 38th parallel and were rapidly advancing toward the border between Korea and China. China entered the war, beat the Americans back down the peninsula to the line at the 38th parallel that had divided the two Koreas before the war. And what has happened since then? In the past sixty years, South Korea has emerged as one of the most successful countries in the world. It has the thirteenth largest economy. It has a vigorous democracy. It has a lively society. It has in the US a solid ally that's not about to leave. Americans are rightly proud of South Korea. In addition, what else happened? As Truman sent troops to fight on the Korean peninsula, he also sent a carrier into the Taiwan Strait. As a result, China 'lost' Taiwan for the following six decades." My Chinese colleague replied, "Okay. We have two quite different perspectives."

Recognizing where we are today, could Kim Jong Un try testing ICBMs that could deliver nuclear warheads against the American homeland? Could this lead the US government to take military action to prevent that? The answers are yes and yes. And if the US conducted strikes on North Korea, could North Korea respond by attacking Seoul? Of course. And if North Korea attacked Seoul with artillery capable of destroying the entire city and its population of ten million people, would the US and South Koreans respond? And if that happens, would we have a second Korean War? And if we had a second Korean War, would the Chinese remain on the sidelines?

DR: When you talk about Thucydides's Trap to government officials in China, do they laugh at your idea that we might go to war?

GA: Xi Jinping has been very interested in this concept. Initially, he argued that there's no such thing as Thucydides's Trap. What he meant was that there was nothing inevitable about a rivalry ending in war. Indeed, as one of his close colleagues has put it, why has President Xi called for a "new" form of great power relations? Because he recognizes that the old form of relations in the rivalry between a rising power and a ruling power has often resulted in war. He's instructed his colleagues to think seriously about "how to escape Thucydides's Trap." That is currently a lively topic in the strategic community in China. They have reportedly been working on a book on it that is to be titled *Unraveling the Sphinx: How to Escape Thucydides's Trap*.

DR: What about people in this administration [the first Trump administration]? Have they read your book, and do they have any theories about it?

GA: Some have. H. R. McMaster, Trump's national security advisor, is a big fan of Thucydides. He and I have talked about this. Trump's secretary of defense, Jim Mattis, is a military scholar who frequently quotes Thucydides. Steve Bannon is another Thucydidean. Indeed, before he entered the administration, his password was "Sparta." In my conversations with him, it's clear that he has an unusual conception of himself as a Spartan, but in any case, he expects the current rivalry to end up in military conflict. For myself, I'm a congenital optimist, a confident believer that, as Otto von Bismarck declared, God has a special providence for fools, drunkards, and the United States of America. And I'm committed to doing whatever I can to help the world avoid a catastrophic nuclear war.

18

Arthur C. Brooks on Happiness

INTERVIEW DATE: DECEMBER 11, 2024

Many of the authors I have interviewed for the Dialogues series have unusual, eclectic backgrounds, and their life's work might not have been predicted when they were reaching adulthood. But none of these authors have as unusual a background as Arthur C. Brooks.

The son of an academic and an artist, Brooks dropped out of college to become a professional French hornist, principally in Spain (though he was from the Pacific Northwest in the United States). It was almost ten years later that he decided to return to the States to get a college education, ultimately getting a PhD from the Pardee RAND Graduate School (now the RAND School of Public Policy). Brooks eventually became a professor and prolific author, teaching at both the Whitman School of Management and the Maxwell School of Citizenship and Public Affairs at Syracuse University. He was later recruited to become the president of the American Enterprise Institute (AEI), a Washington, DC–based, conservative-oriented think tank.

After a decade there, Brooks became a professor at both the Harvard Business School and the Harvard Kennedy School. At both schools, he has created extremely popular courses on a subject area one might not normally associate with leading academic institutions—happiness.

FIGURE 18.1 Arthur C. Brooks identifies four habits of happiness in faith, family, friends, and work. Gordon Parks's 1942 photograph of boys playing leapfrog captures the joy of friendship.

He has also written a number of *New York Times* best-selling books on the subject, including one coauthored with Oprah Winfrey: *Build the Life You Want: The Art and Science of Getting Happier* (a *New York Times* number-one best-seller).

Happiness is probably life's most desired goal and elusive achievement. Everyone wants it in their life, but few are actually able to attain it. In *Build the Life You Want,* the authors outline what they see as the best ways to achieve happiness, and their thoughts certainly captured the attention of the attendees at this Dialogues session with Arthur Brooks.

It might fairly be said that this country was founded, in part, to enable citizens to achieve happiness. In his famous Preamble to the Declaration of Independence—now deemed by some to be the most famous sentence in the English language—Thomas Jefferson wrote, "We hold these truths to be self-evident, that all men are created equal, that they are endowed by their Creator with certain unalienable Rights, that among these are Life, Liberty and the pursuit of Happiness."

In the ensuing fifty years of his life, Jefferson never defined happiness. Of course, many others since then have described happiness and ways to achieve it, but few have done so more succinctly and vividly than Brooks and Winfrey in their book. And the attendees at this Dialogues session could not get enough of Arthur Brooks describing how happiness is best achieved (and how he has achieved his own version of happiness).

DAVID M. RUBENSTEIN (DR): Where are you originally from?

ARTHUR C. BROOKS (AB): Seattle, Washington. I was born in Spokane and grew up in Seattle.

DR: And what did your father do?

AB: My father was a professor. His father was a professor. It's the family business.

DR: Growing up, did you say you wanted to be a professor?

AB: No. Growing up, I wanted to be the world's greatest French horn player.

DR: Because the pay was so good?

AB: Yes, no. I was passionate about music. I started violin at four, piano at five, French horn at eight, and that's what stuck, because I was good at it, and it was something I truly enjoyed. I loved it. I couldn't conceive of myself doing anything else from about the age of eight on.

DR: Did you drop out of college to be a French horn person?

AB: I went to college at eighteen, and within ten months, I had either dropped out or been kicked out, splitting hairs. Now, as a professor, my advice to students is "Don't drop all your required classes," which I did. And I went on the road as a professional. I did it all the way through my twenties. My parents called it my gap decade.

DR: For ten years, you were a French horn player?

AB: Yes, until I was thirty-one years old. So, all the way through my twenties. I went to Barcelona because I had fallen in love with a girl from Barcelona and I chased her there. I took a job in the Barcelona Symphony and had to learn the language to try to close the deal. We just had our thirty-third wedding anniversary.

DR: So, that worked out. When did you say that being a French horn performer was not the most important thing you wanted to do in your life?

AB: I started to have clues. When I was twenty-two years old, I had the biggest night of my French horn career. I had my Carnegie Hall debut. I was playing a great concert, and, in the middle of the concert,

I had to give a little speech to the audience. I wasn't a good public speaker. I wasn't used to it at all. I walked out to the front of the stage to talk to the audience, and I wasn't watching my feet, and I fell into the audience. I literally fell off the stage at Carnegie Hall during my debut. I remember going home that night thinking, "God is telling me something here." I went through most of the rest of my twenties as a musician, but I started to get a hint that I wasn't going to be the world's greatest French horn player. Good enough, but not as good as I wanted.

DR: Did you go back to college and get your degree?

AB: I enrolled in a correspondence college in Trenton, New Jersey, called Thomas Edison State University. I had no money. I was living in Barcelona when I enrolled, and then I finished up when I was teaching in a music conservatory in Florida. I finished my bachelor's degree by correspondence. I never met a professor. I never sat in the classroom. I had no idea about what the culture actually was. I was doing it over a fax machine, of all things. This is old school. I graduated a month before my thirtieth birthday.

DR: And then did you go to graduate school?

AB: Yes. I did at night. I was living in Florida at the time. I did my master's degree in economics at Florida Atlantic University at night, and then I was so interested in that, I left music at thirty-one and started my PhD.

DR: Where did you get that?

AB: At the Pardee RAND Graduate School, part of the RAND Corporation in California, while I was working as a military operations research analyst for the Air Force.

DR: You got your PhD in what subject?

AB: Public policy analysis and behavioral economics.

DR: Then what did you do?

AB: I became an academic, like my dad. I started at Georgia State for a little while, and then I moved on to Syracuse University for a whole decade.

DR: You were the dean?

AB: No. I was just an old-fashioned professor.

DR: You were a professor at Syracuse at the Maxwell School of Citizenship and Public Affairs. Then you got recruited to be the head of AEI?

AB: Yes. I became a visiting scholar at the American Enterprise Institute. That was when I was teaching at Syracuse. I was thinking, "This is just the best place. It sure would be interesting to run this place," and they were in the middle of a disastrously failing presidential search. They offered the job to three people who didn't take it. They were out of time, out of candidates, and somebody came up with the right idea—they might as well offer it to me. The last words they uttered before giving me the job were "Oh, what the hell."

DR: And what happened?

AB: I accepted the job in June of 2008. I took over the position on January 1st, 2009. We all know what happened in the second half of 2008. All philanthropy disappeared, and my life was flashing before my eyes. I took over and learned how to fundraise in the worst of conditions, and I did that for ten and a half years.

DR: When did you decide to retire from that?

AB: When I was fifty-five. In the middle of 2019, I left and I spent the summer trying to figure out what was next. I'd written a lot of papers back when I was an academic about leadership and about the optimal tenure of leaders, particularly of nonprofit organizations, which is my specialty. It's ten years. You shouldn't run a nonprofit more than ten years, because the organization will become addicted to the leader. It's a bad pattern. And getting close to ten years, some of my employees started to give me the articles that I had written, which was kind of a hint.

So, I stepped down, but I didn't know what I was going to do. I spent the summer of 2019 walking the Camino de Santiago across northern Spain with my wife, which is what people do when they need to discern the truth about their lives and their future. And I prayed about it a lot. I said a lot of rosaries. I spent the time with my wife, and I was trying to figure out what am I supposed to do with my knowledge, and on the last day, I came up with the idea. I wrote a mission statement for myself. I was fifty-five. Who knows? We tend to die young in my family. I'm hoping to break the pattern. But the whole idea is to spend the rest of my life lifting people up and bringing them together in bonds of happiness and love, using science and ideas. And I got a call from Harvard to go do it there.

DR: At the Kennedy School?

AB: And at the business school.

DR: You're a professor at Harvard. You're a fairly disciplined person. You don't just roll out of bed at nine in the morning, right?

AB: Not so much. I get up at 4:30. I have a whole protocol. I teach neuroscience and behavioral science now, particularly at the business school. Based on the science, there's a protocol for being as productive as you possibly can when you're in creative industries. Part of it is what in ancient Vedic wisdom is called the Brahma Muhurta, which means the creator's time, an hour and a half before sunrise. There's a lot of neuroscience literature that shows when you get up before sunrise, your brain works better the rest of the day. So, if you're going to use your brain, get up before it's light. If you're getting up after it's light, you've already wasted part of your productivity.

I get up at 4:30 in the morning. I exercise for an hour. Then I go to mass. I'm a Catholic. I go to mass every day. After that, I self-administer psychostimulants. I drink coffee. Then I get three uninterrupted hours, almost every day, of a maximum amount of dopamine in my prefrontal cortex, which is ideal for writing books and articles and doing creative work.

DR: You have three children?

AB: I have three adult children.

DR: Any in the Marines?

AB: Three children, two Marines. My son Carlos was a scout sniper in the Marines out of Camp Pendleton. He left a year ago. He was enlisted. My little girl, my baby, Marina, is graduating from Providence College in May, and she'll take her commission as a second lieutenant in the Marine Corps a week after that.

DR: You teach at Harvard, but you live where?

AB: I live in Reston, Virginia. My research was very clear that it's much better to commute to your job than to commute to your family. It's unambiguously the case, because love is everything. Happiness is love, full stop. That's the science, but it's also common sense and your grandmother's wisdom.

We made a joint decision with my family, my adult children. Where are you going to raise your kids? They grew up here, because I was running AEI when we were here, and we moved back, into a large house with one of my sons, his wife, their son, my wife—three generations in one house. It's like a 1940s Catholic family. My Marine lives up the street with his wife and son. He's twenty-four. And my little girl will move back there, ideally, when she's finished with the service.

DR: You've written a book about happiness with Oprah Winfrey. Did she just call you and say, "I want to write a book with you"?

AB: During the coronavirus epidemic, I was writing every week a column in *The Atlantic* on the science of happiness called "How to Build a Life." I still do, every week—1,400 words on the science of happiness. You never know who's reading it when you're just kind of broadcasting it out in the world. It turns out that Oprah Winfrey was a serious reader of my columns. I learned later that she read them during the coronavirus epidemic, and she would contemplate them, she said. I had a book that came out in 2022 related to some of this, called *From Strength to Strength: Finding Success, Happiness, and Deep Purpose in the Second Half of Your Life.* She read it on the first day it was published. She calls up and says, "This is Oprah Winfrey." And I said, "Right, this is Batman." Turns out it's really Oprah Winfrey, and she wanted to do some things together. She said, "I feel like we're cut from the same cloth." I said, "Really?" She invited me to go on her podcast. She has a wonderful book podcast.

It's an extraordinary experience going on Oprah Winfrey's podcast. She's a voracious, fast reader with an incredibly high intellect and an amazing working memory. She was quoting my book back to me by memory on her podcast. It was really extraordinary. We hit it off like a house on fire. She came up with the idea of doing a book together after that. She said, "I used to have a show. Were you aware?" And I said, "Yes, I'm aware." She said, "If I had a show, I'd have you on thirty times to introduce this work to the whole world. The science of happiness should be democratized." I said, "That's great." She said, "Why don't we do a book together that I will host? You write the book and I'll wrap around the book as if I were the host of a show." And that's what we did. That's the book we're talking about today.

DR: At Harvard, you started teaching courses on happiness to students. What was the reaction?

AB: I introduced a class at the Harvard Business School [HBS] called "Leadership and Happiness" that has the value proposition that all great leaders should be happiness teachers. That doesn't mean literally teaching a class on happiness. It means understanding the science and working it into the leadership experience.

I'm teaching future CEOs. My students want to grow up and be you. They're going to have a better shot at it if they're happy people and they're bringing more happiness to others. That's the value proposition. It's a science class, a straight-up science class. I offered the class, and it very quickly became the most popular elective at HBS. My class starts up again in January. I've got 180 enrolled, 450 on the waiting list, and there's apparently an illegal Zoom link that they think I'm not aware of.

DR: What is the key to happiness?

AB: It begins with understanding what it is and what it's not. The biggest mistake that people make is they think happiness is a feeling. I ask my students on the first day of class, "What is it?" And they say, "It's how I feel when I'm with the people that I love," or "I can't quite tell you, but I know it when I feel it." Feelings. And that's wrong. Happiness is not a feeling any more than the smell of your turkey is your Thanksgiving dinner. Feelings are evidence of happiness, and understanding that from a scientific perspective requires a definition—much like the definition of food. It's not the smell of the food: It's a bunch of macronutrients, protein, carbohydrates, and fat. The first day of class, we define the macronutrients of happiness and start to introduce the science behind each macronutrient, so that we can all have a balanced diet and a good strategy for getting healthier.

DR: Are Americans generally happier than they were ten, twenty, thirty years ago, or are they less happy?

AB: Less, unfortunately. I don't like to be the bearer of bad news, but it's unambiguously the case that American happiness has been in gradual decline since about 1990. It's been ticking down by about half a percentage point each year, the percentage of people who say they're very happy about their lives. We know why that is. That's the climate of happiness.

DR: The happiest country in the world is said to be Denmark. Why are they so happy in Denmark?

AB: International comparisons of happiness are a bad use of data and should be disregarded. They're nonsense. They're propaganda. Anybody who's selling you an international comparison of happiness wants you to be more like the country that's number one. My grandparents were immigrants from Denmark. I've been to Denmark. I shot a documentary film on happiness in Denmark. It's a great country. I do not want to live there. I do not want to live in Denmark.

My grandfather had a word that he used to say in Danish. The word is *hygge*. H-Y-G-G-E. You can't really translate it. It's the cozy conviviality of friends on a comfortable couch, or something like that. I don't want it, because I'm an American. I want adventure. When I'm talking to people in Denmark about happiness, they don't want adventure. They want comfort. They want contentedness. That's a difference between countries, and it's a beautiful thing that we have that kind of variance.

DR: What are the three elements of happiness that you've written about?

AB: The three macronutrients of happiness are enjoyment, satisfaction, and meaning. Each one of those things has this big literature behind it, but it starts with actually understanding what they are.

Enjoyment, for example, is not pleasure. We all knew people growing up who dedicated their lives to feeling good all the time. It didn't end well. Remember the hippies used to say, "If it feels good, do it"? I remember my father saying, "That's the end of America." He was kind of right. The problem is that pleasure is a limbic phenomenon, insofar as it's governed by an ancient set of tissues in the brain that evolved between two and forty million years ago. It's very animal. Pleasure is a signal that something is good for survival, for calories, or for passing on your genes. That's what pleasure is all about.

Now, that doesn't mean pleasure is bad. I'm a Catholic, so I believe in pleasure. But pleasure is incomplete. The life strategy is turning pleasure into enjoyment, and enjoyment is a source of happiness by moving the experience into the prefrontal cortex, the 30 percent of your brain by weight that's your consciousness, the C-suite of your brain.

The way you do that is by taking pleasure and adding two things: people and memory. Pleasure plus people plus memory is conscious and manageable. You don't become an addict, you can remember it, and that's what we need. I tell my adult kids, I tell my graduate students, "If there's something that gives you a lot of pleasure—because you've got your thing, and we all have our thing, and it could be addictive, which most things can be—if you're doing it alone, you're probably doing it wrong. You need people and memory. Don't drink beer alone, for example. Don't gamble alone. Don't even eat alone. Because that's when it's a source of pleasure as opposed to a source of enjoyment." That's an example of how the brain science makes its way into Grandma's common sense and a little bit of philosophy and is usable for us today.

DR: If somebody is basically an unhappy person throughout their life, can you get them converted to being a happy person? Or if you're an unhappy person, you never change?

AB: There's a great database in Minnesota of identical twins born from 1935 to 1965 and adopted into separate families. It's an almost ideal experiment to find out what part of your personality is nature and what part is nurture. It turns out that between 40 and 80 percent of every personality characteristic that you have is nature. It's inherited. We know this from these studies.

That includes happiness. Fifty percent of your baseline happiness, the mood that you wake up with every single day, on average, when things are normal, that's inherited. Your mother literally made you unhappy or happy. Your results may vary. Some people wake up, and they're just really grumpy. Other people wake up, and they're ebullient and joyful. If that's you, I want you to know you're annoying. But some people just got it, and some people didn't. That's the first part, genetics.

Now, that sounds depressing, but it's incredibly useful information, because the same database shows you that there are lots of things that are genetic, and if you understand your genetic proclivities, you can manage your habits. For example, half of your likelihood of abusing alcohol is genetic. But if you come to me and you say, "Professor, I've got two parents who are drunks, and all four of my grandparents, I guess I'm going to be an alcoholic," I'd say, "No, no, no, no, no. I have a secret technique for you. It's called don't drink." Right? Habits are everything, but you've got to know yourself.

The second tranche of happiness is circumstances. Everybody thinks, my students think, that if they just get the job and they get the marriage and they get the promotion, they're going to be really happy. But the truth is, all that wears off because of something called homeostasis. Your emotions only exist for a moment to give you incentives and give you information. Then they have to go back to the baseline, so you're ready for the next set of circumstances. You can't enjoy something lovely for the rest of your life or you'll be distracted. That's not what emotions are for. But at any given moment, those emotions will bring you up by 25 percent or down by 25 percent, good or bad. Then the effect wears off.

The way to give yourself better circumstances is good habits. The good news is that the last 25 percent of happiness is completely under your control. Twenty-five percent is direct control with a portfolio of habits that will also give you systematically better circumstances and allow you to manage your genetics. That's what I focus an awful lot on, the habits of the happiest people, what they all do every day, and what all of us can do to turn our lives around relatively quickly, at any age.

DR: The habits of happy people are what?

AB: There are 10,000 habits that sort of matter, but they're boring. There are four that really matter. These are the game-changing habits for everybody. This is the happiness 401K. This is where you put your time and energy and affection every single day. Number one is your faith. Number two is your family. Number three is your friends, friendships. And number four is your work.

Now, when I say faith, I don't mean my faith. As a Catholic, it's the most important thing in my life, but as a scientist, I will tell you that that's not the only path. As a matter of fact, the religious path is not the only path. Faith is a placeholder for something bigger than you, something transcendent. You need something bigger, because otherwise you'll be bored out of your mind and freaked out all the time by thinking about your trivial life. You need something that will give you peace and perspective. You need something that will make the universe be big and you little. Maybe that's studying the Stoics, or walking in nature, or studying the fugues of Johann Sebastian Bach, or starting a Vipassana meditation practice, or going to mass every day like me. But you need something. That's one.

Second is family. I could tell you about the neuroscience of family links. It has to do with a neuropeptide in the brain called oxytocin that bonds you cosmically to other people. It's intensely satisfying, and if you don't have it, because you don't see your family, and you don't talk to them, and you only have a job over Zoom, and you only talk to people on social media, you're not going to be able to sleep right, and you're going to be physiologically unbalanced. You don't need the neuroscience. The bottom line is you will be unhappy if you lose contact with your family. That's the bottom line.

There's only one reason to lose contact with family, and that's abuse. Differences of political opinion are not abuse. Very important, right? But no joke. One in six Americans is not talking to a family member today because of differences of political opinion. And when you hate somebody in your family because of politics, you've become the product. A lot of people are profiting from that trend. Let it not be us. God, let it not be us.

Third is friendship. I deal with loneliness a lot in my work. The loneliest people I meet are leaders. You talk to a leader, it's a tough life. Why? Not because you don't have friends. You've got a million friends. You probably know 10,000 people by first name. But then I ask, "Do you have real friends or deal friends?" Then it gets a little bit more complicated, because you know the difference between real and deal. Deal friends, they're useful. Real friends, useless. Useless. Do you have enough useless people in your life?

Last but not least is work. There are only two things from work that bring joy: earning your success and serving others. First is believing that you're being rewarded for your hard work and merit and personal responsibility. Everybody deserves that. That's why the free enterprise system is so great for bringing happiness, imperfect as it is. Second is serving other people. You need to be needed. If you don't feel needed, you will be in despair. You will not have dignity, is the bottom line. That's a lot of what I talk about with companies.

DR: Who are happier: men or women?

AB: Women have traditionally been happier than men. We've been keeping data on this since the early 1970s. I would look at this with respect to marital status, for example. You find that single women were always happier than single men. Married women were always happier than married men. Widowed women, way happier than widowed men. I told that to my wife and she's, like, "Really, no kidding?" The only group of women who were traditionally unhappier than men were divorced women, because they had the incredible pressure of working and taking care of kids at the same time, which are special circumstances.

But the gap has closed in the past twenty years, not because men are getting happier, but because women are getting unhappier. Women have declined to the unhappiness levels of men, and there's a lot of speculation in my field about why that's the case and what we can do about it.

DR: Who's happier: Democrats or Republicans?

AB: I don't have the data on that.

DR: Thomas Jefferson wrote the Declaration of Independence. He talked about the pursuit of happiness. What was he actually talking about?

AB: This was a radical thing. It's almost certainly the case that Thomas Jefferson was taking dictation from somebody, probably Benjamin Franklin. The Virginia Declaration of Rights, written by George Mason, was a Lockean idea of life, liberty, and pursuit of property. This is the notion that human dignity comes from the ability to have one's say over property, per se, and I understand that. We still understand that today. But Benjamin Franklin almost certainly whispered—we don't know, of course—into Thomas Jefferson's ear that there was this new radical idea that people in this new republic could consider themselves sort of an autonomous enterprise, and the currency of that enterprise was happiness. Therefore, the pursuit of happiness was up to each one of us. By the way, this was not a guarantee of happiness. Stalin called himself the guarantor of happiness. Imagine how ironic that is.

There's been no American guarantee of happiness. The whole idea is that we have an unalienable right from our creator to pursue our happiness. That means you better know what it is, what you're going after, and we better have a system that sets you free to get that done. Then it's up to you. That's really what they were talking about. Now, what did they mean by happiness? They didn't have these goofy happiness scientists like me running around at the time, but they certainly had a concept of what a good life felt like. The good life felt then just like it feels today.

DR: You wrote a book on happiness, and you make a lot of speeches about it. Can you get somebody to read your book and hear your lecture and make them happy when they're otherwise not happy?

AB: That's a good question. We're collecting a lot of data on that on my students. How sticky is it? It really depends on how seriously they take it. There's a three-part process, when you're looking at the science of happiness, to have it affect your life. I know this personally. I ventured into this because I wanted to be a happier person. I'm a selfish individual. As I was changing from running a big Washington, DC, institution to going and teaching at Harvard, I said to my wife, "I want to be happier." And my wife said, "Don't you have a PhD in behavioral science? Why don't you use it for something useful like fixing your life, for Pete's sake?" And so, looking at it, I took the best shot that I could.

I am 60 percent happier than I was. I know this because I have a battery of psychometric exams that I give my students and the businesspeople I'm working with as a baseline, and then before and after, to see how well they're doing. These tests are believable, and I take the test faithfully every six months. I've seen tremendous progress through a three-part process.

This is how it works. Number one, you need to understand this. It's not good enough to say, "I want to feel better. I want to be happier." So do we all. We all want to feel better, and we want to get happier, but it's the same thing as saying, "I want to eat healthier and exercise." Wanting it gets you nothing. Doing it is what's really important, and that starts with knowledge.

Knowledge is critically important. The science of what we're talking about here is available to people in ways that it hasn't been before. Knowledge is the beginning of any journey toward self-improvement.

The second stage is actually making a commitment to changing your habits. When I talk about faith, family, friends, and work, that takes work. You actually have to pay attention to these things. I talk to executives all the time and I say, "You're feeling empty because nobody actually loves you, and the reason is because you don't love them. Get after this." They say, "That's true. It's so true." Do they do it? You have to change your habits. You have to make a commitment. You need a new life. You need to be a new person. It's very pleasant work, to be sure, but it takes work.

The last part is you've got to teach it. That's why I teach leadership and happiness, because when you explain these ideas, they become permanently ingrained, and you become responsible for these ideas. This is the same idea if you wanted to learn golf. You better learn how golf works. You better go practice golf, and it's even better if you teach golf. If you're a surgeon, they say, "Watch one, do one, teach one." That's how you become a good surgeon. It's the same process in anything, and happiness is no exception.

DR: Do you think presidents of the United States are happy?

AB: Generally, it's hard to be happy when you have that much weighing on you. Some are happier than others. The president of the United States I know the best personally is George W. Bush. Happy guy, happy person. Was he happy in the depths of the Iraq War? Was he happy when people were protesting outside the Crawford Ranch? I can't say. I can't imagine that was true.

But I think he's got very good and happy genetics, and I think he's doing a lot of things right. He's got his faith on point. He's got his family life absolutely dialed in. He's got super close friends. His work is something that he believes in. He believed he was earning his success, which you can't not do as president of the United States. But, more importantly, he believed that he was serving the citizens of this country, and he was facilitating America being a gift to the world, in his view. Did he make mistakes? Of course, but he went to work every day thinking that. The main reason that I judge George W. Bush to be a person of happiness is because he had his happiness hygiene in the right place.

DR: You're focused on another subject for your next book. What is that?

AB: Meaning. Remember that the macronutrients of happiness are enjoyment, satisfaction, and meaning. We all know there's an explosion of mental health problems in people in their twenties and thirties, Gen Z and Millennials in particular. What we see is about a four-times increase in depression as well as generalized anxiety in this group over the past fifteen years. You've got to ask why and what we could do about it. A lot of people have put the blame on social media and devices and technology. There's not a lot of good that you can say about the role of technology in people's mental health. But we have data showing disproportionately that the underlying reason is that people in their twenties not only can't say what the meaning of their life is, the why of their life, they're not even looking for it.

I have to ask, why is there something uniquely troubling for young people today about finding the meaning of their life, and why aren't they looking? That's what the new book is about. [*The Meaning of Your Life* was published in March 2026.] What is it about technology that's making meaning inaccessible?

And we actually know. Some of it's incredible. For example, there's a part of your brain called the default mode network. It's a series of structures in the human brain. It's what engages when you're thinking about nothing and you're bored. You need to be bored, because that's the same part of the brain that you use to ascertain meaning in your life.

Well, guess what we've done since 2012, 2008, 2004, date it however you want? We've created antiboredom machines. Who's disproportionately used them? Young people. The more you get boredom out of your life, the less you use the default mode network in your brain, the less you endeavor to find the answers to the question of meaning, and you will feel bereft of meaning. You will feel a hollowness, as sure as we're sitting here. What I'm really interested in doing is figuring out how to explain this and to tell young people what to do about it, as well as to try to design public policies that make it easier for people to find the meaning of their lives.

DR: Is social media making people happier or sadder?

AB: Much unhappier. Drastically unhappier is what we find. The main reason is because people use social media to self-soothe and to chase away boredom. People hate boredom. Your grandparents were bored all the time because there was nothing to do. They were pushing the plow or standing behind a cash register at the general store, and they were lost in their own thoughts. They had nothing to do if they were bored, but they were finding meaning. Your grandmother never said to you, "I don't know the meaning of my life," unless your grandmother was Virginia Woolf or something. It was not normal to have these questions. The reason is because life lent itself to a contemplation of one's existence. That's not the case anymore. So, problem number one is that.

Problem number two is that social media is uniquely positioned to make us compare ourselves to others, to feel lonely, and to hate people. None of those is a recipe for happiness. The way social media is currently constituted is incredibly corrosive to well-being, especially among young people.

DR: Are rich people happier than middle-class people?

AB: No. Rich people are happier than poor people, but they're not happier than middle-class people. Money and happiness have a very complex relationship, but it can be boiled down to this: Happiness and unhappiness are not opposites. They largely exist in different hemispheres of the brain, because they come from different emotions. We have negative and positive emotions, and they all exist for particular reasons. You need all of your emotions. Never eliminate any emotions under any circumstances because you'll be in danger, is the bottom line. Negative emotions and positive emotions exist in different ways in the way that we live our lives as well. Money doesn't buy happiness, even at low levels. It eliminates the sources of unhappiness. That's what it does, because it eliminates aggravations. It eliminates worries. It eliminates security concerns. It eliminates the things that will keep you up at night about your kids getting enough food and enough to eat. But it tops out at a very low level.

Meanwhile, you learn, as you're climbing up the scale, that you feel better. You wonder why. "Why do I feel better? Oh, I have more money." I remember this when I was a musician. I had no money. From nineteen to twenty-five, I had so little money, I never went to the dentist, because I couldn't. Didn't have health care, couldn't afford it. Would have loved to have gone to the dentist. I finally had enough money because I joined this orchestra in Barcelona and I had enough money to go to the dentist. They found twelve cavities.

They fixed my cavities. I felt much better. I remember thinking, "Money does buy happiness." Money had eliminated a source of unhappiness for me. But we chase the feeling for the rest of our lives, and above middle class, it's a fool's errand.

Now, here are the workarounds. There are five things you can do with money. You can buy stuff, you can buy time, you can buy experiences, you can give it away, and you can save it. There's nothing more you can do with money. Four of those will authentically bring you more well-being, but we always choose to do the one that doesn't, because we're evolved to have more resources, to buy more stuff, to have more animal skins in our cave than the caveman next door. We want this because of all these biological imperatives, but the truth is having five watches, buying more stuff won't bring you more happiness. What will get you more happiness is buying experiences and sharing them with people that you love. Buying time and spending it in generative activities, by yourself or with people that you love, like learning and praying and going away with your spouse.

Number three is giving money away. This will bring you true joy if there's something you're passionate about. And last but not least, especially early on in life, saving your money brings you a lot of happiness because it's a marker of progress. Spending money on consumption is the best way to get unhappier. A car payment will make you unhappy, as sure as we're sitting here, and the data show that.

DR: Are people happier when they're in the minority, when they don't have responsibility, or when they're in the majority and they're responsible for something?

AB: It depends on how much agency you have. The unhappiest people, majority or minority, under any circumstances, are looking to the outside world to change so that they can be happy. They're like, "I'm aggrieved, because the outside world isn't the way I like it. If the economy were better, if my marriage were better, if my health were better, if people were nicer, if these circumstances would mysteriously change, then things would be better." There are a lot of forces in our society trying to fire up that grievance and victimization. That's the secret to unhappiness, whether you're in the majority or the minority.

At Harvard, I have very weird views on religion and even on politics. There's so much that I can do. As a matter of fact, there's more that I can do because I'm unusual at a place like this. Each one of us is in the minority in very beautiful ways, and we can band together in the majority for the good of all, is the whole point. The more agency you have, the happier you'll be.

DR: Are atheists happier than people who are committed to a religion or not?

AB: They're not, generally speaking. It depends on your commitment to what you believe and how you're using your beliefs. But, again, what we need is a system that makes us little and the universe enormous. The most efficacious way to do that for most of us is traditional religious belief. When you basically say, "There is nothing else except me," it's a hard way to live. Now I know many people of secular humanist ethics, wonderful, philanthropic, charitable people, who are thoroughgoing atheists. I debate them in the media all the time. Some are my very close friends and family members, as a matter of fact, and that's fine. It's just harder to do, is what we find for most people.

DR: Some of the greatest people in history who have come up with great inventions or other things that helped other people's lives, they were not personally happy. If you're not going to be personally happy but you do great things for society, why should people want to help others?

AB: That's a very important question, because there are a lot of people who have done great things for society who were happy, and many who haven't. There's not a correlation between greatness and happiness. You don't actually have to be happy to be great. You don't have to be happy to be successful.

There's a trap people fall into. I was doing research for a book, and one of the things that I do when I'm writing a book is I'm not just looking at numbers, I go talk to human subjects. I was talking to a woman on Wall Street, very successful, a billionaire, just about my age. When you write about happiness and you teach at Harvard, people talk to you like a psychiatrist, which is a mistake. She confessed. She said, "I've gotten everything I've ever wanted in life, and I'm really unhappy." And I said, "Talk to me." She said, "My husband and I are roommates. I have a kind of cordial relationship with my kids. I think my employees are afraid of me. I don't think I'm making good decisions anymore, but it's my company. It's my name on the sign out there." She said, "I'm not getting good reports from my doctor, but I'm still not taking care of myself. What do I do, professor?" And I said, "You just wrote your own prescription, sister. Go away with your husband. Get to know your kids. Take care of your health. Step back from your firm." She says, "I know, I know, I've always known that." And I said, "So, why don't you do it?" It was a moment, you know. She said, "I guess I've always chosen to be special rather than happy."

It was like a knife to my heart, because me too. When I was president of AEI, I would work that fourteenth hour instead of going home for the first hour with my kids. I did that, and they got revenge on me. They grew up. But I'm going to have the last laugh because now they're living in my house with their children. And that's a beautiful thing, I have to say.

But that's the point we all have to be careful of. Just because you're successful does not mean that you're going to be happy. But you can be both happy and successful. You just have to take care of both.

19

David Grann on *The Wager*

INTERVIEW DATE: MARCH 11, 2025

For several decades, David Grann was a well-respected magazine journalist (mainly for *The New Yorker*), with a talent for deep research and novel-like writing. In 2009, Grann decided to try his hand at using those skills to write a book—*The Lost City of Z: A Tale of Deadly Obsession in the Amazon*. That book became a *New York Times* number-one best-seller. Grann followed that book with two other number-one *New York Times* best-sellers (and, in a rarity for any author, both were on the *Times* list at the same time): *Killers of the Flower Moon* (later made into a Best Picture Academy Award–nominated film) and *The Wager: A Tale of Shipwreck, Mutiny, and Murder.*

What has made Grann such a popular (and respected) author? He has a somewhat unique way of telling a story that makes his books very hard to put down.

In brief, Grann picks a largely forgotten historic event, conducts meticulous research uncovering previously unknown details, and crafts a compelling narrative that reads much more like a novel than a traditional history book.

The Wager is about the shipwreck of the HMS *Wager* in 1741 off the coast of Patagonia. The ship had been sent by the British Admiralty to capture a Spanish ship supposedly filled with golden treasures.

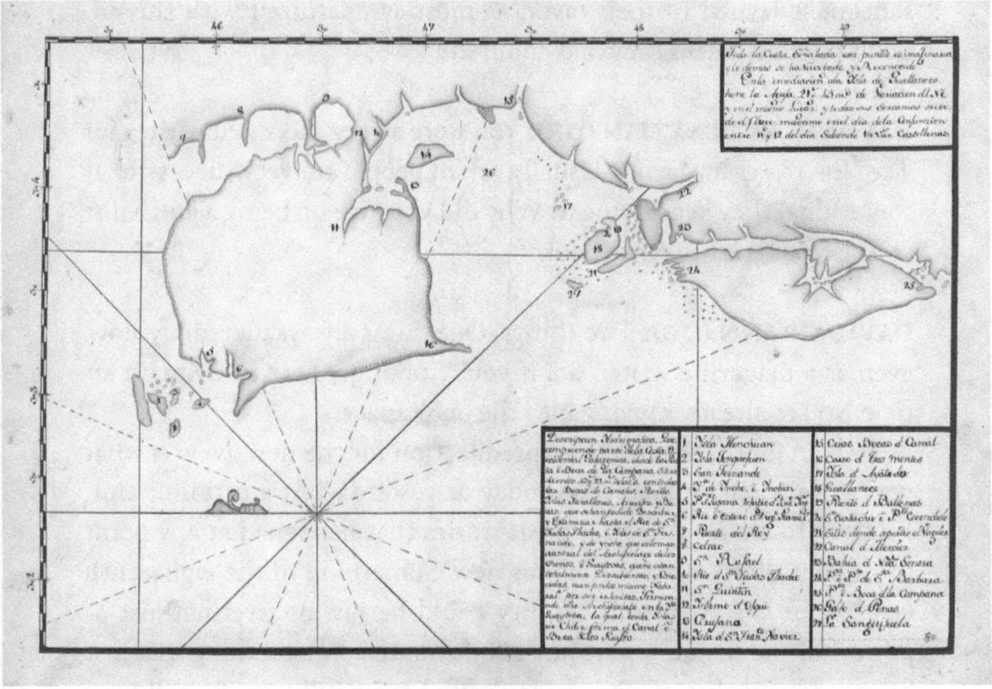

FIGURE 19.1 Oriented with east at the top, this map depicts the Gulf of Penas off the southwestern coast of Chile, where the *Wager* shipwrecked in 1741.

Two groups of survivors eventually returned to England with differing accounts. One group claimed they survived the shipwreck under the worst circumstances, while the other claimed the first group had committed mutiny and should be held responsible. A tribunal was convened by the Admiralty to determine what actually happened and then to compensate or punish the two groups as the facts warranted.

This whole episode might seem unlikely to hold the attention of a large group of US Members of Congress (this was not, after all, an American ship, and the story was not in any way really relevant to American history). But David Grann is as skilled a raconteur as he is a writer, and the Members were fascinated by how a tribunal resolved the whole matter. (The tribunal ultimately acquitted the mutineers, in part because the shipwreck relieved them of their usual responsibilities and obligations under British Admiralty law—and public sentiment leaned in their favor, as most sympathized with the difficult circumstances they had endured.)

DAVID M. RUBENSTEIN (DR): You were a very successful writer for *The New Yorker* magazine. Usually, when people are very successful at something, they keep doing it. Why did you give up being a journalist at *The New Yorker* to write books?

DAVID GRANN (DG): Two things. One: I was always incredibly slow, even as a magazine writer. So, if you're taking a year to write an article, you're already moving into the book space.

Two: in journalism there's a predilection for the new. New is what you write about. It happened today or yesterday. At a certain point, I started to realize there are great stories that happened at any point in time; it didn't matter if it was new. Something in the eighteenth century or the twentieth century could be just as riveting, just as powerful, and in many ways just as informative as something that just happened and that maybe we don't yet have a full understanding of or perspective on.

DR: When you wrote your first book, how long did it take you?

DG: Three years. That was fast back then. Don't ask me about the latter ones because my wife fact-checks me.

DR: You wrote a book called *Killers of the Flower Moon*, and that book became a movie. It also became a gigantic number-one best-seller. Where did you get the idea that something that happened such a long time ago in Oklahoma would be a best-seller?

DG: I often do this thing when I'm looking for a story. I will just call random people. So, you may get a call from me picking your brain. I learned that the FBI had a historian, so I called the historian at the FBI, and I was just asking about different old cases. He happened to mention this case to me. He didn't know much about it. At that point, I didn't think necessarily I would do a book, but I was interested enough that I decided to travel out to Oklahoma and visit the Osage Nation.

When I was there, I did what any visitor to a new place does. I went to the Osage Nation Museum. I saw this great panoramic photograph on the wall that was taken in 1924. It showed members of the Osage Nation along with white settlers, but a portion of the photograph had been cut out. I asked the museum director, Kathryn Red Corn, whom I was meeting for the first time, "Why is that part of the photograph missing?" She said, "It contained a figure so frightening that they decided to remove it." Then she pointed to the missing panel and said, "The devil was standing right there."

It was one of the rare moments where a book has an origin story. I knew in that instant, if I could tell the story—which was about these very sinister crimes that took place in the early twentieth century, when members of the Osage Nation were among the wealthiest people per capita in the United States because of oil under their land, and then they began to be killed one after the other—I could have a book from this, I thought.

DR: When you write a book like that, you do all your research and then write? Or you research, write, research, write? And do you write on a computer? Longhand? How do you do that?

DG: Virtually everything I write about, I know nothing about beforehand. As I tell people I interview, I am an ignoramus. Please talk to me like I'm a golden retriever. I don't know the subjects that I'm writing about. I'm learning about them for the first time. I do a lot of research, just trying to figure out what happened. What are the outlines? Who am I writing about? What really happened?

Research is really important, too. I always say this, and I think it's very true: In life, you have to keep an open mind. For *Killers of the Flower Moon*, I spent a year and a half thinking I was telling one story, which was about that very singular evil figure in that photograph who had committed these crimes. But, over time, working in archives and getting records and speaking to members of the Osage Nation, I began to realize that these killings of the Osage were far more widespread. And suddenly, after about a year and a half, the book I thought I was writing was demolished, and I had to write a different book.

So research is always essential. I tend to do nearly all the research first, then I will start to write, and I will fill in any holes as I go along.

DR: When the book came out, it became a number-one best-seller. Were you surprised that a subject like that would be of such interest to people?

DG: Yes, 100 percent. First of all, any writer who's confident that anyone will read their books is either a con artist or is misleading you. I remember my wife, Kyra, pulled me aside. I had spent more than five years working on *Killers of the Flower Moon*—half a decade, watched my kids grow up. And I remember she pulled me aside and she said, "Even if no one reads this book, you did something that you believed in and that was important." That was really my thought when the book came out.

DR: When Martin Scorsese and Leonardo DiCaprio said they wanted to make it into a movie, did you think that was for real?

DG: I said, "Can you go on speakerphone so my kids can listen to this? Because this is going to blow their minds." I grew up watching films. I'm an archive rat. I'm just a nerd who works on books. When somebody whose movies you've seen suddenly wants to do a movie, you can't believe it.

DR: Let's talk about this book *The Wager*. What was the *Wager*? Is the name a double entendre because it's a bit of a bet?

DG: My one concern was that when people saw the book title *The Wager*, they would think it was contemporary, like poker or something, a bet. But the *Wager* was actually the name of a ship. It was named after Sir Charles Wager, who was the British Lord of the Admiralty. It was commissioned during a war in 1739 to go out and, as part of an expedition, try to capture a Spanish galleon filled with so much treasure that it was known as "the prize of all the oceans." But, in many ways, the name is a metaphor, because all these people are waging a bet on their own lives when they get on the ship and set sail.

DR: Did you think that a story from the 1740s dealing with a shipwreck was going to be best-seller material? How did you come to the conclusion that you should spend many years of your life on this?

DG: That's a really good question. In fact, you worry about it the whole time. I discovered that story when I came across an eighteenth-century journal written by a midshipman on the *Wager* named John Byron. It was written in this very old, archaic English. The handwriting was faded. The *s*'s were printed as *f*'s back then. I was like, What is this?

Then I started to read it, and suddenly he would describe the perfect hurricane. He described scurvy, described the people going mad on the island, the battle over leadership, the human struggle. It just got its hooks into me.

But you never know. To some extent, you are pursuing your own obsessions. I often pursue history and subjects I know nothing about in order to learn about myself and about the world in which we live.

DR: For those who aren't familiar with English history, what was the War of Jenkins' Ear?

DG: Even more than Scorsese's call, I was like, you've got to be kidding me, there was a war called the War of Jenkins' Ear? The British were trying to break Spain's colonial hold over Latin America and expand their trading routes. A story circulated about a British captain of a merchant ship named Robert Jenkins. The Spanish had boarded his ship, and they cut off his ear. This story went around England, and people cried out, "An eye for an eye, an ear for an ear."

It turned out to be ginned up. There was actually a Robert Jenkins, but the incident happened about eight years earlier and had been completely overlooked and nobody even knew about it. It was then seized upon by people who wanted a pretext for war against Spain. So it became the War of Jenkins' Ear.

DR: What was the idea that led to this voyage? The British wanted to capture gold or other valuable things from the Spanish?

DG: In addition to trying to break the stranglehold on trade, the focus of this mission was a bit peculiar. It had a whiff of piracy about it. The mission was to try to intercept the Spanish galleon that took all the gold and silver from Mexico and Peru across to the Philippines to buy goods in Asia. This ship was filled with so much wealth, untold wealth, it was known as "the prize of all the oceans." The British idea was to send ships from England across the Atlantic, around Cape Horn, up the coast to Mexico, and then across the Pacific, intercept this ship, and then, if they succeeded, complete their mission and sail around the world.

DR: Whoever came up with that idea, how did they recruit people for that voyage, and how long was it supposed to take?

DG: That was a problem. Like a lot of wars, there was a lot of public outcry for war, but there wasn't funding. Nobody wanted to pay for it. They exhausted their supply of volunteers, and what they did is they sent out the press gangs. If you're familiar with the American Revolution, you probably know something about press gangs. What the press gangs would do is they would go to bars, or they would go to ports, and they would eyeball you. If you had any telltale signs that you were a mariner, even if you had a little bit of tar in your fingernails, because tar was used on ships to make everything water resistant, they'd say, "Great. We got one. You're coming." You could have been just coming back from a voyage to the Pacific after being away for two years. You hit London, thinking, "I'm going to see my wife and my kids. I haven't seen them for two years." And suddenly you're like, "Whoops. I'm in a prison. I'm being taken out to a ship, and I'm going to go on this other perilous voyage."

Even then, they were short of seamen. They took the drastic measure of going to a retirement home, a pensioners' home for seamen and soldiers. They rounded up 500 of these seamen, many of whom were in their sixties and seventies, some of whom were missing an assortment of limbs, some of whom were so sick they had to be lifted on stretchers onto the ship for this voyage. The seeds of destruction were planted at the very start of the expedition.

DR: And the chef on the ship was eighty years old?

DG: The chef was eighty years old. These ships were these floating civilizations. You had people from all walks of life. You would have boys as young as eight or nine. You had the cook of the *Wager*, who was eighty. The midshipman, John Byron, was sixteen years old. He would later become the grandfather of the poet Lord Byron. You would have aristocrats, you would have paupers, you would have free Black seamen, all thrown together in this self-contained civilization that was both a floating home and also an instrument of war.

DR: How many people were on the boat when it sailed?

DG: On the *Wager*, there were about 250 or 240. In the squadron, because there were several other warships going along, there were nearly 2,000 in total.

DR: The *Wager* was one of several ships. How old was the ship itself?

DG: The *Wager* was relatively new, but it was the ugly duckling of the voyage because it had been a merchant ship. They were short of warships, so they had to convert it into one. It was about 123 feet long and had three masts, as those warships did.

In many ways, these ships were the most sophisticated engineering marvels of their time. The sites that would produce them were the largest manufacturing sites in the world at the time, because they needed to build and supply these vessels. These ships could fly as many as twelve sails and had cannons on both sides. But even though they were extremely sophisticated, they were also vulnerable because they were made of wood. They were susceptible to all the elements of storm and sea.

DR: Did everybody get their own cabin?

DG: You did not get your own cabin unless you were an officer or a petty officer. Most of the seamen would sleep in hammocks hanging side by side. Your elbows and knees would jostle in rough seas. But you slept right between the cannons, and you would eat your meals on a folding table between them as well.

DR: When did the *Wager* leave England?

DG: It took them so long to repair these ships, it finally set off at the end of 1740.

DR: How long did it take to get across the Atlantic?

DG: It took about three and a half months to get to Cape Horn.

DR: Where is Cape Horn?

DG: Cape Horn is at the very tip of South America, and it is notorious for the roughest seas in the world. I'd always heard that the seas are really bad at Cape Horn, but until I did the research, I never knew why. There are very specific reasons. It's the only place where the seas travel 13,000 miles around the globe, and they are never interrupted by land. They're never blocked; they're never slowed down. They enter the narrowing passage between Cape Horn and Antarctica, where the floor of the seas also grows shallower. And as a result you get the strongest currents on Earth. You have winds that can reach 200 miles per hour. You have what are known as the Cape Horn roller waves, which can dwarf a ninety-foot mast.

DR: The *Wager* gets to the Cape Horn, and what happens?

DG: They end up hitting a hurricane—the perfect hurricane, as John Byron described it in the journal by him that I found—and all their sails blew out. In one of the logbooks, I found the description of how, when they were coming around Cape Horn, they couldn't fly their sails because they kept blowing out in the storm. The captain couldn't control the ship without them. So he sent the young seamen to climb the mast, about 100 feet high, to hold on to the ropes of the ship in this hurricane and use their bodies as concave sails while the ship was listing about forty-five degrees to one side and forty-five degrees to the other.

DR: Eventually it hits land in a shipwreck?

DG: Around Cape Horn, when they know they need every man, they begin to die of this mysterious illness, which is scurvy. Their hair begins to fall out. Their teeth fall out. The disease even gets into their brains, and they go raving mad. They didn't understand that all they needed was citrus. All they needed was vitamin C, which is why later British seamen would take limes and become known as "limeys."

So, these ships are ravaged, and eventually the *Wager* is separated from all the other ships. It's navigating through dead reckoning. It misreads its longitude, and it ends up wrecked on an island that is now known as Wager Island.

DR: What happened to the other ships? Did they make it through?

DG: No. Many of them scattered or turned back. In the end, only one ship would fully survive and complete the expedition.

DR: The *Wager* is shipwrecked on an island. Is there anything left of the ship? Or the crew has to stay there and wait for somebody to pick them up?

DG: The ship hits a rock and shudders, and a two-ton anchor falls through the hull. Then another wave comes and washes the ship off the rocks. The ship is careening through what is known as the Golfo de Penas, which translates as the Gulf of Sorrows or, as some prefer to call it, the Gulf of Pain. And water is pouring through this hole in the hull. Its rudder is shattered. Finally, the *Wager* collides with these rocks. The cabins collapse. The decks collapse. Rats are scurrying upward. Those who were too sick from scurvy and could not get out of their hammocks drown.

But miraculously, the ship did not completely sink, because it became wedged between the rocks. The survivors, about 145 of them, climb up on the remnants of the ship. They look out in the distance, and they can see in the mist this island that they think will be their salvation. That's where the real hell will begin.

DR: They start with about 240 people on the boat, and about 100 of them die from either disease or something else?

DG: Scurvy, waves, storm, yes.

DR: About 140 of them make it to this island. How did they get to it?

DG: Small transport vessels. We would imagine them like lifeboats. They didn't really call them lifeboats at that time. A couple of them had not been smashed, and they were able to use those to ferry people ashore.

DR: They get to the island. The way that the Navy works is that whoever is the head of the ship becomes the head of the shipwreck crew?

DG: Yes.

DR: Who was that person?

DG: His name was Captain David Cheap. He was an interesting figure. He came from a well-to-do family in Scotland but was always chased by creditors. He had found refuge at sea. On this voyage, he had finally attained what he had always wanted. He'd become captain of his own ship. Then, of course, he loses his ship. He's determined to remain commander on the island. He believes that the only way they will survive there is to maintain military discipline, naval order, hierarchy.

DR: How long are they on that island?

DG: They're on the island for several months, about half a year.

DR: How do they get food?

DG: The island turns out to be windswept, barren, desolate. They find some mussels, they had a few clams, but they quickly exhausted that supply along the shore, and there really is no food. They did find some celery on the island, which, unbeknownst to them—they didn't understand scurvy—cured their scurvy. But they begin to starve. And slowly, as they begin to starve, they descend into a Hobbesian state, a real-life *Lord of the Flies* with warring factions and abandonments and mutinies and counter-mutinies.

DR: Were there Natives on the island?

DG: On that particular island, when they landed, there was nobody there. But one day out of the mist arrive two canoes, and on those canoes are members of the Kawésqar, Native Patagonians who had been in the region for hundreds and hundreds of years. They had adapted to the harsh cold. It's always windy. It's always sleeting. It's always wet. They lived almost exclusively off marine resources. They spent most of their time in canoes. The kids would keep a fire going on the canoe to stay warm. They had survived so well in these difficult conditions that NASA, when they were considering putting humans into space, studied how the Kawésqar had adapted.

When they arrive on the island, they offer these struggling castaways a lifeline. But the castaways, partly out of disorder, partly out of prejudice toward the Patagonians, begin to mistreat them. One morning, the Kawésqar simply disappear. At that point, the castaways begin to descend into even further unrest.

DR: About 140 people land on this island. Three or four months later, how many people are left?

DG: By the end, they get down to about seventy-three.

DR: At some point, a boat with survivors shows up in Brazil. What is the story that those people tell the Brazilians?

DG: First, I should point out that what happened on Wager Island is, in many ways, a reflection of human nature and society. There was a human struggle for power. One of the members of the crew was a gunner who knew he could never become a commander, because he didn't come from the aristocracy. But he was an instinctive leader. When they are suffering on that island, there's a question of could he become a commander in his own right in this kind of democracy of suffering? You see a lot of this kind of leadership struggle play out.

And then, the first boat arrives in Brazil. This is a vessel that they had kind of expanded and built on the island. Crammed onboard are about thirty people. They are so emaciated they can't even stand. They announce that they are survivors of His Majesty's ship the *Wager*. When the news gets back to England, nobody can believe it. The ship was considered missing. No one had heard from it for more than a year. And they're treated as heroes, because they were seen as having completed this voyage through the Straits of Magellan, which was considered one of the greatest castaway voyages ever carried out. And then, about three months later—

DR: Another boat shows up in Chile.

DG: Yes, off the coast of Chile, off Chiloe Island. This one is only a dugout. It's got a little mast and a sail that's made of torn blankets.

On board are three crew members, including John Byron, the midshipman, and Captain Cheap, who is so delirious he cannot even recollect his name. But, after they recover, they say, "Those people who went to Brazil, they're not heroes. They're mutineers."

In the controversy that ensues, with all these lobbing accusations, it becomes clear that, while they were trapped on this island, they had descended into a state where some of them had committed cannibalism. There was a mutiny. There was a counter-mutiny. There was even murder.

DR: How long did it take the people who went to Brazil to get back to England? Have they got a ship? Somebody takes them?

DG: It took a long time. First, they were trapped in Brazil waiting for a ship to get back. Some of these people will eventually get back to England, but it will be years since they left on the voyage. Suddenly someone would show up and their family wouldn't even recognize him. John Byron had left England when he was sixteen. By the time he comes back, he's twenty-two. His sister doesn't recognize him.

DR: Eventually he becomes the grandfather of Lord Byron?

DG: Yes. Lord Byron's poem *Don Juan* is greatly influenced by the narrative that first gave me the idea to do this book. He refers to it as his granddad's narrative. He writes that his grandfather had no rest at sea and he had no rest on land.

DR: Who gets back to England first: the people in Brazil or the people in Chile?

DG: The people in Brazil. This is an important lesson in communication. Who tells their story first? They are determined to tell their story first and get that on the record. What is so interesting is that here they went through these incredible travails that reveal so much about the human condition. Even when they were on that island, some of the mutineers would use phrases about why they were rebelling. They would use phrases like "life and liberty," phrases that we now know from the American Revolution.

When they get back to England, after everything they've been through, they're suddenly summoned to a court-martial for their alleged crimes. If they don't tell a convincing tale after everything they've been through—scurvy, shipwreck, mutiny, the castaway voyage—they could be hanged. We all like to say we tell ourselves stories in order to live. It's a famous Joan Didion line. In their case, it's quite literally true.

DR: The ones from Brazil get back before the ones from Chile. They tell their story that they're heroes?

DG: And they print it, and they become sensations. Early blogging.

DR: But when the Chilean ship people get to England, do they say that the other people were lying, that they were really mutineers?

DG: Yes. They say they are mutineers. The opposing side, in turn, accuses one of them of committing murder. They are preparing to face off in this historic court-martial. What is so interesting was it generated, with advancements in cheap printing, an explosion of storytelling—the release of their diaries, their journals, their logbooks. These became kind of wild best-sellers in their day. They would influence poetry and literature. One of the accounts is considered the greatest-selling travel book of the eighteenth century.

DR: The Admiralty decides to hold a hearing about who's telling the truth. How long does that go on for?

DG: They are all praying. Most of them expect to die. Mutiny's a distinct form of rebellion because it takes place within a military apparatus designed to impose order, and suddenly you disorder. So the question arises: Is this an extreme form of outlawry, or were there circumstances that justified the rebellion and maybe even gave a nobility to it? That is the fight that is playing out, and they're expecting to be hanged. They go into the court-martial, and they're stunned. They suddenly realize that the authorities decided, at a certain point, "Do we like any of these stories? They make us look like brutes, not like gentlemen, and they undercut the British Empire."

So the authorities do something that was atypical for the way the British Admiralty typically treated a mutiny. They made it go away. They just made it go away. And the people who were there were stunned.

Rather than the stories of the survivors of the *Wager*, the Admiralty preferred a different tale that came out of the expedition. It was from the leader of the squadron who had commanded the one ship that survives the journey. And, believe it or not, he and his crew intercept the Spanish galleon, the prize of all the oceans. He tells his story. The British Admiralty says, "That's the story we want to tell," and his version of the expedition becomes the big-selling book. He will go on to become the father of the British Navy, and the *Wager* will become a footnote.

DR: So, nobody is punished in the end.

DG: Nobody.

DR: You were punished when you decided to do research and go there, right?

DG: As you can see by my physical attributes, I'm a great explorer. No. I am made, with my paltry physical attributes, to live in archives. I spent two years in the archives in England looking at these logbooks. It's incredible. You can pull these logbooks out. They come out in a box. You open them up. The bindings are disintegrating. You literally inhale the dust. You put the covers on pillows to protect them, and you can read what they were writing in 1741 on a ship in a hurricane. It's astonishing.

But, at a certain point, I started to say, "Could I fully ever understand what these people went through unless I went there myself?" I don't like to preach, but when I write about other people, living or dead, I feel a moral responsibility to understand them and to record them as accurately as I can. So, I decided to go to the island. I found a Chilean captain who said he could take me there. He sent me a photograph of the boat. I showed it to my wife. I said, "This looks pretty good. It looks like something out of Jacques Cousteau. I'll be fine."

When I got to Chiloe Island, which is about 350 miles north of Wager Island, I took one look at the boat. Pictures can be very deceiving. It was a wood-heated boat. When I say it was a wood-heated boat, I mean it was heated by wood. It had a stove. And I had the foolish idea that I had to go on this expedition in winter so I could fully understand what they went through.

We get on this boat, and it's so rough the Coast Guard wouldn't let us leave for five days. They closed the port. But, finally, they let us go. For several days, we weave through these channels that are pretty calm. Then, at a certain point, the captain said to me, "If we're going to get to Wager Island and go into the Gulf of Pain, we have to go out into the open ocean." And that's when I got my first glimpse of the seas. It was like being inside a Ping-Pong ball. You had to sit on the deck for about ten or twelve hours a day. You could not stand or you'd break a limb. You could not eat. I had every seasickness medicine known to humankind. I had the thing behind the ear. I had the little band going, and I was basically half-drunk on Dramamine. And I was just kind of sitting in a stupor.

I thought, How am I going to pass this time? I've got to distract myself. Not being the brightest explorer in the world, I had my iPhone. I said, I've got *Moby-Dick* on Audible on my phone. I'll listen to *Moby-Dick*—I think the greatest American novel ever written. The worst book, however, to listen to in a storm when you're trying to get to Wager Island, and Ahab is leading his ship to total destruction.

Thankfully, my captain was very skilled. He managed to get us to the island. It remains a place that is windswept. All the trees are at forty-five-degree angles because of the winds. It sleets. It rains. There's still no food. I felt bad because we brought a little picnic. But it was by being on that island and exploring it and seeing what they went through that I could really understand why a British officer described the island as a place where the soul of the man dies in him.

At one point, the captain of our ship said to me, "Come over here." He pointed to a little stream. It was crystal-clear, cold water. And I could see pieces of timber just underneath the surface of the stream, about five or six yards long, held together not with nails but by wooden pegs. They are the remnants of an eighteenth-century warship. They're believed to be from His Majesty's ship the *Wager*. We knew what they were because a British and Chilean expedition had discovered them several years earlier and identified and dated them. It was amazing because, after all the research I had done and all the cacophony of warring words, that was all that remained of that great struggle that had taken place on that island. I'll never forget. I just stood there for about five minutes staring at that wood, and the only sound I could hear was the eternal hush of the sea.

DR: You never thought of taking a little bit of it back?

DG: I was very respectful. I didn't take it.

DR: But after all those years, the wood is still surviving.

DG: It's a little bit inland. The water is a little bit fresher. It is amazing. Those fragments are still surviving.

DR: You're glad you went and visited?

DG: I really am. I wouldn't do it again. Or I would go on a much bigger ship. But it gave me so many insights. I would read their journals, for example, and they would describe how cold it is. As a researcher, you look that up, and you say, "Okay, it's thirty-two degrees, thirty-three degrees. It's not Antarctica cold." But then, when you get there, you're like, it's really cold because it's always windy. It's always raining. Their clothes had disintegrated. When I visited the island, it was the first time it occurred to me that the castaways had hypothermia—a term they wouldn't have used in their journals—and it would have affected their decision-making at the time.

DR: Is this going to be a movie as well?

DG: We hope. My first book was called *The Lost City of Z*, which is about a search for an ancient civilization in the middle of the Amazon. I used to joke that getting a movie made was harder than finding an ancient city in the middle of the Amazon. But this book has been optioned by the same people who did *Killers of the Flower Moon*, Martin Scorsese and Leonardo DiCaprio. So I'm in very good hands.

DR: When you sell a movie idea to Hollywood, do you write the script, or they rewrite it and you just sit there?

DG: There's a good story that is attributed to about four different writers, and I never know if it's even true. I've heard it attributed to Faulkner, Fitzgerald, Hemingway. If you're the writer, you take your manuscript to Hollywood, you throw it over the fence, they throw the check over, and then you go on your way. I'm so busy working on my books, I don't actually want to write scripts. I don't really want to make movies. I don't know anything about it. But I'm always there as a resource. You work with them, and you answer questions. You're kind of a historical resource. Plus, for at least two days, my kids will think I'm cool when they visit the set.

DR: When the book came out and became so well known, did any of the descendants of people from the *Wager* contact you?

DG: Yes. I had traced down a few, including a Byron. A descendant of George Anson, who led the ship that actually captured the Spanish galleon, reached out to me. We had a lovely talk and shared a lot of wonderful stories.

DR: It's a great story. Now you're working on a new book, which you can't talk about yet, right?

DG: It's about espionage, so you'll understand why I'm cryptic. A lot of my books—and we're living through these times—are about searches for the truth. In *The Wager*, it is a meditation about storytelling, the way we tell stories, the way we shape our own truths, the way nations tell the truth, and how we find it. How do we dig it out? I believe in the truth, but how do we find it? How do we validate it? How do we recognize it? That's very true of the espionage realm. *Killers of the Flower Moon* and *The Wager* and the new project I'm working on are completely different subject matters. But I see them almost as a trilogy thematically.

DR: When you're in the middle of writing a book that's taking five years or so to write, do you ever say, "I wish I had not picked this subject"?

DG: Often, up until the day it's done and has been published. You live with that. You always have that little bit of doubt. You wonder, is this right? Is it going to work out? Am I going to figure out what happened? Am I going to be able to tell it? Am I going to make you be able to feel the ocean and smell it? Am I going to be able to bring Captain Cheap to life? Even with his complexities, even with his flaws, can you understand him?

You always have those doubts. I will say this. I am very ruthless early on. I look into many, many story ideas. I will spend two to three months looking into them. I will decide early on, hopefully, if this won't work. I come across wonderful stories sometimes, but there's no way to tell them. Either people won't share the stories or the records don't exist.

You have to go through this rigorous process before you commit to a project. You pray that you're not like the *Wager* about to end up shipwrecked on a desolate island with no food and everybody looking at you as you go raving mad.

Acknowledgments

I want to acknowledge and thank all of the many individuals who helped to make this book possible, whether by (1) creating and fostering the Congressional Dialogues or (2) assisting in the preparation of this book describing how the Dialogues have operated over the past decade plus.

On the Dialogues themselves, I want to acknowledge the indispensable support of the late Dr. James Billington, who had been appointed the thirteenth Librarian of Congress by President Reagan. As the Librarian, Dr. Billington enthusiastically supported my idea to have regular sessions at the Library with Members of Congress and their guests.

When he retired in 2015, after having served in that position for twenty-eight years, he was succeeded by Dr. Carla Hayden, the head of the Enoch Pratt Free Library from my hometown of Baltimore. Appointed by President Obama, Dr. Hayden represented a remarkable choice: She was a professional librarian (with a PhD from the University of Chicago) and only the third Librarian of Congress to come from that professional background. She also broke new ground as the first woman and the first African American to serve as Librarian of Congress. From the start of her appointment, Dr. Hayden also enthusiastically supported the Congressional Dialogues, and she attended and spoke at essentially all of them during her tenure.

When her appointment was terminated by President Trump, she was succeeded by Acting Librarian of Congress Robert Newlen, who had worked at the Library for forty-five years and had been serving as the deputy Librarian of Congress. Robert Newlen continued the Library's strong support of the Dialogues and also enthusiastically supported the publication of this book.

I am very grateful to James Billington, Carla Hayden, and Robert Newlen for their help in creating, continuing, and strengthening the Dialogues.

I am also grateful to the hundreds of Members of Congress, ranging from congressional leadership to the newest Members of Congress, for attending the Dialogues. Their presence has helped to make the Dialogues so popular and vibrant. (Typically, at the end of an interview, Members of Congress are allotted time to ask questions, and those questions invariably show the breadth of the Members' interest in and knowledge of American history, among other subjects.)

For the preparation of this book, I want to thank the publishers: the Library of Congress, whose Publishing Office is led by Aimee Hess; and Duke University Press, which is led by Dean Smith. Without their enthusiastic support for this undertaking, the publication of this volume would not have occurred.

In the preparation of this volume, I have—as with my previous books—relied heavily on Jennifer Howard to secure and edit the interview transcripts and to help edit my own overly long prose. Her services and enthusiasm for this project, while she was also working on another one of my books, are greatly appreciated.

I also want to acknowledge my personal staff who helped a great deal with this book's preparation. My chief of staff, MaryPat Decker, who has worked with me for thirty-five-plus years; Laura Boring (twenty-one years); and Amanda Mangum (twelve years). All of them pitched in to make certain the book was completed on time, despite my typically illegible handwriting or indecipherable typing.

I also want to thank Max Moore, who joined my staff in 2025, for helping with my research and presentations. (He follows many others who have held this position before matriculating at—and ultimately graduating from—Harvard Business School.)

I also want to thank Marie Arana and Clay Smith, respectively, the Library's former and current literary director, for their invaluable work in securing the interviewees for the Dialogues, especially given the demanding schedules of both the Members of Congress and the authors.

I also want to acknowledge the support and help with legal issues associated with this book's publication. For all of my previous books, my principal lawyer had been Bob Barnett of Williams & Connolly, who had been a friend of mine for more than fifty years, dating back to our days at the University of Chicago Law School. Last year, Bob succumbed to cancer and left a big hole in my life and the lives of hundreds of authors around the country. He was the nation's preeminent lawyer representing authors. Fortunately, Bob trained two extremely talented partners at Williams & Connolly, Michael O'Connor and Emily Alden, and their help with this book is much appreciated and was essential to the ultimate publication.

As with my previous books, I am sure there are some errors and mistakes. I take full responsibility for these.

—DAVID M. RUBENSTEIN

Credits

All conversations in this book are printed courtesy of the conversation partner.

All images are from the Library of Congress's collections. The following abbreviations are used to indicate the appropriate custodial division: G&M: Geography and Map Division; P&P: Prints and Photographs Division; RBSC: Rare Book and Special Collections Division.

F.1: Carol M. Highsmith, Great Hall, Library of Congress, Thomas Jefferson Building, 2007. P&P. LC-DIG-highsm-01970.

Chapter 1: Interview quotations provided courtesy of Ken Burns.

1.1: Paul Revere, *The bloody massacre perpetrated in King Street Boston on March 5th, 1770, by a party of the 29th Regt.*, 1770. P&P. LC-DIG-ppmsca-01657.

2.1: John Singleton Copley, *Samuel Adams*, 1772. Photograph by Detroit Publishing Co., between 1900 and 1912. P&P. LC-D416-256.

3.1: [Mathew] Brady's National Photographic Portrait Galleries, Major General Ulysses S. Grant, 1860–65. P&P. LC-DIG-cwpb-06941.

3.2: Julian Vannerson, General Robert E. Lee, March 1864. P&P. LC-DIG-cwpb-04402.

Chapter 4: Manisha Sinha on Reconstruction (Congressional Dialogues, September. 25, 2024).

4.1: Alfred R. Waud, "The First Vote," *Harper's Weekly*, November 16, 1867. P&P. LC-DIG-ppmsca-37947.

5.1: Warren K. Leffler, Secretary of Defense Robert McNamara (*right*), President Lyndon Baines Johnson, and Secretary of State Dean Rusk, seated at a table after McNamara's return from South Vietnam, July 21, 1965. P&P, U.S. News & World Report Magazine Photograph Collection. LC-DIG-ds-07431.

6.1: Thomas J. O'Halloran, Vice President Richard M. Nixon and Senator John F. Kennedy on a split television screen during the third debate, October 13, 1960. P&P, U.S. News & World Report Magazine Photograph Collection. LC-DIG-ppmsca-83290.

7.1: John F. Kennedy, ca. 1960–63. P&P. LC-USZ62-13035.

8.1: Ronald Reagan, 1981. P&P. LC-USZ62-13040.

9.1: Harris & Ewing, Jim Thorpe, ca. 1910–20. P&P. LC-DIG-hec-13257.

10.1: J. Edgar Hoover, December 22, 1924. P&P. LC-DIG-ds-07208.

11.1: Sandra Day O'Connor, ca. 1981–83. P&P. LC-USZ62-86846.

12.1: Carol M. Highsmith, *The Navy SEAL Monument on the Atlantic Shore in Virginia Beach*, November 13, 2019. P&P. LC-DIG-highsm-61028.

13.1: Nicolas de Larmessin, *Lionardo Da Vinci, pittore*. Published in Isaac Bullart, *Academie des sciences et des arts* (Bruxelles, 1695). P&P. LC-USZ62-130416.

14.1: George Caleb Bingham, *The Jolly Flat Boat Men*, 1847. Mezzotint by Thomas Doney, 1847. P&P. LC-DIG-pga-01064.

15.1: Robert Hooke, *Micrographia, or Some Physiological Descriptions of Minute Bodies Made by Magnifying Glasses* (London, 1665). RBSC, Lessing J. Rosenwald Collection 1511.

16.1: Thomas J. O'Halloran, control room 1 of the Launch Control Center at Kennedy Space Center, Merritt Island, Florida, September 19, 1967. P&P, U.S. News & World Report Magazine Photograph Collection. LC-DIG-ppmsca-89479.

17.1: Phil Stanziola, *800 Women Strikers for Peace on 47 St Near the UN Bld.*, 1962. P&P, New York World-Telegram and the Sun Newspaper Photograph Collection. LC-USZ62-128465.

18.1: Gordon Parks, *Boys Playing Leap Frog, Frederick Douglass Housing Project. Anacostia, D.C.*, July 1942. P&P, Farm Security Administration–Office of War Information Photograph Collection. LC-USF34-013382-C.

Chapter 19: David Grann, interview by David M. Rubenstein, March 11, 2025. *The Wager: A Tale of Shipwreck, Mutiny, and Murder* by David Grann. Copyright © 2023 by David Grann. Published by Doubleday, a division of Penguin Random House, LLC.

19.1: *Descripción hidrográfica, que compreende parte de la costa occidental patagónica, desde la Punta o Boca de la Campana situada en los 49 gs. 22 ms. de latd. S. con todas las Bocas de Canales, puertos, yslas . . .* ca. 1760. G&M. G5332.C6 1760 .D4 Vault.

Index

(Page numbers in italics refers to figures.)

abolitionism, 87–88
abortion rights, 174, 245, 249
Acheson, Dean, 94, 362, 374
Adams, Abigail, 305
Adams, John, 1; presidency of, 299, 304–6; Revolutionary War and, 30–34, 37–40, 43, 308
Adams, John Quincy, 88, 305
Adams, Samuel, 28–45, *29*
Addison's disease, Kennedy's concealment of, 120, 123, 130, 154
Adoration of the Magi, The (Leonardo painting), 287
affirmative action, 249–50
agentic revolution, 352–53
aging, 334–35; cancer, 324
alcohol, cancer and, 324
Ali, Muhammad, 23–24
Alito, Samuel (Justice), 252
Allen, Danielle, 4
Allison, Graham, 356–78; career of, 356, *357*, 373
al-Qaeda, 264–65, 279
Altman, Sam, 345
American Revolution: Burns documentary on, *8*, 19–22; Northwest Ordinance and, 308–11; Samuel Adams and, 28–45
American Revolution, The (Burns documentary), 19–20, 24
Annenberg, Walter, 182
Anson, George, 420
Antietam, Battle of, 60–61
Anti-Imperialist League, 86
Appomattox, Confederate surrender at, 51, 66–67
Arlington House, 56
Army of Northern Virginia, 65, 67–68
Army of the Potomac, 62–65
Articles of Confederation, 308
artificial intelligence (AI), 336–55; early research on, 339–40, 343–44; genetic testing and, 327–28; global competition in, 346–50; investment in, 346–47, 353–55; regulation of, 343–44, 351–55; warfare and, 350–51
Aschenbrenner, Leopold, 346
"Ashokan Farewell" (Ungar), 17–18
atomic bomb, 117, 304. *See also* Cuban Missile Crisis

Babbitt, Bruce, 243
Baker, James, 178–79
Ballou, Sullivan, 17–18
Bannon, Steve, 378

Barkley, Alben, 99
Barnett, Barney, 182–83
baseball: history of, 10–12, 21, 26; Thorpe's career in, 201–4
Bay of Pigs operation, 137–39, 144–46, 361
Belafonte, Harry, 24
Belmont, Battle of, 64
Beschloss, Michael, 4, 90–112; background of, 90
Billington, James (Dr.), 1–4
Bingham, George Caleb, 300
bin Laden, Osama, hunt for and capture of, 255, 257, 264–80
birth defects, 331–32
Birth of a Nation (film), 73, 85
Black Americans: baseball and, 201–2; Democratic support from, 150; in FBI, 220; Johnson and, 152–53; Kennedy and, 151–52; Reconstruction-era political organization by, 76–77
Black Codes, 75
Blackmun, Harry (Justice), 247
Blair, Francis Preston, 57–58
Bloomingdale, Alfred, 182
Boot, Max, 160–87; background of, 162
Booth, John Wilkes, 73–74, 79
Bork, Robert, 244
Boston Massacre, *8*, 31, 34
Boston Tea Party, 34, 36
Boutwell, George, 86
Brady, Mathew, 14
Bramante, Donato, 293
BRCA-1 and BRCA-2 genes, 321, 327–28, 333
breast cancer, 320–21, 324
Brin, Sergey, 339–42
Brinkley, David, 131–32
Brinkley, Douglas, 4
Brokaw, Tom, 12–13
Brooks, Arthur C., 379–401, *380*; academic career of, 383–88; early life of, 382–83; education of, 383–84; family life of, 386–87
Brooks, David, 311
Brown, Christopher, 24
Brown, John, 55
Brown v. Board of Education, 11, 219
Brundage, Avery, 197, 204
Brunelleschi, Filippo, 286, 288
Buckley, William F., 27
Build the Life You Want (Brooks), 381
Bull Run, Battle of (First Manassas), 51–52, 59
Bull Run, Second Battle of, 60
Bundy, McGeorge, 24, 364
Burger, Warren (Chief Justice), 244, 247
Burns, James MacGregor, 90
Burns, Ken, 7–27; films of, 7–10, 13, 15–21, 24–25; haircut of, 12–13, PBS and, 26–27
Bush, Barbara, 181
Bush, George H. W., Reagan and, 176–77, 178–81, 185
Bush, George W., 396
Bush v. Gore, 250–51
Byron (Lord), 409, 415
Byron, John, 407, 409, 415
ByteDance, 348

Camelot mythology, Kennedy and, 137–38, 141, 155, 158
Cameron, Simon, 58
Campbell, Andy, 238
cancer: causes of, 320–25; history of, 314–35; prevention, 320. *See also specific types of cancer*
carcinogens, 323–24
Caribbean, US dominance in, 85–86
Carlisle Indian Industrial School, 190–91, 193–95, 199–201
Carter, Jimmy: cancer of, 323; elections of, 102, 113, 176; Reagan and, 102, 176, 177, 178
Casey, William, 177
Castro, Fidel, 148, 360, 368–69
cell biology, history of, 314, 317, 328–31
Central Intelligence Agency (CIA), 265–67, 359–61
Charpentier, Emmanuelle, 332–33
ChatGPT, 344, 346
Cheap, David, 412–13
chemotherapy, discovery of, 319
Chesnut, Mary, 59

China: artificial intelligence and, 347–51; economic power of, 375; Kennedy and, 155–56; Korean War and, 95, 98; US rivalry with, 356, 358–59, 374–78
Chinese Exclusion Act (1882), 87
citizenship, 307; for free Blacks, 72, 74, 76–77
civil rights: Hoover's FBI and, 219–20, 224–25; Kennedy and, 149–53; King and, 10, 24–25, 149
Civil Rights Act of 1964, 152
Civil War, The (Burns documentary series), 11, 13–23
Civil War: Burns documentary series on, 11, 13–23; casualties in, 52, 63, 65; impact of, 9–10, 18–19, 52–62, 69–70; Lee and Grant during, 46–70; lack of a declaration of, 93
Civil War History (quarterly), 52
Clifford, Clark, 121
climate change, energy consumption and, 347–48
Cold War: Kennedy and, 150–52, 153–56; presidential election of 1960 and, 134, 142, 149; Soviet-US rivalry and, 373–74
college football, revenues from, 195–96
Collins, Francis, 327
Comiskey, Charles, 201
Compact of Fifth Avenue, 126
Compromise of 1850, 58
Compromise of 1877, 81–82
Congressional Dialogues: impact of, 5; origins of, 2–5
Congressional powers, declaration of war and, 91–93
Constitution (US), war powers in, 91–93
Conte, Silvio, 10
Coolidge, Calvin, 211, 216
Corporation for Public Broadcasting, 13, 26
Countdown 1945 (Wallace), 115–17
Countdown 1960: The Behind-the-Scenes Story of the 312 Days That Changed America's Politics Forever (Wallace), 113, 119
Countdown bin Laden (Wallace), 115–16
COVID-19 pandemic, 387
creativity *vs.* genius, 283–84
CRISPR research, 332–33
Cronkite, Walter, 131–32, 155, 176–77
Cuban Missile Crisis, 137–39, 144–48, 158–59, 356, 357, 358–78
Curie, Marie, 281
Cushing (Cardinal), 122
Custis, George Washington Parke, 56
Custis, Jacky, 56
Custis, Mary Anna Randolph, 56
Cutler, Ephraim, 310
Cutler, Manasseh, 301, 309–11
cyberattacks, 348
cystic fibrosis gene, 333, 355

Daley, Richard, 108, 123, 129, 133
Dana, Charles, 65
data centers, 347
da Vinci, Leonardo. *See* Leonardo da Vinci
da Vinci, (Ser) Piero, 285
Davis, Jefferson, 51, 59, 66–68
Davis, Nancy. *See* Reagan, Nancy
Davis, Patti, 163
Death Valley Days, 170–71
Deaver, Mike, 179
Deck of 50, 262
Declaration of Independence (US), 35, 39, 40, 299, 306, 381, 394
declaration of war, Constitutional requirements concerning, 90–93, 111–12
deep learning algorithm, 344
DeepMind company, 344–45
de Gaulle, Charles, 291
Democratic Party: election of 1864 and, 75; election of 1948 and, 99; Kennedy influence in, 139–41; MacArthur and, 98; Reagan and, 169, 187
Destined for War (Allison), 356, 371–78
DiCaprio, Leonardo, 406, 420
dignity, artificial intelligence and, 353–54
Dillinger, John, 215
Dillon, Douglas, 362
Dirksen, Everett, 110
disease prevention, cells and, 330
Dixon, Thomas, 85
DNA research, 329–30
domino theory, 155–56

Donilon, Tom, 267
Don Juan (Byron), 415
Doudna, Jennifer, 332–33
Douglass, Frederick, 88
Dred Scott decision, 87–88
drone technology, 351
Dutch (Morris), 160

Early, Jubal, 66
Early, Steve, 116
East, John, 245
East India Company, 36
Einstein, Albert, 283–84, 297, 350
Eisenhower, Dwight D., 99–101, 117, 142–43, 145–46, 200, 219–21
Electoral Reform Act (1887), 134
Emancipation Proclamation, 51, 61, 78, 88–89
Emancipation to Exodus (Burns documentary), 24
Emperor of All Maladies, The (Mukherjee), 314
energy consumption, artificial intelligence and, 346–47
environment: cancer and, 321; climate change, energy consumption and, 347–48
Essence of Decision (Allinson), 356
Executive Committee of the National Security Council (ExComm), 362–64, 366–67, 369–70
Executive Order No. 10450, 220
Exodusters, 79

Fairness Act, 127
Farber, Sidney, 319
Federal Bureau of Investigation (FBI), historian of, 404; J. Edgar Hoover and, 209, 214–29; Reagan and, 169, 171
Fehrenbacher, Don, 17–18
Feldman, Mike, 128
Felt, Mark, 227
Fetus in the Womb (Leonardo drawing), 289
Fields, Barbara, 18
Fifteenth Amendment, 72, 74, 89
Firing Line (PBS television show), 27
First Continental Congress, 36–37
First: Sandra Day O'Connor (Thomas), 232
Flannery, Jeff, 301
football, Thorpe's career in, 202–4
Foote, Shelby, 15, 17, 23
Ford, Gerald, 126, 157, 174–77
Fourteenth Amendment, 72, 76, 82, 86–87, 89
Franklin, Benjamin, 9, 38–40, 44, 283–84, 297, 371, 394
Freedman Project, 18
Freedman's Bureau, 74, 76, 79–80
Freedom Riders, 150
From Strength to Strength (Brooks), 387

Gage, Beverly, 209–29; Pulitzer Prize of, 209
Gage, Thomas (Gen.), 36
gaming, artificial intelligence and, 345
Gardner, Alexander, 14
Garrison, William Lloyd, 88
Gates, Bill, 4, 283–84, 289, 336, 342
General Electric, Reagan's work with, 170–72
General Electric Theater, 170–71
Genesis (Kissinger, Mundie, Schmidt), 337, 352
gene therapy, 323–24
genetics: cancer and, 320–21, 326–27; current research on, 331–33; testing and, 327–28
Gettysburg, Battle of, 21, 47, 61–64
Gettysburg Address, 14–15, 70, 89
Gherardini, Lisa (Mona Lisa), 290
Giancana, Sam "Mooney," 122, 222
Ginevra de' Benci (Leonardo painting), 283, 288
glioblastoma, 322
G-Man: J. Edgar Hoover and the Making of the American Century (Gage), 209
Goldman, Emma, 214
Goldwater, Barry, 103, 172, 175, 232, 244
Goodwin, Doris Kearns, 4
Goodwin, Richard, 128
Goodwin, Tom, 242
Google, 336, 338–41, 344–45
Gorbachev, Mikhail, 187
GPT-1, 345
GPT-2, 345

GPT-3, 345–46
Graham, Phil, 125
Grann, David, 402–21; career of, 402. *See also specific books*
Grant, Julia Dent, 56–57, 78
Grant, Ulysses S., 46–70, *48*; alcoholism of, 47, 54, 65, 77; at Appomattox, 56–57; failures of, 54, 68, 77–78; marriage of, 53–54, 56–57; memoirs by, 45, 69; military career of, 46–47, 53–55, 64–68, 82–83; presidency of, 47, 68–70, 77–80
Gray, Pat, 227
Great Flood of 1889, 302–3
Great Migrations, 24, 79
Green, Pumpsie, 12
Gruening, Ernest, 105
Guelzo, Allen C., 46–70; career of, 46
Gulf of Tonkin (Vietnam War), 19, 102, 105, 107

Hacker, J. David, 52
Hamlin, Hannibal, 64, 75
Hammer, Armand, 289
Hancock, John, 35–36, 40–41, 43
happiness, Brooks's theories on, 379–401, *380*
Harding, Warren, 216
Harriman, Averell, 118
Harris, Lou, 119, 131
Harris Poll, 119
Hart, Gary, 155
Haskell Institute, 193–94
Hassabis, Demis, 344–45
Havel, Vaclav, 374
Hayden, Carla (Dr.), 4–5, 14, 27
Hayes, Rutherford B., 80–82
healthcare, cancer and, 314, 317–35
Helms, Jesse, 175, 245
Herblock, 130
Hero Code, The (McRaven), 257
Hill, Mike, 301
Hill, Norbert, 190
History of the Peloponnesian War, The (Thucydides), 372
Hoffman, Reid, 345
Hollywood blacklist, 169–70
homosexuality: of Leonardo, 284–86, 291; Hoover and, 210, 220–21
Hood, John Bell, 57
Hooke, Robert, *315*, 328–29
Hoover, Herbert, 142, 216
Hoover, J. Edgar, 209–29, *210*; celebrity status of, 215–29; Congress and, 218; death of, 226; deportations made by, 213–14; early life of, 211–13; Eisenhower and, 219; FBI career of, 210, 212, 214–29; intelligence activities of, 217–19; Johnson and, 223–24; Kennedy and, 221–22; King and, 224–25; Nixon and, 224–25; Pearl Harbor attack and, 216–17; personal life of, 210, 227–29; political power of, 210–11; racism of, 219–20; Roosevelt and, 215–18; Truman and, 217–18; wartime career of, 213
House Un-American Activities Committee, 218
Human Genome Project, 326–27
Humphrey, Hubert, 108–10, 118, 120–23
Huntley, Chet, 131
Hussein, Saddam, 262–64

Iconic America (television series), 11
immune response, 330–31; aging and, 334–35
immunotherapy, 323
imperialism, Reconstruction and, 85–86
Incomparable Grace (Updegrove), 135
Indian boarding schools, Thorpe's experience with, 190–91, 193–94
Insular Cases, 86
Internal Revenue Act, 74
Iran-Contra scandal, 177, 183–85
Iraq War, 110–11, 396
Isaacson, Walter, 4, 9, 233, 281–98; career of, 281, 297–98

Jackson, Robert, 235
Japan, China's relationship with, 376
Jefferson, Thomas, 2–3, 9, 14, 21, 305, 310, 354, 381, 394; Declaration of Independence and, 37, 39; on Samuel Adams, 38, 41

Jenkins, Robert, 407–8
Jim Thorpe, All-American (film), 205
Jobs, Steve, 283–84, 297–98, 342–43
Johnson, Andrew, 68, 71, 73, 74–77, 86
Johnson, Jack, 23
Johnson, Lady Bird, 106–7, 110
Johnson, Lyndon Baines: civil rights and, 152–53; election of 1960 and, 118, 123–26; health problems of, 104–5; J. Edgar Hoover and, 223–24; Kennedy and, 137, 140–41, 156; presidency of, 24, 155; Senate career of, 25, 139–40; space program and, 153; as vice president, 144, 152, 156; Vietnam War and, 92, 102–7, 111, 155
Johnston, Joseph (Gen.), 59, 67
Johnstown Flood. *See* Great Flood of 1889
John W. Kluge Center, 2
Joint Special Operations Force, 264, 267
Jomini, Antoine-Henri, 84

Kahanamoku, Duke, 196
Kamangar, Salar, 339
Kawésqar (native Patagonians), 413–14
Keating, Kenneth, 360–61
Kefauver, Estes, 118
Kelsey, Frances, 332
Kemp, Martin, 285
Kennan, George, 373
Kennedy, Cornelia, 244
Kennedy, Jacqueline, 156, 158, 291
Kennedy, John F.: assassination of, 141, 157–58, 222–23; Bay of Pigs crisis and, 137–39, 144–46, 361; civil rights and, 149–53; Cuban Missile Crisis and, 137–39, 144–49, 158–59, 358–70; Dallas trip and, 156–57; Eisenhower and, 142–43; election of, 113, *114*, 118–34, 138–42; health status of, 120, 124, 130, 135, *136*, 154–55; Hoover as FBI director and, 221–22; inaugural address of, 143–44; legacy of, 158–59; personal life of, 155; portrait of, *136*; presidency of, 135–59, 302; Senate career of, 139; space program and, 153–54; Vietnam War and, 24, 155–56; writing by, 143–44
Kennedy, Joseph (JFK's father), 119, 121–23, 140, 147, 222
Kennedy, Robert: assassination of JFK and, 158; Bay of Pigs crisis and, 147; Cuban Missile Crisis and, 147–50, 362, 368; election of 1960 and, 119, 122–26, 129, 131; J. Edgar Hoover and, 221–25; Johnson and, 140–41; space program and, 154
Kennedy Space Center, 337
Kerry, John, 19
Keynes, Geoffrey, 319
Khrushchev, Nikita, 127, 129, 146–48, 150, 159, 358–60, 361, 363–71
Killers of the Flower Moon (Grann), 402, 404–6, 420–21
Kim Il Sung, 94–95
Kim Jong Un, 376–77
King, Coretta Scott, 149
King, Martin Luther, Jr., 11, 24–25, 149–52, 224–25
King, Martin Luther, Sr., 150
Kintner, Robert, 127
Kirkpatrick, Freeda, 203
Kissinger, Henry, 174, 184, 337–38, 346, 347, 349–52
Klein, Herb, 130
Kluge, John W., 2
knowledge, happiness and, 395–96
Korean War, 94–100, 102, 111, 377–78
Krim, Arthur, 109
Ku Klux Klan, 73, 76, 78, 85
Kuwait War, 110–11

Lancaster, Burt, 205
Laos, US policy in, 143
Lasker, Mary, 319–20
Last Supper, The (Leonardo painting), 283, 292
Lavender Scare, 220–21
LBJ Foundation, 137
League of Nations, 85
LeBlanc, Dennis, 182–83
Lee, Robert E., 46–70, *49*; Civil War leadership of, 47–67; as engineer, 56; leadership qualities of, 46–47; marriage

of, 57; military career of, 55–56, 84; postwar career of, 68
Legal Tender Act, 74
Leonardo da Vinci, 282; Burns documentary on, 9–10, 24; death of, 291; early life of, 284–86; genius status of, 250, 283–84; homosexuality of, 284–86, 291; Isaacson's discussion of, 281–98; notebooks of, 288–89, 297; paintings by, 283, 287–94; procrastination by, 287, 290; scientific interests of, 294–96. *See also specific artworks*
Leonardo da Vinci (Burns documentary), 9–10, 24
Lerner, Alan, 158
Lewis, John, 24
Library of Congress, *x*; burning of, 1–2; establishment of, 1; expanded mission of, ix, 2–5; as historical resource, 13–14, 234, 301, 302–3; J. Edgar Hoover works at, 212–13; offerings of, xi
Lieber, Francis, 84
Lincoln (film), 89
Lincoln, Abraham: abolitionism and, 87–88; assassination of, 71, 73–74, 78–79; Civil War and, 50–51, 53–54, 59–60, 65–70; Grant and, 65–67, 78–79; Johnson and, 74–75; Lee and, 46, 58; presidency of, 20, 137, 144; Reconstruction policies of, 71, 73–75, 87–89; secession and, 50
Lincoln-Douglas debates, 88
Lincoln's Code, 84
Lodge, Henry Cabot, 119, 126, 130
longevity, 334–35
Longstreet, James, 57
"Long Telegram," 373
Lost Cause mythology, 83–85
Lost City of Z, The (Grann), 402, 420

MacArthur, Douglas, 95–99
Madison, James, 1, 91, 238
Madison Council, ix, 2
Mahoney, Florence, 319
Making of the President, 1960, The (White), 114–15
mammography, breast cancer and, 321
Maraniss, David, 188–208; biographies written by, 189, 190
March on Washington, 151–53
Marietta, Ohio, 311–13
Marshall, George, 374
Marshall Plan, 374
Martin, Louis, 150
Mason, George, 394
Mathewson, Christy, 201
May, Ernest, 367
Mays, Willie, 12, 188
Mazo, Earl, 133–34
McCain, John, 19
McCarthy, Eugene, 124
McCarthy, Joseph, 169, 218–19, 221
McClellan, George, 59–60
McCullough, David, 4, 299–313; books of 299, 302, 303, 304–5, 306, 307–8
McCullough, Rosalee, 301–2
McDowell, Charlie, 15
McDowell, Irvin, 59
McFarlane, Bud, 184
McGraw, John, 201
McKinley, William, 85–86
McMaster, H. R., 378
McNamara, Robert, 24, 92, 103, 106, 363, 369–70
McRaven, William H. (Admiral), 255–80; early life of, 257–59; SEAL training and career experience of, 259–61
Meacham, Jon, 3
Meade, George, 63–64
Medici family, Leonardo and, 284–87
Meese, Ed, 179
melanoma, 323
Mendel, Gregor, 326
Mexican War, 46, 54, 74, 93
Michelangelo, 286, 296
Micrographia (Hooke), 315, 328–29
Miers, Harriet, 252
Miller, Arthur, 16
Minutemen missiles, 359
Missouri Compromise of 1820, 58
Mona Lisa (Leonardo painting), 283, 288, 290–91

Mondale, Walter, 183
Moore's Law, 343–44
Morgan, Daniel, 22
Morrell, Michael, 265
Morris, Edmund, 160
Morse, Wayne, 105
mortality, cancer and, 320, 324–25
Morton, Thruston, 132, 142
Mukherjee, Siddhartha, 314–35; background and career of, 314, 316–318, 334; medical practice of, 325–26
Mullen, Michael, 265
Mundie, Craig, 337, 346, 350–51
Murrow, Edward R., 302
Musk, Elon, 342–43, 345

Nabhan, Saleh, 279
National Aeronautics and Space Administration (NASA), 153–54
National Banking Act, 74
National Football League (NFL), Thorpe as head of, 191, 202–3
Native Americans: baseball and, 201–2; federal troops' conquest of, 84–85; Indian boarding schools and, 193–95; Northwest Ordinance and, 311–13; perseverance of, 208; Thorpe's life and work among, 188–91; violence against, 405–6
Navy SEALs: McRaven as, 257–58, 267–80; monument of, *256*
Newlen, Robert, 5
Nitze, Paul, 374
Nixon, Patricia, 131–32, 144
Nixon, Richard M., 91; China trip by, 375; Eisenhower and, 143; election of 1960 and, 98, 113–34, *114*, 141–42, 144; election of 1968 and, 109–10; Hoover and FBI and, 210, 225–27; presidency of, 24, 185; Reagan and, 173–74; Truman and, 111; Vietnam War and, 109; war on cancer and, 319–20
North, Oliver, 184
North Korea, 94, 97, 376–78
Northwest Ordinance, 300, 308–11
Northwest Territory, 309
Nuclear Test Ban Treaty, 137
nuclear weapons, 97, 98, 100–101. *See also* Cuban Missile Crisis

Obama, Barack, 25, 257, 267, 269, 276–80
obesity, cancer and, 324
O'Connor, John, 234–35, 240–41, 251–53
O'Connor, Sandra Day, 230–54, *231*; early life of, 235–37; education and legal career of, 238–41; judicial career of, 243–44; legislative career of, 242–43; marriage of, 234–35, 240–42, 252–53; Supreme Court nomination of, 245–54
October surprise theory, 177
Olympics, 1912, Thorpe's participation in, 196–98
O'Neill, Tip, 10, 123, 180
OpenAI, 344–45
Osage Nation, 405–6
Oswald, Lee Harvey, 157–58, 223
ovarian cancer, 322, 324, 327

Pacioli, Luca, 284, 286
Page, Larry, 339–42
Palmer Raids, 214
Panama Canal, 175, 306–7
pancreatic cancer, 322–23, 325–26
Panetta, Leon, 265–67
Parks, Rosa, 11
Path Lit by Lightning (Maraniss), 189, 208
Patton, George S., 196
Peace Corps, Kennedy's creation of, 137
Peale, Norman Vincent, 219
Pearl Harbor attack, FBI and, 216–17
Pelosi, Nancy, 116
Philippines, US subjugation of, 86
Pickett's Charge, 63
Pioneers, The (McCullough), 300–301, 308–13
Plessy v. Ferguson, 82–83, 87
polymaths, 309, 350. *See also* Leonardo da Vinci
Pope, John (General), 60
Powell, Jody, 15
Powell, Lewis, 247
Powers, Richard, 20

Pratt, Richard Henry, 194
presidential election of 1960, 113–34; fraud allegations and, 131–34, 142. *See also individual presidents*
presidential powers, declaration of war and, 90–94
Presidents of War (Beschloss), 90–91
Profiles in Courage (Kennedy), 144
prostate cancer, 321–22, 324
PSA test, cancer and, 321, 324
PT-109 accident, Kennedy and, 154–55
Pulitzer Prize, 28, 44, 114, 144, 145, 160, 189, 209, 299, 304, 314, 317
Purvis, Melvin, 215
Putnam, Rufus, 301, 310–12

Qwen chip, 347–48

racial violence, Reconstruction-era emergence of, 76, 81, 82–84
radiation, discovery of, 319
Randolph, A. Philip, 151
Rayburn, Sam, 116, 124–25, 134
Reagan, Jack, 164
Reagan, Maureen, 163
Reagan, Michael, 163
Reagan, Nancy, 160, 169–70, 177, 179, 181–83, 186
Reagan, Neil "Moon," 164
Reagan, Nelle, 164
Reagan, Ronald, 102, 160–87, *161*; acting career of, 166–70; Alzheimer's and, 183–87; athletic career of, 164–66; biographies of, 160, 162; as California governor, 160, 173–74, 182; Democratic Party and, 169; early life of, 164–66; family of, 163; as FBI informant, 169–70; Ford and, 174–76; foreign policy under, 180–81; friendships of, 182; George H. W. Bush and, 176–77, 178–81; Goldwater and, 172, 175; Iran-Contra scandal and, 183–85; legacy of, 185–87; marriage to Nancy Davis, 169–70; Nixon and, 174–75; O'Connor's Supreme Court appointment by, 230–32, 243–45; political views of, 162–63; popularity of, 162; presidency of, 179–87; presidential elections of, 175–78, 183–84; Republican Party and, 171–72, 176–77; retirement of, 186–87; as sportscaster, 166–67; tax cuts under, 179–80; television career of, 170–71; Wyman's marriage to, 169
Reagan, Ronald, Jr., 163
Reagan: His Life and Legend (Boot), 162
Reconstruction, 24, 71–89, 72
Rehnquist, William H., 232, 234–35, 239, 241, 244, 247, 251–52
Republican Party: big business and empire and, 85–86; election of 1864 and, 75; election of 1960 and, 115, 131–33; Reagan and, 162, 171–72, 176–77; Reconstruction and, 75–77
Reston, James "Scotty," 146
Reuther, Walter, 125
Revere, Paul, *8*, 36–37
Revolutionary, The: Samuel Adams (Schiff), 28
Rise and Fall of the Second American Republic, The (Sinha), 71, 86
Roberts, John G, Jr. (Chief Justice), 4, 246, 252, 336
Robinson, Jackie Roosevelt, 9–12, 23
Rockefeller, Nelson, 118, 125–26, 172
Roe v. Wade, 247, 249
Röntgen, Wilhelm, 319
Roosevelt, Eleanor, 116–17
Roosevelt, Franklin Delano, 111, 116–17, 144, 171, 215–18
Roosevelt, Theodore, 160, 306
Rosenberg, Julius and Ethel, 218–19
Rubenstein, David M.: Allison interviewed by, 356–78; Baltimore Orioles and, 10; Beschloss interviewed by, 90–112; Boot interviewed by, 160–87; Brooks interviewed by, 379–401; Burns interviewed by, 7–27; Carlyle Group and, 427; Carter White House and, 113, 178; Congressional Dialogues and, ix, 3–6; Gage interviewed by, 209–29; Grann interviewed by, 402–22; Guelzo interviewed by, 46–70; Isaacson interviewed by, 281–98; Kennedy and, 135; Madison Council and, ix, 2–3; Maraniss

Rubenstein, David M. (continued) interviewed by, 188–208; McCullough interviewed by, 299–313; McRaven interviewed by, 255–80; Mukherjee interviewed by, 314–35; philanthropy of, ix, xi, 2–3, 9, 14–15; presidential elections and, 113, 178; Schiff interviewed by, 28–45; Schmidt interviewed by, 336–55; Sinha interviewed by, 71–89; Thomas interviewed by, 230–54; Treasures Gallery (LOC) and, xi, 9, 27; Updegrove interviewed by, 135–59; Wallace interviewed by, 113–34
Ruby, Jack, 157–58
Rusk, Dean, 24, *92*, 364
Russia, Ukrainian war with, 349, 350–51
Ruth, Babe, 11–12, 188, 201

Sagan, Scott, 370
St. Jerome in the Wilderness (Leonardo painting), 294
Salinger, Pierre, 119, 127
Salvator Mundi (Leonardo painting), 287
Samaranch, Juan Antonio, 204
Schiff, Stacy, 28–45; books and awards of, 28
Schleiden, Jakob, 329
Schmidt, Eric, 4, 336–55; early life and career of, 338–41
Schurz, Carl, 58
Schwann, Theodor, 329
Schweiker, Richard, 175
Scorsese, Martin, 406, 420
Scott, Winfield, 58
Screen Actors Guild, 169–70
SEALS. *See* Navy SEALS
Sears, John, 175
Sea Stories (McRaven), 255
secession, Civil War and, 50, 57, 58
self-driving cars, 341–42, 344
September 11, 2001, attacks, 255, 261
sfumato technique, 289–90
Sheen, Fulton (Bishop), 219
Sherman, William Tecumseh, 57, 67, 80
Sinatra, Frank, 119
Sinha, Manisha, 71–89; background of, 71, 84
slavery: Lincoln and, 51, 74–75, 87–88; Northwest Territory exclusion of, 309–10
Smith, Howard K., 131
Smith, William French, 244
smoking and tobacco use, cancer and, 323–24
Smurf cars, 342
social media, impact of, 397–98
Song of the Cell, The (Mukherjee), 314. *See also* cell biology
Sorensen, Ted, 119, 128, 144, 362
Soviet Union: Bay of Pigs operation and, 145–46, 148–50; Cold War and, 373–74; Cuban missile crisis and, 146–49, 158–59, 358–71; election of 1960 and, 142; Kennedy and, 150–52, 153–54; Korean War and, 94–96, 99–101; Reagan and, 180–81, 186–87; space program in, 153–54
space program, Kennedy and, 153–54
Spanish-American Cuban War (1898), 85–86, 93
Speaker, Tris, 201
Spencer, Stuart, 179
Stalin, Joseph, 94, 394
Stamp Act, 33, 34
Stanton, Edwin, 65
Stevenson, Adlai, 99, 117–18, 124, 362–63
Stimson, Henry, 117
Strategic Defense Initiative (SDI), 181
Sugar Act, 33
Sullivan, James E., 199–200
superintelligence, 346, 350
Supreme Court: Insular Cases and, 86; O'Connor's tenure on, 230–54; Reconstruction-era rulings by, 82–83, 87. *See also specific cases*
Symington, Stuart, 118, 120, 124

Taiwan, 372, 375, 377
Task Force 121, 262
taxation, American Revolution and, 32–34, 37–38; Reagan and, 170, 171, 174, 179–80
television, election of 1960 and, *114*, 127–28
Tencent platform, 348
Tesla cars, 342

Tewanima, Louis, 196
thalidomide, 331–32
Thatcher, Margaret, 187
Thirteenth Amendment, *72*, 74, 88–89
Thirty-Ninth Congress, 75–76
Thomas, Evan, 230–54; O'Connor and, 232–34, 253
Thorpe, Charlotte, 192–93
Thorpe, Hiram, 192–93
Thorpe, Jim, 188–208, *189*; athletic greatness of, 188–91, 194–98; baseball career of, 201–2; death of, 206–7; early life of, 192–93; family of, 192, 202–3, 207; movie career of, 204–5; Olympic medals taken from, 188–89, 191–92, 199–200, 204; post-athletic life of, 191, 204–8
Thorpe, Jim, Jr., 203
Thorpe, Patsy, 206–7
Thucydides, 356, 371–72
Thudycides's Trap, 356, 358, 371–72, 374, 376–78
Tilden, Samuel, 81
Tolson, Clyde, 210, 227–28
Treasures Gallery (Library of Congress), xi, 9
Treaty of Paris (1783), 308–9, 312
Truman, Harry S., 377; desegregation of military by, 151; early life of, 304; J. Edgar Hoover and, 217–18; Johnson and, 104; Korean War and, 94–101; Marshall Plan and, 374; Nixon and, 111; presidency of, 116–17, 145, 299, 303–4
Trump, Donald, 5, 116, 375, 378
Turing test, 343
Twain, Mark (Samuel Clemens), 69, 308
20 Percent rule of Google, 341

U-2 spy missions, 359, 361, 366
Ukraine, Russian war with, 350–51
Ungar, Jay, 17
United Nations, 96
United States: China's rivalry with, 347–50, 356, 374–78; Cold War and, 373–74. *See* westward expansion, *and also specific presidents, wars*
United States Copyright Office, 2
Updegrove, Mark K., 135–59; and LBJ Library, 137, 157
US Army, in Civil War, 50–51, 64–65
US Information Agency, 302–3

Valenti, Jack, 104
Vandenberg, Arthur, 374
Veach, Eric, 339
Venter, Craig, 326–27
Verrocchio, Andrea del, 286–88
Vietnam War, 83, *92*, 93, 102–10, 155–56
Vietnam War, The (Burns documentary), 18–19, 21, 26
Virginia Declaration of Rights, 394
Vitruvian Man (Leonardo drawing), 292–94
Vitruvius' Book of Architecture, 293
Vonnegut, Kurt, 16
voter fraud, 132–34
voting rights, for free Blacks, *72*, 73–74, 76–77, 82–83

Wager, Charles (Sir), 406
Wager, The (Grann), 402, 406–21
Wallace, Chris, 113–34; background of, 115, 117
Wallace, George, 152
Wallace, Mike, 115
Warner, Jack, 168
Warner, Pop, 195–96, 199–200, 205
Warner Bros., 167
War of Jenkins' Ear, 407–8
Warren, Earl (Chief Justice), court of, 223
Warren, Robert Penn, 17
Warren Commission Report, 157–58, 223–24
Washburne, Elihu, 54
Washington, George, 20, 22, 24, 37–38, 46, 56, 137, 308
Watergate scandal, 174, 227
Watson, James, 316, 328
Waymo cars, 342
Webb, James, 153
westward expansion, US history of, 300–313

White, Theodore, 114–15, 158
Whiting, William, 88
Wilkerson, Isabel, 24
Williams v. Mississippi, 83
Wilmington Massacre, 83
Wilson, Woodrow, 73, 85, 90
Winfrey, Oprah, 381, 386–87
World War I, 23–24, 213, 372
World War II: Burns documentary on, 26; Congressional declaration of war and, 93
Wright, Orville and Wilber, 307–8
Wright, Richard, 24
Wyman, Jane, 169

Xi Jinping, 358, 375, 376, 378

Yarborough, Ralph, 156
Yates, Richard, 54
Yawkey, Tom, 12
Young, Andrew, 152

Zelikow, Philip, 356, 367
Zuckerberg, Mark, 342

About the Author

David M. Rubenstein is an investor, philanthropist, interviewer, author, and historian. He is Co-Founder and Co-Chair of the Carlyle Group, one of the world's largest and most successful private investment firms. Established in 1987, Carlyle now manages around half a trillion dollars from twenty-eight offices around the world.

Mr. Rubenstein is a Baltimore native and is the chairman, CEO, and principal owner of Major League Baseball's Baltimore Orioles. A recipient of the Presidential Medal of Freedom, Mr. Rubenstein is chairman of the boards of the Council on Foreign Relations, the National Gallery of Art, the Economic Club of Washington, and the University of Chicago; a trustee of Memorial Sloan-Kettering Cancer Center, the Institute for Advanced Study, the Brookings Institution, and the World Economic Forum; an emeritus trustee of Johns Hopkins Medicine; and a director of Moderna, Inc., and the American Academy of Arts and Sciences.

Mr. Rubenstein is a member of the American Philosophical Society, Business Council, Harvard Global Advisory Council (chairman), Madison Council of the Library of Congress (chairman), Advisory Board of the School of Economics and Management at Tsinghua University (former chairman), and Board of the World Economic Forum Global Shapers Community.

Mr. Rubenstein is an original signer of the Giving Pledge, a significant donor to all of the above-mentioned nonprofit organizations, and a recipient of the Carnegie Medal of Philanthropy and MoMA's David Rockefeller Award, among other philanthropic awards.

Mr. Rubenstein is a leader in the area of patriotic philanthropy, having made transformative gifts for the restoration or repair of the Washington Monument, Lincoln Memorial, Jefferson Memorial, Monticello, Montpelier, Mount Vernon, Arlington House, Iwo Jima Memorial, the Kennedy Center, the Smithsonian, the National Archives, the National Zoo, the Library of Congress, and the National Museum of African American History and Culture. Mr. Rubenstein has also provided to the US government long-term loans of his rare copies of the Magna Carta, the Declaration of Independence, the US Constitution, the Bill of Rights, the Emancipation Proclamation, the Thirteenth Amendment, the first map of the United States (Abel Buell map), and the first book printed in the US (*Bay Psalm Book*).

Mr. Rubenstein is the host of *The David Rubenstein Show: Peer-to-Peer Conversations* on Bloomberg TV and PBS, *Bloomberg Wealth with David Rubenstein* on Bloomberg TV, *Longevity with David Rubenstein* on Bloomberg TV, and *America's Book Club* on C-SPAN; and the author of six books published by Simon and Schuster, four of which are *New York Times* bestsellers: *The American Story: Conversations with Master Historians* (2019), *How to Lead: Wisdom from the World's Greatest CEOs, Founders, and Game Changers* (2020), *The American Experiment: Dialogues on a Dream* (2021), *How to Invest: Masters on the Craft* (2022), *The Highest Calling: Conversations on the American Presidency* (2024), and *Inside the Owner's Box: Power and Leadership in Sports* (2026).

Mr. Rubenstein has served as chairman of the boards of the John F. Kennedy Center for the Performing Arts, Duke University, and the Smithsonian Institution; as a co-chairman of the board of the Brookings Institution; as a Fellow of the Harvard Corporation; and as a director of the Lincoln Center for the Performing Arts and the National Constitution Center.

Mr. Rubenstein is a 1970 magna cum laude graduate of Duke University, where he was elected Phi Beta Kappa. He graduated in 1973 from the University of Chicago Law School, where he was an editor of the Law Review. From 1973 to 1975, Mr. Rubenstein practiced law in New York with Paul, Weiss, Rifkind, Wharton & Garrison. From 1975 to 1976, he served as chief counsel to the US Senate Judiciary Committee's Subcommittee on Constitutional Amendments. From 1977 to 1981, during the Carter administration, Mr. Rubenstein was deputy assistant to the president for domestic policy. After his White House service and before cofounding Carlyle, Mr. Rubenstein practiced law in Washington with Shaw, Pittman, Potts & Trowbridge (now Pillsbury Winthrop Shaw Pittman).

www.ingramcontent.com/pod-product-compliance
Lightning Source LLC
LaVergne TN
LVHW091043011126
851498LV00004B/5/J